Fire Starters

Fire Starters

one year devotional
through the
New Testament

GPH™

Gospel Publishing House
Springfield, Missouri
02-0450

How busy are you?

Between school, extracurriculars, homework, housework, church, youth group, maybe a job—is there time for anything else except eating and sleeping? Hopefully you find a little free time for fun and friends. But what about God? Sure, He's always there, and you have His constant attention. But does He have yours? Do you get alone daily with God and give Him your undivided attention? As with any friendship, getting to know God takes time.

A guy named Martin Luther instigated what's known in church history as the Reformation. He helped change the way people viewed their relationship with Jesus by emphasizing God's grace and our personal access to God's Word. When once asked what his plans for the following day were, Luther answered: "Work, work, from early until late. In fact, I have so much business I cannot get on without spending the first three hours in prayer." Of all the important things going on in his life, Martin Luther knew there was nothing more important than getting to know God and taking time to hear from Him.

If you're too busy to spend time with God, then you're busier than God intends for you to be. It's not that He requires you to carve out three hours a day to pray. God is always there, so when it comes to His special time alone with you, He's more concerned with quality than quantity. He wants your best time, not your leftover time. Part of trusting God is giving Him time off the top, then watching Him make the most of the rest of your day.

For now, let's consider one small piece of your day—devoted solely to listening, learning, and gaining inspiration from God. This book will help you make the most of that time by providing a pattern for purposeful Bible study, prayer, and personal application of spiritual truth.

SO, GET READY . . .

"Therefore, prepare your minds for action" (1 Peter 1:13).

Each day's FIRE Starter begins by having you READ a short passage from the Bible—the written record of God's personal revelation and plans for us. It could be argued that if you don't know God's Word—the Bible—you don't really know God. Used daily, this book will take you through the entire New Testament in one year.

Following the Bible reading, the THINK section describes a brief scenario or poses questions to get you thinking about how the passage relates to your life. As you approach the Bible with an open mind, you can learn how to be more like Jesus.

GET SET . . .

"Set your mind on things above, not on earthly things" (Colossians 3:2).

When learning God's Word, before you can make effective application, you must make proper interpretation. The RESPOND section contains a series of questions to help you delve deeper into the passage: Who's involved? What's going on? What's the author trying to communicate? And what does it have to do with you?

"I meditate on your precepts and consider your ways. I delight in your decrees; I will not neglect your word" (Psalm 119:15,16).

In a biblical sense, to meditate means to "chew" on God's Word mentally, pondering what it means and how it applies to your life. You'll notice that some questions contain brief responses in parentheses. These are meant to spark your thinking and not to convey all implications or answers. You can find more complete commentary in the FIRE Bible Student Edition.

Following the questions, each FIRE Starter gives you a specific way to PRAY, relating to issues from your study. Keep in mind that prayer is a two-way conversation with God. It's not just a matter of what you say to Him, but what He wants to say to you. Take time to listen for God's response.

GO!

"Do not merely listen to the word, and so deceive yourselves. Do what it says" (James 1:22).

For God's Word to become part of your life, you must live what you learn. The final segment of each FIRE Starter challenges you to ACT on at least one specific point of application, putting into practice the spiritual principles of that day's Bible passage. Any time you read or hear something from the Bible ask yourself, "What difference should this make in my life, and what should I do now that God has shown me this?" Remember, if you don't use it, you'll lose it.

For in-depth, downloadable versions of these daily FIRE Starters in which the questions relate directly to specific study notes in the FIRE Bible Student Edition, go to fbse.ag.org.

The FIRE Bible Student Edition contains:

- ·· 20 major themes tracked through Scripture.

- ·· a simple, but detailed, cross-reference system.

- ·· personal Bible study tips.

- ·· over 80 background and key issue articles.

- ·· easy-to-read charts, illustrations, and maps.

- ·· the most thorough study notes of any student Bible.

- ·· Campus Missions (discipleship and evangelism) training and cross-referencing of five core values: PRAY / LIVE / TELL / SERVE / GIVE.

Matthew 1:1-25

THINK: Do you ever feel that because of your past failures or what you've been through that God could never use you for a great purpose? Jesus came to earth to relate to your pain so that you could relate to His purposes. Look back at Old Testament passages that highlight the lives of Jesus' ancestors. You'll find that many of these individuals have major character flaws and failures in their past (e.g., Jacob, who lied; Rahab, the prostitute).

RESPOND: What does the title "Christ" refer to when connected to Jesus? *(Greek:* christos *means "anointed," which is like saying chosen, commissioned, empowered, set apart for special service.)* What does it mean that Jesus was the "son of David"? *(Matthew demonstrates that Jesus was a legal descendant of David by tracing the family history of his earthly father, Joseph, who was from King David's family line.)* Why did Matthew list Jesus' ancestors in this way? *(Jewish custom traces family history through one's paternal line—that is, His earthly father's side.)* Considering the variety of people in Jesus' family line, what does this tell you about God and the people He can use to serve His highest purposes? How can this provide comfort and encouragement to you? What does the name Jesus mean and what is its significance in relation to Christ? *(Jesus is the Greek version of the Hebrew name* Yeshua *[Joshua], translated "the Lord saves." Christ in Greek is the Hebrew equivalent of "Messiah," referring to the Savior the Jews were waiting for.)* Why did Jesus have to live and suffer as a human, and how does that relate to you?

PRAY: Give God thanks for His forgiveness and for the assurance that the hurts and failures of your past do not have to stand in the way of God's ultimate plans for your life. If there is anything that is hindering your personal relationship with Jesus, confess it to Him and submit to His purposes.

ACT: Demonstrate God's love through an act of kindness or word of encouragement to someone who may seem spiritually distant or "unreachable." Pray for that individual and do something practical to help them. If you have the opportunity, let the person know that God loves them and you are praying that they discover God's plan for their life.

Fire Starter

Matthew 2:1-23

THINK: Have you ever gotten out of one tough situation only to encounter another one right away? Perhaps you feel that this is just life as usual for you? Jesus understands. He never promised that life would be easy. In fact, some of the people God uses the most are those who have been through the toughest trials. But God expects you to trust Him. He is completely able to bring you through any challenge and circumstance. But God's protection often requires obedience to God's direction (verses 13,14,19-22).

RESPOND: Who were the Magi? *(They were most likely highly educated religious leaders from Persia or southern Arabia, now Iran.)* Who were the chief priests and teachers of the law? *(Chief priests were temple ministers in charge of worship. Teachers of the law were Jewish scholars trained professionally in the history and application of Old Testament law.)* What lesson can you learn from Jesus' family's escape to Egypt? *(They had to obey God's direction, though it meant leaving their home country.)* Why might God allow you to face opposition or go through things you don't understand? How can the experience of Jesus' family right after His birth help you to understand and cope with some of the problems, difficulties and opposition you might face? What can you learn from Joseph and Mary's actions and responses?

PRAY: Ask God to help you be sensitive to His direction and to trust Him when facing challenges, particularly those that seem to require a change in plans or direction. Thank Him for providing protection, even though you don't always understand His methods or reasons.

ACT: Think of a problem or tough situation you are currently facing. Instead of removing the apparent obstacle or opposition, could God be trying to give you guidance and direction to work through it? Perhaps He will lead you into an unexpected course of action? Ask God for wisdom. Then listen for His guidance and be prepared to act. Thank God for what He will teach you through the situation.

Fire Starter

Matthew 3:1-17

THINK: If you've already accepted Jesus as the Forgiver of your sins, how much have you grown since that time in a spiritual sense? Are you continuing to grow deeper in your personal relationship with Jesus, and does your life reflect that on a daily basis?

RESPOND: What does it mean to repent, and how does that relate to a person's relationship with God? *(To repent is to "turn around." But it's not just turning from sin; it's turning to God through Jesus.)* What does it mean to "produce fruit" in a spiritual sense? *(Your outside behavior, should match your inside—mind, character, heart.)* Who were the Pharisees and Sadducees? *(Pharisees were Jewish leaders who followed the entire Old Testament Law plus their own interpretations of it. Sadducees were political leaders. If they believed in God at all, they didn't believe He bothered supernaturally with peoples' lives.)* What does it mean that Jesus "will baptize you with the Holy Spirit and with fire"? *(Focused submission to the Holy Spirit gives us the power to live for God and be Christ's witnesses. "Fire" refers to both God's purifying presence and refining work in our lives.)* Why was Jesus baptized? *(To show everyone watching that He was set apart for God and to set the example of submitting to God's purposes.)* What do the events surrounding Jesus' baptism reveal about the character and uniqueness of God? *(All three persons in the Trinity are present, being Who they are individually, but One in purpose.)*

PRAY: Ask God to help you understand His Word and to apply it to your life daily. If you are aware of any way in which your beliefs and behavior don't line up or that you are not obeying something God has told you, ask Jesus to forgive you and to help you make a definite change.

ACT: Make a conscious and determined effort to obey God in ways that you may have previously overlooked or neglected. Also, if you have not yet been baptized in water since surrendering your life to Christ, talk to your pastor about doing so as a means of following Jesus' example and identifying with Him.

Fire Starter

Matthew 4:1-25

THINK: Think of the times when you seem to be most vulnerable to spiritual attack and temptation. How do you typically hold up under the pressure? God has given you tools for success and an example to follow in overcoming even the toughest temptations. The devil tried to take advantage of Jesus and distract Him from His mission, just as he will try to do to you. But if you follow Jesus' example, He will give you victory over the enemy's fiercest attacks.

RESPOND: What was Satan's goal in tempting Jesus? *(Satan did and said what he thought it would take to provoke Jesus to sin.)* In what ways had Jesus prepared for Satan's attacks? *(Jesus obviously knew God and knew His Word long before He faced these temptations.)* How did Jesus' use of God's written Word differ from Satan's? *(Whereas Satan quoted Scripture correctly but out of context, Jesus both quoted and used God's Word correctly.)* What does this passage reveal about Satan, how he will attack you spiritually, and how you can resist his attacks? What can you learn from how Jesus' first disciples responded to Him (cf. verses 20,22)?

PRAY: Ask Jesus to help you recognize times when you are most susceptible to spiritual attack and temptation. Pray that God will help you fill your mind with His Word and bring it to mind when you face difficulty and temptation. Also, ask God to use you to bring help and healing to hurting people.

ACT: Bring your Bible with you today and take it out when you have spare time. Find a verse that is special to you and memorize or recite it throughout the day. Also, stay alert for anyone who may be hurting physically, emotionally or spiritually. Don't be afraid to tell them that you'll pray for them. If God gives you an opportunity to talk about a spiritual issue, trust Him to guide your conversation.

Fire Starter

Matthew 5:1-20

THINK: In what ways are you trying to find satisfaction and significance in life? This passage challenges us to consider the types of people who find true joy and fulfillment as part of God's kingdom. Their character, values and behavior are vastly different from those who try to find happiness and success apart from a relationship with Jesus. Think about how life would be different—for you and for others—if you applied Jesus' instructions from this passage.

RESPOND: People who pursue worldly goals, such as material wealth or power, never seem to get enough. How does this contrast with those who pursue God's standards and purposes? *(Your desire for righteousness directly influences your character and behavior.)* What does it mean to be meek (as Jesus instructed us to be)? *(It's having the attitude, "Yes, Lord, You are the boss of me," acting like it, and being okay with it.)* What does it mean to "hunger and thirst for righteousness" and how does this bring spiritual satisfaction? What special connection do "the pure in heart" have with God? What kind of influence can you have on others if you demonstrate the character traits described in this chapter? What does it mean that Jesus' followers are "salt" and "light" in the world? *(In the same way salt enhances flavor and light helps people see where it's dim or dark, true Christians benefit others and help people see Jesus more clearly.)* How does your life and "light" stand out in your home, school, and neighborhood?

PRAY: Ask God to help you develop character traits that will give others an accurate impression of Jesus. Pray for the strength to endure the opposition that is sure to come from following His purposes.

ACT: Select one of the character traits mentioned in this passage that you need to develop more fully in your life. Make a conscious effort to practice this trait today. Pay particular attention to how your attitudes, actions and conversation should differ from those who don't follow Jesus. Look for ways to serve and assist others in ways that demonstrate Jesus' compassion.

Fire Starter

Matthew 5:21-48

THINK: God's laws and commands are not obsolete standards of the past; they are reflections of God's character, desires, standards and purposes. Because of that, the ethical and moral principles of God's Laws still apply today. Just as Jesus' perfect life fulfilled all the requirements of God's Law, the Holy Spirit also empowers the lives of Jesus' followers so that they too can live in a way that upholds the spiritual principles and truths of the Law. (Review verses 17-20.)

RESPOND: As a follower of Jesus, what should be your attitude, relationship and response to God's Law? In what ways does Jesus set an even higher standard than the one set by God's Old Testament Law? How are a person's thoughts and motives related to his or her behavior and overall relationship with God and others? What does it mean to "lust" over another person? What does Jesus say about this, and how can you overcome this tendency *(Consciously think of people as sacred, loved by God and pursued by the Holy Spirit, just like you. Treat them as someone worth honoring.)* What does Jesus say about how you should treat your "enemies" and why? *(Don't mirror back what someone is dishing out, whether a condescending attitude, a nasty remark, or an unprovoked attack. Jesus isn't saying to be a doormat. But if at all possible, show kindness and respect, without either belittling or attacking them.)*

PRAY: Ask God to help you guard your thoughts, attitudes and motives so that they result in actions that please Him and reflect His purity and graciousness toward others.

ACT: While it's not a sin to be tempted, it is wrong to dwell on ungodly and impure thoughts. Don't set yourself up for failure. Avoid situations that stir up improper attitudes and desires. This includes the images that you look at from various media. Also, watch your conduct to ensure that your behavior does not inspire ungodly thoughts, desires and actions in others.

Matthew 6:1-18

THINK: If you are a Christian, why do you serve Jesus? Think about your deepest motivation for following Christ and doing things for God. Do your acts of service reflect authentic love for God and a desire to please Him? Consider the reasons and motives behind your prayers. Do they tend to be self-serving—focused on your own needs and concerns—or are they aimed at honoring God and fulfilling His purposes?

RESPOND: What are the problems with doing good things primarily because of what others might think or notice? *(God doesn't honor impure motives.)* Does Jesus' challenge to "pray . . . in secret" mean that you should keep your personal relationship with Jesus private? *(While we don't want to hide the fact that we follow Jesus, we can know Him so much more deeply and hear His voice more clearly when we pray privately.)* How would you explain to someone your reason for following Jesus? What can you learn from Jesus' prayer in verses 9-13? Why is forgiving others so important to your relationship with God? *(Forgiving others not only shows them God's character, it frees us from resentment that can take hold of our life.)* What is fasting and how can it play a significant role in your prayer life and spiritual discipline? *(Abstaining from food for a set period of time to focus on God through prayer and meditation can help us hear His voice more clearly and know Him better.)*

PRAY: Using Jesus' prayer in verses 9-13 as a guide, use your own words, situations and perspective to pray in a way that honors God and focuses on His purposes for your life and your current situation. Consider fasting a meal and spending that time with God in prayer.

ACT: Do something completely selfless for someone today—something that reflects God's love and kindness but is not likely to benefit you in any way other than the satisfaction of serving Jesus and following His example. If you have an unresolved problem with anyone, take the first step to settle the issue and forgive any offenses.

Matthew 6:19 through 7:6

THINK: Consider how you spend the majority of your time and effort. Then think of your greatest dreams and aspirations. Do you sometimes find yourself worrying about things God promised to take care of in verses 25–32? What kind of images and influences are you allowing into your life by what you look at and watch? Are God's priorities and desires the driving and defining factors in your life?

RESPOND: What does it mean to store up treasures in heaven (verses 19,20), and what does that have to do with the spiritual condition of your heart (verse 21)? How are the things you look at and watch affecting your thoughts, attitudes, actions and relationship with Jesus? *(Images are permanently retained in our minds. Ask yourself, "If I look at what I'm about to look at, how will it affect me or my relationship with God and others if the images pop up in my mind later?")* In what ways might a person "serve" money (verse 24)? Why does God tell us not to worry about the provisions we need in life? *(It's okay to use a budget; in fact, it's wise. But to obsess over money and possessions is worry on mental steroids!)* What does it mean to seek God's kingdom and righteousness? *(Seek: [verb] attempt to find, desire, obtain, or achieve something. This is active, not passive!)* In what ways is it appropriate for Christians to make judgments? In what ways it is not appropriate? How should we approach people if we truly want to inspire change?

PRAY: Ask God to help you stay focused on lasting and eternal priorities. Ask Him to help you be patient and gracious toward others. Express thanks to God for His continual care and provision in your life.

ACT: Make a conscious effort to avoid watching or looking at anything that would not please God and uplift you spiritually. Consciously avoid being critical of anyone today. Instead, hand out as many genuine compliments as you can to encourage others.

Fire Starter

Matthew 7:7-29

THINK: Are you as persistent in seeking what God wants from you as you are about getting what you want from God? Does your time in God's Word simply help you to know about God, or to actually know Him personally? Do you sometimes get more excited about the opportunities and experiences you have as a Christian than about spending quality time with Jesus and getting to know Him better?

RESPOND: What is Jesus trying to say by telling you "ask," "seek" and "knock"? What does it show when we keep asking, seeking and knocking? What does it mean that the road to life is narrow and few find it? *(Since following Jesus requires humility, selflessness, servant-hood, and sacrifice, let's be real: do the majority of people come by those things naturally? For all of us, those traits result from hard choices we make day after day in big and little ways.)* What do you do when you have doubts about whether someone is really speaking God's truth? *(When you have doubts, ask, [1] Do they think and speak more highly about God or experiences/results?, [2] Are they more concerned with taking care of themselves or pointing people to Jesus?, [3] Do they compromise biblical teaching?, [4] Are their beliefs based on supernatural experiences alone or do they back what they believe with Scripture?)* How can you ensure that your relationship with God is on solid ground? How can putting God's Word into practice help you weather the storms of life? What kind of plan or strategy do you have for remembering and applying what you learn from your time in God's Word?

PRAY: Ask God to help you do more than just gain knowledge from His Word, but to also help you retain and apply what He shows you on a daily basis. Also, pray that you continue to rely on God for direction and discernment.

ACT: Make a deliberate effort to apply something God has shown you through His Word today or recently. Think of something you felt He wanted you to do, but you never quite put it into action.

Matthew 8:1-27

THINK: Think about the people at school, work or in your community who seem to be shunned by others. Like Jesus, are you willing to reach out with compassion and "touch" those who may be rejected by others? Then consider this: Do you take Jesus at His Word, or do you tend to want "proof" of His power before trusting Him with difficult situations and choices? Remember, there is nothing you can "give up" for God that He will not ultimately replace with something greater and more fulfilling.

RESPOND: What was significant about the fact that Jesus touched the man who had leprosy? *(Answer honestly: would you want to touch someone with a grotesque, oozing, bad-smelling skin condition? Jesus does.)* Why would Jesus tell the man not to tell anyone what had happened? What were some of the outstanding aspects of the centurion's faith? *(Here's a guy most people today would call "Chief," or "Commander," but he is smart enough to know who the real boss is. He recognizes that Jesus has the power and authority to command healing and he's humble enough to ask. God loves that!)* Is God calling you to befriend or demonstrate compassion to someone whom others avoid or reject? Considering how many people wanted to see Jesus and how many others witnessed and experienced His power, why did they find it difficult to truly follow Him?

PRAY: Pray for someone you know who needs physical healing. If you have opportunity, don't hesitate to tell the person that you are praying for them. Ask Him to fill you with His active compassion for those who need a touch from God.

ACT: Reach out and befriend someone who seems socially isolated and left alone by others. Allow God to push you out of your comfort zone in regard to the people you typically associate with and the ways you would ordinarily trust God to use you.

Fire Starter

Matthew 8:29 through 9:17

THINK: Are you up for an adventure? Do you dare to trust God beyond what is obvious or convenient? And do the people you hang out with encourage your faith in this respect? Do you spend too much time with people who don't think they need God and not enough time with people who would probably admit that they need His help? And when you are with Christians, how much of an effort do you make to introduce those you come in contact with to Christ so that He can help and heal them?

RESPOND: Why do you think the people of the Gadarenes pleaded with Jesus to leave them after an obvious miracle? In what ways are you allowing God to push you beyond your comfort zone in respect to your spiritual growth and service? Do you know anyone who needs to experience Jesus' help and forgiveness and is probably ready to receive His help? What could you do or say to reach out and let that person know that Jesus can help them? *(Ask God to give you creative ideas for this. Don't automatically assume giving money is the answer, though it may be at times. You don't have to be best friends with everyone, but you can build everyone up by your kindness and show of respect. Who could use a kind note taped to their car windshield or slipped into their locker? If you drive, does someone need a ride somewhere?)*

PRAY: Ask God to help you reach the people around you who are in desperate need of a relationship with Jesus. Pray that God will give you boldness and creativity in building relationships and leading others to a point where they can see their need for Jesus.

ACT: Spend time today with people outside of your typical circle of friends—people who seem to realize they are missing something in life and may be open to Christ. Whether or not you have an opportunity to talk about spiritual matters, make a new acquaintance. Perhaps you could invite him or her to join you at a youth group event.

Fire Starter

Matthew 9:18-38

THINK: Do you need a miracle or know anyone who does? Jesus' healing power is not limited by a person's condition or circumstances, or by people's reactions or expectations. He responds to humble faith and He works out of compassion for individuals, not a need for attention. How much do you trust Jesus when you or those close to you need healing? Keep in mind that true faith does not rely on what you think will happen; instead, it leaves the situation in God's hands, regardless of what the outcome appears to be.

RESPOND: What is your first response when facing illness in your own life or those close to you? Does this response indicate faith in God? Why or why not? Why do you think Jesus told the crowd to leave the house (verse 24)? Why do you think He asked the formerly blind men not to talk about what happened (verse 30)? What do you think was Jesus' main motivation for performing these miracles? What does Jesus mean when He says, "The harvest is plentiful"? *(There are plenty of people ready and willing to hear the gospel message and learn more about Jesus, especially when He is presented in a way they can understand or, at least, which makes them curious to learn more.)* What evidence do you see that people are spiritually lost and helpless? How should you respond to these spiritual realities (verse 38)?

PRAY: Pray for several people you know who need miracles. Follow Jesus' instruction (verse 38) and ask God to send more workers into the spiritual harvest. Make yourself available as part of the answer to that prayer.

ACT: Pay particular attention to the individuals and crowds around you today. Try to view them with Christ's compassion— as people who are lost and looking for direction that only He can give. Trust God for the opportunity to talk about spiritual issues with someone who does not yet know Jesus.

Fire Starter

Matthew 10:1-23

THINK: Do you ever feel like everyone is in charge of you and you don't have authority over anything? The fact is that God has given you His authority to accomplish His work, bringing hope, healing and the message of new life through faith in Jesus Christ. With that in mind, consider the life, love and blessings that God has given you. How much of this are you passing on to others?

RESPOND: What authority did Jesus give His disciples and how were they to use it? *(Jesus gave His disciples the authority to cast out demons and heal people in His name. We, like Jesus' disciples, have His authority, but it's not our power; it's His.)* What did it mean for them to preach, "The kingdom of heaven is near"? *(Jesus has the same authority on earth as He does in heaven. Whatever God is doing in heaven, we want the effects of it on earth.)* Do you think that the powerful signs and miracles mentioned in verse 8 are still necessary and available today? Why or why not? If so, why are these things not often evident in the lives of Christians? How do you prepare for spiritual opposition and how do you ensure that you can hear the Holy Spirit when He wants to speak through you? *(It's funny how sometimes God's Spirit will plant thoughts and words in our minds to share with others. When we're open to God using us in that way, He will.)*

PRAY: Ask God to work through you in whatever ways He chooses to help others find the healing, joy and fulfillment of a personal relationship with Jesus. Ask Him to prepare you for the opposition you will face in taking a stand for Christ.

ACT: Think of a specific way in which God has helped or blessed you. Now think of someone who needs similar help, healing, relief or inspiration. Go to that person today, or contact them, and follow the Holy Spirit's direction in sharing God's love and power with them. Be prepared to back your prayers and concern with practical action.

Matthew 10:24–42

THINK: Be honest. Does following Jesus ever seem tougher than you thought it would be? Jesus never promised that you wouldn't face spiritual attack, opposition and persecution. However, He is completely aware of what you are going through and promises that you don't face these things on your own. That's why He gives you the power of the Holy Spirit to guide and enable you to serve Him with ultimate effectiveness.

RESPOND: In what specific ways are you striving to be more like Jesus (verse 25)? What does the Bible teach about hell? *(God's Word teaches that hell is a place of eternal punishment and separation from God for those who reject God.)* Why do you not have to be afraid of what any person can do to you? *(Followers of Christ know that ultimately, their lives are in God's hands. Even in the worst case scenario, God has their best interest in mind and, as they trust Him, He will ensure their safe passage to heaven.)* What does this passage indicate about your value to God? What did Jesus mean when He said, "I did not come to bring peace"? *(Even though Jesus gives His followers peace with God, following Him is at odds with the world's value system.)* In what ways does Christ and His message bring contention and division among people? How can you ensure that your love for Jesus always exceeds your love for anyone or anything else?

PRAY: Thank Jesus for His great love. Ask Him to help your love for Him grow as you spend time in His Word. Pray for boldness to face persecution. Give thanks for the opportunity to grow in faith through times of opposition.

ACT: Think of one way to demonstrate Jesus' character toward someone who has given you trouble in the past. If you recall a situation in which you were timid or even ashamed of your relationship with Jesus, make an effort to redeem that situation. You might be surprised at what kind of a door this can open to share Christ.

Fire Starter

Matthew 11:1-30

THINK: Do you ever wrestle with doubts about God's purposes or His work in your life? Even John the Baptist—the one who prepared the way for Jesus—struggled with doubts and insecurity during extremely difficult times. But Jesus understood. He assured John that God's work was being done, and He defended John's legacy of fearlessness and faith. John boldly proclaimed the message of Jesus, and eventually gave his life for his Friend and Lord.

RESPOND: Why do you think John sent his followers to question Jesus? What did Jesus mean when He said that "he who is least in the kingdom of heaven is greater than he (John the Baptist)"? *(John was born before Jesus. It's as if he straddled the time between the old and new covenant [agreement between God and man]. Jesus ushered in a new covenant with mankind, replacing the old covenant. Any believer born in and after Jesus' time would benefit from the authority, power, grace, and freedom this new covenant brought.)* What does it mean that "the kingdom of heaven has been forcefully advancing, and forceful men lay hold of it"? *(Promoting God's mission on earth is active, not passive.)* In what way is God's truth hidden (verse 25) from people who are only wise in a worldly sense? In what sense does Jesus provide rest for those who are weary?

PRAY: Ask God to help you overcome any doubts you might have regarding God's work and your relationship with Jesus. Pray for courage, intensity and perseverance in pursuing God's purposes for your life. If you are spiritually weary in any way, ask God to refresh you as you spend time with Him.

ACT: Instead of being reactive with your faith and simply responding to situations or opportunities, focus on being proactive—pursuing and creating opportunities to demonstrate Jesus' love and communicating His message. Take the first step and do something that may be uncharacteristically bold for you regarding your faith. Don't be pushy or obnoxious, but find a way to honor God in a deliberate way today.

Matthew 12:1-21

THINK: When Jesus walked the earth, He was a polarizing figure. People responded to Him in extreme ways. No doubt, some followed Jesus solely out of fascination or because of what He could do for them. But others recognized Jesus as Lord and put their faith in Him as their only Source of hope and spiritual salvation.

RESPOND: Why were the Pharisees so upset by what Jesus and His disciples were doing? *(Jesus was upsetting the entire "rule of law" by introducing new ideas that basically wiped out the need for multiple ritual sacrifices and rule-keeping as the means to gain God's favor and blessing.)* What is the true principle and purpose behind a weekly Sabbath, or day of rest? *(Sabbath is more than not working. It's focusing on God and resting.)* Is this purpose still valid for Christians today? How so? In what ways did the Pharisees miss the point of the Sabbath—and of Jesus' mission—distorting its true meaning? *(The Pharisees took Sabbath laws to the extreme, burdening people with odd rules God never required, such as how far a person could walk on the Sabbath. Imagine telling your parents, "I can't help with lunch because the cooking pot weighs too much, and I shouldn't carry more than sixteen ounces on the Sabbath.")* Why were the Pharisees more obsessed with their rules and traditions than with actually helping people who were in desperate need, such as the man with the withered hand?

PRAY: Give thanks to God for giving you times of rest and refreshment. But also ask Him to keep you from being distracted by your own ideas, concerns and benefits. Pray that you will always be able to recognize the good things He wants you to do for others as a means of demonstrating God's mercy and compassion.

ACT: Throughout the day, look for opportunities to represent Jesus by doing good for others. As much as possible, keep the focus off yourself, and do all you can to benefit those around you with random acts of kindness that help and encourage.

Matthew 12:22-50

THINK: The Pharisees were so consumed with themselves—their traditions, positions, comforts and ways of life—that they completely missed Jesus' identity, even to the point of mistaking good for evil and evil for good. They could not comprehend the true nature and purpose of God's kingdom. Are you currently at risk of missing God's plans and purposes because you're caught up in your own image or concerns?

RESPOND: Jesus often refers to "the kingdom of God." What does He mean by that? *(God's ultimate purpose and ways now and in eternity represent, in part, the kingdom of God.)* What does Jesus mean that "blasphemy against the Spirit" is an unforgivable sin? *(To blaspheme is to treat God with disdain and persistently reject His Spirit's power and work in one's life.)* How should your thinking be affected by the fact that you are accountable to God for the words you speak (verses 33-37)? What does it mean for a person to be possessed by a demon or "evil spirit"? *(People can, by continually allowing demonic influences to gain power over their lives, become possessed and bound by demonic spirits. Demonic spirits must submit to Jesus' absolute authority, which is why Christians should respect but not fear the demonic realm.)* Why is it important after Jesus has freed a person spiritually that he or she remains faithful to Jesus and continues to grow in a relationship with Him?

PRAY: Ask God to help you keep your focus on His kingdom rather than on your own concerns or things that would distract you from following His plans for your life. Ask God to help you guard your words so that they are not careless or hurtful toward Him or anyone else.

ACT: Go throughout the day making a conscious effort that everything you do honors and promotes God's kingdom and purposes. If you encounter situations that need a miracle or extraordinary solution, trust God to demonstrate His power in that situation. Also, try to say things that reflect your devotion to Christ and that benefit those around you.

Matthew 13:1-23

THINK: Consider some of the most effective speakers and teachers you've heard. What makes them good communicators? Most likely, they use concepts you can relate to and give real-life examples of how the message connects to life. They probably use stories and word pictures to make their points. Jesus did this as well as anyone, using what the Bible calls parables (from the Greek word parabole meaning "placing beside" as if comparing). Jesus wants you to relate to His message and to comprehend the truth. Though some of His stories may seem like riddles, God will help you understand His Word if you truly desire to fulfill His purposes for your life.

RESPOND: What are parables and how did Jesus use them? *(Parables are stories that teach to make a point.)* Why do you think Jesus used parables, or illustrative stories, to describe God's kingdom and how it relates to life on earth? How and why do you think people's hearts become calloused and their eyes closed so that they cannot comprehend God's truth or the nature of His kingdom? What kinds of things keep people from retaining God's message and experiencing spiritual life and growth? How can you make sure that your life is like good soil that retains God's message and produces spiritual growth?

PRAY: Pray that the cares of life would not harden your heart or close your eyes to God's truth. Ask God to help you understand His Word so you can apply it to your life and be fruitful in your relationship with Jesus.

ACT: Think of any way in which worldly concerns and distractions have kept you from retaining and applying something God has told you or shown you in His Word. Turn that situation around by dealing with or removing the distraction. Then take action. Do what God has asked and apply what God has already shown you so you can grow in that area of your life.

Matthew 13:24-43

THINK: Do you like word pictures and stories? Jesus did. He used many parables (i.e., brief, illustrative stories) to teach lessons and principles about how God's kingdom operates and what things will be like for His people on earth until Jesus returns. Not all of these stories are easy to understand, but Jesus reveals the meaning to those who are ready to listen and follow His instructions, warnings and guidance. Jesus will have such followers throughout the world, and all will encounter similar challenges.

RESPOND: What do the "wheat" and "weeds" represent? *(The "wheat" represents people following and teaching God's Word, as well as their good deeds. The "weeds" are Satan's tactics and people he influences to thwart God's plans and distract people from following God.)* What is Jesus' point in describing wheat and weeds growing together (verses 24-30,36-43)? Why doesn't God remove the weeds immediately, but instead allows evil to co-exist among His people? *(Christ's followers must be wise to the fact that there will always be people who, whether out of ignorance or bad motives, promote a false doctrine.)* Is evil always obvious? Why or why not? How does this situation test Jesus' true followers? How can the weeds affect God's kingdom if His people are not careful? How and why are Christians often influenced by ungodly people around them? What ultimately happens to the "weeds" and to the "wheat"? *(Everyone will face God's judgment.)*

PRAY: Express thanks to God for allowing you to be part of His kingdom. Ask Him for spiritual insight and discernment so you can detect the "weeds" around you. Pray for strength and determination to resist and overcome evil's influence.

ACT: Don't expect a weed free environment in order to grow spiritually. But inspect your own life for weeds—those you need to pull out—and make sure the weeds around you are not choking out your devotion to Christ or hindering your fruitfulness for God.

Matthew 13:44 through 14:12

THINK: What do you value most in life? Using very simple parables, Jesus leaves little doubt about how much His followers should treasure their part in God's kingdom. Jesus paid the ultimate price to provide you with a place in His kingdom as a gift. However, you must surrender all that you are and make Jesus your absolute highest priority and authority in order to fulfill your ultimate purpose. People may reject you for following after Christ, but remember, Jesus understands what it's like to be rejected (see verse 57), and He is always with you.

RESPOND: In regard to God's kingdom, what does it mean that those who found the treasures went and sold everything they had? *(Being part of God's great kingdom here on earth is worth any worldly treasure. Having Him in our lives and accomplishing His purposes on earth should be our highest priorities.)* What evidence is there in your life of how much you value God's kingdom? Why do you think that the people in Jesus' hometown took offense at Him (14:57)? What does that mean to you? What lessons can be learned from the tragic result of Herod's party? *(Herod had reservations about his "gift" to Herodias, but was bound by tradition to keep his word. It's better to suffer the embarrassment of going back on a bad decision than to suffer and cause suffering to others because of your decision.)* How can you do your best to avoid situations and circumstances and behaviors that may lead to unwise decisions and ungodly behavior?

PRAY: Express to God how much you value your place in His kingdom. Thank Jesus for understanding what it's like to experience rejection and for giving you strength to endure it.

ACT: If there is anything hindering your relationship with God or preventing you from accomplishing His purpose, give it up to God today and place your whole heart in His trustworthy care. Also, if you are putting yourself in tempting situations that could provoke foolish decisions, make a deliberate choice to avoid these things as much as possible from now on.

Fire 🔥 Starter

Matthew 14:13-36

THINK: Have you ever experienced a tough time or tragedy and afterward felt like you needed to get away for a while? Jesus' friend and forerunner, John the Baptist, had just been executed and Jesus needed some private time, likely to spend in prayer with His Father. But the crowds, as usual, did not allow Him the alone time. How would you have felt in Jesus' situation? Would you have had the same compassion for people as Jesus did? Notice how Jesus responds to the challenge of "inconveniences" presented by the action and attention of other people.

RESPOND: What spiritual principles can you learn from Jesus' miracle of feeding the crowd of thousands with five loaves and two fish? What does this tell you about Jesus' ability to do great things in and through your life? Throughout His time on earth, Jesus often looked for time alone to pray. What does His example mean to you? What can you learn from Peter's experience of walking on the water (verses 28-31)? What do Jesus' words, "Don't be afraid" (verse 27) mean to you personally?

PRAY: Ask God to give you the patience and compassion He had for people, even when they seem too needy, too demanding or too inconvenient. Thank Jesus for His miraculous power—for the fact that He can do very much with very little. Pray for a greater awareness of His presence to keep you from all fear.

ACT: Go out of your way to show compassion to someone who may be hurting or simply in need of a friend. If you've wanted God to do something extraordinary, look at what you have "in your hand" right now. It may not seem like much, but if you're willing to let Jesus use it, you may soon experience the miracle you've been waiting for. Take some extra time to spend alone with God today.

Fire Starter

Matthew 15:1-28

THINK: Have you ever felt the need to fake something? You may at times be able to fool a lot of people, but you can never pull one over on God. It's one thing to worship in words or songs, but it's another thing to live in a way that is truly worthy of identifying with Jesus.

RESPOND: In what ways can traditions be good? In what way can they get in the way of good or even be bad? In what ways do people sometimes honor God with their lips, while their hearts are far from Him? *(Anyone can follow the rules. God truly cares for you and wants to interact with you by being involved and influencing your daily life.)* What can you do to ensure that your speech and conversation honors God and reflects a pure heart? Jesus' words and actions toward the Canaanite woman may have seemed harsh, but He had a purpose for responding to her as He did. What was His reasoning and what did the woman's words and actions tell you about her? *(The woman passed Jesus' test of her faith in that she made it clear she was willing to take whatever He was willing to give. She understood that even the slightest action from Jesus is more than we can do for ourselves.)*

PRAY: Ask God to help you keep your heart in right relation to Him so that your words and actions reflect love for and devotion to God. Pray with a peaceful but persistent faith that leaves your requests in God's hands but continues to believe that He will do what only He can. Ask God to test your faith as He sees fit.

ACT: Make a note to yourself that will help you remain conscious of your conversations throughout the day. Ask God to keep your motives pure in serving Him. Be conscious of situations throughout the day that may test your faith and character. Pass these tests and grow stronger spiritually by responding in a way that honors God.

Fire Starter

Matthew 15:29 through 16:12

THINK: Once again, just as He had been with the crowd of over five thousand (Matthew 14:13-21), Jesus was moved by compassion for the people and proceeded to do a miracle, providing very much with very little—and having plenty left over. Yet, despite miracles like this and all of the healings Jesus performed, there were still many people—including His disciples—who struggled with a lack of faith. Many of the religious leaders still weren't satisfied and demanded to see another sign from Jesus.

RESPOND: How could people witness such powerful miracles, hear such godly teaching, and experience such genuine compassion, yet still have doubts or even hateful feelings about Jesus? Why did the Pharisees and Sadducees want a miraculous sign from Jesus (16:1)? Do you think it would have changed their perception and attitude toward Him? Why or why not? Why did Jesus not give them what they wanted? In what way did the disciples show a lack of faith by worrying about bread? What did Jesus mean when He told them, "Be on your guard against the yeast of the Pharisees and Sadducees? In what way was their teaching like the yeast? *(Yeast is a fungus that turns sugar into alcohol and carbon dioxide. A small amount affects the whole batch of whatever it's being used in. Somehow it works in a recipe. But the Bible is comparing yeast to the corruption of the Pharisees and Sadducees. Their power-hungry, nit-picky rules affected their entire community.)*

PRAY: Consider what Jesus has done in your life and what you have known Him to do for others. Thank Him for His power and compassion. Ask Him to help you overcome any doubts or lack of faith.

ACT: If there is any area of your life in which you have struggled with a lack of faith toward God, ask Him to forgive and help you. But even more, take a step of action that somehow demonstrates that you are trusting God in that situation or area of life.

31

THINK: To be part of Christ's true Church—His worldwide community of followers—is to be part of the most powerful spiritual "institution" on earth. However, our local churches, which are made up of imperfect people and sometimes centered around human structures and ideas, often lack the power and influence Jesus describes in this passage. But God's power is still available to any of His followers whose lives are built on a solid foundation of faith in Jesus and the bold profession of His message.

RESPOND: Where did Simon's confidence in Christ come from? Why do you think God revealed this to Simon (Peter)? What did Jesus really mean when He said, "On this rock I will build my church"? *(The truth of Peter's confession of "Christ, the Son of the Living God" is what God's Church is built on. Without Christ, there would be no New Testament church.)* What does it mean that "the gates of Hades will not overcome it (the Church)"? *(Nothing can stop Jesus' Church from overcoming the powers of death and hell.)* What does it mean that Jesus has given His followers "the keys of the kingdom of heaven"? *(The "keys" symbolize God's authority, given to believers to use in His name, for His purposes.)* Why did Jesus rebuke Peter so strongly for refusing to accept the fact that Jesus must suffer?

PRAY: Ask the Father to reveal more of Jesus' power, love and character to you, and then to help these traits become a part of your life so that Christ becomes more evident to those around you. Ask Him to help you fill your role in His Church with passion, power and excellence.

ACT: As a follower of Jesus, you have access to all the power and authority you need to be victorious against the forces of evil. Keeping in mind that the Church is to be on the offense and not simply on defense against Satan's kingdom, determine that you will approach your life as a Christian not in a passive way, but in an active way.

Fire Starter

Matthew 17:14 through 18:14

THINK: One of the biggest lies and deceptions Satan uses is to convince people that he doesn't exist. But the Bible talks a lot about the devil and his forces of evil. Jesus expects His followers to use the power and authority He gives them to defeat evil, but they must demonstrate uncompromising faith in God. He must be both the source and the focus of our faith in order for it to be ultimately effective.

RESPOND: What was Jesus' point in saying that His disciples needed more faith, but then saying, "If you have faith as small as a mustard seed . . . Nothing will be impossible for you" (17:20,21)? How can you grow in faith? *(Our goal isn't to have faith in faith, or even in God's power, but rather in God himself. It's not the amount, but the focus of our faith which matters.)* In what ways are God's measure of "greatness" vastly different from the world's standards? In what ways must people become "like little children" in order to be part of God's kingdom? *(Christians should be continually maturing and learning about Jesus and God's Word.)* In what ways might people cause others to sin, and why is that such a serious offense against God?

PRAY: Ask God to remove anything in your life that may be hindering your faith and to build your faith as you spend time in His Word. Ask Him to keep you humble and childlike as you depend on God.

ACT: Think of something that you are trusting God for right now. Make sure that the focus of your faith is not so much the situation or need, but in God himself. Leave the situation in His hands and begin praying that God will be honored in the situation. Also, examine your life to see if you need to deal with or remove anything that could possibly cause another person to compromise their conscience and defy God.

33

Fire Starter

Matthew 18:15–35

THINK: Forgiveness can certainly be tough—both giving it and receiving it. Either way, it's a humbling experience. But Jesus expects His followers to take the initiative in extending forgiveness and working to reconcile differences and disputes in relationships. But sometimes our best efforts to do so are not enough to repair the damage. In these cases, Jesus lays out a biblical pattern for resolving issues, enacting discipline, and restoring godly relationships among people in the church. Though it might seem that people would welcome and appreciate forgiveness, Jesus illustrates how some resent the need to offer as well as receive forgiveness.

RESPOND: Why is there special power among God's people when they join together in prayer and agree in faith? *(Wherever Jesus is, anything is possible—change, help, healing, provision, etc. He promised to be present whenever two or more believers pray together.)* What was Jesus' point in telling His disciples to forgive "seventy-seven times"? Why would the man who had been forgiven of a very large debt turn around and immediately refuse to forgive someone of a very small debt? *(Let's face it: to need forgiveness for anything requires a humble attitude. Perhaps the man in this parable confused humility with humiliation. Some people find being humble humiliating, when in truth, humility is one of the keys to God's heart.)* Why does God take the issue of unforgiveness so seriously?

PRAY: Pray that God keeps you humble enough to both offer and receive forgiveness when necessary. Thank Jesus for providing forgiveness for you through His sacrificial death on the cross.

ACT: If you have an issue or dispute with anyone—or you know of anyone who has an issue with you—take the initiative in asking for and offering forgiveness. Do so graciously, not expecting an apology or anything in return. Also, make a point to show kindness to someone who has wronged you in the past.

Fire Starter

Matthew 19:1-15

THINK: A marriage between a man and a woman represents the first and deepest personal relationship established by God outside of His own relationship with mankind. From the beginning, God had a definite design for this special union. But ever since mankind rebelled against God, people have defied and distorted God's plans regarding all sorts of human relationships. Only by following God's design and relying on His help can we find true fulfillment within a marriage or any other relationship.

RESPOND: What does this passage say about God's plans and intentions for marriage relationships? In what ways do people's attitudes and actions defy God's plans for marriage? Why does God take the break-up of a marriage so seriously? What does this passage indicate about the conditions in which God allows for divorce? *(Marital unfaithfulness—because of adultery or continual, flagrant abuse—is grounds for divorce. It's still a tragedy, but God gives grace to those whose spouses have been unfaithful.)* In what ways does God's forgiveness provide hope and healing for those who have experienced the tragedy of divorce? Why was Jesus so adamant about ministering to children?

PRAY: Pray for couples you know who may be struggling in their marriage, that they would look to God and find resolution in their relationships. Pray for friends who have been hurt by divorce. If your own family has been hit by this tragedy, ask God to bring emotional healing to all involved. Pray that from here on, your family members will learn to depend more fully on God and to follow His plans for their lives.

ACT: Prepare for healthy relationships in your future by relying on God to help you make wise and unselfish decisions in all your relationships. Take time to compliment any couples you know, including your parents, who have exemplified godly devotion in their marriage.

35

Matthew 19:16 through 20:16

THINK: Like the man in this passage, many people wonder what it takes to have a relationship with God. Some who already claim to have "eternal life" think they can earn a relationship with God by doing good things. Jesus already paid the price with His own life. Receiving eternal life is a matter of the heart. It means accepting God's gift without reservation and surrendering your life to His purposes. Ultimately, God desires that you love Him in such a way that nothing in your life takes priority over a relationship with Him, and nothing stands between you and His purpose for your life.

RESPOND: Judging by his questions, what seemed to be the rich man's impression of how to have eternal life? Even though eternal life with God is not something we can earn by effort, why did Jesus say that all the rich man lacked was to sell his possessions and give to the poor? *(Jesus probably knew that the man's wealth was more important to him than anything else.)* What could possibly be a hindrance in your own life if you aren't careful? Why is it so "hard for a rich man to enter the kingdom of God" (verse 24)? In what ways will the first be last and the last be first in God's kingdom? *(God values things in people that aren't always rewarded in the world—character, integrity, God-honoring living, marital faithfulness, and a heart continually turned toward God.)*

PRAY: Ask God to aim His searchlight into your life and reveal anything you're holding on to that may be hindering your relationship with Him or keeping you from fulfilling His plans for your life.

ACT: Follow up on your prayer. Respond to God by removing or giving up whatever may be holding you back so you can experience life to the fullest—now and for eternity.

Fire Starter

Matthew 20:17-34

THINK: What does it take to be great? Consider the concept that many people have of greatness. What are some of the ways people attempt to achieve greatness by worldly standards? Think about some of the people whom the world tends to regard as great leaders and achievers. Would most of these individuals be "great" in God's eyes? Many people aspire to be great at what they do, which can certainly be a good thing. But those who desire to follow Christ must reassess their concept of greatness so that they measure success by God's standard.

RESPOND: Why do you think Jesus told the disciples ahead of time what was going to happen to Him? What did Jesus mean when He asked the disciples if they were prepared to drink from His cup (verse 22)? Why were the other disciples mad at James and John? What did this indicate about their spiritual maturity and what they needed to learn about leadership? How does a person become "great" in God's kingdom? *(The kingdom of God is full of paradoxes [which are similar to oxymorons, like dress pants, altogether separate, dull roar, and awfully nice]. Two such kingdom paradoxes are found in verses 26 and 27.)* How is God's measure of true leadership and authority different from the world's? How did Jesus ultimately model these principles in His own life? What can you learn from how the blind men responded to Jesus and how Jesus responded to them (verses 29-34)?

PRAY: Ask God to help you do your best at whatever you do, but to keep you humble in the process. Ask God for wisdom to discern true greatness and for help in following Jesus' example of servant leadership.

ACT: As a means of reflecting Jesus' character and influencing others for Him, look for opportunities throughout the day to serve others in practical ways. Resist the tendency to be prideful about your efforts. If you are not actively involved in a service role at your church, talk to a leader about finding a place of ministry.

Fire Starter

Matthew 21:1-32

THINK: Approaching things from God's perspective will seldom be popular, but it will change lives. Throughout His life and ministry on earth, Jesus demonstrated that God's view of authority, power, position and leadership was vastly different from the world's concept. Though Jesus accepted His rightful place as God's Son, He exemplified humility in all He did. He didn't care what people thought about His approach when it came to delivering His message or fulfilling His Father's plan. In order to influence others as Jesus did, you must not worry about people's perceptions. Instead, you must pursue God's purposes.

RESPOND: Why did Jesus ride into Jerusalem on a donkey? What did the crowd's actions reflect about their view of Jesus at that point? Do you think the people comprehended Jesus' true mission and purpose? Why or why not? Why did Jesus respond as He did in the temple area? What does this indicate about His mission and purpose? *(Greed, hypocrisy, and disrespect in God's house are no more appropriate or pleasing to Him than they are outside of church.)* What do you think Jesus was trying to teach His disciples about faith by His actions and words regarding the fig tree? *(There is a direct link between the focus of our faith and answered prayers.)*

PRAY: Ask God to help you become more like Jesus in humility and in passion. Pray that you will not follow your own emotions, but that you will be stirred to action by the things that God is passionate about. Ask God to strengthen your faith and dependence on Him as you spend time in prayer.

ACT: Be careful in your actions and conversations throughout the day to ensure that you are not behaving in an arrogant, prideful or selfish way. When you find your emotions being stirred, stop to consider how Jesus might feel and how He would react in your situation. Then respond in a way that honors Him.

Fire Starter

Matthew 21:33 through 22:14

THINK: Regardless of how patient and gracious God is toward people, most will ultimately reject His persistent offers to be a part of His kingdom. They are preoccupied with their own interests and endeavors and they show little interest in God's plans for their life. Ironically, in their attempt to get all they can for themselves, they end up missing their ultimate purpose and passing up the greatest reward.

RESPOND: If the servants represent God's prophets, who is "the stone the builders rejected" (21:42)? What do you think it means that "he who falls on this stone will be broken to pieces, but he on whom it falls will be crushed"? *(Ultimately those who reject and defy Jesus will be crushed under His judgment.)* Who are the "few" and in what sense are they "chosen"? *(The invitation for salvation through Christ is for everyone. However, not everyone accepts the invitation. Accepting God's invitation by an act of one's free will makes them part of God's "chosen" people, inheriting eternal life!)*

PRAY: Give thanks to God for extending to you the gracious invitation to be part of His kingdom. Pray for friends who have not accepted the invitation or have outright rejected God up to this point. Pray that they will accept Christ before it's too late. Ask God to use you to reach them, regardless of the cost.

ACT: As you go through the day, view the people around you like those on "the street corners" (22:9) whom the king invited to his banquet after others had turned down his invitation. As a willing servant, deliver God's invitation without prejudice, keeping in mind that the invitation went out to "both good and bad" (22:10). You could take the first step in bringing someone closer to Christ simply by inviting a new friend to join you for lunch or to come with you to youth group this week. If you have not personally accepted God's invitation, you can do so right now by asking Jesus to forgive your sins and take charge of your life.

Matthew 22:15-46

THINK: Throughout His ministry, Jesus faced deception and trickery from the religious leaders of His day. In their attempt to satisfy God in their own way, they completely overlooked Jesus' true identity and purpose. As a result they tried to use insincere flattery and their own interpretations of the Law in an attempt to trap Jesus by His own words. If He came across as too supportive of the Roman government, He might alienate himself from the people who felt oppressed by that government. But if He appeared to defy the Romans, they could accuse Him of rebellion or treason. But Jesus saw through their deceit and gave replies that silenced His critics.

RESPOND: Why did the religious leaders and others try to flatter Jesus with smooth words while trying to trick Him into saying something incriminating? How was Jesus able to deflect their questions and avoid their trap? How did knowing God's Word help Him? In what sense are all of God's laws and messages summed up in the commands to love God completely and love others selflessly? What does it mean to "love your neighbor as yourself"? *(Loving your neighbor as yourself means, among other things, pointing them to Jesus, doing what's best for them, helping in the way they need [which isn't always the way they want], and treating them the way you want to be treated.)*

PRAY: Ask God to always keep you honest with Him. Pray that He will help you retain His Word so that it can help you overcome deception. Ask God to strengthen and deepen your love for Him and to reflect His love in your motives, attitudes, words and actions toward others.

ACT: Do something completely selfless for at least two people today. Put their concerns, needs or interests ahead of your own and expect nothing in return. Treat everyone you encounter the way you would prefer to be treated. Make this your regular practice as a means of honoring God.

Matthew 23:1-39

THINK: Do you ever catch yourself doing things simply to please or impress other people? Jesus strictly warns His followers not to seek popularity and positions. (Anyone can be a "good" person, following the rules. Rule following, however, isn't the key to God's heart or eternal life. All of our lives we should ask the question: What matters most to God? As you read the Gospels, make a list in your journal or one of the blank pages in the back of your Bible of how Jesus answers this important question.) In this passage, Jesus may come across as harsh to those who are not what they appear to be. Yet He is motivated by sincere compassion (verses 37,38) for those who may be influenced by insincere and hypocritical people.

RESPOND: What kind of problems might a person who constantly seeks recognition or affirmation from others encounter? How can being humble lead to honor? Why is it so important for those who claim to know God and follow Christ to "practice what they preach" (verse 3) and to live what they believe? What is a hypocrite, and what harm can such a person do to the cause of Christ? *(Hypocrisy is like bringing a shade across the true image of Jesus. Nothing can hide Jesus, but hypocrisy makes it hard for people to see Him as clearly. By the way, the word* hypocrite *is derived from a Greek word which means an actor in a play. Think of it this way: Don't act like a Christian; just be one.)*

PRAY: Ask God to help you live in a way that is consistent with your faith in Christ. Ask God to help you resist the temptation to seek popularity or recognition and to eliminate any inconsistency in your life that could distract others from accepting and following Christ.

ACT: Examine your life to determine if there is any way in which you are being hypocritical and are at risk of misleading others spiritually by your example. Ask God to forgive you, then determine to make a distinct change so that your behavior mirrors your belief.

Matthew 24:1-35

THINK: Jesus answers His disciples' question about the sign of His return and "the end of the age" (verse 3) by describing several indicators and events that will characterize the last days before He takes His followers from the earth. Toward the end of the Tribulation, more horrific signs will signal Jesus' literal return to earth to conquer evil and rule in peace at the end of time as we know it. Judging from conditions in the world today, it appears that Christ's return is fast approaching. Note: many details of Christ's coming—and the end times in general—are not revealed in this passage. In some cases, the timing or order of events is uncertain.

RESPOND: What are some of the conditions that will be evident in the last days before Jesus returns? What will happen with Christ's message? *(The good news of forgiveness through Jesus' death and resurrection will have been shared to the entire world.)* What is Jesus' primary purpose in describing these times and events? Why will people be so easily deceived in the last days, even though God's Word offers plenty of warning? *(When you realize how easily people—even you and I—can be deceived, "read your Bible" becomes more than a convenient Sunday School answer. It becomes essential.)* What evidence is there of increasing hatred and opposition toward Christ's followers? What should you do to prepare for these times?

PRAY: Pray for the spread of Christ's message around the world, which will precede His coming. Pray that God uses you to spread the message with a sense of urgency in your corner of the world right now. Pray that people would be more open to God as they see some of the end-time conditions described in the Bible.

ACT: Familiarize yourself with the "signs of the end of this age" in verses 4-14. Note how these relate to specific occurrences in the world today. Use some of these issues to spark conversations with friends about spiritual matters. Look for the opportunity to talk specifically about knowing Jesus and being ready for His return.

Fire Starter

Matthew 24:36-51

THINK: Do you know what's coming in the days ahead? In this passage, Jesus continues to describe the events surrounding His second coming. Jesus' statements here have a double reference, with implications to two distinct "stages" of end-time events. The first stage is the "rapture" when Jesus returns suddenly at an unknown time to take His faithful followers from the earth prior to the Tribulation period. The second stage is His return to earth at the end of the Tribulation.

RESPOND: Why will Jesus' return take people off guard? What does it mean to "keep watch" for His return? *(People like to say, "I was born ready," when asked if they're ready to do something or go somewhere. Jesus wants us to stay ready for His return. This is actually active, not passive. We're to live as though we're preparing for His immediate return every day.)* Why is Christ's coming compared to a thief breaking into a house? How should the fact that Christ will return for His followers at an unknown time affect the way you live right now?

PRAY: Pray that God would keep you alert to Christ's soon return so that you will remain faithful to Him. Pray for people you know who do not have a personal relationship with Jesus, asking God to use you to reach them with the message of forgiveness and new life before it is too late.

ACT: Think of someone close to you who does not have a personal relationship with Christ and would be left behind when He returns. If you see that person today, make it a point to spend time with your friend and try to talk about things that might lead to a discussion of Christ and the salvation He offers. If you won't see the person, make a point to call or send a note or e-mail of support and friendship.

Fire Starter

Matthew 25:1-30

THINK: Over the last couple days you've considered Christ's challenge to be ready for His return. Does that simply have to do with accepting His forgiveness and beginning a new life? Of course it starts there, but being prepared for the coming of Christ is more than a one-time decision. It involves a continuously devoted relationship with Jesus and persistent faithfulness with the resources and opportunities God has given you to serve Him.

RESPOND: What were the essential differences between the wise and foolish virgins in Jesus' parable? How does this serve as a warning to many in the Church who claim to know Christ at this time? What does the oil represent? *(The oil represents genuine faith, a right relationship with God, and the Holy Spirit's presence and influence in our lives.)* According to the parable of the talents, what is the measure of faithfulness and reward in God's kingdom? What do the talents represent? *(In the New Testament days, a talent was first a measurement of weight, then a unit of coinage. Today, you can think of talents, not only as the gifts God has given you that benefit those around you, but also your abilities, time, resources, and opportunities to serve God and people in ways that matter most to Him.)* What misconceptions did the wicked, lazy servant have about the master, who, in general, represents God? How is one's place in God's eternal kingdom impacted by his or her faithfulness and devotion to God's kingdom now?

PRAY: Ask God to help you remain faithful by constantly growing in your relationship with Him and by making the most of the time, talents, resources and opportunities He has given you to serve Him.

ACT: Take a quick inventory of your life to see if you are being completely faithful with what God has entrusted to you. Do you have an interest, talent or opportunity that you are not fully utilizing to honor God and benefit others? It's time to take action. Talk to your parents or youth leader about serving God and people in meaningful, practical ways.

Fire Starter

Matthew 25:31-46

THINK: The judgment described in this passage likely occurs after Christ's physical return to earth, but before the beginning of His earthly reign. Of all the parables, analogies and illustrative stories Jesus uses to describe God's kingdom and the end times, this is one of the few that describes what will take place "on that day" (Matthew 7:22)—when Christ actually judges individuals for their time on earth and pronounces their eternal destiny. This account of end-time judgment emphasizes how Jesus expects His followers to respond to people who are hurting or in need.

RESPOND: According to this passage, what is one of the primary criteria of God's judgment of people—both those who know Him and those who don't? Who are "the least of these" (verses 40, 45)? Although good works cannot save us, all accounts of judgment described in the Bible indicate that our actions and responses to opportunities on earth will affect our reward or punishment. Why are acts of compassion so important to God (verses 35-46)? Even those who did the right thing were seemingly oblivious to when they acted with compassion. What does this reveal about their character and way of life?

PRAY: Ask God to keep you constantly aware of those around you who are hurting or in need. Thank Jesus for the opportunity to serve Him in practical ways by showing active compassion to others.

ACT: Make a deliberate effort to show kindness and active compassion to people who could use help or a friend, people others tend to overlook. Grab a couple of friends (whether Christian or not) and surprise the maintenance personnel at school or church by asking for several large trash bags to pick up trash around the building(s) before or after school or during lunch. Leave a thank you note or card of encouragement on the desk or locker of a classmate, teacher, or other school personnel—choose someone who needs it most or expects it the least! Babysit free for a family who can't always afford to hire a sitter.

Fire Starter

Matthew 26:1-30

THINK: Jesus came to earth to meet needs. His mission was ultimately to meet our greatest need—the forgiveness of our offenses against God and the restoration of our relationship with Him. Seldom did people show concern for Jesus' desires and few ever catered to His needs. When people did make the time, effort and sacrifice to do something special just for Jesus, their kindness stood out from the crowds. This passage describes one such time.

RESPOND: What is the Passover and what does it represent? *(The Passover celebration recounts the historical account [see Exodus 12] in which the "angel of death" passed over Hebrew homes sprinkled with lamb's blood.)* Why did the leaders plot to arrest Jesus secretly? What made the woman's actions so significant that Jesus said her story would be told wherever His message is preached? *(It meant a great deal to Jesus that this woman sacrificed something of such value just for Him; not to impress anyone in the world or the Church, but for Him alone. Her tender act symbolized selflessness, sacrifice, devotion, and intimacy—all traits that make for a powerful, thriving relationship with Jesus.)* Why do you think Judas was willing to betray Jesus? In what way did the bread at the last supper represent Jesus' body? Why did Jesus have to shed His Blood in order to provide forgiveness of sins? *(Since Old Testament days, God has always required blood sacrifice to pardon people for their sins [see Heb. 9:22]. Our sin actually requires the penalty of death and separation from God. Jesus is the only One who could provide the perfect 'blood sacrifice' for mankind.)*

PRAY: Express thanks to Jesus for the ultimate sacrifice of His life for your sins so you could have a personal and eternal relationship with Him. Ask God to always help you see what is most important to Him.

ACT: Think of something special you could do just for Jesus. Perhaps you could spend some extra time with Him in a place that is special to you. Maybe you could engage in conversational prayer while you work through a favorite activity.

Fire Starter

Matthew 26:31-56

THINK: Jesus already knew what it was like to be misunderstood. He was familiar with intense sorrow. He had faced extreme rejection. But He was about to experience a level of suffering that no one else has ever known. This was the purpose of His coming to earth, and He was prepared for it. Still, as He took upon himself the weight of all the sins of all humanity for all time, He would endure unimaginable grief and isolation. He did this willingly so that we would have the opportunity to escape spiritual death and eternal isolation from God.

RESPOND: How could Jesus' closest disciples desert Him during His greatest time of hardship, especially after all they had been through with Him? What did Jesus mean when He asked, "My Father, if it is possible, may this cup be taken from me"? *(Since Jesus came to earth specifically to die on the cross, it's unlikely He was asking God to change the mission. What's more likely is that Jesus wanted to avoid the spiritual, mental, and emotional torment of separation from His Father.)* What can you learn from Jesus' example (verses 39,42)? Why did Jesus say that it's important for His disciples to pray (v.41)? Why did Jesus not resist arrest when it was within His power to do so?

PRAY: Give thanks to Jesus for all that He willingly endured to provide you with eternal life. Pray that He will give you the strength to stand with Him, regardless of any grief and rejection you might face. Pray that, just like Jesus, you will be prepared to do God's will, whatever it may be.

ACT: Perhaps there is an aspect of life in which you've sensed God's will and desire for you, but you've hesitated to follow His direction. It could be something "big," like what He wants you to do for a career, or it could be "small," like helping a family member or befriending a classmate. Step out and trust God. Give yourself completely to His purpose, regardless of cost, and let God use you however He chooses.

47

Fire Starter

Matthew 26:57-75

THINK: Have you ever been accused of something that you did not do? How did you feel? Did you try to defend yourself? What was your attitude toward those who misunderstood or lied about you? Did you suffer any consequences? Consider how your feelings and reactions may have differed from Jesus' response in this passage, when the consequences He was about to face were more horrendous than any you've ever faced. Remember, Jesus endured all this for you. Rather than speaking up and silencing His accusers, He took their abuse and willingly prepared for the suffering He was about to face in your place.

RESPOND: Why do you think that people were willing to give false testimony about Jesus (verse 60)? Why do you think Jesus remained silent and did not respond when falsely accused (verses 62,63)? Why were Jesus' accusers so furious when Jesus affirmed that He was God's Son? How do you think Jesus felt when they beat, mocked and ridiculed Him? How do you think He felt specifically toward His accusers who did these cruel things? Why did Peter deny Jesus so emphatically after he had once insisted that he would never do such a thing (cf. verses 33,34)? How do you think Peter felt after his staunch denial?

PRAY: Ask Jesus to help you face misunderstanding, injustice and persecution with the same grace and courage He did. Pray for the boldness to acknowledge Jesus to anyone who associates you with Him.

ACT: Think of a time when you were misrepresented, lied about or put in a position you didn't deserve. It's okay to defend yourself to a degree and to seek justice in most situations. But if you retaliated or responded in away that was not Christlike, confess your failure to Jesus. Depend on Him for a gracious attitude as you revisit the situation, making apologies and trying to set things right with anyone else who was involved. This will demonstrate Jesus' character and could even allow you to influence others for Him.

Fire Starter

Matthew 27:1-26

THINK: Most of the time when our decisions and actions get us into trouble or cause problems, we never expected or intended the consequences. In fact, had we known what would happen, we may have handled the situation much differently. But seldom can we undo the wrongs that result from foolish and regretful choices. Sadly, much pain and regret stems from instances when we give in to our own selfish desires or the pressure to please others. If you are unwilling to endure the pressure of doing what's right, you will have to endure the consequences of doing what's wrong.

RESPOND: Why did Judas seem to have regrets after Jesus was condemned? *(It could be that Judas thought people would demand Jesus' release or that Jesus would somehow get out of being condemned.)* What could you learn from Judas' actions about doing things for the wrong motives, even when you may not intend the consequences? Why did Jesus offer no reply to the false testimonies, and why was Pilate so amazed by this? Why would the crowd want a notorious criminal like Barabbas released while calling for Jesus' execution? Why was Pilate willing to compromise what he knew was right and turn Jesus over for execution? *(Like someone protecting his reputation or a politician who makes decisions based on opinion polls, Pilate followed the crowd. Washing his hands in a bowl didn't change the wrongness of his decision.)* In what way does this resemble how people often respond to pressure from others?

PRAY: Ask God for the wisdom and strength to always do what's right, regardless of the pressure, the cost, or what anyone else thinks.

ACT: Be conscious of the decisions you make today and why. Try not to do anything out of selfish motives or because you feel pressured by others or because you want to impress someone. Do the right things for the right reasons in the right ways.

Matthew 27:27-44

THINK: Why did Jesus suffer so intensely? Keep this in mind as you consider what Jesus went through: None of His suffering was due to His own wrongdoing. He did not have to endure any abuse for His own sake; He did it all for us. He loved us so much that He suffered in our place, to pay the price for our offenses against God. We never could have covered this cost ourselves. Our own death would simply give us what we deserve, sealing our separation from God forever. Jesus' sacrifice provided the only hope we have of forgiveness, new life and a personal relationship with God. Because He suffered and died for us, we can live eternally with Him.

RESPOND: How does it make you feel, knowing that Jesus suffered as He did for you? How would you have felt in Simon's place (verse 32), being forced to carry Jesus' cross? What was the significance of Jesus being crucified with criminals? Why would those who passed by Jesus' cross feel inclined to add insults to His injury? What did Jesus really mean when He talked about rebuilding the temple in three days (verse 40)? What irony is there in statements like these: "He saved others . . . but he can't save himself . . . come down now from the cross and we will believe in him" (verse 42)? Would there have been any purpose or benefit from believing Jesus if He had not ultimately suffered?

PRAY: Give thanks to Jesus for dying in your place and paying the price for your sin. Thank Him for the opportunity and privilege you have to live for Him—even when you face grief and rejection for His sake.

ACT: As you always should, make a conscious effort to think, talk, and act in ways that reflect Jesus' character and demonstrate your faith in Him. Whenever you find it difficult to put your faith into practice or to take a stand for Christ, consider what He suffered for you and be encouraged to endure hardship for Him.

Fire Starter

Matthew 27:45-66

THINK: As Jesus was dying on the cross, He endured more than the intense physical torture of crucifixion; He also experienced the spiritual anguish of an unimaginable sense of isolation from His Father. We cannot begin to comprehend the sense of abandonment that Jesus felt as He carried the full weight of guilt and punishment for every sin that has ever been committed or ever will be. Those who accept Jesus' sacrifice for themselves and surrender their lives to Him find forgiveness and eternal life through a personal relationship with God.

RESPOND: How did our sin affect Jesus physically, mentally, emotionally and spiritually? What's the significance of the temple curtain tearing in two at the precise moment of Jesus' death? *(Previously, only the high priest had access to the "Most Holy Place"—God's presence. Because of Jesus, there is no longer a veil, or barrier, between people and God.)* What's the significance of some godly people being raised to life when Jesus died? *(After all those people were raised from the dead, there was no way people could deny the power of God. Now all Christ followers have assurance of bodily resurrection after we've died, by the time Jesus returns.)* What did the women's actions (verses 55,56,61) indicate about their devotion to Jesus? What were the chief priests and Pharisees really worried about when they asked Pilate to secure Jesus' tomb?

PRAY: Express gratitude to Jesus because He died forsaken so that you would not have to be forsaken. Praise Him for restoring your relationship with God and for calling you to share His love and life with others. Pray for those you know who have not accepted Christ and are still living in a state of separation from God.

ACT: In light of the fact that Jesus gave His life to bring you to God, determine that you will devote your life to bringing others to God. Look for a way today to help someone you know grow in their understanding of God or in some way come closer to accepting Jesus for themselves.

Fire Starter

Matthew 28:1–20

THINK: This passage communicates the truth about an event that is absolutely essential to authentic Christian faith—the resurrection of Jesus Christ. Without the resurrection, all other aspects of the Christian message would be essentially powerless and Christian faith would be in vain (1 Corinthians 15:16–19). Thankfully, the resurrection is a reality, providing ultimate hope for Jesus' followers and laying a firm foundation for their God-given mission to spread Christ's message of forgiveness and new life to all the world.

RESPOND: Why is Jesus' resurrection absolutely crucial to those who put their faith and hope in God? What does the resurrection prove? *(Christ's resurrection proves, among other things, that He is God's son, guarantees our forgiveness and access to God, verifies every biblical prophecy about Jesus' resurrection, ensures a heavenly inheritance for all believers and our own resurrection from the dead.)* Why were the women "afraid yet filled with joy" (verse 8)? Even after seeing Jesus after His resurrection, why would some people still doubt (verse 17)? How should the fact that Christ has "all authority in heaven and on earth" affect the lives of His followers? *(Without His authority, believers have no claim to authority.)* What does Jesus' final command—His "Great Commission"—indicate about the goal and responsibility of each of His followers? What does it mean to be and to make disciples of Christ? What does Jesus' promise that "I am with you" mean to you personally? How should it affect your life?

PRAY: Praise Jesus for the privilege and authority He has given you to communicate His message and to represent Him. Thank Him that He is always with you as you aim to accomplish His purposes.

ACT: Accept your mission and responsibility to take Jesus' message of forgiveness and new life to your corner of the world. List five people you know who have not yet accepted Jesus. Commit to pray for these individuals daily. Build relationships with them. Look for opportunities to serve them and to share your personal experience with Jesus.

Fire Starter

Mark 1:1-20

THINK: Before Jesus began His public ministry, John the Baptist prepared the way and previewed the message. That message was simple: turn from your own way and turn toward God and His way. Jesus, God's son, made the way for you to have a personal relationship with God by giving His own life to pay the price for every wrong you've ever done. If you confess your wrongdoing and surrender your old life to Jesus, He will give you new and eternal life through the power of the Holy Spirit who wants to live in and through you.

RESPOND: In relation to God, what does it mean to repent? *(Repentance is first admitting your sin. Then, it's not only turning away from sin, but turning to God to help you not live in sin. You can't do one without the other.)* How would Jesus baptize people compared to how John baptized them? *(Whereas John baptized people in water to outwardly signify their surrender to a God-honoring life, Jesus baptizes His followers with the Holy Spirit, cleansing them inwardly, empowering them to live a God-honoring life.)* What are some things we can learn about the nature and character of God from the events surrounding Jesus' baptism? How would you explain the concept of the "Trinity"? *(All three persons in the Trinity—God the Father, Jesus the Son, and the Holy Spirit—exist distinctly and simultaneously, united in purpose.)* What can we learn from how Jesus' first disciples responded to His call (verses 18,20)?

PRAY: Give Jesus thanks for allowing you to be part of His kingdom. Pray that His authority, power and purposes will be at work through your life and that He uses you to bring others into His eternal kingdom.

ACT: If there is anything in your life for which you need to repent, confess it to God and ask for His help in making a complete change. If you sense God asking you to do something, don't hesitate to act, respond to His call immediately, like His first followers.

Fire ✹ Starter

Mark 1:21-45

THINK: Have you ever known of someone who had a position of authority but seemed to lack compassion or concern for people? Jesus is someone you can know personally who has ultimate power and authority over everything. Yet not only does He have the ability to help and heal, He also has the desire to show compassion and do what's best for you in every situation. Even more, He has the ability and the desire to demonstrate His power and compassion through you.

RESPOND: What is the "synagogue"? *(Meaning "gathering place," it was a place for worship, teaching, prayer, and community.)* How was Jesus' authority different from that of the teachers of the Law? What does Jesus' response to the demons (verses 25-27) tell us about Him? *(Jesus shows that there's no middle ground when dealing with demonic influences, whether in community or personally. He dealt with demons quickly, succinctly, and left no room for negotiations as far as the person involved went.)* Why did Jesus not permit the demons to speak of His identity? What difference do you think Jesus' prayer life made in His ministry? What can we learn from how the man with leprosy approached Jesus (verse 40) and from how Jesus responded to him (verses 41,42)? Why did the people keep coming to Jesus regardless of where He was?

PRAY: Praise Jesus for His awesome power and authority over all things, including the forces of evil in this world. Ask Him to have His way in your life and to give you compassion for people that allows you to influence them for God. Pray for someone you know who is facing spiritual opposition or is in need of help and healing.

ACT: Do more than pray. Reach out to someone today who needs to experience Jesus' power and compassion. Don't wait for someone to cross your path. Go to him or her and offer an encouraging word and do something practical to help. Let the person know that you are praying. If appropriate, pray for them on the spot, in person.

Fire Starter

Mark 2:1-22

THINK: There are a lot of people in the world who don't think they need God. Some simply want to live life on their own terms. Others may not totally disregard God, but they think that their own efforts are good enough to assure them favor with Him. As a result, they fail to entrust their lives and spiritual salvation to God's Son, Jesus, who provided the only true way to eternal life with God. Sadly, many people not only reject Jesus themselves, they make it difficult for others to find hope and fulfillment through Him. Then again, there are people who not only follow Jesus, they do what they can to help others find forgiveness, hope and new life through Him. Which of these descriptions fits you best?

RESPOND: What can we learn about bringing people to Jesus from the story of the healing of the paralyzed man (verses 1-12)? What does Jesus' response to the teachers and Pharisees tell us about His mission on earth (verses 16,17)? What did Jesus mean when He said, "I have not come to call the righteous, but sinners."? *(None of us are "righteous" on our own. Jesus was emphasizing that those who are right in their own eyes may not see their need for a Savior, but there's hope for those who recognize their sinfulness and need for forgiveness.)*

PRAY: Pray for someone you know who sees no need for God in his or her life. Pray that God will open your friend's eyes to the love and existence of God.

ACT: While many people see no need for Jesus, there are likely those around you who are looking for hope and would be open to Him. Think of someone who has a need and may be ready to consider Christ. Then think of a way to help bring him or her closer to receiving Jesus. Befriend this individual and learn his or her story. You could also invite this person to church or to an event with friends.

Fire Starter

Mark 2:23 through 3:12

THINK: How often do you find yourself getting angry, and what kinds of things make you angry? Do you usually feel right in getting angry, or do you frequently regret it? And what kinds of consequences often result from your anger? Like any emotion, anger can arise for a variety of reasons and lead to any number of outcomes—some good and some bad. Anger itself is not often the issue. Something deeper usually triggers it. While you cannot always control the circumstances, you can control your emotions so that you respond appropriately to people and situations.

RESPOND: What is the Sabbath and how did God design it to benefit people? *(God established the Sabbath as a blessing for humans, a way to keep us focused on Him, to give us one day to rest from our work, just like He did. The Sabbath is primarily an act of worship, which God deserves. But you have to admit, there's a lot of common sense behind it, in terms of helping us keep priorities straight and living a well-balanced life.)* Why was Jesus angry at those who were trying to find a way to accuse Him (cf. 3:5)? Why were some of the leaders more concerned about their laws and traditions than with the desperate need of the man in 3:1–6? Is anger a good thing or bad thing for a Christian? Explain. *(Jesus' anger in this situation left no doubt as to what He believed was unjust and dishonoring to God. This doesn't mean we can justify taking violent action against those who are evil. But to hate evil itself is Christlike when we do what we can to overcome it in godly ways.)* What should a Christian's attitude be toward evil, hypocrisy, and injustice?

PRAY: Ask God to help you control your emotions and to respond to situations and circumstances in ways that are appropriate, beneficial and God-honoring. Pray for anyone who is trying to get the best of you.

ACT: Make a conscious effort throughout the day to control your frustration and anger at all times. If you are currently facing situations in which anger is justified, think of practical and constructive ways to redirect your emotions. Let your actions speak louder than your emotions and find a way to affect positive change in the situation.

Mark 3:13-35

THINK: There is a difference between religion and following Jesus. Religion has to do with rules and routines aimed at reaching God. But following Jesus is not about religion; it's about a relationship in which God made His way to people and opened the way for us to come freely to Him. As a follower of Jesus, your primary concern should be to fulfill His ultimate desire, which is for you to be with Him. Everything else you do for God must flow out of your relationship with Him.

RESPOND: What is an apostle? *(Apostle translated from the Greek word* apostolos *is "messenger" from* apostellein *"sent forth." Jesus sent the apostles out to represent Him.)* What was Jesus' primary calling for His original twelve disciples, and for His followers today? *(A disciple of Jesus' first purpose is to "be with" Jesus, secondly to serve and learn from Him.)* What is one aspect of the authority Jesus gave His disciples and what did this involve? What does Jesus mean by the statement, "If a house is divided against itself, that house cannot stand" (verse 25)? Whom does Jesus consider to be part of His family (verse 35)?

PRAY: Ask God to help you remain aware of your primary purpose and main motives for serving Him. Pray that you will never allow the things you do for God to get in the way or take priority over your time with God. Then ask Him to help you do what He wants you to do out of love and gratitude toward Him.

ACT: Consider all the things you will do this week that are associated with your faith and serving God. How much of this will be spent not just doing things for God or about God, but literally being with God and developing your personal relationship with Him? While time is not always the main issue, it can be one of the best indicators of your priorities. Take extra time today and this week to spend with Jesus.

Fire Starter

Mark 4:1-20

THINK: God never intended for it to be hard to receive His message. But when it comes to following through on that commitment and actually growing in a relationship with Him, God's Word never promises that it will be easy. In fact, the Bible warns of many obstacles and forms of opposition that will try to deter and destroy your devotion to Jesus. But it also promises that if you rely on God and remain deeply devoted to Christ, you will grow spiritually and be fruitful in serving God.

RESPOND: What does the "Parable of the Sower" teach about how people can respond to God's Word and what that has to do with spiritual growth? *(Life change depends on how a person receives and responds to God's Word. Some will hear but not understand; others will believe, begin a relationship with Jesus, but for one reason or another, not take steps to grow; and some will grow for a while, then become distracted and turn away from Christ.)* What are some of the enemies of God's Word? What "thorns" can come up in a person's life, choking out his or her commitment to God? What kinds of things lead to or influence half-hearted commitments to Christ? Why would a person make a "halfway" commitment to Christ? How can you prevent this in your life?

PRAY: Ask God to help you sincerely respond to and effectively retain His Word by putting it into practice. Pray that you will have the wisdom, strength of character and devotion that will prevent worldly attractions and concerns from choking out your devotion to Him.

ACT: Examine your life and present circumstances. Consider your current priorities and time commitments. Examine your recent attitudes and behaviors. If anything is detracting from your devotion to God and stunting your spiritual growth, deal with it immediately. Pull the spiritual weeds from your life so you can be fruitful for Christ.

Mark 4:21-41

THINK: Have you ever asked God to take you deeper spiritually or to help you understand more about Him and His purposes? Then ask yourself this question: What am I doing with what He has already shown me? Many times, Christians ask God to reveal more to them about His Word, yet they are not necessarily doing anything with what they already know. Why should God keep showing us more if we are not fully utilizing what He has shown us already? Certainly, God will keep taking us deeper spiritually if we keep depending on Him and are determined to apply His Word to our lives in specific and practical ways.

RESPOND: Jesus says, "Consider carefully what you hear." He then goes on to say, "Whoever has will be given more; whoever does not have, even what he has will be taken from him." What does Jesus mean by this? *(Real Christians rely on God to learn and apply His truth to their lives. If they don't, they risk losing the effect and influence of what they've already been shown and taught.)* What are the dangers of not doing something and failing to grow spiritually with what we already know of the Word? *(The more we act on what He's already shown us, the more He will reveal to us. Failing to apply His truth can eventually harden our hearts, making us less responsive to His Word and His Spirit's promptings.)*

PRAY: Ask God to help you understand His Word as you read it and hear it taught. But more than that, ask Him to help you apply what He shows you, so it makes a real difference in your life and causes you to grow spiritually.

ACT: Think of some things God has shown you recently from His Word, in your own study time or through preaching and teaching. Have you responded to these challenges and applied God's truths to your life? If there is anything that God has revealed to you that you have not yet worked into your life, take action today, and do something practical with what you know, before you forget it or become hardened to it.

Fire Starter

Mark 5:1-20

THINK: Few people question the fact that evil exists. Thankfully, God is all-powerful and He will help us overcome evil if we rely on Him. That doesn't mean our lives will be free from pain and hardship, which will always be a part of life in a world that defies God. But Jesus came to free us from being trapped and enslaved by evil. Oddly, people often choose to remain under evil influences, because God's plans and purposes seem to disrupt their way of life. But God knows what's best. If we let Him have His way in our lives, we'll experience the fulfillment He intends, regardless of the difficulties we face.

RESPOND: Aside from literal demon possession, what are some more common and subtle ways in which people suffer because of Satan's evil work and influence? What does this passage reveal about Jesus' power over the forces of evil? Why do you think the people asked Jesus to leave them, even after they had witnessed the results of His power? *(It's sad that the community seemed to be more afraid of Jesus' extreme display of power, which clearly inconvenienced them and upset their economy, than they were happy about the man's deliverance. Perhaps they would have been forced to explain certain ways they'd treated him. You don't have to be like people in order to simply show love and respect to them. In fact, that's what Jesus did [Romans 5:8].)*

PRAY: Give God praise for His power and authority over evil. Ask Him to help you never put you own concerns and convenience over His plans and purposes for your life and the lives of those around you.

ACT: Perhaps God has wanted to do something specific in or through you, but you have resisted His plans because they do not seem convenient. It could be something as "big" as a career choice or as "little" as befriending someone at school who is much different than you. Don't hesitate any longer. Accept God's plans and follow the Holy Spirit's direction. Then watch God do something powerful and supernatural through you.

Mark 5:21-43

THINK: It's probably safe to assume that all of those who believe in God would like to witness more miracles. But we may not even recognize most of the supernatural ways in which He guides, protects and works in our lives every day. The fact is, we may miss the most extraordinary things God wants to do through us, because we give up hope or because we do not patiently wait for Him to work in His own time and way. But when people humbly approach God and dare to grow in their faith regardless of the circumstances, God will eventually honor himself through them in undeniably powerful ways.

RESPOND: What lessons can we learn about godly faith from the people described in this passage and from Jesus' interaction with them? Why did the woman's touch (verses 27-32) stand out so distinctly to Jesus? *(She didn't want to use or manipulate Jesus. This woman didn't whine or demand, as though she was entitled to Jesus' favor. But she knew He was the One who could heal her. Her faith was so simple and pure, and she was so humble in the way she approached Jesus. How do you approach Jesus when you need something only He can provide?)* In what ways does Jesus offer hope and comfort to those who trust Him, even before they see answers to their prayers?

PRAY: Ask God to strengthen your faith. Offer bold and daring prayers for situations in your life or in other's lives that may seem hopeless at present. Then give God thanks for answering these prayers in His own time and way.

ACT: If you or someone you know is facing a desperate situation, or simply needs help or healing that only God can provide, don't hesitate to trust Him, regardless of what the circumstances seem to indicate. Don't hesitate to enlist others to pray with you or to let others know that you are praying for them. That way, when God answers, everyone involved will know that He is the One who deserves all honor for the miracle.

Fire 🔥 Starter

Mark 6:1-29

THINK: Do you ever find yourself taking God for granted? There are few things God values more than the faith of those who love and follow Jesus. The fact is, God wants to do powerful works through His people—things so extraordinary that few could deny God is responsible for these things. But Jesus' followers must trust Him completely if He is to use them in this way. They must obey the instructions in His Word and not worry what others think. Then, God will do things that will be difficult for anyone to take for granted.

RESPOND: Why didn't Jesus perform many miracles in His hometown? In what ways did Jesus fill the role of a prophet? *(Jesus was empowered by the Holy Spirit. He knew God's Word. He referred to and understood prophecies that had already been fulfilled as well as prophesied events that did, in fact, come to pass.)* Why is a lack of faith so serious and destructive among God's people? *(Unbelief sometimes gets in the way of what God wants to do in people. It's not that God can't, but that because God has given us free will, He allows us to choose what we believe.)* When Jesus sent His disciples out to do ministry, why do you think He instructed them to "Take nothing for the journey"? Why were the disciples able to do extraordinary works and do you think Jesus expects the same of His followers today? Why or why not? Why do you think Herod was impressed by John and tried to protect him, even though he did not really accept John's warnings?

PRAY: Ask God to teach you to trust Him more fully, even though learning to do so will be difficult. Ask Jesus to honor himself in your life, and pray that people will never give you credit for what God chooses to do through you.

ACT: Put aside your assumptions and expectations as well as the fear of what others might think. Dare to trust God for something that would certainly fail apart from Him.

Fire Starter

Mark 6:30–56

THINK: The biblical account of Jesus' words and works makes it obvious that crowds of people from nearly every walk of life were desperate to see Jesus and to witness His miraculous power. But are people in most societies today this anxious to encounter Jesus and to experience His power? Consider the impression that many people have of Jesus and where they get that first impression. Remember, Jesus hasn't changed. He still has compassion for people and still wants to help and heal in miraculous ways.

RESPOND: Why wouldn't the people give Jesus a break (verses 30–33)? How did Jesus respond to the crowds, even though their presence was not convenient? What does this reveal about Jesus? What does it mean that the crowds "were like sheep without a shepherd (verse 34)"? In what ways does Jesus involve His followers in His miracles? *(We should be ready at any time for Jesus to have us partner with Him in His work in peoples' lives. You may hear of a need . . . a student who needs tutoring, a family in need, a friend who could use a ride somewhere. Jesus may say in not so many words, "You take care of it in My name.")* Why does He do this? What does the fact that they collected twelve baskets of leftovers show about Jesus' miracle-working power?

PRAY: Ask God to help you live in such a way that His compassion and power are evident in your life. Thank Him that His provision is always more than enough to meet the need.

ACT: Make a conscious effort to view those around you through Jesus' eyes of compassion. Understand that people are searching for significance, but they need someone to lead them to Jesus. Let everything you say and do today provide an accurate view of Jesus. If you've been praying that God would work in someone's life, do something specific to help that person. Your actions may be part of a miracle God wants to do for that special person.

Fire Starter

Mark 7:1-23

THINK: Serious problems arise when rules, rituals, and routines get in the way of a person's relationship with God. In the case of the Pharisees and teachers of the Law, physical cleanliness was not the problem. Rules and routines have a place, and Christians should still live by the moral and ethical principles of God's Law. But following these will not help anyone gain God's favor or attain spiritual salvation, which is not possible apart from faith in Christ. Following God's commands and living by His standards are things we should do out of love and gratitude toward Him. But we can only do this with His help.

RESPOND: What seemed to be the Pharisees' main concern and why? *(They took what originally were protective or God-honoring rules and tacked on "extra" rules, some that simply served their purposes and kept them in a state of superiority over people.)* How would you describe "legalism"? In what ways can religious people sometimes substitute outward acts for proper inner attitudes? How do people's traditions differ from God's commands? What kinds of things can come from within a person, making him or her spiritually "unclean"? *(Whatever you dwell on affects your attitudes and seeps into your heart.)* Why is the issue of what goes into our physical bodies vastly different than what goes into our minds? *(When you "feast" on books, movies, or conversations that rip apart morality, honor, and intimacy with God, it affects your thought life and consequently, your heart.)*

PRAY: Ask God to help you (1) follow His commands out of love and gratitude, (2) keep spiritual routines from taking priority over true worship and godly living, and (3) help you guard what goes into and comes out of your mind and heart.

ACT: If any of your activities or routines—good or bad—have taken priority over true godly living, make a distinct change. Be sure that you are doing things out of sincere love for God and not for the sake of appearance only. If you have been doing or viewing anything that fills your mind with spiritual impurity, stop it immediately.

Mark 7:24 through 8:13

THINK: Throughout the Gospel accounts of Jesus' life, two things are typically evident when Jesus performs miracles for people— His compassion and their faith. Jesus does these extraordinary works because He feels sincere empathy for people who are hurting, suffering or in need. But He does expect something from us when we come to Him with our needs. Jesus expects us to entrust our lives and situations completely to Him. And He wants us to demonstrate persistent dependence on Him, even when we do not understand everything or see immediate results.

RESPOND: In what way did the Greek woman demonstrate great faith? Was Jesus being disrespectful to the woman, or was He trying to accomplish something else in the way He interacted with her? *(The "children" refers to Israel, whom God's message of salvation was first intended for. She lets Jesus know that she "gets it" and is willing to settle for whatever He's willing to offer her, even if it's leftovers. Her persistence and strong faith touches Jesus' heart and is an example for us.)* Why must God's people be perseverant and persistent in their prayers? Why do you think that Jesus took the man away from the crowd to heal him (verse 33)? In what ways did Jesus demonstrate compassion for people? How did His compassion affect His ministry and relate to His miracles?

PRAY: Give Jesus thanks for His intense compassion. Then pray for something or someone that you may not have prayed for in a while because you had forgotten about the situation or given up hope for an answer.

ACT: Think of someone who has likely been praying for something specific (i.e., healing, spiritual salvation of a family member, etc.) for a long time and has probably wrestled with doubts and hopelessness. Contact that person and humbly offer a word of encouragement. Let them know that you will pray for him or her, and do so on the spot if you are talking over the phone or in person. Make sure to make it clear that you are available to help out in any way that is needed.

Fire Starter

Mark 8:14–26

THINK: Why is it that some people would not believe in God or accept Christ no matter how much evidence they had of His existence? Yet, there are others who would never give up their faith in God or love for Jesus despite a lack of visible signs or answers to their prayers. The difference comes down to an attitude of the heart that is the essence of genuine faith. Faith in God makes the difference between those to whom God ultimately reveals himself and those who never experience the joy and fulfillment He offers.

RESPOND: What can happen among Jesus' followers if they are not on their guard against leaders whose message contradicts the message of Jesus as revealed in the Bible? Why were the disciples—like us—often slow to understand Jesus or to comprehend His capability, even after witnessing His great power and compassion? Why do you think that some people receive healing immediately, while others receive it gradually, and still others may not seem to receive it at all as they expect? *(He's the Great Physician, but if that's all He is to us, we've missed the point of what communion and relationship with God is all about. Even so, God's desire and power to heal us is part of His nature and plan through Christ's death and resurrection. Trust that He is able and knows what's best in the life of whomever you're praying for—including yourself!)*

PRAY: Ask God to give you discernment so you can detect and avoid insincere spiritual leaders and false teaching.

ACT: Think of a friend or acquaintance who has struggled with the issue of faith in God. Let the individual know that you are thinking of him or her and praying that God would reveal himself in a fresh way. If you can, do something practical for that special person as a means of demonstrating God's love. You never know what God will reveal as a result of your prayers and acts of kindness.

Fire Starter

Mark 8:27 through 9:13

THINK: Have you ever given up something of little value in exchange for something of tremendous value? Did you consider that a big sacrifice? Not likely. If you've followed Jesus for any length of time, you've likely discovered that His plans don't always seem to make sense. Even Jesus' closest followers failed to comprehend God's plan. Jesus knew He would suffer, be rejected, and ultimately face death at the hand of His opponents, but that was not acceptable to some of His followers. They didn't realize that Jesus had to give His life in order to give us life.

RESPOND: Why did Peter rebuke Jesus for talking about His impending suffering and death? Why did Jesus rebuke Peter so strongly in return? *(Remember when Satan tempted Jesus in the wilderness? Peter came close to a repeat performance without the power and illusion Satan conjured up. In both cases, had Jesus succumbed to the temptation to avoid suffering, God's entire plan to buy us back from death would've been completely blown. We can keep that in mind when we're tempted to complain about or avoid suffering.)* What did Jesus mean when He said that anyone who wants to follow Him "must deny himself and take up his cross"? How can you guard against being ashamed of Jesus?

PRAY: Ask God to help you understand His purposes so you don't resist them in any way. Pray for the willingness to put aside your own plans so as not to be distracted from following God's plans. Pray for boldness to identify with Jesus.

ACT: Do something bold—not foolish or obnoxious—to identify yourself with Jesus in a definite and distinct way. Wear an item of clothing with a Christian message, do a school project on a Christian theme, start a conversation about spiritual issues, or invite some new friends to a ministry event. Make sure that the rest of your life is consistent with Christ's character and message so you give people an accurate impression of Him.

Fire Starter

Mark 9:14-32

THINK: The Bible talks a lot about faith—how much God values it, how much we need it, and how much it can accomplish if directed properly. Yet, as frail humans, we often struggle with doubts about what God wants to do in and through us. As we wrestle with our own inadequacies, reservations, and limitations, we must separate these issues from our confidence in God's capability. Though we may sometimes wonder if God will do certain things, we should not question the fact that He can do whatever He desires and whatever is needed in any situation.

RESPOND: What responsibility does Jesus put on us in order to see miracles? When Jesus says, "Everything is possible for him who believes," what responsibility does the believer have? *(Our faith and prayers should be based on God's purposes and His divine will, not our foolish whims or selfish desires.)* In what ways can Jesus still work with our faith, even though it may be weak or mixed with questions? *(God knows that people will doubt sometimes, but we shouldn't obsess over it. Instead, talk to Him about it and trust Him.)* In regard to faith, what's the difference between doubting ourselves and doubting God? What kind of prayer was Jesus talking about? *(Effective praying includes sincere faith that God hears and is able to answer our prayers, praying in Jesus' name, praying in line with God's will, living in obedience to God, and being persistent.)*

PRAY: Ask Jesus to help you grow in faith, and though you may struggle with doubts about yourself, pray that you will not question His ability. Ask Him to help you become more disciplined and diligent in your prayer life, and to help keep your desires in line with His will so that your faith is focused on the right things.

ACT: Think of a situation in which you've struggled with doubt or a lack of faith. Demonstrate full confidence in God by taking some sort of practical action to show that you've given the situation completely to Him.

Fire Starter

Mark 9:33-50

THINK: Who is watching you and what kind of influence are you having on them? You may not feel that anyone is looking to you for anything. But you will make an impact on someone, somewhere, by your example, especially if they know you follow Christ. Your greatest potential influence may be on kids younger than you, perhaps your siblings or other kids in your church or neighborhood. Whether you realize it or not, you have a responsibility to lead people to Jesus by your example. Will you make it easier or more difficult for those around you to find Jesus?

RESPOND: What traits and behaviors make someone "great" in God's kingdom? What responsibility do you have toward those who may be influenced by your example? Does Jesus really expect you to remove your hand, foot, or eye if it causes you to sin? What is He trying to tell us with these extreme examples? *(Jesus uses this hyperbole—overstatement—to help us take sin seriously as well as the consequence of sin.)* What does this have to do with spiritual purity, discipline, boldness and influence? *(Everyone will be tested and tried through suffering or persecution. But our obedience to God and God's grace in our lives keeps and purifies us through those trying times.)*

PRAY: Ask God to keep you from being prideful or selfish as you serve Him, and to put other people ahead of yourself. Then ask Him to search your life and reveal anything that needs to be removed so that you do not influence others negatively and so you can fulfill His plans for you more effectively.

ACT: Do something for a kid or someone else who may look up to you that will give them a better idea of what a Christian should be like and what Jesus himself is like. Be conscious throughout the day of how your attitudes, words and actions may influence others. If you are doing anything that could cause someone else to doubt or defy God, put an abrupt end to that behavior.

Mark 10:1-31

THINK: Have you ever been accused of being childish? Typically, that's not a compliment. But in a very distinct way, God wants His people to be like little children in their humility and openness toward Him and in their simple approach to faith. If your priorities begin to get out of line, God will work to expose the problems and to rid your life of anything that could keep you from following His purposes and experiencing the life He intends for you.

RESPOND: What does it mean to have a hard heart (verse 5), and how can it cause broken relationships? What do verses 6-9 tell us about marriage and how God feels about divorce? *(God requires us to take our life-long marriage vows seriously. Any basis for divorce besides biblical reasons makes that divorce a sin. The fallout from divorce in the lives of everyone involved should cause you to take the marriage commitment very seriously.)* In what ways should God's people be like children? *(To be like a child in God's kingdom is to approach Him with a simple, humble, trustful, and wholehearted faith.)* How can possessions hinder a person's relationship with God and keep him or her from being part of His kingdom? What did Jesus mean that those who give up things for Him will receive a hundred times as much in return? Why is it important for Jesus' followers to realize that they'll experience both reward and rejection, blessing and suffering, grief and glory as part of His kingdom?

PRAY: Ask God to keep your heart soft toward Him and others and to help you accept His Word and purposes in a simple, humble, trusting, and childlike way. Pray that you will be prepared to accept both the blessing and the persecution that you will encounter as a result of following Jesus.

ACT: Remove anything from your life or possessions that are getting too much of your time, attention and priority, or could hinder your relationship with Jesus in any way.

Fire Starter

Mark 10:32-52

THINK: From the time He walked the earth, Jesus inspired a range of reactions unlike anyone else who has ever lived. From unreserved love to unwarranted hatred, from unbridled joy to unparalleled sorrow, from profound faith to intense fear, people responded to Jesus with a wide array of emotions. But this was consistent with His life's mission, which was a paradox—a seeming contradiction—as He would be wounded for our healing and die to give us life. But those who accept Jesus' life and live by His teaching will find fulfillment beyond anything they could comprehend.

RESPOND: Why do you think the disciples were astonished and why were those who followed afraid (verse 32)? What did Jesus mean when He asked James and John, "Can you drink the cup I drink or be baptized with the baptism I am baptized with?"? *("Can you drink the cup I drink?" is actually a Jewish saying meaning to share another's fate.)* What was Jesus trying to teach His disciples about being in positions of leadership and authority? *(Jesus set the example of greatness through his life, the way He treated people, and ultimately, His death. He knows what it yields for us and others when we have this "servanthood" mindset and model for living.)* How did Jesus exemplify His teaching (verse 45)? In what way can serving affect a person's influence?

PRAY: Ask Jesus to prepare you for the ways you may suffer for His sake. Pray for humility and an attitude that doesn't worry about getting recognition, but instead is ready to serve others as a representative of Christ.

ACT: Look for as many ways as possible today to represent Jesus by serving others. Perform random acts of kindness. Do things that others don't want to do. Serve without being asked. If anyone questions why you are doing any of these things, don't hesitate to let them know that Jesus has helped you and you want to pass His goodness on to others.

THINK: People have a lot of misconceptions about Jesus. But we do not have to speculate about Jesus or wonder what He's really like. He has revealed himself clearly through His written Word—the Bible. We see Him respond with both gentleness and severity. We witness His matchless mercy, but we also get a glimpse of His righteous judgment. Through it all, we see what matters most to Jesus and what should matter most to His followers.

RESPOND: How did the crowd feel about Jesus at this point and what did they expect of Him? What do Jesus' actions in the temple (verses 15–17) tell us about His character, passions and mission? *(Jesus' passionate reaction makes clear how seriously He takes dedication to God and preserving God's honor. It's been said that these temple merchants took advantage of foreigners, literally doing what Jesus accused them of, using God's house as a "den of robbers.")* What are God's intentions for His places of worship? In what ways must we ensure that our churches and ministries are open to all who desire to know and honor God? What conditions does God put on true faith, godly belief and answered prayers? *(We cannot fabricate or manipulate simple faith; it's God-given, or God-generated, and developed by the Holy Spirit as we pray and put our faith in action. True faith is God-focused and free of resentment or unforgiveness toward others.)*

PRAY: Ask Jesus to give you His passion for sincere worship and prayer. Ask Him to help you seize every opportunity to stretch your faith by trusting His methods and timing. Pray for a forgiving spirit toward those who offend you.

ACT: Have you in any way taken your church for granted or not shown proper respect for God's house? If so, ask God to forgive you. Then make a change to ensure that you never hinder anyone from worshipping or receiving from God anywhere you are involved in ministry. Also, make sure that you take full advantage of the opportunity for worship, prayer and service with other believers, and that you are genuine and sincere in all of these expressions.

Mark 11:27 through 12:17

THINK: It's long been popular, even expected, among younger people—particularly during the teen years—to test boundaries and to question authority. Wise youth recognize when this is appropriate and when it's not. And wise leaders do not fall into the trap of unproductive argument and combative conversation in an effort to assert their authority. Instead, they gauge their responses, ask informed questions and lead by example. They don't demand respect because of their position; they inspire respect by persuasive passion. No one better demonstrated this than Jesus. Many religious leaders of Jesus' time questioned His authority and opposed His teaching because it exposed their hypocrisy. But Jesus saw through their veiled attempts to trap Him with words. He responded with thought-provoking insight that silenced His critics, amazed the crowds and inspired confidence in those who followed Him.

RESPOND: Why did the religious leaders seem so concerned about the source of Jesus' authority? What was their motive for questioning Jesus? Why do you think Jesus put a question back to them rather than answering their question? How does Jesus fit the description of the capstone? *(A capstone is "the uppermost stone of a structure" You can't build a building without a capstone. In the same way, Christianity simply isn't complete without Christ. Christianity is because of Christ.)* In what way were the Pharisees and Herodians being insincere with Jesus? What was amazing about the way Jesus answered them?

PRAY: Pray for an attitude of sincerity in all you do. Ask God to expose any hypocrisy in your life and to help you get rid of it. Give Jesus praise for being the capstone and solid foundation of His Church.

ACT: Think about your greatest interests, your biggest endeavors and your loftiest goals—the things that get a good share of your time and attention. Is your relationship with Jesus the foundation of these activities, aims, and efforts? Make sure that your priorities are based on God's purposes for you and that you seek to honor Christ above everything else in all aspects of your life.

Fire Starter

Mark 12:18-44

THINK: The Bible is packed with practical instruction, guidelines and direct commands from God. All of these principles are aimed at revealing His character and principles, helping us to experience productive and fulfilling lives, and pointing us to our need for God. But Jesus summed up all of God's life instructions in two basic commands: "Love the Lord your God with all your heart and with all your soul and with all your mind and with all your strength," and "Love your neighbor as yourself" (verses 30,31). By following these two primary directives, God's people—with His help—will fulfill the requirements of God's perfect Law.

RESPOND: In what ways did the Sadducees not understand the Scriptures or the power of God (verse 24)? What does it mean to love God with all your heart, soul, mind, strength? *(Jesus doesn't love God or people conditionally or partially. God wants us to love Him in the same way—wholly, expressed with one's whole self, not part of himself or part-time.)* What does it mean to love your neighbor as yourself? In what ways do these two commands summarize and encompass all other commands? Why did Jesus take so seriously the hypocrisy and insincerity of the teachers of the Law, and why would they be judged severely (verses 38-40)? In what way did the poor widow give much more than all of the rich people (verses 41-44)? How does God measure the value of giving?

PRAY: Ask God to give you a greater understanding of what it means to love Him with every aspect of your being, and to love others as yourself. Praise Jesus for His amazing love for you.

ACT: Find a way to use your strength or intellect to honor God. Perhaps you can volunteer for a chore at home or church. Maybe you could share a ministry idea with a leader, write a paper on a Christian theme or create a poem of worship to God for your journal. Also, do something for someone else that you would like them to do for you.

Fire Starter

Mark 13:1-37

THINK: Have you ever noticed that whenever world events or catastrophes resemble descriptions given in the Bible of end-time events, people suddenly become interested in spiritual issues and what God says in His Word? Don't wait for a sign or event to point you to God's Word or inspire you to trust Him. Learn the Word now. Be prepared, be alert, and be ready at all times for Jesus' return.

RESPOND: In what ways are the times we live in now like the times described in this passage? Why does Jesus give repeated warnings to "watch out" (verse 5), "be on your guard," and "be alert" (verses 5,9,23,33,35,37)? What must you do to guard against deception in the days ahead? *(There are so many false doctrines floating around, mixing biblical truths with man-made rules, compromising God's Laws to help people feel better about themselves. How can you know any of this if you don't read and know what God's Word says?)* What will happen before the end comes (verse 10)? Why don't Jesus' followers have to worry about what to say when persecuted and standing before others as a witness for Christ (verse 11)? In what way do you sometimes "sleep" spiritually? What helps you "wake up"? *(A Midwest coffee chain, Caribou, puts this phrase on some of its mugs: "Life is short. Stay awake for it." As followers of Jesus, we can be motivated by remembering that life, for us, is eternal. Life before Jesus returns is short, in comparison to eternity. Stay awake and stay ready for His return!)*

PRAY: Ask God to keep you alert and on guard against spiritual deception as Jesus' return approaches. Pray for a greater understanding of His Word so you can discern truth from error. Ask Jesus to help you do your part to spread His message before He returns. Thank the Holy Spirit for giving you the words to say when testifying about Jesus.

ACT: Look through a newspaper, news magazine or website. Notice how many items fit descriptions of last days events (e.g., wars, natural disasters, violent acts, immorality).

Fire Starter

Mark 14:1–26

THINK: Did Jesus lack concern for the poor? Certainly not! No one will ever care more for the poor—or for any of us—than Jesus. He proved His ultimate compassion by laying down His life, providing us with what we really need: the opportunity for forgiveness, hope, new life, and a personal relationship with Him. His whole time on earth was aimed at fulfilling that purpose. Along the way He continually gave of himself to comfort, heal, enrich, and restore countless lives. But knowing that His time on earth was short, Jesus infinitely valued the isolated moments when individuals disregarded the peer pressure and did something extra-special just for Him. These individuals seized opportunities that few others recognized, and Jesus would not deny them the privilege of ministering directly to Him.

RESPOND: Why did Jesus accept the woman's extravagant gift when others condemned her for wasting her resources? In what way did the bread Jesus served at His last supper symbolize His own body (verse 22)? What did Jesus mean when He referred to "my blood of the covenant"? What is a "covenant"? How did Jesus Christ establish and seal a covenant with us through His death? *(A covenant is a "life agreement" in which people pledge themselves to each other [e.g., marriage]. The "old covenant" was God's way of maintaining a right relationship with people, based on His Laws and promises, as well as on peoples' obedience to Him. The "new covenant" is God's plan of salvation for people, based on Jesus' life and sacrifice.)*

PRAY: Express thanks to Jesus for suffering and giving His life so you could be forgiven of your sins and have an eternal, personal relationship with Him.

ACT: Take time to think of and do something special just for Jesus. This may involve a tangible ministry gift or, better yet, a gift of extra time with Him personally. Perhaps you can spend time in conversational prayer at a favorite quiet spot. Try writing a song or poem of praise and adoration to Jesus, thanking Him for His personal sacrifice by which He provided you with eternal life.

Fire Starter

Mark 14:27-52

THINK: Do you ever worry that you won't have the guts to stand up for Jesus if confronted with the prospect of severe consequences or persecution? Perhaps you've gotten discouraged in the past because you've backed down in your faith when faced with very little pressure. Well, you don't have to wonder if you will have the strength; God promised to provide that. But you do your part by staying in tune with God through consistent time in His Word and prayer.

RESPOND: What did Jesus mean when He told His disciples, "You will all fall away" (verse 27)? Why would this happen? What did Jesus later challenge the disciples to do that could have kept them from failing during the difficult hours and days ahead? *(Sometimes prayer is the only thing that will keep us from falling into temptation or depression.)* How do you develop and maintain a strong prayer life? *(There's more than one time and one way to pray. But one thing to keep in mind is, don't wait until an emergency to pray. Pray regularly. Praying a few sincere minutes a day will bring you closer to God than praying fervently for an hour when a crisis hits. Of course, God wants you to spend more than a few minutes with Him throughout the day as you mature in your spiritual journey. But the point is, He wants to be with you regularly, not sporadically.)*

PRAY: Pray for the strength to resist falling away from Jesus when times get tough and you face pressure to deny your faith in Him. Commit to spending consistent daily time talking and listening to God.

ACT: Do something bold to identify with Jesus today. It might help if throughout the day you take every opportunity during your free time to focus on God in prayer. You can pray silently on your way to class, or take time in study hall or during a work break to read your Bible. If someone notices you doing this, it will almost certainly spark a conversation.

Fire Starter

Mark 14:53-72

THINK: Most people find it difficult to keep quiet when others spread rumors or tell lies about them—especially when the remarks are made to their face. Even with petty, insignificant issues it's still hard not to respond defensively. But sometimes false statements can do serious and significant damage to a person's reputation. Even in these instances, however, the situations seldom involve anything life-threatening. But in today's passage, we see Jesus in just such a situation: He is falsely accused and facing the prospect of certain death if He offers no defense. Amazingly, Jesus keeps quiet. Certainly, He could have countered His critics with profound questions or insights, leaving them speechless, as He had done many times before in public. But this time He would not respond to the lies. He would only affirm the truth of His identity. Why would Jesus remain silent at this time? It had everything to do with fulfilling His mission to rescue you.

RESPOND: Why do you think people were willing to falsely testify against Jesus, and why were there conflicting accounts (verses 56-58)? Why do you think Jesus remained silent in the face of the accusations, but when questioned by the high priest He admitted that He was the Christ, the Son of God (verses 61,62)? Why did His accusers refuse to accept Jesus as God's Son, and instead abuse Him so shamefully (verse 65)? How would you have felt if you were Peter, having so emphatically denied his friend and mentor, Jesus (verses 66-72)?

PRAY: Give Jesus praise as the eternal Son of God. Express to Him how thankful you are that He stood up to ridicule, rejection and abuse and never denied His mission to suffer and die for your offenses against God.

ACT: Whenever someone says or does something that bothers you, offends you or outright hurts you, resist the urge to talk back or retaliate in any way. In fact, respond graciously in every situation. This could set a better example and make a more powerful impact for Christ than most things you could say to people.

Fire Starter

Mark 15:1-20

THINK: Have you ever noticed how fickle people can be—how quickly their moods, opinions and behaviors can be swayed depending on the situation or how others respond to them? Have you also noticed how people will do things when they are with a group or in a crowd—things they would never do, or even consider, on their own? Call it peer pressure, a group dynamic, a herd mentality—call it whatever you want—but it's a sad reality that unrestrained crowds tend to throw aside inhibitions and bring out the worst in people. And when a few lose control, others often follow, all for the sake of two extremes—getting attention or trying to blend in. Christ's followers, however, must dare to be different, resisting the inclination to imitate destructive behaviors. Instead, they must lead by example and seek to influence others for good.

RESPOND: Why do you think the crowd—some of whom had likely witnessed Jesus' ministry and even celebrated Him before—was so easily persuaded to ask for Barabbas' release and for Jesus' crucifixion (verses 9-14)? Why did Pilate eventually hand Jesus over to be crucified (verse 15)? How are we sometimes like Pilate? Why do you think the soldiers were abusive to Jesus, when they likely had little or no previous interaction with Him? How do you think you would have handled yourself as a soldier in that situation? Would you have joined in the ridicule? Why or why not? Why do people so easily engage in destructive behavior when they are with a group or crowd?

PRAY: Ask God for boldness and strength of character to avoid destructive situations and to resist pressure from people to behave shamefully. Ask for wisdom in choosing the friends and groups with whom to keep company.

ACT: When you are with a friend or in groups today, make a conscious effort to resist negative pressure to say or do anything that might displease God or hinder your witness for Him. Instead, be a leader and try to influence your groups for good, helping to bring out the best in those around you.

Fire Starter

Mark 15:21-47

THINK: Why did Jesus endure all the rejection and pain He encountered during His life and ministry—particularly as His death approached? He certainly didn't deserve the abuse, and He didn't pursue this path of opposition for His own sake, other than the fact that He wanted to relate to us in a personal way. But that was not possible without God's intervention. He could not have a relationship with people who have chosen to go their own way and defy Him. That's what sin is, and it separates us all from God. Ultimately, our sin warrants death and eternal separation from Him. The only way to restore that relationship was for God himself to provide the perfect payment for the penalty of sin. He did this by sending His Son, Jesus, to suffer sin's ultimate consequences in our place. Jesus died to provide forgiveness and new life for those who entrust themselves to Him. That's the message of hope His followers have the privilege of sharing with everyone else, including those who continue to reject Him.

RESPOND: Why would people heap insult upon injury as they passed by Jesus? For whom did Jesus suffer and endure all of the shame, and why? Do you think that those who mocked Jesus would have believed Him if He would have saved himself from death? Why of why not? Why didn't Jesus save himself (verse 31)? Whom did He save instead through His death?

PRAY: Express gratitude to Jesus for enduring the shame of your sin against God, and for opening the way for you to be forgiven and have a personal relationship with God.

ACT: Whenever you hear someone make a negative, derogatory or insulting comment about God, Christianity, faith, spiritual issues—even if they use God's name casually as a curse word— take a moment to pray silently for the individual. Ask God to reveal himself in an undeniable way to him or her. If you feel that it's appropriate, say something that may influence the person to rethink their words or opinions. But be kind and gracious as you do.

Fire Starter

Mark 16:1-20

THINK: Since we have full access to God's written Word, we may sometimes find it difficult to relate to the emotions and experiences of people we read about in the Bible. After all, it's always easier in retrospect to over-dramatize situations, to excessively glorify people's faith, and to criticize their failures. But certainly we would have emerged with different perspectives had we actually been there and lived through events described in the Bible.

RESPOND: What do the women's actions during Jesus' ministry (Mark 15:40,41) and surrounding His death tell us about their character and commitment to Him? *(They obviously didn't expect Jesus to rise from death. Jews didn't practice embalming, so this anointing of His body was a tender act of love on their part.)* How would you have felt if you were with the women? Why did Jesus' followers refuse to believe He was alive (Mark 16:11-13), even though He had told them He would rise from the dead (Mark 10:34; 16:7)? Are the signs Jesus spoke about (verses 17-19) still valid today? What signs do you think accompanied the disciples' preaching (verse 20)? Are these signs still evident? Why or why not? *(God's power has not diminished. Supernatural activities will continue to occur until Christ's return.)*

PRAY: Ask God to help you become better acquainted with His Word and to remember and apply what you study. Ask Him to help you follow the example of the women who stuck by Jesus through the darkest hours. Ask Jesus to work through you in powerful ways to confirm the message He has called you to spread.

ACT: Follow the example of the women who served Jesus' needs and the example of Jesus, who meets your needs. Look for people who have apparent needs—physical, emotional, relational, and spiritual. Pray for them as you encounter them, asking God to do miracles, even for those who don't know Him yet. Serve others in practical or tangible ways. Perhaps this will spark spiritual conversations. Believe that God will do things so powerful that people will not be able to explain them apart from Him.

Fire Starter

Luke 1:1-25

THINK: When people are trying to prove a case—like in court—what kinds of evidence do they look for? When people are confirming a story for a news article or non-fiction book, what sources do they value most? They want eyewitnesses who can provide a firsthand account of events and confirm facts. Only then can they assemble the most complete and accurate story. Like all of the Holy Spirit-inspired authors of Scripture, Luke did just that when he wrote his account of the good news (gospel) of Jesus. As a result, his is the Bible's most comprehensive and extensive record of Jesus' unique life and powerful ministry.

RESPOND: Why is it important that the biblical record of Jesus' life and ministry is based on carefully investigated eyewitness accounts (verses 2,3)? In what ways had Zechariah and Elizabeth demonstrated faithfulness and devotion to God? In what ways would John's birth and life be unique? In what ways would John help turn people to God and prepare them for God's purposes? *(John wouldn't have made it as a motivational speaker today. He probably would have attracted as many picketers outside his speaking engagements as listeners. But back then, he helped people see their offenses against God. He challenged them to get back in right relationship with God.)* Why is the relationship between fathers and their children so important? What does this indicate about God's intentions for the family unit? What are a father's responsibilities in regard to his children?

PRAY: Give God thanks for making His Word available to you. Pray that your heart will always accept God's purposes, regardless of how impossible they may seem. Also, ask God to strengthen your family relationships.

ACT: Talk to someone about your first-hand experience with Jesus. Also, do something deliberate and practical to enhance your relationship with a family member—preferably for a parent, if that is possible. Show them proper respect and do what they ask of you. But you may also help a brother or sister with a task or write a personal note of appreciation to family members.

Fire Starter

Luke 1:26-56

THINK: How do you think you would have responded if an angel appeared to you with the news he brought to Mary? Would you have believed and accepted the message? Scholars and historians speculate that Mary was a young woman—likely still a teen—when the angel brought this message to her. Age is not an issue with God. In the Bible, some of the greatest missions of faith were accomplished by youth. God still works like that today.

RESPOND: What was Joseph and Mary's relationship at the time the angel Gabriel first appeared to Mary? *(They were betrothed. Betrothal in Bible days was as legally binding as marriage, only nullified by divorce.)* What did the angel mean when he said that Mary was "highly favored" (verse 28) and that she had "found favor with God" (verse 30)? *(Mary, though respected and honored as the mother of Christ, should never be worshipped like Christ.)* As a virgin, how would Mary conceive a son? *(Pure and simple, Jesus' birth from a virgin was a supernatural act of God.)* What does Mary's response to the angel tell us about her? What do Mary's words in verse 47 reveal about her relationship to God? *(Though Mary found favor with God, she was still human and a sinner in need of a savior, like everyone else who ever lived—besides the Savior.)*

PRAY: Ask God to help you live in such a way that you "find favor" with Him. Pray that you remain humble and dependent on Him through times of both blessing and suffering. Ask God to help you take Him at His Word.

ACT: Has God asked you to do something which you have not yet done? Perhaps He has shown you something directly from His Word but you've not taken it at face value and acted upon it. Ask God to forgive you for a lack of faith; then take immediate action. If there is any area of life in which you've harbored ungodly pride, ask God to help you learn and demonstrate humility.

Luke 1:57–80

THINK: Put yourself in Zechariah's place and consider how you might have felt and what you might have done under the following circumstances. First of all, would you have taken the angel at his word, or would you have had a few questions as well? Then think about how you would handle the inability to talk. How long could you go without getting extremely restless? Could you handle it for months—particularly during an extraordinary event like having a child if you were at an advanced age? And what would be the first thing you'd say when you were able to speak again?

RESPOND: What was the first thing Zechariah did when he was once again able to speak (verse 64)? Why is this significant? Who inspired Zechariah's prophetic words in verses 67–79? What was the main thing for which Zechariah praised God? How would people receive "the knowledge of salvation" (verse 77)? Why is God's forgiveness so vital to us? What does it mean to serve God "in holiness and righteousness" (verse 75)? *(Holiness includes moral purity, integrity, disunion from evil, and devotion to God. Righteousness means maintaining a right relationship with God, doing what's right by His standards, not the world's.)* How would you describe the concepts of holiness and righteousness, and how should these traits affect your everyday life?

PRAY: Praise God in your own words for His forgiveness and salvation. Ask Him to help you—in the power of the Holy Spirit— to demonstrate true holiness and righteousness in all you think, say and do.

ACT: Ask God to search your heart and life and expose any area in which you are not practicing and demonstrating moral purity, spiritual integrity, separation from evil and complete dedication to God. Make the necessary changes starting today.

Fire Starter

Luke 2:1-20

THINK: Jesus' birth was a big event. No doubt about it. But extraordinary as it was, Jesus' birth was not glamorous. Certainly, there were spectacular elements—such as the angelic announcement—but the setting was crude and the people involved were profoundly common. Yet, that was all part of the life-changing message Jesus came to convey. That message is not just for the elite; it is for the ordinary person. In fact, Jesus came to serve the needy and help the hurting. His good news is for all people. Anyone can receive it, and anyone can share it.

RESPOND: How do you think people viewed Joseph and Mary as they were expecting a child during their engagement (verse 5)? How would this situation test their faith and character? For whom did He come into the world (verses 10,11)? What does the title "Christ" mean? *(The word* Christ *translated from Greek means "anointed" which refers to the presence, blessing, and power of God.)* What does it mean that Christ would be a Savior (verse 11)? What is significant about the fact that Jesus' birth was announced to shepherds? After seeing Jesus, in what way is their response a lesson to all people who hear and receive Christ's message?

PRAY: Express to Jesus how thankful you are that He came to be your Savior. Pray for the boldness to not worry about other people's impressions of you as you fulfill God's purposes. Ask Him to help you respond to His message as the shepherds did—with humility and unabashed joy—anxious to share the good news.

ACT: If there is any aspect or situation of your life in which you've been overly concerned with people's impressions of you—particularly in regard to your faith—make a deliberate choice to change your attitude. Trust God for the strength of character to let your faith show. View yourself like the simple shepherds who first heard the message of Jesus and had no higher priority than to spread the word about what they had experienced.

Fire Starter

Luke 2:21-52

THINK: How young is too young to grasp God's purpose and mission for one's life? If true Christianity is about knowing Jesus and following His example, then even a child can begin to comprehend and fulfill God's plans. And that means having the ability to influence and inspire others—of all ages—to consider God's purpose for their own lives. God is calling you to impact your world right now. Jesus has been where you are and He can help you become aware and prepared for His ultimate plans for your life.

RESPOND: How do Joseph's and Mary's actions at the temple set an example for parents today? What was Simeon waiting for, and how does this relate to our situation today? *(Even as Simeon was waiting for the appearance of the Messiah, so we today, await our Messiah to return.)* What does the incident with Jesus and the teachers at the temple reveal about Jesus and His life's mission? *(This is earliest record of Jesus' acknowledgement of His special relationship with God, the Father, and the mission God had sent Him to earth for. Yet, Jesus was still obedient to his parents, and left when they came to get Him.)* What do the statements in verses 40 and 52 tell us about Jesus' development during the years before His public ministry began? How does this relate to you?

PRAY: Ask God for wisdom and for favor with people of all ages so you can influence them for Christ. Pray verse 52 into your life, that you would grow in wisdom and stature, and in favor with God and men.

ACT: Is there anything you've hesitated to do for God or any area of service you've refrained from because of your age, social status or other concern? Take a mature step to become involved in that particular venture or ministry. If there is an area of your church's ministry in which no young people are involved, volunteer to be a part of it. Watch how the congregation gets inspired to see its youth serving in all aspects of ministry.

Fire Starter

Luke 3:1-38

THINK: Do most people who know you realize you're a Christian? How about those who don't know you well, but are near you at school, work or around town—can they tell by your behavior that there is something different about you? Jesus wants His followers' lives to be distinct, in a positive and persuasive way. He wants their personal relationship with Him to be evident in how they relate to others. But the difference He desires can only develop through the presence and power of the Holy Spirit within the individual lives of Jesus' followers.

RESPOND: What does John mean when he says, "produce fruit in keeping with repentance"? What are the consequences of not doing this (verse 9)? What types of behaviors can demonstrate that people have taken this challenge to heart (verses 10-14)? In what ways does John's view of Jesus and of himself serve as an example to us (verses 15,16)? In what way would Jesus' baptism differ from John's? *(Whereas John baptized people as an outward sign of surrender to God, as we still do today, Jesus' ministry of baptizing believers in the Holy Spirit is an inward work of cleansing and empowering, and a continuing ministry in this present age.)* What's the significance of the Holy Spirit descending on Jesus at His baptism? *(Since Jesus was conceived by and filled with the Holy Spirit, it made sense and was significant that at His baptism He was personally empowered by the Holy Spirit for His ministry.)*

PRAY: Ask God to help you interact with others in a way that demonstrates the sincerity of your devotion to God. Pray that the power of the Holy Spirit will saturate your life and help you to influence others for Him.

ACT: Think of a practical way to demonstrate that your life is different than it would be apart from Christ. Perhaps you can demonstrate more generosity by sharing something tangible with others. Maybe you can be more diligent in your job and more gracious to your employer. You could also strive for a better attitude around your family at home.

Fire Starter

Luke 4:1-13

THINK: What tempts you? And what are you doing—if anything—to deal with and overcome temptation? Keep in mind that God does not intend for you to win the battle on your own. He has given you the wisdom of His Word and the strength of His Spirit to help you overcome ungodly passions that war against your soul. Today's passage reveals key spiritual strategies—directly from Jesus' experience—to help you be victorious through the most trying times.

RESPOND: What were the keys of Jesus' power over temptation (verses 1,4,8,12)? What human needs and desires did these temptations appeal to? In defeating these temptations, what does Jesus demonstrate about what's really important? *(Jesus' response to temptation affirms His belief that what matters most in life depends on God's plans and purposes.)* How does Jesus' kingdom differ from worldly kingdoms? *(Jesus' kingdom is spiritual, founded in His peoples' hearts. It is attained through suffering, self-denial, and humility rather than power, popularity, or personality.)* Did Satan really have the ability or authority to grant what He promised Jesus? Why or why not? How did Satan use Scripture to tempt Jesus? What does this passage reveal about how Satan's forces will tempt you, and the way you can defeat him?

PRAY: Ask God for wisdom and power to overcome the temptation to give in to selfish preoccupation with physical desires, personal comforts, and pride. Pray for insight to see through Satan's twisted tactics and his misuse of God's Word. Pray that you will be full of the Holy Spirit and the knowledge of God's Word so you can win the battle over temptation.

ACT: Think of an area of weakness in your life in which you have been especially vulnerable to temptation. Ask God to expose any way in which your behavior or practices may be contributing to the problem. Then make some changes. In addition, use the concordance or subject index in the back of your Bible to find specific passages that pertain to your temptations. Mark and memorize these passages so you can use them to defeat the devil's attacks.

Fire Starter

Luke 4:14–44

THINK: People seem to love superheroes. Even prime time TV is full of shows that portray seemingly average people with extraordinary abilities they use to change the world. But God's people don't have to live in a fantasy world to experience ultimate power or to accomplish world-changing missions. If you are a true follower of Jesus, the Holy Spirit lives in and through you, empowering and commissioning you to accomplish great things and to impact the world for Him.

RESPOND: What does it mean to be "anointed" (verse 18)? *(To be anointed is to be "commissioned" with the power of the Holy Spirit for service.)* How was Jesus' ministry—and that of His followers—aimed at meeting human need? What Source of power must Jesus' followers have in order to continue the same works? Why would it have been difficult for those in Jesus' hometown to accept His ministry and authority? In what way do you think Jesus' message had distinct authority, and how was that authority evident to the people? *(Jesus' authority was given to Him by His Father. Jesus didn't use His authority to oppress others. And He specifically told His followers not to use the authority He conferred on them to control or dominate people.)* What do Jesus' confrontations with demons—and the demons' responses (verses 34,35,41)—reveal about Jesus' identity, power, authority, and mission?

PRAY: Ask Jesus to anoint you with the power of the Holy Spirit to accomplish His purposes for your life. Pray for greater sensitivity to people's needs, and ask God to use you to minister to and meet those needs for His honor.

ACT: Keep in mind that Jesus intends for you to be anointed (i.e., commissioned and empowered for service) by the Holy Spirit. Look for someone today to whom you can be Jesus' representative, bringing encouragement, help, and healing. If you can meet the person's need in a tangible way, do so. Offer encouragement to someone who needs a friend or pray personally for someone who is hurting or in need. God may be ready to do a miracle through you.

Luke 5:1-16

THINK: Are you a "think-before-you-act" type of person, or are you overly spontaneous? It's probably best to be a little of both, without being extreme either way. In the Bible, you'll find a lot of challenges and instructions to consider things carefully. Yet, when it comes to exercising faith in response to God's commands, callings, and revelations of power, He expects people to respond without hesitation. It's that kind of faith that gets God's attention and demonstrates a person's desire to follow Jesus regardless of the cost.

RESPOND: What does Simon's response in verse 5 tell us about him, and what can you learn from his example? What did Jesus mean when He said, "from now on you will catch men"? What seemed to be some of the characteristics Jesus saw in those whom He chose as His closest disciples? *(Strikingly, Jesus seems to have chosen people who were simply willing to put everything aside to follow Him. Do you qualify?)* What can you tell about Jesus from His response to the man with leprosy? Why do you think that Jesus often withdrew to lonely places to pray? *(Jesus' relationship with his Father was the source of His ability to carry out God's mission on earth.)* What do you think happened during His prayer times? How did Jesus' prayer life affect His ministry? How does Jesus' discipline of prayer serve as an example for you?

PRAY: Pray for the willingness to put aside anything in your life that may hinder you from pursuing God's purposes and to always respond to Him in faith, without hesitation.

ACT: Perhaps you've had a distinct sense that God wants you to do something—to make a decision, to get involved in something, to give up something, to talk to someone, to settle a difference—but you've hesitated to act. Don't wait any longer. Follow the example of Jesus' first followers. They were far from perfect, but they responded to Jesus and followed Him without hesitation. Also, find a secluded place where you can spend some extra quiet time hearing from God without distraction or interruption.

Fire Starter

Luke 5:17-39

THINK: Have you ever gotten stuck in a rut? While this can be the easy, comfortable route, it also tends to be boring and void of adventure. God certainly doesn't intend for His followers to take that route. Yet many Christians lack the supernatural power that was evident in Jesus' life and ministry. Perhaps that's because so few are willing to break their routine, get out of their comfort zone and pay the price of extreme faith.

RESPOND: Why did so many religious leaders want to see Jesus? How would you describe "the power of the Lord" (verse 17) and why was it present with Jesus in such a distinct way? How are those who brought the paralyzed man to Jesus an example to you and your Christian friends? What did Jesus mean when He said, "It is not the healthy who need a doctor, but the sick"? In His wine analogy, what did Jesus mean when He said, "The old is better" (verse 39)? *(Many Jews, like many people today, were reluctant to embrace "new wine"—the gospel—having become complacent and comfortable with their old traditions.)* In what ways did the Pharisees and teachers overlook the true purpose of God's law and how Christ fulfilled it? Why are some people stuck in their old ways to the point of resisting anything better, particularly God's plans for their lives?

PRAY: Pray for a friend who does not yet have a personal relationship with Jesus, that he or she would see the futility of their own way and find hope in the new life Jesus offers.

ACT: Think of an area of life in which you're stuck in an old rut and reluctant to change, even for the better. You may be hanging on to a familiar attitude or an old habit. Or you may be afraid to take a bold new step into a ministry venture at church. Then again, you may need to make a simple change to become more disciplined about your health or lifestyle. Break out of your old routine and start doing something better today.

Fire Starter

Luke 6:1-16

THINK: Do you ever feel like you need a break? God certainly knows and understands that you do, and He's provided just what you need. But you may not be taking advantage of it. You may get so busy with unnecessary things that you end up taking breaks from the necessary things, like your time alone with God. Maybe you're so caught up in doing what you think God expects, that you miss the good work He puts right in front of you. As a result, you may miss a miracle. One way to guard your priorities from getting out of whack is to take the opportunity God gives you every week to focus more intensely on worshipping Him, finding encouragement from other Christians, and refreshing yourself.

RESPOND: How did the Pharisees miss the purpose of God's Sabbath—the day He gives for worship, rest and refreshment? *(The Pharisees' own extreme interpretation of the Sabbath blinded them to God's true intent. The Sabbath is more benefit than ritual, blessing than rule.)* What kind of opportunities does the Sabbath, or "Lord's day" provide for His people? What did Jesus do before choosing those who would be His closest followers? What do you think it takes to be a close follower of Jesus? What lesson can you learn from His example in this situation?

PRAY: Give God thanks for the opportunities He gives you for worship and refreshment—physical and spiritual. Pray about a decision you are facing and trust God to help you choose wisely. Pray that your own ideas, behaviors and agendas never get in the way of anyone getting to God or receiving what they need from Him.

ACT: Spend some extended time in prayer regarding a significant decision you have to make. Make plans that the next time you are at church, you will do something specific and out of the ordinary to help, serve, encourage or inspire at least one other person or a whole group of people. Also, be sure to take advantage of the day God gives you to rest and refresh yourself physically and spiritually.

Luke 6:17–49

THINK: Do you have any enemies? Or maybe just a few people that get on your nerves? While God wants you to strive for peace with others, there's reason for concern if you seldom encounter opposition for your faith. If this is the case, your faith may not be showing. Jesus expects His followers to be different, in a positive way, from those who don't know Him. This inevitably brings resistance. But it also provides an opportunity for true Christians to shine Jesus' light into a spiritually dark world.

RESPOND: Who does God eventually bless, comfort and satisfy? Why do God's ways often not make sense to people? What can those who endure rejection and persecution for their faith in Jesus look forward to? What does it mean to love your enemies, and why does Jesus command this? What does this passage teach about judging others? *(Judging in this context isn't saying we can't call things what they are. Jesus doesn't require us to turn a blind eye to peoples' faults, especially if it means they could negatively influence us. But even when being honest about someone's faults, we should do so with grace toward the person, humility before God, and honesty about our own faults.)* What does it teach about dealing with your own faults before trying to help others with theirs (verses 41,42)? What does Jesus mean when He talks about good or bad "fruit" in a person's life (verses 43–45)? What does the heart have to do with this? Why is it vital to practice God's Word as opposed to just reading or hearing it?

PRAY: Pray that God would demonstrate His power through you as you pursue His purposes and put His Word into practice. Ask Him to help you love those who oppose you and to show you how to influence them for Jesus.

ACT: Demonstrate kindness to someone who has hurt you or given you a hard time. If you have unfairly judged anyone, apologize first to God, then to the other person. Do something generous for someone without expecting anything in return.

Fire Starter

Luke 7:1–35

THINK: Are you the type of person that wants proof? Do you tend to have a "believe-it-when-I-see-it" attitude about things that seem far-fetched or out of the ordinary? Actually, that's not a bad mindset regarding many things in life. But you've got to let it go when it comes to demonstrating faith in God. That doesn't mean you turn off your intellect or never struggle with doubts. But when you truly trust God's power and authority in your life, you can rest in confidence that He's taken care of your needs even before you see the proof.

RESPOND: Why was Jesus amazed by the centurion's faith? *(The high-ranking centurion recognized Jesus' ultimate authority and didn't hesitate to approach Jesus with respect and humility.)* Why is this kind of faith important in approaching Jesus and receiving from Him? What does Jesus' compassion for the widow reveal about God's heart for hurting people? *(God has a special place in His heart for widows, orphans, and those abandoned. God blesses those who make a place in their hearts for them, as well. See Psalm 68:5.)* Why do you think that John, who prepared the way for Jesus, struggled with doubts (verses 18–20)? How did Jesus encourage John? Under what circumstances is true faith in God best tested? What did Jesus mean when He said, "wisdom is proved right by all her children"? *(You've heard the saying, "The proof is in the pudding." People could see the "fruit" or positive result of both John's and Jesus' ministries.)*

PRAY: Ask Jesus to help you grow in humility and faith as you spend time with Him in prayer.

ACT: Think of an area or issue in which you have not demonstrated faith like the centurion. Perhaps you've been waiting for some sort of indication or sign before taking a step that you know God wants you to take. Maybe you've been doing things in your own time and way. Turn this around and take the action you believe God desires, even before you see the evidence you desire. Trust God to honor your faith and confirm His plans.

Luke 7:36–50

THINK: How often have you stopped to consider just how merciful God has been to you and how much God's forgiveness means to you personally? No matter how good or bad any of us think we've been throughout our lives, on our own we're all hopelessly separated from God just the same. If you've accepted the forgiveness and new life Jesus purchased for you at the price of His own perfect life, then you must realize that you owe Him everything. Jesus doesn't expect you to dwell on a past from which He's liberated you. But the more you grasp the hopelessness of your former condition apart from Christ, and the more you consider His love revealed when He gave His life on the cross, and the more you lay hold of the inner assurance that you are now forgiven and cared for by God himself, the more your faith and love for Jesus will grow and endure.

RESPOND: In what ways did the woman display boldness and devotion to Christ, disregarding what other's thought of her actions? How did the Pharisee's attitude toward himself and toward Jesus differ from the woman's attitude toward herself and toward Jesus? What response from the woman really allowed her to be saved (verse 50)? What kind of attitude and awareness can help you develop deeper love and devotion to Jesus? *(Never forget what Jesus has saved you both from and for.)* How does receiving forgiveness from Jesus affect your love for Him and your faith in Him?

PRAY: Express thanks to Jesus for His love and forgiveness and ask Him to keep you constantly aware of the mercy and compassion He has shown you. Ask Him to help you view others with similar compassion.

ACT: Extend forgiveness to someone who has hurt or offended you. If possible, settle things in person. Otherwise, try to call or send a note. Be gracious and apologize if necessary for harboring any bitterness or resentment toward the person. Don't worry about what he or she or anyone else thinks as you extend forgiveness.

Fire Starter

Luke 8:1-21

THINK: Think about things you had to have or be part of—but they have no place in your life today. Would any of these have changed your life dramatically? Probably not. However, what God starts in you will change things for eternity. But you must persevere in your relationship with Jesus, not giving up when things get tough or you lack enthusiasm. God won't give up on you, but He expects you to make the most of what He's given and to act on what you know of His Word. That way, your relationship with Jesus will grow and endure, and He will entrust you with even more (verse 18).

RESPOND: How are the actions of the women who followed Jesus an example for all followers of Christ? How can you show gratitude to Jesus? How can you contribute to ministry in practical ways? In what ways can "life's worries" choke a person's commitment to Jesus? *(When responsibilities, material things, or pleasure consume our thoughts and priorities, they can easily become "choking agents" against our active dedication to Jesus.)* What does it take on your part to "produce a crop"—to grow and mature and endure spiritually (verse 15)? What does Jesus mean when He talks about putting a light on a stand instead of hiding it under something (verse 16)? Whom does Jesus consider to be part of His family?

PRAY: Pray that the activities, cares and worries of your life will not distract you and rob you of your devotion to Jesus. Ask God to help you develop the strength and discipline to persevere in your faith.

ACT: Put aside some extra money and make a contribution beyond your current commitment to a missions effort of your church or youth ministry. If you are not currently active in ministry or service in your church, talk to one of your leaders and make plans to get involved. If there is any issue, concern, or activity in your life that is crowding out your commitment to Christ, ask Him for help in dealing with or getting rid of that distraction.

Fire Starter

Luke 8:22-39

THINK: What amazes you? Whatever it is, it's likely to get your attention. And whatever gets your attention has potential to influence you and even to change your life. In fact, if amazement turns to inspiration, and inspiration becomes passion, it can literally control your life. So what are you passionate about? What drives your dreams? Is your relationship with Jesus the controlling influence in your life? Do His love, power and purposes continue to amaze you? If so, your relationship with God will remain fresh, allowing Him to do amazing things through you.

RESPOND: Why do you think that the disciples' view of Jesus at this point was a mixture of fear and amazement (verse 25)? In what ways should Christ's followers continue to have a sense of amazement toward Him? What does it mean to be demon-possessed? *(Demon possession is when an evil spirit takes control of a person's body and personality.)* What does the demons' interaction with Jesus reveal about the Lord? Aside from literal demon possession, in what other ways do the forces of evil enslave, control and abuse people, spiritually and otherwise? Why would the people ask Jesus to leave their region after they had obviously witnessed His life-liberating power?

PRAY: Ask God to give you a continual sense of wonder and amazement regarding Jesus and His purposes—not because you don't expect great things—but because He is an awesome God who is worthy of your praise.

ACT: As you go through the day, notice the people around you in every situation and setting. Consider how the forces of evil seem to have control or influence over so many. Some of the effects are apparent in people who are angry or rebellious. Others may be dealing with obvious pain or desperate situations. Some are simply lonely or depressed. Behaviors and lifestyles reveal that people are deceived spiritually. As you pass and encounter people, pray silently that God will reveal himself to them in a special way and that they might turn to Him for hope and new life.

Fire Starter

Luke 8:40-56

THINK: Do you ever feel the need or pressure to prove yourself? It's not a comfortable feeling, and it can cause a lot of anxiety and insecurity. Wouldn't it be nice to be free of concern over what people think or what is expected of you? That freedom comes from knowing exactly who you are, what you are capable of and what your purpose is. No human has ever been more self-aware than Jesus. Neither has anyone been more aware of the people, problems and needs around Him. And certainly, no one has ever been more capable and compassionate in meeting those needs. Jesus didn't do things for people out of a need to prove himself or to show off His miraculous power. Rather, He responded to individual's faith because He loved them and wanted to honor to His Father through them.

RESPOND: What does the healing of the woman who touched Jesus' clothes tell us about how God's power can work through an individual? What does this situation teach about godly faith (verses 43-48)? If you were in Jairus' place, do you think you would have been able to accept Jesus' words, without any fear or doubt, that your daughter would be healed? Why or why not? What do these instances of healing reveal about Jesus and about God's character? In what ways do they challenge your faith? Why do you think that Jesus ordered the parents not to tell anyone what had happened (verse 56)?

PRAY: Ask God to continually work in you and prepare you to be used by Him in powerful ways. Ask Him to strengthen your faith and trust in Jesus. Pray also that you will develop Jesus' character more and more, and that you will demonstrate His compassion to people who are hurting and in need.

ACT: Call or visit someone you know who is ill or needs physical healing of some sort. Spend a little time encouraging them, but also let them know that you simply want to pray with them. Do so on the spot, and then continue to pray throughout the week.

Fire Starter

Luke 9:1-17

THINK: Do you ever feel as if you have little or nothing to contribute to God's purposes or that your role in ministry is insignificant? Perhaps these feelings have kept you from serving more fully in your church. Regardless of your self-perception, God intends for you to participate in His purposes. He has equipped you to do things that no one else can do quite like you. Consider the powerful ways in which He used common individuals—like His first followers. Then, surrender yourself completely to God so He can use you as He chooses.

RESPOND: What does Jesus' commissioning of the Twelve reveal about His purpose for all of His followers? Why did He tell the disciples, "Take nothing for your journey" (verse 3)? On whom were they to depend? What did the preaching of God's kingdom involve? *("Preaching the gospel" involved healing the sick and casting out demonic influences—prayerfully, and in Jesus' authority, breaking the power of darkness from peoples' lives.)* How do you think most churches measure up to this New Testament pattern? Do you think Jesus expects His followers today to be involved in the same sort of ministry as His first followers? Why or why not? Are you doing your part to represent New Testament Christianity? How so? Why would Jesus tell His disciples, "You give them something to eat," when referring to the massive crowd?

PRAY: Ask God to help you comprehend and fulfill His mission for you. Pray that you'll continually rely on the Holy Spirit for power and guidance. Pray that God's power will be evident through the ministries of your church.

ACT: If you're currently involved in a ministry, strengthen your commitment by (1) spending time in prayer every week for that ministry, (2) giving that ministry your best effort, and (3) encouraging others to dream about how God could use all of you in a more powerful way. If you're not currently involved in a ministry, set up an appointment with a ministry leader to talk about how God wants you to use your gifts and strengths for Him. Imagine God working in your life so He can work in someone else's!

Fire Starter

Luke 9:18-36

THINK: What do people think of when they see you or hear your name? Does your faith in Jesus have anything to do with it? When your identity gets so wrapped up in Jesus—when people think of you, they think of Him—that's when your devotion likely has what it takes to endure. While you can't control other people's perceptions, you can demonstrate a passion for Christ that's difficult to deny.

RESPOND: What does it mean for a follower of Jesus to "take up His cross daily"? *(More than belief only, the commitment to share in Christ's attitude of sacrifice and servanthood is part of what it means to take up one's cross daily.)* What kinds of personal costs or sacrifices are associated with following and serving Jesus? How can your identity become wrapped up in your relationship with Jesus? What do crosses often symbolize to people today? How does this view differ from what the Cross represented for Christians in the early days of the Church? How does a person save his or her life by losing it? In what ways do people—even Christians—act ashamed of Jesus? How can you guard against this in your life? Why did Peter react as he did as he witnessed Jesus' transfiguration? What was wrong with Peter's request? What was the significance of this event?

PRAY: Ask God to help you lose your own identity in your relationship with Jesus. Ask Him for strength to endure rejection and suffering for Jesus. Pray that your life will give people an accurate impression of Jesus.

ACT: Every time you see a cross today, consider what it seems to represent to those who wear it or display it. Every time you see one, give Jesus thanks for how He gave His life for you. Also, find a practical way you can identify with Jesus today through an activity or action involving other people, preferably people who do not know Christ yet.

Fire Starter

Luke 9:37–62

THINK: Have you ever been jealous of anyone at church who got an opportunity you would have liked or received recognition you felt was undeserved? Perhaps you've been skeptical of someone's ministry or motives based solely on prejudice. Such attitudes are not uncommon, but they are destructive because they influence our attitudes toward God. They also keep us from appreciating and celebrating what He's doing through the church to bring help, healing and inspiration to others. No matter how good your intentions are, your attitudes toward both Christians and non-Christians must be humble, gracious, and aimed at bringing others closer to Christ.

RESPOND: Why couldn't Jesus' disciples exercise authority over the demon that controlled the boy? What was Jesus teaching us using the child as an example (verses 47,48)? Why do you suppose the disciples felt as they did toward others who were driving out demons in Jesus' name (verse 49)? How is jealousy over ministry sometimes evident among Christians? What are the consequences of such behavior? Why did Jesus rebuke His disciples for their attitude toward the Samaritans? How can Christians' enthusiasm for Jesus sometimes be misguided in their attitudes and actions toward non-Christians? *(Christians aren't to be known for what or whom they're against more than what or whom they're for. In our zeal, there's no place for violence, antagonism, condescending, or prejudice, especially in the name of Christ.)* What was Jesus trying to teach in verses 57–62 about following Him?

PRAY: Confess any selfish pride you've held on to. Ask Jesus to help you avoid competition or jealousy in ministry. Pray that your enthusiasm for God never becomes misguided in a way that pushes people away from Him.

ACT: If you've harbored any jealousy, resentment or a bad attitude toward someone regarding ministry or Christian service, ask God to forgive you. Then, contact that person to confess your attitude and apologize. If you've been impatient, unkind, or difficult toward anyone because of their non-Christian behavior, make a personal apology to them as well.

Fire Starter

Luke 10:1-24

THINK: Do you work better alone or with others? Do you prefer self-guided projects or team efforts? God made us each unique, and depending on your distinct personality and the task at hand, both styles have a place. But when it comes to accomplishing God's purposes, He's designed us to function and find fulfillment by working with other believers. That way, we benefit from each other's gifts, encourage one another, and keep each other accountable.

RESPOND: What are the benefits of ministering with a partner or team? What did Jesus mean when He said, "The harvest is plentiful, but the workers are few" (verse 2)? How can you contribute to the spiritual harvest? What does verse 16 say about receiving or rejecting those who speak the truth from God? Why do you think the seventy-two were so amazed by how God used them, especially after witnessing Jesus' authority many times? What did Jesus mean when He said, "I saw Satan fall like lightning from heaven"? *(Jesus literally witnessed Satan's downfall before creation. Also, every time the disciples helped free anyone from spiritual bondage, Satan was once again defeated. That hasn't changed.)* What is the greatest cause for rejoicing among Jesus' followers? What did Jesus mean when He said that His Father had "hidden these things from the wise and learned, and revealed them to little children"? *(The simple truth of life with God isn't over the heads of those who humbly accept his Word.)* What does verse 22 indicate about the only way we can know and relate to God the Father?

PRAY: Ask God to help you connect with others who are devoted to Christ. Pray for wisdom and accountability. Also, ask God to raise up more workers in the ministries in which you take part through your church. Ask God to make His power and purpose evident through those ministries in your community and around the world.

ACT: Talk to a ministry leader about being part of a team which prays and serves in genuine, effective ways.

THINK: Have you noticed how an accident draws a crowd? Traffic will come to a near standstill as people slow down to gaze at the wreckage. In a strangely perverse way, people are intrigued by tragedy. Then again, people may be exposed to so much grief and carnage—both real and dramatized—that in an equally strange way they become desensitized to the desperate needs all around them. Consider how you respond when you see people in need. Do you feel sorry for them? Do you wonder how they got into the situations? Do you think of how God could help them? Are you ever willing to go out of your way to provide at least some of the help that's needed?

RESPOND: In what way was the teacher trying "to test Jesus" (verse 25)? What do you think was his real motive? How can following the commands in verse 27 bring life (verse 28)? In what way do you think the man was trying to "justify himself" (verse 29)? What can you learn from the parable of "The Good Samaritan"? How can you be a neighbor to people in need? Why is it significant that the Samaritan was the one who did the right thing? In what way did Mary choose the better and more necessary thing in relation to serving Jesus? What does this teach you about serving God and arranging your priorities?

PRAY: Ask the Holy Spirit to guide you into opportunities to help and serve others. Pray for wisdom to keep your priorities straight, and to not get so caught up in doing things for Jesus that you don't take time to be with Him.

ACT: Look for ways to help and serve others today. Don't wait for opportunities to come to you, pursue them. Keep in mind that this won't be convenient. It may even cost you. Be especially considerate of anyone who has given you a hard time in the past. If anyone asks why you're helping, don't hesitate to say that you're trying to pass on the kindness that God has shown you.

Fire Starter

Luke 11:1-13

THINK: When Jesus' disciples wanted to be more like Him, effectively ministering in the power of the Holy Spirit, they did not ask Him, "Lord, teach us to do miracles," or "teach us how to relate effectively to others," or even, "teach us to have great faith." No, they asked, "Lord, teach us to pray." By spending extended time with Jesus, it was obvious to them that the source of His miraculous power and supernatural guidance was that He had spent time communicating with His Father.

RESPOND: Why do you think Jesus disciple's asked Him to teach them to pray? Following Jesus' example, what are some of the things we should pray for? How should we approach God in regard to our daily needs and provisions? What is Jesus trying to teach about faith through the story of asking a friend for bread (verses 5-9)? Is God reluctant to answer our prayers? Why or why not? *(God requires persistence on our part to help us grow in trust and dependence on Him, which in turn deepens and strengthens our faith.)* What can persistent prayer develop in your life? Why is dependence on God so vital in seeing answers to prayer? In what ways is God a good Father?

PRAY: Pray for something that you have not prayed for in a while—perhaps you had given up hope or gotten weary of asking. Don't feel that you are begging God for an answer, as if He is reluctant to respond. Instead, let your ongoing prayers in this matter be an ongoing expression of dependence on God.

ACT: Focus on each phrase of "The Lord's Prayer" (Luke 11:2-4). Restate or write each one to apply to your life today. For example, "Father, while I have an earthly father, because of Jesus, I'm able to call You my heavenly Father," and so on. Then set aside some extra time every day this week specifically for prayer. Remember, this time should be spent not only speaking to God, but listening as well for His response and direction.

Fire Starter

Luke 11:14-36

THINK: You've probably used a camera before, but can you explain how it works? Basically, you get what you see. Whatever the lens takes in is the image in the viewfinder and becomes the image on the photo paper or computer screen. In a similar way, your eyes are like a lens to your soul. Physically, they register images in your brain; but spiritually, your eyes take in light or darkness that affects your entire being.

RESPOND: Why did some ask for a sign from Jesus, even after they had seen His power over the demon? What does Jesus mean when He says, "He who is not with me is against me"? Can a person remain "neutral" in the conflict between good and evil? Why or why not? Though demonic powers cannot possess true followers of Christ, in what ways will they continually attempt to influence them? Why is it crucial for those who have accepted Christ to turn from sin and obey God's Word (verse 28)? What does Jesus mean when He says, "Your eye is the lamp of your body"? *(Eyes are like cameras, "filming" everything for imprint on the brain. Whatever's imprinted affects us in some way, for better or worse.)* How does what you view through your eyes affect your entire being? How can you ensure that your eyes stay "good" spiritually (verse 34)?

PRAY: Pray for boldness to engage in the battle against evil, confident that you will be victorious in the Holy Spirit's power. Pray for God's help in guarding what you see so that your eyes receive things that light your life spiritually.

ACT: Examine your life (interests, hobbies, entertainment, etc.). Ask God to reveal ways in which you're taking in ungodly images that will dim or darken or your spirit. Make the necessary lifestyle changes to ensure that your eyes are full of spiritual light. If in any way you've tried to "ride the fence" between following God and doing your own thing, ask God to forgive you. Surrender to Christ and get completely on God's side.

Fire Starter

Luke 11:37-54

THINK: Are you serving God inwardly as well as outwardly? Think about your church involvement. Consider the image you've tried to convey to others regarding your Christianity. Is what they see an accurate reflection of what's going on inside? That's not to say you can't be facing struggles, doubts or painful issues. But are you trying to fake like you're not? If so, don't give up. Confess your hypocrisy to God and let Him help you change—from the inside out.

RESPOND: What does Jesus mean that some people clean the outside of things but the inside is "full of greed and wickedness" (verse 39)? In what ways can people appear to be spiritually clean, even though they may not be? What do you think Jesus means when He talks about giving what's inside the dish to the poor (verse 41)? Is Jesus saying that the Pharisees should not worry about giving God a tenth of what they have, but should only be concerned with love and justice toward others? Why or why not? *(Jesus is saying they should give their tithe in addition to these other choices.)* Why is it important to do both—to give God His due and to demonstrate true compassion for others? How would you have felt if you were a teacher of the Law in Jesus' time? Would you have taken His challenge to heart, or would you have been insulted and resented Jesus like the others?

PRAY: Ask God to keep your heart sincere toward Him so that you can be spiritually pure, inside and out. Pray that you will never resist or resent the tough challenges you come across in God's Word. Instead, ask for the wisdom and diligence to obey God without hesitating or complaining.

ACT: If there is any way in which you've tended your outward image and neglected your inner spirit, or if you have allowed spiritual impurity or insincerity to remain in your life, ask God to forgive you. Then, make some changes, obey God and allow Him to keep you clean, inside and out.

Fire Starter

Luke 12:1-21

THINK: Are you hiding something? Are you pretending to be something you're not? It might not seem like a big deal to you, but it's a huge deal to God. Remember, you may fool people, but you can't fool God. In fact, the Bible speaks frequently about fearing God and focusing on eternity, rather than worrying about what people think and focusing on what's temporary.

RESPOND: In what ways do some people "live a lie"—particularly in a spiritual sense? What does hypocrisy reveal about a person's attitude toward God? *(It reveals that a person doesn't fear God with respect or reverence.)* What does it mean to fear God, and why is this understanding so vital? *(The fear of God is deep reverence for his character, judgment, and power, and the humble awareness that, apart from Christ, we have no hope of an eternity with God.)* How does this relate to Jesus instruction, "Don't be afraid" (verse 7), when it comes to trusting God's care for us? Why don't Jesus' followers have to worry when sharing or defending their faith in Him (verses 11,12)? What is greed, and why is it so destructive?

PRAY: Ask God to expose and help you remove any hint of hypocrisy from your life. Pray that you will live with a reverent fear toward Him that drives away every other fear. Pray also that you'll never become preoccupied with a desire for worldly wealth, but that your priority will be to gain eternal riches toward God.

ACT: Have you ever felt that God provided an opportunity to talk with someone about your faith in Him, but you hesitated? Trust the Holy Spirit for the words to say, and then obey God. If you've been a hypocrite, confess it to God and to the other person. This could open a door to talk even further about Jesus. Also, if you've been greedy or materialistic, give that area of your life to God. In fact, take some money that you would have used to get more stuff and give it to missions instead.

Fire Starter

Luke 12:22-48

THINK: What are you worried about? Is anything causing you tension or anxiety? While most people would admit that worrying never accomplishes anything positive, it still seems to be a fact of life in many circumstances. Yet God doesn't intend for His followers to be consumed with worry. In a very real sense, worrying means taking responsibility for something God never intended—or at least not in the way He intended. From the basic necessities to the toughest trials, God has everything under control, which means, as a follower of Jesus, you have nothing to worry about.

RESPOND: How would you define "treasure" as used in this passage? *(Your treasure is what you value and pursue most, proven by your priorities. What captivates you? What gets your attention? Those fall into the "treasure" category of your life.)* How can you store up lasting treasures? What does Jesus mean when He says, "Be dressed ready for service" (verse 35)? Why must you be ready at all times (verse 40)? What does the parable about the wise and unwise managers teach about handling opportunities and responsibilities? *(You can grow, using time, resources, and responsibilities wisely, or you can grow careless, wasting time, money, and responsibilities on things that don't matter.)* What do verses 47 and 48 indicate about the relationship between our responsibility and our reward or punishment from God?

PRAY: Give God thanks for providing for your needs. Ask God to give you the desires and discipline to store lasting treasure in heaven. Pray to stay alert for Jesus' soon return so you'll be faithful to fulfill your God-given responsibilities.

ACT: Entrust to God any need or situation that currently worries you. Any time this concern arises, go to God in prayer as an indication of your dependence on Him. Also, take a brief inventory in your mind of things that get most of your time, attention and resources—including your money. If this exercise reveals that your priorities are skewed, shift your focus and make changes. Start putting your efforts and affections toward things that will matter for eternity.

Fire Starter

Luke 12:49-59

THINK: Is fire good or bad? It can be neither. It can be both. It depends on how it's used. Fire can destroy a home or consume a pile of rubble. It can cook food, warm the body and even seal a wound. Yet it can also leave permanent scars. Fire can melt metal, altering or destroying the original form. Yet, when rough metal becomes liquefied, the fire causes impurities to rise to the top, where they can be skimmed off and eliminated. The metal can then be forged and molded into something new, strong and precious. That's what God does with our lives if we let Him. But one way or another, God's fire will put each of us to the test.

RESPOND: In what way did Jesus' birth bring peace—particularly in a spiritual sense—to those who respond to God's gracious offer of forgiveness and new life through faith in Jesus (see Luke 2:14)? In what sense did Jesus coming disrupt people's lives? What did Jesus mean when He said, "I have come to bring fire on the earth" (verse 49)? *(In this verse, fire is associated with judgment and division.)* In what ways does God's fire purify and refine people's lives? In what ways does fire represent judgment? In what sense does Jesus' life and ministry actually bring division in the world? Why are people in the world at odds with those who follow Jesus? What could verses 57–59 indicate about your relationship with others? What could they indicate about your relationship with God?

PRAY: Ask God to put you through His refining fire, eliminating impurity and preparing you for His highest purposes.

ACT: Make a conscious effort to display the spiritual peace that God has brought to your life. If your faith has led to any tension between you and those close to you, don't push, but make a special effort to show kindness and graciousness to them. Also, if God reveals during your prayer time any spiritual impurities or rough edges, accept His help in removing these issues and refining these areas in your life.

Fire 🔥 Starter

Luke 13:1-21

THINK: Like never before, people today seek involvement in charitable causes to make our world a better place. Ironically, people are bombarded as never before with images of immorality, violence and destruction—much of it for the sake of information and entertainment. Because they are involved in decent causes, many young people are lulled into believing that their heart is in the right place. All the while, they are becoming more desensitized to the true value of life and the desperate needs around them. Jesus' followers must recognize real needs, responding with real hope and help—physically and spiritually.

RESPOND: What will happen to people who don't repent (i.e., admit their sin, turn from their own ways, and entrust themselves to Jesus as Savior and Leader of their lives, verses 3–5)? How does the fig tree story apply to people who claim to believe in Jesus but lack sincerity and spiritual fruitfulness? What does this reveal about God's patience? What does this passage reveal about Jesus' attitude toward hurting people? How can you remain sensitive to people in need? What do the parables of the mustard seed and yeast indicate about the growth and influence of God's kingdom? What do they say about the influence of deception and evil among Christ's followers? *(Yeast represents distorted doctrine. We need to study and know God's Word so we don't buy into false teaching.)* How can Christians and churches guard against deceptive and destructive influences?

PRAY: Confess and repent of any known sin in your life. Ask Jesus to give you sensitivity and compassion for hurting people and to show you what you can do to help. Pray for discernment to recognize and resist spiritual deception.

ACT: Ask God to lead you to people today who are hurting or have significant needs and to guide and provide you with a way to offer practical help. Be sure to pray, either on your own or even with the individuals in need. If any habit in your life is desensitizing you to the desperate needs all around, eliminate that distraction starting today.

Fire Starter

Luke 13:22-35

THINK: Many people claim that we are free to choose whichever path to God we like—as long as it involves significant effort to do good and does not hurt anyone else. Yes, we are free to choose a path in life. God has given us that liberty. It's also true that the invitation to know God—or could we say the "door" through which we come to know Him—is open. But it is also narrow, as is the path that leads to life and eternity with God. People cannot come to God in their own way or on their own terms. Many will try, but unless they accept Jesus and surrender their lives to Him, they'll never really know God or fulfill His purposes for their lives.

RESPOND: What does it mean that the way to be saved is through a "narrow door" (verse 24)? How might people try to enter God's kingdom but not be able to do so? How will it be that some people claim to have associated with Jesus, yet He will say, "I don't know you" (verses 25-27)? What was Jesus' "goal" as He refers to it in verse 32? What does Jesus' sorrow in verses 34 and 35 reveal about people? *(Jesus' sorrow affirms peoples' free will to either follow or reject Him.)*

PRAY: Pray for people you know who are attempting to please God in their own way—through good works or other beliefs. Pray that they come to know Jesus personally, relying on Him for forgiveness and eternal life.

ACT: If you've been trying to reach God on your own terms, ask Him to forgive you. Accept the sacrifice that His Son, Jesus, made in your place, to pay the price for your offense against God. Surrender your old way of life to Jesus in exchange for the new life and purpose He has for you. Then determine to follow Jesus with His help. Tell your youth leader or pastor that you have a fresh desire to know and follow Jesus. Ask them to pray for you.

Fire Starter

THINK: What are you doing to get ahead? After all, that's the way of the world isn't it? It certainly is for a lot of people. But it shouldn't be a concern for Christ's followers. In fact, Jesus warns that self-centered attempts to come out on top will ultimately come crashing down. On the other hand, when His followers set pride aside and put their success in God's hands, He will often reward their efforts and fulfill His highest purposes through their lives.

RESPOND: Why were those at the Pharisee's house carefully watching Jesus (verse 1)? Why did Jesus ask the Pharisees and teachers of the Law if it was okay to heal on the Sabbath? Why did they not respond? Why does exalting oneself have no place in God's kingdom? *(Self-promotion usually means we're not promoting God's image. Christ followers who have a lot of pride cause themselves as well as others to stumble.)* How does a person gain honor in God's kingdom? What is the significance of doing things for people who cannot repay you (verses 12–14)? Why do people often neglect or reject God's invitation to be part of His kingdom? What does the story of the great banquet indicate about those who will be part of God's kingdom? What role do you and other followers of Jesus have in the invitation process?

PRAY: Ask God to keep you humble and aware when you may be trying to exalt yourself in any way. Give thanks for the opportunity to deliver God's invitation to eternal life. Ask God for help and boldness in doing this.

ACT: If there is any area of your life in which you've pridefully attempted to exalt yourself or put yourself ahead of others for selfish reasons, ask God to forgive you. Then back off from your own way and put your success in God's hands. Still do your best, but only as a means of honoring God. Do what you can to help others succeed along the way. Also, try serving as many people as possible today.

Fire Starter

Luke 14:25 through 15:10

THINK: While Jesus was on earth, a lot of people followed Him at one time or another. But when things got tough and His challenges a little too intense, the crowds dwindled. It became apparent that being a true disciple—a disciplined learner and devoted follower—of Christ involved more than most were prepared to give. But those who were willing to put everything else aside to stick with Jesus found their reward in the opportunity to become more like their Leader.

RESPOND: What did Jesus mean when He said that anyone who would follow Him must "hate his father and mother, his wife and children, his brothers and sisters—yes, even his own life"? *(Jesus is emphasizing that we're to love Him way more than anything or anyone else in comparison. We're not to literally "hate" our family, but to love and be loyal to Jesus more than anything or anyone else.)* What does this passage reveal about the personal demands of discipleship? *(Christianity isn't a wishy-washy religion. Being a disciple of Jesus means we prioritize what God wants over anything.)* What do the parables about the lost sheep and lost coin illustrate about God's priorities and the purpose of Jesus' earthly mission? How does this passage challenge?

PRAY: Pray that no interest, activity or relationship in your life will compare to your love and devotion to Christ. Commit to God all of your relationships, possessions, plans and desires so that He can do as He chooses with these things and so He can use you for the purpose for which He created you.

ACT: In your journal or one of those blank pages in the front of your Bible, write down one or two ways you can incorporate the following into your life: Know and live God's Word, Boldly identify with Jesus, Show people what Jesus is like, Be different in positive ways, Make choices that reflect integrity, Inspire people to think about Jesus. Now, of all the things you thought of (and hopefully wrote down) which can and will you do today?

Luke 15:11-32

THINK: Have you ever lost something really valuable? How did you feel when you realized it was missing and what did you do? Get mad? Cry? Panic? Did you get others to help find it? If and when you found it, how did you respond? If losing things is a miserable feeling, imagine losing track of someone you love. Then imagine reuniting with the person.

RESPOND: What does the parable of the lost son reveal about the eventual consequences of sin (i.e., going our own way and defying God)? In what ways do people demonstrate a desire to do as they please, "free" of God's constraints? What did the lost son need to realize before he was ready to change (verse 21)? What does it often take for people to come to their senses spiritually? What does it mean to be spiritually "lost"? *("Lost" in this story refers to being lost in relation to God. Life apart from God equals spiritual death; life with Him means life.)* What does this parable reveal about God's attitude toward lost people? How should this affect your attitude? *(Keep praying for friends and family who are far from God. Jesus never gives up on them; neither should you.)* In what way does the older son represent some Christians? In what way is the older son like people who appear to live for God but don't really know Him or His purposes?

PRAY: Pray for a friend, family member or someone you know who once knew God, or was near to knowing Him, but is currently away from God and doing their own thing. Pray that the person will come to his or her senses, recognizing the need for God and returning to Him.

ACT: Contact the person you prayed for. Ask how he or she is doing and make a point to be available if needed. Don't feel the need to press him or her about spiritual issues unless they seem open and you feel God directing you to do so. However, let the person know that you're praying for them.

Fire Starter

Luke 16:1-31

THINK: Are you making the most of your resources and relationships? When you're with Christians are you taking full advantage of opportunities to worship and serve? Are you sharpening your God-given gifts and helping others to grow and excel with theirs? And when you're around those who don't know Jesus, are you doing all you can to show them what Jesus is like and to inspire them to consider Christ for themselves?

RESPOND: Why did the master commend the dishonest servant? In what ways do worldly people sometimes do more with their abilities, resources and relationships than godly people? *(Jesus illustrates, in a way many can understand, that sometimes non-Christians are better about using their abilities. Christians can and should learn to use their resources, abilities, and possessions to promote spiritual and eternal interests.)* How should the way Christians handle their resources and relationships differ from the practices of people who don't follow Christ? *(The wealth of Christians should benefit God's kingdom, including helping the needy.)* How does being trustworthy with possessions relate to spiritual issues? How can a person become a slave to money, and how does this relate to one's relationship with God? How do God's values differ from what people typically value (verse 15)? In what ways does Jesus' teaching call you to an even higher standard than the Law (verse 18)? What does the story of the rich man and Lazarus indicate about how our life choices and circumstances now can affect eternity?

PRAY: Ask God to help you be wise and responsible with the gifts, resources and opportunities He's given you. Pray that you'll keep worldly resources in perspective, using them to honor God and to influence other people for eternity.

ACT: In all of your interaction today with people—particularly, those who don't likely follow Jesus—do something to influence them in a positive way. Show simple kindness to all. Befriend those who could use encouragement, and include them in your activities with Christian friends. Initiate spiritual conversations with anyone who is open.

Luke 17:1-19

THINK: Jesus' followers should be known for helping to relieve others of their hurts and offenses by extending compassion and forgiveness. As a follower of Jesus, you must always guard your behavior so as to help reconcile people to God, not alienate them from Him.

RESPOND: In what ways do people often cause or influence others to sin or defy God? *(People are innately sinful; we don't need help breaking God's laws. It's bad enough when someone sins alone, but to encourage or cause, by their example, another person to do what's wrong is far worse.)* Why do people often try to involve others in their sinful and destructive activities? What can happen in your own life and spirit if you refuse to forgive? What can forgiveness do for the person who receives it? What can it do for the person who offers it? When Jesus responded to the disciples' request to increase their faith, what did His answer indicate about the amount of faith we need for great things? If the amount of faith is not the main issue, what are the keys to exercising faith? What do verses 7-10 indicate about the attitude you should have in regard to serving God? Why do you think only one of the lepers returned to thank Jesus? How does this story challenge or inspire you (see 1 John 4:19)?

PRAY: Ask God to give you a continual attitude of mercy and forgiveness. If someone has hurt you in the past and the situation is still unresolved, pray for God's help in dealing with any lingering pain so that the situation does not continue to hurt or destroy you. Pray that the other person will accept forgiveness and get right with God.

ACT: If you've been a bad influence on anyone, ask God to forgive you. Apologize to those involved, and ask for their forgiveness. If someone has offended you, forgive them—in person if appropriate. Also, consider God's many benefits and blessings to you. If you've taken anything for granted, take time to express gratitude to God for His goodness.

Luke 17:20 through 18:14

THINK: To listen to some believers you'd get the impression that faith is knowing exactly what will happen and getting what you pray for right away. After all, God hears us the first time; we don't have to beg Him for what He already knows we need. But God longs for our company and our conversation. And He wants us to keep bringing our requests to Him time and again—until we see how He chooses to answer. He expects us to demonstrate persistent dependence on Him. That's the essence of real faith.

RESPOND: What does it mean, "the kingdom of God is within you"? *(The nature of God's kingdom is neither political nor material; rather, His kingdom is spiritual. Gaining the kingdom of God is less a matter of effort and position and more of transformation of our hearts and minds. It's not what we do for God; it's something He does in us.)* How is God's kingdom and the way it operates different from worldly kingdoms and the way they operate? When Jesus comes to take His followers from the earth, and then finally returns to judge the world, why and how will people be unprepared? *(Even though God called Lot and his family out in a very obvious and dramatic way, Lot's wife was still attached in some ways. Her eyes were on an earthly city rather than a heavenly kingdom. What about you? Is your heart more attached to earthly things than to Jesus?)* In what ways will Jesus' final return be vastly different from when He first walked the earth (verses 24,25,30–35)?

PRAY: Ask God to reveal the reality and character of His kingdom through you in powerful and persuasive ways, bringing hope, healing and new life to those who have yet to find their place in God's kingdom.

ACT: Spend some extra time today with God in prayer. Talk to Him about several things that have been on your mind for a while—things you may not have prayed for lately. As you pray, listen for God's response and guidance.

Luke 18:15-43

THINK: Somewhere during the teen years childish wonder gives way to adolescent anxiety and playtime is replaced by peer pressure. Then comes the responsibilities and concerns of adulthood, multiplying stress, skewing priorities and turning youthful innocence into so-called worldly sophistication. Thankfully, God understands our need to reclaim some of the simplicities of childhood—uninhibited amazement, boundless idealism, and humble dependence. In fact, these are the kinds of qualities that characterize those who find their place in God's kingdom.

RESPOND: Why do you think people brought babies to Jesus? Why did the disciples try to prevent this? What does Jesus' response reveal about His values? In what ways does God's kingdom belong to people who are like children? What do you think the rich man hoped Jesus would say about receiving eternal life? What did this man really lack (verse 22) in order to gain treasure in heaven? Why do you think the man was unable to let go of everything to follow Jesus? What are some things that keep people from following Him? Why do people have a difficult time letting go of things to serve God? In what ways does following Jesus bring greater fulfillment and reward than anything we could put aside for His purposes (verses 29,30)? Why were the disciples unable to comprehend Jesus' predictions of suffering and death (verse 34)? In what ways did the blind man show great faith in Jesus? *(For one thing, the man was persistent and didn't let the crowd shout him down. By addressing Jesus as "Son of David" he was acknowledging Jesus as the Messiah who would be a descendant of King David.)*

PRAY: Thank Jesus for the opportunity to follow Him. Ask Him to expose anything in your life that's taking too much priority and could keep you from complete devotion to God and His purposes. Give this thing or area to Jesus.

ACT: Allow God to search your life, exposing anything that could hinder you from fulfilling His highest purposes. Adjust your priorities accordingly. Also, take time to interact with and encourage any children you encounter today.

Fire Starter

Luke 19:1-27

THINK: What are you doing with your God-given gifts, resources, and opportunities? Are you using them to benefit others, or are you squandering them on selfish interests? Above all, are you using them in a way that honors God and promotes His purposes? Those who depend on God and make the most of what they have will be entrusted with even more—not necessarily from a worldly point of view, but from an eternal perspective. However, those who don't use what they have will eventually lose it (verse 26). Don't let laziness, pride, self-consciousness or fear keep you from investing what God has entrusted to you.

RESPOND: How did people likely feel about Zacchaeus (Zacchaeus was a government agent squeezing tax dollars out of the people, taking more than he should have)? What do Zacchaeus' actions and quick response indicate about his attitude toward Jesus? How does this story challenge your attitudes about spiritually lost people? How can you tell that Zacchaeus' faith was genuine? *(True spiritual conversion results in positive changes in peoples' lives.)* What does this passage reveal about the purpose of Jesus' earthly mission? What does the parable of the ten minas teach about our responsibilities to God? In what ways was the unfaithful servant's view of the master completely inaccurate (verses 21-23)? How does the way we use what God has given us in this life affect what happens to us now and in eternity?

PRAY: Ask God to give you an attitude of greater compassion and openness to people of all types who don't know Him. Ask God to help you be faithful with all the opportunities and resources He's given you to honor Him.

ACT: Think of people you know who seem far from God. Reconsider your attitude toward them and any judgments you've made regarding their openness. Some of these individuals may be ready to receive Christ, but could be testing you to see if your faith is real. Befriend these individuals and trust God for the opportunity to lead them to Jesus.

Fire Starter

Luke 19:28-48

THINK: As Jesus entered Jerusalem for the last time, people lined the streets, full of expectation. Jesus knew that His earthly ministry was nearing an end, but the crowd had other ideas. Many assumed He would rise to power and rescue them from Roman tyranny. But the masses misunderstood the spiritual nature of God's kingdom and would ultimately reject Jesus as their Deliverer. Knowing this, Jesus was overcome with grief—not for himself, but for them. Judgment would eventually come as a result of their rebellion. God's heart still breaks for the lost and rebellious.

RESPOND: Why did Jesus ride into the city on a donkey? *(Jesus' entrance on a donkey not only fulfilled prophecy from Zechariah 9:9, but showed His kingdom really was "not of this world.")* In what way did this symbolize God's kingdom and how it differs from earthly kingdoms? Why did Jesus weep as He neared Jerusalem? What does this reveal about God's heart for people? Why did the people ultimately reject Jesus? What kind of peace had He come to bring, and why were they unable to recognize it? What do Jesus' actions in the temple reveal about His priorities and purpose for the Church? *(Jesus drove out those who were disrespecting God's house and polluting its true spiritual purpose.)* What can happen in our congregations if we tolerate deceit, irreverence, and worldliness in our churches?

PRAY: Ask Jesus to give you His intense compassion for those who do not know or accept Him. Ask God to help you do what you can to reach and influence those who don't know Him while there is still time.

ACT: As you walk the halls of your school, or go through your workplace, or are out in the community, try to view the people around you as God sees them—through eyes of intense compassion. Allow yourself to sense God's sorrow over their spiritual helplessness and the judgment they'll face if they persistently reject Christ. Let these feelings inspire you to encourage people, meet their needs, and start conversations that may lead them to consider Christ.

Luke 20:1-19

THINK: Do you ever challenge those in authority over you, pushing the boundaries of respect and acceptable behavior? It seems that a lot of people tolerate this kind of conduct, especially from teens and young adults. There are times to question the powers that be, but God doesn't smile on irreverent behavior, particularly when it defies His authority. God doesn't have to prove himself to anyone. Yet, for those whose hearts are open to His Son, Jesus, His works speak for themselves. As people accept Jesus and entrust their lives to Him, God opens their eyes to the wonder of His works and enlightens their minds to the wisdom of His Word.

RESPOND: Why do you think the religious leaders questioned Jesus' authority? What did this reveal about them? *(For the Pharisees, it was like, "How dare this young upstart act like he knows what's best in our temple!" Jesus condemned the very practices the Pharisees allowed and even participated in.)* How does the parable of the tenants describe how people through the ages have treated God's prophets and eventually His Son? Who is "the stone the builders rejected"? How has that stone become a foundation? *(Those who reject Christ will suffer being crushed under His judgment. But for those who surrender to and serve Him, Jesus becomes the basis of everything they say and do.)* Why are people often offended by Jesus? How will rejecting Jesus ultimately "crush" people?

PRAY: Pray for people you know who have rejected Jesus or are currently opposed to following Him. Pray that Jesus' passion, power and purposes will become evident to them, particularly through your life and example. Pray that they will not find ultimate fulfillment or another foundation for their lives apart from Jesus.

ACT: Do something practical to show kindness and compassion, or to provide help and encouragement, to any of those you just prayed for. Let them see through your example that true authority, power, and leadership in God's kingdom are a result of humility, service, and honor to God.

121

Luke 20:20 through 21:4

THINK: Have you ever been around someone who seemed bent on getting people into trouble? Perhaps he or she avoided blame and punishment by getting others to do the "dirty work." Such people are often shrewd and come across innocently to unsuspecting victims or accomplices. The religious leaders of Jesus' day were like that, but Jesus saw through their deception and foiled their attempts to trick Him time and again. Interestingly, Jesus doesn't really tell His followers how to answer such people or how to turn the tables on them. Instead, He says to avoid them altogether.

RESPOND: What is a Christian's responsibility in regard to his or her government? *(Unless the man's law requires us to disobey God's commands, we're to submit to government regulations and secular laws.)* In what ways do you think relationships with other people will be different for God's people in eternity, and why? What is the connection and relationship between the Messiah (i.e., "Anointed One," Savior, Christ) and King David? *(While, in human terms, Jesus is a descendant of King David, David's statement in Psalm 110:1 affirms that the Messiah is the Son of God.)* According to Jesus (verses 45–47) what types of people should you avoid and why? In what way was the widow's offering much greater than all the others put together? How does God determine the value of a gift? In what way does the widow's example challenge you personally?

PRAY: Pray for those in governmental leadership on the national, state and local levels. Pray for individuals by name, asking God to give them wisdom. Also, give thanks for the hope of resurrection and eternal life with Christ.

ACT: Get a newspaper or magazine or log on to a news Web site and notice the stories related to government. Use this as a guide in praying for government leaders, their situations and the decisions they must make. Also, set aside some money that you would have used for something else—not just your "extra" income, but something that will truly be more of a sacrifice—and give it to your church or to missions.

Fire Starter

Luke 21:5-38

THINK: Most products are manufactured with some degree of "planned obsolescence," which means they're expected to wear out after a period of time. That way, manufacturers are assured of selling more parts and products in the long run. Look through all your old stuff and see what's become of things you once had to have and couldn't live without. That will serve as an object lesson that nothing endures forever. Nothing, that is, except for the truth and reality of God's Word (verse 33)—the only thing worth staking your life on.

RESPOND: Why shouldn't you stake your hope and affections on earthly things? What are some signs of the end times? Though many of the signs and events described in this passage relate to the Tribulation period (after Jesus takes His Church from the world), which ones do you see already? How can persecution provide opportunities to honor God (verse 13)? Does Jesus guarantee that His followers won't face physical harm or persecution for their faith in Him? *(Jesus promises spiritual security for His followers, but faithful believers will face persecution in various forms throughout their earthly lives. We are assured that God is neither absent nor blind to persecution of His children, and works through all things for their good [Romans 8:28].)* What does this passage say about the truth and endurance of God's Word (verse 33)? Why and how must God's people remain alert and on guard in the last days?

PRAY: Pray that you'll not become distracted from devotion to God by earthly concerns and that you'll be alert to the signs around you, which indicate that Christ's coming is near. Ask God to give you discernment regarding what's right and true so that you will not fall for deceptive ideas and teaching.

ACT: Look through a newspaper, magazine or online news source (as you may have done for yesterday's reading). Notice issues and events that fit the general description of end-time occurrences. Then, look further to see if you can detect any information or ideas that are deceptive or contradictory compared to biblical truth.

123

Luke 22:1-38

THINK: A contract is a legal agreement with another party, outlining specific benefits, obligations, and potential penalties for both sides. To initiate the contract, you put up payment or collateral—something of value to guarantee your side of the deal. A covenant is similar to a contract, but more than a legal agreement, it's a "life agreement" in which two parties pledge themselves to each other. God has established a covenant with you, pledging His love, loyalty and life. His Son, Jesus, has even covered your payment, sealing the covenant with His own life's blood. That was the price of entering a relationship with God. If you accept the terms of this covenant, entrusting your life to Jesus, you receive the benefits of forgiveness and eternal life with Him.

RESPOND: In what ways is Judas' example a caution to all Christians? *(The account of Judas's suicide is a sobering reminder that we must be on guard against Satan and his lies. We must always look to Jesus and believe in Him regardless of our circumstances.)* What's the significance and symbolism of "the cup" and the bread at Jesus' last supper (verses 19,20)? What is the "new covenant" Jesus established with us? *(His sacrifice, rather than animal sacrifices and other Old Testament rituals, has become payment for our sin.)* How did Jesus initiate that covenant, and what is the significance of His blood? What constitutes greatness in God's view? How does Peter's failure challenge you? *(No believer is immune from being tempted by Satan.)*

PRAY: Pray that you never become disillusioned or self-confident to the point of turning your back on Jesus. Pray instead to remain humble and willing to serve, following Jesus' example and showing others what it means to know Him.

ACT: Do something today to serve an individual or group over whom you might normally have status, position or leadership. Help a teammate who looks up to you with a particular skill. Assist a person who is new on the job with a difficult task. Do something special for a youth ministry team in which you have a leadership role. You could even do a household chore for one of your siblings.

Fire Starter

Luke 22:39-65

THINK: Have you ever been hurt or even betrayed by a close friend? How did you feel? Now turn it around. Have you ever abandoned a close friend or betrayed the confidence of someone who trusted you? How did you feel about that? If you really care about a relationship, being the betrayer probably feels worse than being betrayed. But each of us, if left to ourselves, is capable of turning our back on a friend—even if that friend is Jesus. No matter how good your intentions, unless you continue to grow and build spiritual strength, you are at risk of losing your devotion to Christ. So don't compromise your commitment by getting careless or over-confident. Instead, get it together with God by devoting time to His Word and prayer.

RESPOND: Why did Jesus want His disciples to pray with Him? How could prayer have helped them? In what ways does Jesus' instruction about prayer serve as a challenge to you personally? How can prayer help you avoid and overcome temptation and evil? Why do you think Peter followed those who took Jesus away? Why, then, would he not admit that He had been with Jesus? *(Peter, though he believed in and loved Jesus, suffered weakness in this situation.)* How would you describe Peter's emotions after denying Jesus so emphatically? What do you think you might have done and how would you have felt if you were in Peter's situation?

PRAY: Pray that you would never abandon your faith and commitment to Christ during difficult times or because of pressure from others. Pray that God would give you wisdom to avoid tempting situations as much as possible, and for moral strength to overcome temptation when pressured to give in or back down spiritually.

ACT: Take extra time throughout the day to pray, particularly for areas of life in which you've struggled with weakness and temptation. (Don't contribute to the problems by unnecessarily exposing yourself to temptation.) As you encounter difficulties or temptations, pray silently for God's help to overcome them. Listen for God's guidance—and follow it.

Luke 22:66 through 23:25

THINK: How are you at handling peer pressure? Do you typically do what you know is right, or do you take the path of least resistance? Jesus' road to the Cross was paved by people who didn't have the backbone to stand up for what's right. As a result, Jesus suffered at the hands of those who were morally weak and completely wrong. Ironically, He didn't just suffer because of them, He suffered for them. In fact, He willingly gave His life for us all, bearing the weight of our sin, which was more pressure than any of us could have handled.

RESPOND: Why do you think the religious leaders could not accept Jesus as God's Son? Were their accusations true? Who was Pilate, and what can we tell about his character from this passage? *(Pilate was the Roman governor. It seems Pilate was at a crossroads, in that he was aware of Jesus' innocence, but perhaps for "political correctness" and convenience and because of his own weakness, he succumbed to the demands of the crowd.)* Who was Herod, and what was his motive for wanting to see Jesus? Why do you think Jesus refused to speak to Herod? Why did Herod ridicule Jesus after being so anxious to see Him before? Why do you think Herod and Pilate became allies on that particular day surrounding the events with Jesus?

PRAY: Pray for wisdom to recognize the best course of action in any given situation. Ask God to give you strength to resist pressure from others who would push you to go against what He wants and what you know is best.

ACT: Think of situations in which you are currently facing pressure to do the wrong thing. Make a deliberate choice either to remove yourself from those situations or to once and for all make the right choice despite the pressure. Depend on God for strength to take a stand and for the words to say if any of these situations requires a verbal response to people. Trust that God can turn these situations into opportunities to influence others for Christ.

Luke 23:26-49

THINK: One of the surest signs of the depravity and corruption of the human heart is the fact that people take pleasure in violence, blood, and death. We see it today as millions find pleasure and entertainment in media depicting violence, brutality, and death. Jesus died to change this attitude of the heart and to demonstrate true love for life and humanity. Yet, even as He hung on the cross, onlookers gazed in contempt, watching Him suffer a horrible death. Amazingly, He died for them; He died for us all.

RESPOND: What did Jesus mean when He said, "For if men do these things when the tree is green, what will happen when it is dry" (verse 31)? *(In treating Jesus with disdain and rejection while He was with them, people were unknowingly inviting judgment and suffering as the just penalty.)* How does Jesus' death restore people to relationship with God? What did the attitude of the second criminal reveal about his heart and his view of Jesus? What does Jesus' reply to that man reveal about the simplicity of receiving forgiveness and new life? *(Those who trust Jesus for salvation are with God after their physical death. Salvation is the result of faith in Christ, period. As in the case of the man on the cross who asked Jesus to remember him, our righteousness isn't what saves us.)* What do Jesus' words in verse 46 reveal about His death? What can you discern about Jesus by His last sayings from the Cross?

PRAY: Express gratitude to Jesus for His personal sacrifice that makes your forgiveness and relationship with God possible. Commit to sharing that simple message so others too can know Him and experience eternal life with Him.

ACT: Read or sing a familiar hymn about the sacrifice Jesus made for you or create an original artwork honoring Jesus in your own way. You may choose to focus on a particular aspect of His suffering and death, for example, basing your work on one of Jesus' last sayings on the cross.

Fire Starter

Luke 23:50 through 24:12

THINK: The miracle of the Resurrection is unique to the Christian faith. Many consider this claim so outrageous that they refuse to believe. But the facts defy skepticism. In reality, Jesus' resurrection is among the most historically verified events in history. For those who consider the facts and choose to put their faith in Christ, His resurrection is their source of inspiration, power, and hope—both now and for the life to come. Because Jesus is alive, Christianity is a life-transforming experience with eternal benefits.

RESPOND: Why did the women follow Joseph as he took Jesus' body to the tomb? Why do you think that the women—and the rest of Jesus followers—did not remember Jesus' prediction of His resurrection until after it had taken place (verses 6–8,11)? What facts confirm Jesus' resurrection? *(The resurrection has been historically verified. Many security precautions were taken to ensure that no one could steal Jesus' body. If Jesus' enemies had taken it, they would have displayed it publicly to prove Christ a fraud. After Jesus rose, He stayed on earth for forty days, witnessed by over five hundred people.)* How are the lives of those who follow Jesus today a testimony of the reality of Jesus' resurrection? In what way does the empowering of Jesus' followers by the Holy Spirit—starting on the day of Pentecost—confirm the fact of Jesus' resurrection? *(If Jesus had not risen, the Holy Spirit could not have been poured out at Pentecost and wouldn't be active in the lives of believers today.)* How does Jesus' resurrection continually give hope?

PRAY: Give Jesus thanks for His resurrection and the life, hope, and power it provides for those who put faith in Him.

ACT: Take time to research and investigate some other reliable ministry resources highlighting historical facts that back the biblical account of Jesus' resurrection. These facts can encourage your faith and may provide you with some talking points if you ever need to discuss or debate with anyone the reality of Jesus' resurrection.

Fire Starter

Luke 24:13-35

THINK: How many times have you heard something that sounded too good to be true? More times than you could count, probably. And how did most of those claims turn out? As expected—too good to be true. Sadly, most of us have become accustomed to tuning out things that seem beyond belief. In many cases, this is for the best. But sometimes, our skepticism causes us to miss out on things that are truly extraordinary—even miraculous. This is certainly true if we don't take God's Word at face value. A lack of faith can keep us from understanding, receiving and experiencing God's best. And that's not just unbelievable—it's unacceptable.

RESPOND: Do you think that the men on the road to Emmaus had already given up hope? Why or why not? Why did some still have a difficult time believing the women's original report about Jesus rising from the dead, even after others had confirmed some of the facts? Even though many Old Testament prophets had spoken about Christ's suffering, why did so many of His followers seem to miss the necessity of all that? Why do you think that the men sensed "a burning within us while he [Jesus] talked with us on the road and opened the Scriptures to us" (verse 32)? What kind of effect can the truth of God's Word have on human hearts and lives?

PRAY: Ask God to give you a more trusting heart toward Him and His Word. Ask for insight to understand what God has revealed in the Word and for wisdom to see how it applies to your life in specific ways. Then ask Him for the faith and discipline to apply what He shows you.

ACT: Glance back quickly through Luke's Gospel and find a passage that you previously found difficult to understand or relate to. Review any related *Fire Bible: Student Edition* study notes. Ask God to give you deeper insight into the passage and to show you what difference He wants it to make in your life. Then listen to God and put His Word into action.

Fire Starter

Luke 24:36-53

THINK: Remember when you were really young and couldn't wait for the day when people would start trusting you with greater privileges and responsibilities? There is One who is ready to entrust you right now with the highest privilege and greatest responsibility. God has a mission for you. Are you up to the challenge? You won't be on your own; He will guide, equip, and empower you to accomplish His plans.

RESPOND: Why do you think the disciples had to actually see Jesus and be reminded of prophecies about Him before they were willing to believe? What must a person do to receive forgiveness from God? *(Repentance comes before forgiveness. Repentance is a heart and attitude change from self-will to surrender to God's will.)* What's the mission to which Christ calls His followers? What's the primary message they are to deliver? Where are they to start? Why is it important to start fulfilling Jesus' instructions right where you are now? What was the Father's promise that Jesus spoke about and what would it provide for His followers? *(God followed through on His promise to send His Spirit to empower His followers to resist evil, do good, and enjoy Him.)* Why was this so important? What's the significance of God's or Jesus' blessing on His followers?

PRAY: Ask Jesus to open your mind so you can understand His Word in a deeper way. Commit to always taking God at His Word and to putting His Word into practice. Ask Jesus to give you the boldness to deliver His message as you rely on the power of the Holy Spirit.

ACT: Write the names of five friends who don't know Jesus on an index card or the inside flap of your Bible. Commit to pray for them weekly throughout the school year. Build authentic, caring relationships with them and commit to being a positive influence in their lives. Learn to communicate your personal experience with God and the message of Jesus to your friends. Look for opportunities to talk about Jesus in a natural way.

Fire Starter

John 1:1-18

THINK: John's Gospel is unique among the four Gospels (Matthew, Mark, Luke, John). It gives deeper insight into the "mystery" of Jesus as both God and man. As one of Jesus' twelve original disciples and a member of what might be called Jesus' inner circle (along with Peter and James), John describes events as an eyewitness. His writing has served as a vital and authoritative statement about "the truth" as it literally came to life in Jesus Christ.

RESPOND: In John 1:1, who is called "the Word," and why? *(Jesus was the personal "Word" through whom God spoke all things into existence and the personified, not to mention perfect, representation of God's nature and character.)* In what way does Jesus give light to people? What does it really mean to "believe" in Jesus? *(Saving faith is practical and active. Believing, in a biblical sense, is trusting Christ with one's life and future, obeying and serving Him selflessly.)* What's the significance of the fact that "the Word became flesh"? *(Humanity intersected and fused with Deity when Jesus came to earth. Jesus allowed himself to experience human temptations and limitations, yet without sinning. In this way He not only relates to people, He also modeled what it means to live abandoned to God.)* What does it mean that "grace and truth came through Jesus Christ" and how does that affect your life?

PRAY: Worship Jesus as the eternal Word of God. Thank Him for coming to show us what God the Father is like and for revealing undeserved grace and uncompromised truth. Thank Him for allowing you to become a child of God.

ACT: Sit for a few minutes in a totally dark room. Then turn on a lamp or room light and notice the difference. Take time to contemplate how Jesus brought light to a spiritually dark world. Think about how His light exposes sin, reveals truth, and illuminates the way to God. Ask God to show you how to better reflect His light to others. Think of a specific person to whom you can be a light for Christ in words and actions.

Fire Starter

John 1:19-51

THINK: Do you ever wonder what Jesus' first followers were like, or what it would have been like to be one of them? Most who followed Jesus were common people who humbly dared to trust Him without reservation. They didn't do extraordinary things to attract Jesus' attention, but showed extraordinary faith simply by taking Him at His Word, responding to Him without hesitation, and eagerly telling others about Him.

RESPOND: In what way did John prepare the way for Jesus? (Note that when the book refers to John, it means John the Baptist, rather than John the disciple and author of this Gospel.) Why is Jesus called the "Lamb of God"? *(Lambs were used as Old Testament sacrifices, especially the Passover, as "atonement" or payment for sin. Jesus is the "Lamb" provided by God to pay for the sins of the world.)* When the Holy Spirit came down like a dove on Jesus at His baptism, what did that confirm about Him (verse 34)? What does it mean that Jesus baptizes His followers with the Holy Spirit? *(This baptism signifies empowering for all believers, enabling them to communicate Christ's message of salvation to others.)* What's the significance of Peter's name? Why do you think Nathanael and the others were so confident of Jesus' identity right away? What example does this set for others who want to follow Jesus?

PRAY: Give Jesus thanks for coming to earth to be the sacrifice for your sin and offenses against God. Ask Jesus to help you be like His first followers—quick to respond to Him, to trust Him and to eagerly tell others about Him.

ACT: Perhaps God has shown you something that you have not yet acted on or put into practice. Follow the example of Jesus' first followers. Take God at His Word and respond to Him without hesitation. Depend on the Holy Spirit for help and direction, and do what He's told you to do. This may involve talking to someone about Jesus. One way to break the ice could be to invite them to a youth event at your church.

Fire Starter

READ: John 2:1-25

THINK: Have you ever seen God work in ways that seemed "out of character"—unexpected in light of your own impressions of God? Many Bible passages don't fit people's perceptions of God—including times when Jesus expresses emotions. Yet these provide a glimpse of God's personality and passions. In this chapter, Jesus goes from celebration to indignation (or anger). Unlike us, Jesus always has justifiable reasons for His actions, revealing God's personal and relational nature. He wants us to know Him in a way that happens only through times of personal worship and prayerful interaction with God and His Word.

RESPOND: As Jesus began a public ministry, how do you think He interacted with people in social settings, like a friend's wedding? Why do you think Jesus' mother approached Him when the wine ran out? What did Jesus mean when He said, "My time has not yet come"? What does it mean that Jesus' miracle "revealed his glory" (verse 11)? How did Jesus feel about what He saw in the temple, and why? Does His reaction surprise you? Why or why not? What does this incident reveal about Jesus' character, passions and priorities? How does Jesus' attitude regarding the temple (verse 17) affect your attitude toward church? Why did the Jews want a "sign" (verse 18)? What sign would Jesus ultimately give (verses 21,22)? When people believed Jesus based on miracles, what does it mean that He "would not entrust himself to them, for he knew all men" (verses 24,25)?

PRAY: Thank Jesus for His miraculous power and concern about all aspects of your life. Pray for deeper reverence and passion for times of worship, prayer, ministry, and encouragement in church. Thank Jesus for making you worthy of His trust and for entrusting himself to you as you demonstrate faith in Him.

ACT: Don't knock any tables over, but worship and serve with greater passion, intensity and purpose when you're in church this week. Worship God wherever you are today. Make an effort in social settings to do and say things that bring honor and positive attention to Jesus.

Fire Starter

John 3:1-21

THINK: God loves you and wants to have a personal relationship with you. He even sent His Son, who sacrificed His own life to make that relationship possible. Receiving that relationship is a person's only hope of reclaiming his or her purpose in life and avoiding the permanent consequences of defying God. If you confess your sins, accept God's offer and entrust your life to Jesus, you will find forgiveness, fulfillment, and life forever with Him.

RESPOND: What does it mean to be "born again"? *(Regeneration, spiritual birth and renewal, or being "born again" means a person's life is spiritually renewed through faith in Jesus Christ. A person who is truly born again will no longer go along with unbiblical beliefs and practices, but is now empowered to think, talk, and live rightly.)* What's the significance of being "born of the Spirit"? *(Many believe Jesus was talking about being purified by the Holy Spirit; for others, it is a reference to the new birth.)* What does it mean that people "loved darkness instead of light"? What evidence do you see of people choosing to live in darkness (verse 20)? Why do those who live by the truth come out into the light (verse 21)? What evidence is there of what God has done in your life?

PRAY: Express your gratitude to God for His great love in sending Jesus. Thank Jesus for saving you from the consequences of sin and providing a way for you to be spiritually born again into a personal relationship with God. Pray that your faith will continue to be strong and active as you aim to serve Him.

ACT: Stand outside somewhere so you can feel and observe the effects of the wind. Though you can't necessarily see the wind itself, you notice its activity and perhaps even hear its sound. Consider how this illustrates the way the Holy Spirit's activity should be evident in your life. Now, go through the day with an intense awareness of how your faith and the power of the Holy Spirit is—or is not—apparent to those around you in your attitudes, words, and actions.

John 3:22-36

THINK: It seems that most people try to get more out of life by investing more in themselves. Of course, you should always strive to do and be your best, but that's only possible when you focus less on yourself and more on Jesus. It may not make sense in worldly terms, but with God, less is more. When your life becomes less about you and more about Jesus, that's when you start becoming all you were created to be.

RESPOND: In what ways is John the Baptist's attitude toward Jesus (verses 27-30) an example for all followers of Jesus? Looking at your own life, in what ways must Jesus become greater and you become less (verse 30)? To whom did God give the Spirit without limit (verse 34)? *(Even though Jesus was fully human, He had to manage the same way we should: totally dependent on the Holy Spirit's promptings, power, and leading. Jesus would later baptize His followers with this same Holy Spirit! Everyone has access to God's Spirit!)* How was that evident in Jesus' life? How and why do people reject Jesus? What does it mean that such people will not see life and why? In what ways must you be careful not to disregard Jesus or fail to submit to Him? In what specific area of life do you need to submit to Jesus and obey Him more fully?

PRAY: Ask Jesus to help you focus less on yourself so that He will show through you in greater ways. Praise Jesus for His authority over all things. Pray that you will always remain submissive to God and obedient to His Word.

ACT: Ask God to expose an area or two in your life where there is too much of yourself and not enough of Him. Perhaps you are already well aware of these areas and tendencies. Take deliberate steps to humble yourself and submit to God's guidance and control in these areas. Find ways to draw attention away from yourself and your own desires and plans, and instead bring honor and positive attention to God.

Fire Starter

John 4:1-26

THINK: What does worship mean to you? True worship involves more than singing songs, reciting prayers, or verbalizing words of praise in a worship service. It involves a lifestyle that truly honors God and brings positive attention to Him. True, godly worship is a heartfelt expression of praise from your spirit to His. It is the appropriate response to God's powerful presence and matchless character.

RESPOND: What can we identify about Jesus and His purpose from His conversation with the Samaritan woman? *(Jesus was committed to His heavenly Father's purpose to bring people from all cultural backgrounds into relationship with himself.)* Why do you think Jesus started the conversation? What's the "living water" Jesus talked about (verses 10,11)? What does it mean to drink that water, and what does that have to do with your personal relationship with Jesus? Why does a person who drinks the living water no longer thirst? What did Jesus mean about Samaritans worshipping "what you do not know"? *(Because the Samaritans' Bible contained only the first five books—the Pentateuch—they had a limited knowledge of God.)* What does it mean to worship God "in spirit and in truth"? *(Our spiritual attitude is more important than the location of worship; and the depth and humility with which we worship, reflecting deep inner devotion to God, holds more meaning and value than the style.)*

PRAY: Ask Jesus to help you reach out to spiritually thirsty people, regardless of their background or your perceptions. Ask Him to give you a thirst for a deeper relationship with Him, characterized by a lifestyle of sincere worship.

ACT: Ask God to guide you into conversations today with people who need a friend, have a need, or are searching for answers. Initiate conversations by expressing sincere interest in others and what they are doing. Trust God to direct you into deeper conversations about spiritual matters. Also, take time when you're on your own throughout the day to worship God in your own words, acknowledging His attributes like love, wisdom, purity, power, justice, etc.

Fire Starter

John 4:27-54

THINK: How are you at getting into conversations about spiritual issues? Can you relate to people who are very different from you? Do you willingly talk about the good things God has done in your life? These are some key questions to consider if you hope to influence others to follow Jesus. You don't have to have an extremely outgoing personality to reach people for Christ, but you must be willing to take the initiative and step outside of your comfort zone. As you trust God, He will guide your words and efforts. He may even use you to influence an entire community for Him.

RESPOND: Why were Jesus' disciples surprised to find Him talking to the woman? *(Jewish teachers didn't typically converse with women publicly. There was also animosity between the Samaritans and Jews at the time.)* What did Jesus mean when He said, "I have food to eat that you know nothing about"? What did Jesus mean when He said that the fields are ripe for harvest? When God allows you to influence others for Him, what should be your attitude and why? In what ways might you reap the spiritual benefits of others' hard work (verse 38)? What happened as a result of the Samaritan woman's testimony about Jesus (verse 39)? In what way should followers of Jesus learn from her example? When believing God for a miracle, what should be the focus of your faith?

PRAY: Ask Jesus to give you an eagerness to spread His message and to tell others what He's done for you. Thank Him for the privilege of being part of the process of leading others to Him.

ACT: Reach out to someone with whom you might not typically associate and simply start a conversation. Focus on developing a friendship and trust God to help you influence this person for Him. Start a Bible or prayer group at school or work. If you're already involved in a group, encourage its members to talk more openly with others about the good things God does for them. Then watch your group's influence spread.

Fire Starter

John 5:1-30

THINK: A lot of people talk about relating to God, but people cannot relate to God without receiving His Son, Jesus, who is himself God. The Father has entrusted all life, authority, and judgment to His Son. If a person does not respond and relate to Jesus as the Forgiver of their sins and Leader of their life, it doesn't matter what else they think or believe about God.

RESPOND: How is the account of Jesus healing the man at the pool encouraging? What can you learn about healing and faith from this situation? *(The Bible shows that healing occurs at one of three points: the faith of the one in need, the faith of others on behalf of the person in need, and/or the faith of the one empowered to bring the gift of healing from Jesus.)* How will true followers of Jesus view the issue of sin in their own lives? *(Following Jesus doesn't mean we'll never sin again. However, we won't continue in persistent, intentional sin over and over.)* What can you learn from Jesus' example of dependence on His Father (verse 19)? What claims does Jesus make in verses 18–27 that show how He relates to and is equal with God the Father? What does it mean to truly "hear" and "believe" God's Word? *("Hearing and believing" imply listening, responding, and acting on what you've learned.)* Though our own efforts and works cannot save us spiritually, why are good works still important?

PRAY: Pray for the healing of someone who has been ill for a long time. Ask God to expose persistent sin in your life and help you remove it promptly. Pray that you stay dependent on God for wisdom, guidance, and strength in every aspect of life. Praise Jesus for His righteous life and judgment and for the fact that He is God.

ACT: Visit or contact the person you just prayed for, simply to see how he or she is doing and to have casual conversation. Encourage him or her with kind words and even pray one-on-one if the opportunity arises.

Fire Starter

John 5:31-47

THINK: Do you feel the need to gain approval from certain people in order to feel better about yourself and your accomplishments? Consider the fact that what typically impresses people is not at all what impresses God. For this reason, those who seek honor and approval from people will almost certainly not receive honor and approval from God. And God's approval is the only approval that matters.

RESPOND: Who and what provides an even greater testimony than John the Baptist's about the fact that Jesus was sent by God the Father (verse 36)? Can studying and knowing God's Word give a person spiritual life? Why or why not? *(While knowing and following God's Word is critical to one's spiritual health and influence on others, it does not save anyone. We are saved when we surrender to and devotedly follow Jesus.)* Why must Jesus' followers not be motivated by other people's praise or approval? What are some of the dangers of desiring or accepting praise from others? How does Jesus confirm the truth and validity of Old Testament in this passage? *(Jesus validated the Pentateuch and that Moses was God's scribe of Old Testament history. If people don't believe in the Holy Spirit inspired truths of the Old Testament, they won't submit to Jesus' New Testament words.)* Why is this important and how should it affect your view of the entire Bible? *(All of God's Word points to Christ and His fulfilled purposes.)*

PRAY: Ask Jesus to help you resist the desire for praise and approval from others. Instead, pray that you will always live in a way that honors God and is honored by Him. Also, ask Jesus to help you understand the vital historical and spiritual connection between the Bible's Old and New Testaments.

ACT: Be conscious throughout the day of anything you might tend to do to impress others or to get their attention. Instead of being concerned with others perceptions and approval, handle each of these situations in a way that will please and honor God, providing others with a good example of Jesus' character.

Fire Starter

THINK: Do you believe in miracles? If you believe the Bible, it would be tough not to. Do you ever wonder why we don't often experience the same types of miracles today? Perhaps we have too many things figured out. If God doesn't act as we expect, we simply follow another one of our options. But with what we know from God's Word, He may expect us to get more involved in potential miracles. He doesn't expect us to have things figured out. A simple act of faith and dependence on Him may be all He's waiting for. When we realize just how much God can do with so little, we'll willingly place in God's hands whatever we have so we can watch Him do amazing things with it.

RESPOND: In what way was Jesus testing Philip by asking where they could buy food for the crowd (verses 5,6)? How would you have responded in that situation? What can you learn about miracles and the way God works from this passage? *(Miracles honor Jesus, verifying His truthful message and validating His identity as God's Son and mankind's Savior; they convey Jesus' compassion and love; and they mark the open door for salvation.)* In what ways could you imagine God doing very much with very little in your life if you were willing to place what you have in His hands? Why would Jesus resist the people's intentions to set Him up as their king (verse 15)? How could that action have interfered with God's plan and Jesus' real purpose?

PRAY: Ask Jesus to give you the faith to trust God for great things, regardless of what you have, feel, or see.

ACT: Think of a situation in which you need a miracle or a definite answer from God. Is He telling you to do something specific or to contribute to the solution in some way? Whether or not it seems like your contribution or response will make a difference, follow God's direction anyway. Do or give what you can, and trust God to take care of the rest.

Fire Starter

John 6:25–59

THINK: Even when you're not hungry, you eat because you know it's necessary—and you probably enjoy it. Apply this reasoning to your spiritual life. If you're truly hungry, you'll feed your spirit through time with God in His Word and prayer. If you're not taking this time on a regular basis, its either because you're not hungry for God, you don't enjoy time with Him, or you don't realize how necessary it is for your spiritual life, health, and well-being. So indulge your spiritual appetite and see how God's Word satisfies a hungry soul.

RESPOND: How can you work for food that doesn't spoil but "endures to eternal life" (verse 27)? What does Jesus mean when He declares, "I am the bread of life"? *(Each "I am" statement Jesus made in the Gospel of John reveals something specific about His personal ministry. Calling himself "bread" emphasized that He can and will sustain and nourish people spiritually.)* How would you describe "God's will" and how it relates to your life personally? *(God's desires and plans based on His character and purposes are the highest goals we can pursue and attain in life.)* Why is it so important to respond when you sense the Holy Spirit drawing you to God? How can you continue to feed on Jesus in order to grow spiritually?

PRAY: Ask Jesus to help you focus your efforts on things of eternal value. Pray for the Holy Spirit's guidance and power so you can fulfill God's perfect will. Thank Jesus for being the bread of life that satisfies your spiritual hunger.

ACT: Take your Bible with you, and during free time, feed your spirit on God's Word. Try reading in Proverbs, which is filled with practical wisdom for youth. Make a conscious effort today—and every day—to do things God's way rather than your own way. And if you've sensed God's Spirit drawing you to Jesus—perhaps to accept His forgiveness and new life for the first time—don't resist any longer. Entrust your life to Him and let Him restore your ultimate purpose.

141

Fire Starter

John 6:60-71

THINK: Certainly, Jesus followers are to live by His example, being kind and gracious to people in an effort to reflect Jesus' character and influence others to follow Him. But Christians must also realize that God's Word and way of life will always be offensive to people. That doesn't mean that Jesus' followers set out to oppose people, but even when Christians do everything right in their conduct toward others, they'll still face resistance and rejection. Jesus' followers must understand that as they live by God's standards, their lives will stand in sharp contrast to those who choose to defy God and go their own way. This should not surprise of offend anyone who lives to honor Jesus.

RESPOND: What statements from Jesus seemed too hard and offensive to some of His followers? What does Jesus mean when He says, "The Spirit gives life; the flesh counts for nothing"? How does this relate to Jesus previous statements in verses 53-59? According to this passage, what feeds you and gives life spiritually (verse 63)? What might Jesus have meant about knowing from the beginning who would betray Him, and how would this relate to Judas' choices and actions concerning Jesus? *(This may mean that Jesus always knew what Judas was made of and his inclinations. It may also refer to a point in time when Judas began to drift away from an original commitment and devotion to Christ.)* Why did many who had previously followed Jesus turn back and no longer follow Him from this point on (verse 66)? How does Peter's response in verse 68 serve as an example to all who desire to follow Jesus?

PRAY: Ask Jesus to give you the strength, determination, and dependence on Him that will keep you loyal to Him no matter how difficult things may get.

ACT: Continue the exercise from yesterday by keeping your Bible with you and feeding on it during your free time. Also, perhaps you've struggled with your attitude toward something in God's Word that has offended you or been tough to accept. Ask God to forgive you and to help you meet the challenge and be obedient so you can grow deeper in your relationship with Him and in your understanding of God's Word.

Fire ✦ Starter

John 7:1-24

THINK: How does it feel to be misunderstood? Jesus can relate. Even His own family misunderstood His mission, and the world system in general hated Him without even knowing Him. Certainly, those who are willing to identify with Jesus ought to be sensitive to the pain caused when people misjudge others. Even so, as a follower of Jesus, you must strongly resist the tendency to judge by mere appearances.

RESPOND: Why did Jesus' brothers respond to Him as they did? Was it Jesus' intention to become a public figure (verse 4)? Why or why not? Why does the world hate Jesus? *(Jesus condemned all forms of immoral behavior. And nobody likes being told they're wrong. Yet, Jesus cares more about peoples' souls, lives, the affect of sin on them and those around them, and more than their self-esteem—their self-respect. Even in mercy, like Jesus, let's be as honest and uncompromising when it comes to calling sin what it is.)* How will following God's plans and purposes for your life help you understand God's truth? According to verse 18, how can you tell whether a person is sincerely ministering for God or for selfish reasons? Why do people tend to judge by appearances (verse 24)? How can you help to ensure that you make right judgments about things rather than relying on appearances?

PRAY: Ask Jesus to help you discover His desires and purposes as you spend daily time in His Word. Pray that you'll rely on His Word to help you make right judgments about situations, people, beliefs, and behaviors.

ACT: Are there people who you don't know very well or situations that you're not extremely familiar with, yet you've still formed negative opinions or made distinct judgments about these people or things? While you need to be wise about relationships that could negatively impact you, consider the possibility that your judgments are not accurate or appropriate. As you encounter these people and situations—even today— make a deliberate effort to become better acquainted so you can understand and respond in more appropriate and Christ-honoring ways.

THINK: How dependent are you on God? In your everyday life do you typically carry on as if you can make it without Him? Consider how completely Jesus depended on His Father for strength, guidance, and encouragement. Are you following Jesus' example so that God fulfills His purposes and impacts the world through your life?

RESPOND: Why was Jesus so dependent on His Father? If Jesus—God in human form—needed to rely completely on His Father for strength and guidance, what does that mean for you? What was Jesus' view of Scripture? What did Jesus mean that "streams of living water will flow from within" those who truly believe in Him (John 7:38)? *(Jesus was talking about the Holy Spirit who would be poured out after He left earth [cf. verse 39].)* Why do very religious or very educated people often misunderstand or reject Jesus (verses 47,48)? What was the religious leaders' motive in bringing the adulterous woman to Jesus? How did Jesus' response deflect their deception? Did Jesus' excuse or overlook the woman's sin? Why or why not? What did Jesus offer the woman, and how does that relate to you? What do Jesus' instructions to the woman—"Go now and leave your life of sin"—mean for all followers of Christ?

PRAY: Give God the Father thanks for sending Jesus to give His life for you and show you the way to true life. Thank Jesus for forgiving you and for giving you wisdom and strength to continually overcome sin as you rely on Him.

ACT: Be kind and encourage someone who is typically isolated or rejected by others because of their reputation, social status or lifestyle. Don't condone bad behavior or let it influence you negatively. But let the person know, by your words and actions that someone cares and is not out to judge them prematurely. If you get into a conversation, don't hesitate to let the person know in some way that you are a follower of Jesus.

Fire Starter

John 8:12-30

THINK: A lot of people talk about God, claiming to believe in Him. Many say they pray. Some even give God credit for their abilities and accomplishments—even if those accomplishments compromise biblical principles. Yet, for all of the talk about "God," Jesus' name seldom comes up in the same context. So where do they get their perception of God? If you get it from the Bible, it's tough to miss the fact that we can't relate to the Father apart from Jesus. As God's only Son, Jesus is the One who reflects and reveals what His Father is like. In fact, Jesus is himself God, with all the authority and attributes of His Father. You can't take Jesus out of the God equation without arriving at the wrong answer.

RESPOND: What does Jesus mean when He says, "I am the light of the world," and that those who follow Him will never walk in darkness? *(Jesus removes spiritual darkness and deception by revealing the right way to God through faith in himself.)* How does it challenge and inspire you when Jesus says, "If you do not believe that I am the one I claim to be, you will indeed die in your sins" (verse 24)? What can you take personally from the fact that Jesus said, "I do nothing on my own but speak just what the Father has taught me" (verse 28)? Why did Jesus have to depend completely on the Father? In what way does this challenge you?

PRAY: Thank Jesus for providing spiritual light in your life. Pray that you remain dependent on God for guidance regarding what to say and do so you can influence others to accept and depend on Christ.

ACT: Practice going through the day with your spiritual eyes and ears open, looking for God's direction and listening for His voice. Go with a sense of being in constant communication with God. But keep in mind that the most vital part of communicating with God is listening and responding to His guidance. Say and do whatever you sense God telling you to do.

Fire Starter

John 8:31-47

THINK: "You will know the truth, and the truth will set you free." Most people in our society are familiar with that expression in one form or another. It's one of the countless well-known phrases lifted from the pages of the Bible—though most people haven't a clue what it really means. He's talking about the ultimate truth revealed in God's Word and embodied in the Person of Jesus himself. He is the truth that people must know in order to truly be free.

RESPOND: According to verse 31, what must you do to demonstrate that you are a true follower of Jesus? Why didn't many people recognize their need for the freedom Jesus spoke about (verse 33)? In what ways does sin enslave people? *(Whether people see or admit it, without a personal relationship with Jesus, they are slaves to sin.)* How can a person find freedom from sin? Why were the people who argued with Jesus so mistaken in their notion that they were children of God? How can we know if a person is truly a child of God? *(Evidence of being God's child is one's devoted attitude toward and love for His Son Jesus.)* What's the evidence that a person truly loves Jesus? Who does Jesus say that a person belongs to if he or she refuses to accept the truth about Jesus (verse 44)? What does a person do if he or she truly belongs to God (verse 47)?

PRAY: Ask Jesus for the discipline to live by the teaching in God's Word. Thank Him for the freedom that comes from following Him. Pray that you'll always demonstrate love for Him by obeying His Word and refusing to take part in deceit.

ACT: If you've not lived up to the truth of something God has specifically shown you in His Word, take immediate action to put His truth into practice. If you've lied or been deceitful in any way toward another person or situation, ask God to forgive you. Then make things right with any others who are involved by telling the truth.

John 8:48-59

THINK: What is God like? The fact is, God has not made it difficult to get a good glimpse of what He's like and even to relate to Him on a personal level. As you may have considered in your study over the last few days, God has revealed himself clearly through the Person of Jesus Christ, His Son. If you want to know what God is like, look to Jesus through God's Word and prayer, surrender yourself to His purposes and follow Him.

RESPOND: What does Jesus mean when He says, "if anyone keeps my word he will never see death"? How can you "keep" God's Word? How does God's Word provide life? What is the significance of Jesus' statement that "before Abraham was born, I am"? *(In the Old Testament God introduced himself to Moses as "I Am." Jesus both affirms His eternal nature [not, "I was," but "I Am"] and His identification and sameness with God.)* What other characteristics and attributes does Jesus possess as God? In what ways do these traits affect you? How do they provide comfort? How do they inspire faith? How do they help you stay devoted to Jesus?

PRAY: Thank Jesus for His life-giving Word, and ask Him to give you insight so you can understand and obey His Word. Praise Him as the all-powerful and eternal Son of God.

ACT: List God's traits, then ask (and answer) yourself. For example, "How do I see that God is omnipresent (everywhere at once), omniscient (all-knowing), and omnipotent (all-powerful, having ultimate authority) in specific circumstances?" *(Knowing this means you can trust Him, and trust that He's aware of what's going on, that He has a plan for every individual, and that He's capable of carrying that plan out.)* Do the same with some of these attributes of God (look them up if you don't know what they mean): transcendent, eternal, unchangeable, holy, triune, good, love, merciful, compassionate, patient, truth, just. As you go through the day, notice the evidence of His attributes. Make this an ongoing practice.

147

Fire Starter

John 9:1-41

THINK: "How can a loving God allow suffering and evil to continue?" "Why do bad things happen to good people?" Because humankind has rebelled against God and chosen their own way over His, sin and evil have taken hold and turned the world upside down and backward from the way God created it. Disorder and destruction have become the norm. The fact that good exists at all—and can even come out of suffering—is proof of God's love and patience toward a world that continues to defy Him.

RESPOND: Why do you think that Jesus' disciples suspected that someone's sin had caused the man's blindness (verse 2)? Judging from this passage, why does God sometimes allow suffering? Why doesn't God always make His purposes apparent to us at first? How can God be honored in people's lives through difficulty and suffering? How can people actually benefit spiritually through these kinds of trials? In what way was it a blessing for the man to be thrown out of the synagogue? *(Staying in that religious but spiritually lifeless environment may have squelched the man's hunger for Christ.)* How is this a lesson to those in lifeless churches and unbiblical religions? What did Jesus mean when He said that He came "so that the blind will see and those who see will become blind"? *(Jesus had a way of exposing peoples' hearts and motives. People who are humble enough to admit their need for Christ find life and healing. Those who don't remain spiritually blind.)*

PRAY: Thank Jesus for taking you through difficulties in ways that honor Him and bring you closer to God. Thank Him for the privilege of enduring insults and opposition that come as a result of your faith and His work in your life.

ACT: Ask God to help you understand His purposes through suffering—your own and other peoples' suffering. Encourage a couple of individuals today who are going through very difficult times. Pray for these individuals on the spot if you feel they are open to that.

John 10:1-21

THINK: People often knock Christians by referring to them as a bunch of blind followers. But in reality, everyone is following or pursuing something—or someone. People are either following God and His truth, or they're falling for a lie from the devil. Most voices that people listen to are spreading the lie and leading them blindly down a path toward destruction and death. They're being robbed of real life and don't even know it. Wouldn't you rather endure the insults, while following Jesus on a path leading to ultimate fulfillment and eternal life?

RESPOND: In what way is the description of the good and true Shepherd a picture of Jesus' relationship with His people? What did Jesus mean when He said that the sheep listen to the Shepherd's voice but do not follow a strangers' voice? What does Jesus mean in saying, "I am the gate" (verses 7, 9)? In what ways do Satan and his forces kill, steal and destroy? In what ways does Jesus give life "to the full" (verse 10)? What's the significance of Jesus' claim as "the good shepherd"? *(Jesus affirms himself in Old Testament prophetic passages that point to himself [Psalm 23:1, Isaiah 40:11, Ezekiel 34:23; 37:24].)* How did Jesus ultimately fill this role, proving His love for His "sheep" (John 10:11,15,17)? What does this passage illustrate about false spiritual leaders and how you can detect them? How can you take comfort in the fact that Jesus knows His sheep? What does verse 18 indicate about Jesus' power and love for us?

PRAY: Thank Jesus for His care over you and for knowing you personally and individually. Also, thank Jesus for coming to give you life to the fullest.

ACT: As you go through the day, notice all the evidence you can of how the devil is robbing, killing, and bringing destruction on people. Look for signs of this in people's lives, in situations, and in various forms of media. Pray for God's help and healing in these situations. Take action to help and encourage anyone you can. Talk about your faith if the situation arises. This will take a sense of boldness and adventure, which is part of living life "to the full" (verse 10).

John 10:22-42

THINK: Who are you listening to? There are a lot of voices in the world vying for your attention, bombarding you with a myriad of messages aimed at influencing you in one way or another. Some are worthwhile; many are not. Some you choose to listen to, and some you can't seem to ignore. It can be difficult to hear what's really important through all of the noise. As you sift through the chatter, consider whether what you hear builds you up, benefits you spiritually and brings you or anyone else closer to God. Above all, does it help you to discern God's voice, or does it distract you from hearing Him. Perhaps it's time to tune out some noise so you can tune in to God.

RESPOND: What does Jesus mean in saying, "My sheep listen to my voice"? How do people truly "hear" and listen to Jesus? What do the words "listen" and "follow" imply (verse 27)? *(Having spent time regularly with Jesus, true followers recognize His voice. Through prayer, listening, and reading God's Word, they learn to discern His guidance by consistently doing what He tells them, based on His Word and His character.)* What comfort and encouragement can you take from verses 28 and 29? In reality, what is the only thing that can remove you from the life and purpose God intends for you? *(Death is not the ultimate end for Jesus' followers. No circumstance or power—except one's own choice to abandon Jesus—will undo a person's spiritual salvation.)*

PRAY: Ask Jesus to help you always listen and discern His voice and to follow His lead. Thank Him for giving you eternal life and for the fact that no one and nothing—outside of your own choice—can take you away from Him.

ACT: Once again, as you may have practiced a few days ago, go through the day making a conscious effort to listen for God's direction in all you do. (Listening to God's side of the communication is a vital prayer discipline.) This does not mean that you have to stop for a length of time before every decision. Remember, don't just aim to hear but also to follow God's direction, obeying what you sense He's saying to you.

John 11:1-16

THINK: Are you a patient person? If not, you're probably well aware of the fact that God's timing seldom fits your preferred schedule. Yet, if you try to get ahead of God—or if you give up too soon and aren't ready to respond at all—you could forfeit a valuable lesson and miss what God has in store for you. Remember, God's most extraordinary works will never happen the way you expect. They'll go far beyond your plans, expectations and imagination.

RESPOND: Why is an apparent tragedy or terminal illness not a hopeless situation for a person who knows Jesus? *(Death is never the final outcome for God's people and holds no ultimate power over them.)* Why do people who are deeply devoted to God still suffer deeply at times? *(Life is not devoid of suffering and God's people are not devoid of life. As Jesus himself said, "He causes his sun to rise on the evil and the good, and sends rain on the righteous and the unrighteous" Matthew 5:45.)* Why did Jesus not leave for Bethany as soon as He received the message about Lazarus? *(As insensitive as it seemed at the time, Jesus' delay would strengthen the faith of this family and those present when Jesus raised Lazarus from the dead. Jesus' timing in their lives, and often in ours, seems to be questionable, seems to show a lack of concern, and sometimes seems to be downright way off. But God doesn't always tell us His plans or reasons for doing things; however, we can trust that He will respond in wisdom and love for our benefit.)*

PRAY: Thank Jesus for His love and friendship. Thank Him for doing things in His time—the right time—and ask Him to help you trust Him, regardless of the circumstances. Pray for someone who has recently faced a tragedy. Ask God to do something through this situation to honor himself and bring people closer to Him.

ACT: Are you currently facing a situation in which you feel that God is silent or unresponsive. Exercise your faith and demonstrate dependence on God by entrusting the situation to Him once again. Ask Him to honor himself and to help you grow closer to Him as you wait for His answer. Then consider what God might be preparing to do in this situation.

151

Fire Starter

John 11:17-57

THINK: Why are people so fascinated with the supernatural? Most are open to spiritual issues on some level, even if it has nothing to do with God as revealed in the Bible. Perhaps the underlying reason for curiosity about spirituality is humankind's innate desire and hope for something beyond this life. For Christ's followers, this is more than wishful thinking, because their hope is assured. It is a reality that has been guaranteed by the resurrection of their Leader. Jesus is the only One to have conquered death, and He is the only One who can grant eternal life.

RESPOND: How would you describe Martha's faith based on her statements in verses 21-24,27? *(Martha understood that when Jesus is present, things are different.)* What does Jesus mean in saying, "I am the resurrection and the life. He who believes in me will live, even though he dies; and whoever lives and believes in me will never die."? What can you tell about Jesus from His response to Mary and the other mourners? What can you learn from His example? What comfort can you take from the fact that "Jesus wept"? What does the raising of Lazarus from the dead reveal about the nature and character of Jesus? *(We can look at what Jesus did for Lazarus as the example of what God will do for all His children who have died.)*

PRAY: Thank Jesus for the hope of resurrection so you can live with Him forever. Ask Him to give you faith to trust Him in desperate times as well as in normal times. Pray also for a greater sense of empathy and compassion for people who are hurting and need comfort, hope, or a miracle from Jesus.

ACT: Find a way to demonstrate compassion for someone who is hurting. If you know someone who is currently grieving over a tragedy, try to encourage him or her. This may involve an action, a written note, simple words of kindness, or just being with the person. Also, think of anyone you know who has gone to be with Jesus. Give God thanks for bringing them home to heaven and for the fact that you'll see them there.

Fire Starter

John 12:1-19

THINK: If you've attended church for any length of time, you've probably seen a lot of people offer praise and worship to God. No doubt the expressions have been varied. Some people tend to be contemplative and reserved, while others seem more emotional and exuberant. Both sincere worship and shallow worship can assume a variety of forms, postures and expressions. The difference is that truly sincere and fully devoted worshippers are willing to take their expressions of affection outside of the typical worship context. In everyday life settings they do things that truly honor and exalt Jesus. Sincere worshippers are not inhibited by what other people think of their passion for Jesus, and they are prepared to honor Him even when it costs them dearly.

RESPOND: What do Mary's actions toward Jesus indicate about her devotion to Him? What were some of the unusual aspects of Mary's actions, and what do they reveal about her character and attitude toward Jesus? *(Mary's demonstration of sacrifice, devotion, and love were unusual because oil was usually poured on the head, and a respectable woman usually wouldn't let her hair down in public. Both of these behaviors showed her humility and that she didn't care what anyone else thought.)* Why did Jesus rebuke Judas and accept Mary's extravagant gift? What are the dangers of basing one's faith in Jesus on specific signs or miracles? How can you develop and demonstrate deep devotion to Jesus, like Mary and her family had?

PRAY: Ask Jesus to help you develop a more bold yet humble devotion to Him—a devotion that is willing to demonstrate love and appreciation for Jesus, regardless of what others think.

ACT: Think of something special you can do to express devotion to Jesus. It could be anything from volunteering to minister in some way at church, to serving someone in need, to writing a poem, or creating a piece of art in honor of Him. This should cost you in some way—time, effort, money, or willingness to overcome fear or self-consciousness.

John 12:20-50

THINK: What are the most important things in your life—the relationships, the possessions, the activities, the skills? How do you know that they're important to you? Chances are they get the bulk of your time, attention, passion, and resources. But do these priorities have eternal value, and if so, are you investing in them as such? And how do these things line up with your relationship with God and His priorities?

RESPOND: How would Jesus be "glorified" by what was about to happen to Him? *(Once Jesus rose from the dead, He returned to His place of glory and honor with His Father in heaven.)* Why was His death necessary and what would it accomplish? What does it mean, "the man who loves his life will lose it, while the man who hates his life in this world will keep it for eternal life"? How should your attitude toward earthly interests compare to heavenly interests? What does it mean to "serve" and "follow" Jesus? *(Serving and following Christ is active, not passive, fueled by time with Him, obeying his teaching, and identifying with Him, no matter the cost.)* Why would a person desire praise from people rather than honor from God? What does it mean to "hear" but not "keep" Jesus' words (verses 47,48)?

PRAY: Ask Jesus to help you establish your priorities so that nothing in this world compares with your devotion to Him and your desire to lead others to Him. Pray that you never trade honor from God for acclaim from people.

ACT: As you go through the day, consider how you could approach each task or activity in a way that will have a more lasting impact. For example, instead of just finishing a task, do it in a way that encourages or inspires others. Instead of eating with the same friends, invite someone who may need a friend to join you. Instead of spending an hour playing video games, work on a ministry effort, or simply spend time praising God to some worship music. Whatever you do, try to give more time to things of eternal value.

John 13:1-30

THINK: Have you ever had to do something for someone that, even as you were doing it, you were honestly thinking, I shouldn't have to do this—it's beneath me—I'm better than that. Well, consider Jesus, the eternal Son of God through whom all things were created, as He stooped to wash His followers' feet. That was only one of countless ways He served people and met their needs when He walked the earth. And He continues to meet your needs. Is it beneath you to follow Jesus example of servanthood? One of the best tests of how willing you are to be a servant is this: How do you respond when you're treated like one?

RESPOND: What was so extraordinary about Jesus demonstration of servanthood in washing His disciples' feet (verses 3-5)? In what way was this act symbolic, and what example does it set for Jesus' followers? Why did Jesus tell Peter, "Unless I wash you, you have no part with me"? *(Jesus was referring to the spiritual cleansing provided by His death.)* In what ways are Jesus' followers to "wash one another's feet"? In what way can you show acceptance to those whom Jesus sends (verse 20)? Why do you think the other disciples never seemed to suspect or anticipate Judas' deception and betrayal? Why and how must Christ's followers be cautious regarding who they trust and associate with?

PRAY: Ask Jesus to help you follow His example of humility and servanthood in your interaction with others.

ACT: Throughout the day, find several ways to serve others— particularly other Christians—as a means of showing your love and appreciation for them. You could help a friend with homework during study hall, do something for a sibling at home, stop by church after school and help your pastor, or assist an elderly neighbor with a household chore.

Fire Starter

John 13:31 through 14:14

THINK: Most people in the world are offended by the view that there is only one way to God. Popular consensus says that there are any number of equally valid faiths and paths to "God." Those who hold this misguided notion are not just rejecting a Christian worldview; they are rejecting Jesus' own claim. Perhaps the only way they'll consider the truth is if they begin to see the reality of Christ's life and love in those who claim to follow Him.

RESPOND: What does it mean to "love one another" as Jesus loved us? *(Regardless of church affiliation, Christ's followers should be distinguished as people who consider each other brothers and sisters, treating each other with kindness and respect. Of course, Christians should treat everyone with kindness and respect.)* How would you describe this love? *(Authentic, godly, self-giving love that promotes the welfare of others marks true disciples.)* In what ways would Jesus' followers do "greater things" than He did while on earth? In what way are these things still a credit to Jesus? What does it mean to ask for things in Jesus name? *(Doing anything in Jesus' name indicates that you understand who He is and what He's capable of; that you're His representative, acting on His behalf, in His power.)*

PRAY: Ask Jesus to help you develop a more selfless and sacrificial love for other Christians so that non-Christians get an accurate view of Jesus' love through you. Thank Jesus for preparing a place for you in heaven and for His promise to return for you. Pray with an intense awareness of Jesus' authority, power, and love for you.

ACT: Make a deliberate effort to show kindness to everyone today (as you always should). Go out of your way to show particular kindness to fellow Christians, especially those at school or work with whom you might not typically spend time. Keep in mind that it's not your job to prove that Jesus is the only way. It's Jesus' own claim. People must choose whether or not to take Him at His Word.

John 14:15-31

THINK: It's one thing to claim to love and follow Jesus and to say that He lives in you. But it's another thing to prove it. And while proving to someone else that God is real may be a difficult thing, proving that you really love Him is not so difficult. You must simply do what He asks and desires of you. Of course, that will not always be easy. Your human nature tends to resist God's intentions, and pressure from others as well as ungodly spiritual forces push you to do things your own way. But if you've chosen to follow Jesus, He's given you His presence and power through the Holy Spirit, who enables you to obey God and demonstrate that your love for Him is real.

RESPOND: What will you do if you truly love Jesus? How should this affect your daily life? What will Jesus do for those who love Him? Who is the "Counselor" and how does He fill that role? Why is it vital to obey Jesus? *(Obedience is a reflection of our love for Jesus. Obedience guards us and maintains a level of grace and freedom in our lives that disobedience diminishes.)* What will the Spirit do for Jesus' followers (verse 26)? How is the peace that Jesus gives different from the world's peace (verse 27)?

PRAY: Ask Jesus to help you obey Him completely and without hesitation. Thank Jesus for the power, guidance, and comfort of the Holy Spirit. Also, thank Him for giving you true peace, beyond anything the world could offer.

ACT: Perhaps you sense that God has told you to do something—either directly through His Word, through prayer, or by guidance from the Holy Spirit—but you have not yet acted on God's command or instruction. Demonstrate true devotion to God by taking Him at His Word, doing what He desires and trusting Him to help you.

Fire Starter

John 15:1-17

THINK: Have you ever picked flowers because they looked pretty? How long did they stay that way—a few days at best? In reality, no matter how nice they looked, they started dying and stopped producing from the moment they were detached from their source. The same is true of people. No matter how they appear, they'll wither and die spiritually unless they are connected to their life Source. But if you are joined to God through a personal relationship with Jesus, you'll grow as He intended and God will produce something beautiful through you.

RESPOND: How does the analogy of the vine and branches illustrate Jesus' relationship with His followers? What does it mean when Jesus tells His followers, "Remain in me"? *(Jesus' followers are responsible for maintaining closeness with Him as the Holy Spirit helps them.)* What warning does Jesus give about staying connected to Him? *(Jesus didn't teach, "once in the vine, always in the vine." He gave a direct but loving caution that believers can walk away from Him, choosing to abandon their relationship with him. As a result, they are "cut off" or separated from Him until and unless they choose to recommit themselves to Him.)* Why is vital for you to continue to grow spiritually? For what purpose has God chosen and appointed you (verse 16)? What does it mean to "bear fruit" spiritually?

PRAY: Ask Jesus to help you stay strongly connected to Him by obeying His Word, following His purposes, and growing continually in your relationship with Him.

ACT: Pay attention to plants and trees today. Notice how the leaves and flowers connect to the main stems or branches, and how branches connect to the trunk. The outer parts can only sustain life as they remain attached to the main source. Consider how this illustrates your relationship with God and your ability to be spiritually fruitful. Sit under a tree and read the Bible for a few minutes, reviewing today's passage.

John 15:18 through 16:16

THINK: With all the emphasis on tolerance in contemporary culture, the world seems determined to rid society of hate. On the surface, this may seem like a noble quest. Yet ironically, even as the world aims to eliminate hate toward almost everyone, it's becoming more tolerable to despise Christians, as they are often perceived to be a source of intolerance. But none of this should come as a surprise to Christ's true followers. Jesus told them to expect and be prepared for such treatment as long as they are in the world.

RESPOND: Who or what is "the world" (16:8), and why does the world hate Jesus and His followers? *("The world" represents those who choose not to follow Christ and the system set against God and His principles. What Christians, as imperfect as they are, stand for—values, standards, behaviors, lifestyles, and ultimate goals—is often in conflict with society overall. Those believers who refuse to compromise godly standards will always bring discomfort to people who don't live by God's standards.)* What does it mean that Jesus' followers do not belong to the world? In what ways should Jesus' followers be different from those who don't follow Him? Why did Jesus warn His followers ahead of time that they would face rejection (verses 1,4)? Why was it good that Jesus left earth? *(The outpouring of the Holy Spirit hinged on Jesus' ascension after His resurrection.)* What are the advantages of having the Holy Spirit with you? How will the Holy Spirit guide you into truth? How will He enhance your relationship with Jesus?

PRAY: Ask Jesus to give you strength to endure the opposition and hatred you'll face as His follower. Thank Him for giving you power and encouragement through the constant presence of the Holy Spirit.

ACT: As you go through the day, take mental note of all the ways you can which indicate how the world resists and opposes God, His principles and His purposes. As you do, make a conscious effort to think, talk, behave, and interact with others in ways that identify with Jesus. While your actions don't need to stand out as odd, there should be distinct differences in your life compared to those who do not follow Jesus.

Fire Starter

John 16:17-33

THINK: Are you looking for trouble? Hopefully not. But regardless, trouble will find you—as long as you live in this world. Christians often seem surprised when faced with adverse circumstances through no fault of their own. But Jesus told His followers that they would encounter trouble—even more so because of their faith. Life will be tough, but it will cause you to depend on Jesus and to fully appreciate the peace and joy He provides in the midst of present circumstances and the ultimate victory that can be yours for eternity.

RESPOND: Why can't the world rob you of the joy of your relationship with Jesus (verse 22)? What does it mean to ask for things "in Jesus name"? *(Praying in Jesus' name involves promoting His honor and purposes in whatever we're asking. Prayer in His name should show Jesus' character and line up with His desires and purposes.)* How would you describe the Father's love for Jesus' followers? What does God's love mean to you personally? In what ways will you have trouble in the world— particularly because of faith in Jesus? How does Jesus give peace in the midst of trouble? How did Jesus overcome the world (verse 33), and how can you also do so as His follower?

PRAY: Thank Jesus for the hope, joy, and peace He gives—that no one can take away—in the face of grief and trouble.

ACT: Take notice today of things in the media, in advertising, in your studies, at work, etc., which reflect the beliefs, practices, and priorities that the world seems to promote and celebrate. Consider how your attitude as a follower of Christ should be toward these things. You definitely should not be arrogant or judgmental, but neither should you simply accept or concede to these things. Perhaps some of these should cause you to grieve—not out of hopelessness, but out of compassion for those who are deceived and caught up in the world's ways. Let these issues turn you to prayer. Ask God to open people's eyes to His truth and to use you to graciously influence others for Him.

Fire Starter

John 17:1-26

THINK: If you were preparing to leave your closest loved ones and about to face the toughest time of your life, do you think you might have some parting words? Jesus knew He was about to be arrested, tried and executed, and here we read how He prayed for His followers—including you—as He faced His final hours. In this prayer, Jesus expresses some of His most intense longings for you, including His desire for you to know God in a deeper way and the necessity of being in unity with other believers.

RESPOND: What can you tell about Jesus' deepest desires for His followers from His prayer? According to verse 3, what is the essence of Christ's gift of eternal life? *(More than deathless existence, eternal life is enjoying God and knowing Him intimately.)* When and how does this life begin? What does eternal life mean to you in the present? In the future? In what way are you, as Jesus' follower, "not of the world" (verses 14,16)? The most frequent request in Jesus' prayer is for His followers to "be one" as He and His Father are (verses 11,21-23). *(Unity is key in Christians accomplishing God's purposes on earth and confirming His message.)* What type of unity is Jesus referring to, and why is this so important among Christ's followers? In what way does Christian unity validate the message of Jesus? How can disunity among Christians affect those within the Church and those outside the Church?

PRAY: Thank Jesus for His gift of eternal life—the opportunity to have a personal and eternal relationship with God. Commit to taking full advantage of this gift by getting to know Jesus more deeply through God's Word, prayer, and faithful living. Pray for unity among Christians, and ask Jesus to help you never be the source of unnecessary division.

ACT: Throughout the day, practice praying in a constant and conversational way. Much of this will be silent, and most of your attention will be rightly focused on listening for God's direction and not simply talking. In addition, if you have unsettled differences with other Christians, fulfill Jesus' desire and restore unity to these relationships by asking for and extending forgiveness.

Fire Starter

John 18:1-27

THINK: Psychologists say that we all have an innate tendency to react one way or another when facing intense pressure and confrontation. It's called the fight or flight response, and you'll lean toward one extreme almost automatically. Neither is completely good or bad; there's a time for both. While you should be bold in the face of challenge, you shouldn't be combative toward others. And while there are times to turn the other cheek to avoid a fight, you must not be timid in standing for what's right. The problem is that on your own you'll tend to react the wrong way at the wrong time. But as Jesus' follower, the Holy Spirit helps you overcome this misguided tendency and do what honors God in even the most extreme situations. This will be evident later, as the Holy Spirit comes and transforms Peter completely.

RESPOND: What do Jesus' words, responses, and attitudes surrounding His arrest tell you about His character and readiness for what was ahead? What did Jesus mean when He said, "Shall I not drink the cup the Father has given me?"? How would you explain the contrast between Peter's boldness and defiance when the soldiers came for Jesus (verse 10) and his denials of Jesus in the courtyard (verses 15-18,25-27)? How do you think you would have reacted in both situations? Would you have been as bold in the one and as cowardly in the other? Explain.

PRAY: Thank Jesus for willingly facing ridicule and rejection in standing up for truth and suffering for you. Ask Him to give you the boldness to also stand for truth and to never deny your faith in Him.

ACT: Do something to boldly identify with Jesus. Carry your Bible. Wear a shirt with a Christian theme. Invite people to a ministry event, or talk about spiritual issues. Do whatever you do sincerely, not just for show. Ask God for opportunities to talk about your faith and to let others know that you love Jesus and aren't ashamed to identify with Him.

John 18:28 through 19:16

THINK: What will people think? Whether or not we'd like to admit it, we all worry about that at times. Regardless of how unique and independent we pride ourselves on being, we tend to be concerned about others' opinions and perceptions of us. That's understandable to a degree. But when these concerns cause us to defy our better judgment and compromise our connection to Christ, we risk making some tragically life-altering choices.

RESPOND: What was ironic and hypocritical about the Jews' not going into the palace because they wanted to eat the Passover (verse 28)? In what way do people today sometimes show more concern for religious formalities than for authentic spiritual truth and behavior? In what ways is Jesus kingdom "not of this world"? *(Jesus' kingdom did not originate here on earth, nor was its purpose either world domination or political sovereignty.)* What does this mean for Jesus' followers regarding their relationship with God and their relationship to the world and earthly authorities? In what ways are people today still searching for an answer to Pilate's question in verse 38? How do the reasons people rejected Jesus then compare with the reasons people reject Him today? *(Jesus doesn't fit some peoples' expectations.)* What was Pilate most afraid of (verses 8,12,16)? In what ways are people today like Pilate and like the Jewish leaders?

PRAY: Thank Jesus for giving you a part in His eternal kingdom, and for enduring humiliation to secure that place for you. Ask Him for wisdom to recognize God's truth and boldness to stand up for it. Also, pray for your political leaders and those in positions of authority in your life.

ACT: If you're currently doing (or not doing) something out of fear of what others might think, change your behavior and boldly do what will honor Jesus. The same goes for any way in which you are being phony or hypocritical. Confess any deceit to God and to others involved, and start living in a way that's authentic, honest, and sincere.

Fire Starter

John 19:17-42

THINK: Have you ever been in a situation so stressful or intense that you pretty much forgot about everything and everyone else around you, because you were completely caught up in your own issues and concerns? Consider the fact that Jesus endured as much pain, agony, humiliation, and isolation as anyone ever has, as He took our punishment and bore the weight of sin for all humanity when He died on the cross. Yet His mind was not focused on His own pain, but on others' needs. He forgave His accusers and even had the presence of mind to arrange for His mother's care. To the very end of His earthly life, Jesus brought help and healing—through His own perseverance and pain—to those around Him. And because of His sacrifice, you too can find help and hope in your most trying times.

RESPOND: What did Jesus' statements from the Cross to His mother indicate about His character and concerns? What was the full significance of Jesus' statement, "It is finished."? *(In making this concise statement, Jesus signaled and declared the completion of His mission on the cross, fulfillment of His earthly purpose, as well as Old Testament prophecy concerning the Messiah's suffering, and decisive victory over Satan and every demonic force to come.)* In what way is Jesus' "finished" work also ongoing? How has Jesus' completed work impacted your life, and how does it continue to do so? How does John's own eye-witness account (verse 35) add validity to His Gospel account?

PRAY: Thank Jesus for suffering in your place and for finishing the work He started, showing you the way to God and opening the door for you to enter a personal and eternal relationship with Him.

ACT: Do something practical to help or show appreciation to every member of your immediate family. If any of these relationships are broken or strained, you may need to be more deliberate or discreet in the way you handle this. Still, an act of kindness and compassion may help in healing a wounded relationship. If they know about your faith, then these actions may influence family members to consider Christ in a way they never have before.

John 20:1-18

THINK: Do you picture Jesus' followers as older people or younger? Illustrations depicting Bible characters often portray the disciples as long-bearded, middle-aged men—which is highly unlikely. In fact, this passage may lend itself to a somewhat odd observation, but it seems that with all of the running back and forth—both men and women—they were probably a bit younger and more inclined to fast-paced action. Of course, there were other indications of youthfulness, beside the fact that Jesus was only in His early thirties, His closest followers were intense, idealistic, and adventurous. Some were prone to inhibited emotion and all were willing to stake their lives on what others saw as a big risk at best. Though they didn't realize it at the time, life was just beginning for Jesus' followers.

RESPOND: Why did Jesus have to rise from the dead (verse 9)? *(Had Jesus not risen, His followers would have no hope and their faith and testimony would be useless [1 Corinthians 15:12-19].)* How would His mission to bring spiritual salvation and eternal life have been incomplete without the resurrection? What hope does Jesus' resurrection give you personally? How does it inspire you to serve Him?

PRAY: Thank Jesus for His resurrection and for conquering death for you. Thank Him for the new life He now gives you. Ask Him to help you take advantage of the opportunity to spread the hope of this life to others.

ACT: Have you made a practice of talking to people about Jesus since you've accepted Him and allowed Him to change your life? Your conversations could include both Christians and non-Christians with whom you're willing to talk about God's goodness to you. Consider how often such conversations include sharing your faith with those who don't know Jesus, leading them closer to accepting Him for themselves. Try to talk to at least one person today about Jesus or spiritual matters.

Fire Starter

John 20:19-31

THINK: I'll believe it when I see it! Have you ever had that attitude? Perhaps you've often said those very words. Healthy skepticism and reasonable caution have their place. And under the circumstances described in this passage, it's understandable that many of us may have had doubts until coming face to face with Jesus. But the Lord expects a higher level of faith from His followers—particularly now that we have the full account of events in His Word. We're able to recount the miracles He performed and the prophecies He fulfilled.

RESPOND: Jesus' followers were still fearful (verse 19) and probably confused. How do you think you would have felt under these circumstances, following the execution of your leader and friend, and then having received a report that He was alive? How would you have reacted to seeing Jesus alive? What was significant about Jesus breathing on them and saying, "Receive the Holy Spirit"? *(This was the first time Jesus' disciples received the spiritually renewing presence of God's Spirit—the same Spirit that raised Jesus from the dead [see Romans 8:11]. The inner presence of the Holy Spirit is part of the new life all Jesus' followers receive when they surrender their lives to Him.)* What actually happened in their lives at that point? If you were in Thomas' position, do you think you would have believed the other disciples' without seeing Jesus for yourself? Why or why not? What was significant about Thomas' declaration to Jesus, "My Lord and my God!"? How does God enable us to believe in Jesus even though we've never seen Him (John 20:29)?

PRAY: Express gratitude to Jesus for giving you the faith to believe in Him. Ask Him to continually strengthen that faith as you take Him at His Word and as you trust Him—even when you don't see immediate effects of that faith.

ACT: Perhaps fear or lack of faith has kept you from making a certain decision or taking a specific action you feel that God wants you to take. If so, it's time to break away and let God help you overcome these fears and doubts. Take action today to begin fulfilling what you feel are God's intentions in this situation.

Fire Starter

John 21:1-25

THINK: Jesus' most vital concern is that we love Him. All the determination and good intentions in the world cannot replace love as the primary motivation for serving Christ. If your love for the Lord is lacking, you'll labor in frustration to fulfill what you feel is your spiritual duty, and eventually your relationship with God will collapse. But as you spend time with Jesus and your love for Him grows, you'll gain the power and inspiration to fulfill your God-given purpose—no matter what you encounter or endure along the way.

RESPOND: In what sense are your efforts unproductive—or not all they could be—until they're done God's way (verse 6)? How do Jesus' appearances following His resurrection (verse 14) help to confirm the biblical account of Jesus and His ministry? Why did Jesus persistently ask Peter, "Do you truly love me?"? How do you think this made Peter feel? In what way was Jesus demonstrating compassion for Peter and preparing him for future challenges? *(Jesus knew that Peter, who had denied Him before the Crucifixion, wouldn't last in his commitment to Christ if he wasn't confident of his own love for Jesus.)* How are Jesus' questions to Peter significant for you? (Our love, just like Peter's, must be a matter of mind and choice as well as heart and devotion.

PRAY: Thank Jesus for His incomparable love for you. Ask Him to strengthen and increase your love and devotion to Him—even when that requires going through painful and challenging times. Also, ask Him to help you pass His love on to others—particularly those who do not yet have a personal relationship with Him.

ACT: Commit all of your work to God. Whether it's job tasks, school studies, or responsibilities at home, ask God to help you and to have His way in all of your work. Do something specific to demonstrate your love for Jesus. This may involve a personal project such as a prayer letter or creative artwork. Consider doing something that will also inspire others in their relationship with God.

Fire Starter

Acts 1:1-26

THINK: The Book of Acts is a continuation of Luke's Gospel, picking up the story after Jesus ascended back to heaven. Acts is essentially an account of how Jesus' followers—in the power of the Holy Spirit—continued to spread Jesus' message and reproduce His work. Acts provides a general history of the beginning of the Church—the worldwide community of all true followers of Christ—which He established to convey His life-transforming message throughout the earth.

RESPOND: When the author, Luke, says that he wrote about "all that Jesus began to do and to teach," what does that statement imply? *(Jesus continues to work in peoples' lives and teach people through the Holy Spirit and through His own followers.)* What are some of the proofs Jesus gave His followers that He was alive? What additional proofs do we have today? What was the gift that Jesus' followers were instructed to wait for? What would this gift provide for Jesus' followers? *(The main purpose of the baptism in the Spirit is to give power to communicate the gospel message to people.)* What does it mean to be Jesus' "witnesses"? How does the Holy Spirit enable Jesus' followers to do this? *(The Holy Spirit makes the personal presence of Jesus more real to believers and witnesses both to and through Christians to convince others of God's righteousness.)* What hope and promise did Jesus' followers receive when He left earth (verse 11)? What did Jesus' closest followers do constantly as they joined together? How is this an example and a challenge for Jesus' followers today?

PRAY: Ask Jesus to continue His powerful work through you. Give God thanks for the gift of the Holy Spirit, who provides power for you to spread the message about Jesus.

ACT: The Holy Spirit's power is foundational to your life and service for Jesus. Regularly rely on the Holy Spirit, listening for and obeying His promptings as you live for and serve Jesus. Commit to some sort of consistent prayer time with others in your church and perhaps as part of a prayer or Bible group at your school or work.

Fire Starter

Acts 2:1-36

THINK: Acts 2 is a key passage in the Bible for many Pentecostals worldwide. A Pentecostal perspective is based on a firm belief that Christians today can and should experience the purposes and power of God's Holy Spirit in the same way Christ's followers did in the first century Church.

RESPOND: What was the atmosphere surrounding the Holy Spirit's arrival *(Pentecost—it was the second great festival of the Jewish year—a celebration of harvest when the first yields of grain were presented to God as offerings. For Christians, Pentecost represents the beginning of God's spiritual harvest of souls—people turning to Him personally.)* What was significant about the extraordinary signs accompanying the Spirit's arrival? *(Because God had previously demonstrated His presence and power through fire, the sign of tongues may have assured Jewish believers that what was taking place was, indeed, from God.)* What's the significance of being "baptized in" or "filled with" the Holy Spirit? *(This initial "outpouring" of the Holy Spirit—when God sent His Spirit to fill, empower, and work through His followers— was the beginning of the fulfillment of God's promise in Joel 2:28,29 to pour out His Spirit on all His people.)* In this passage, what's the initial physical evidence of being baptized in the Holy Spirit? *(Speaking in tongues.)* Who can be baptized in the Holy Spirit and what indication does Joel give that the baptism in the Spirit is still available for every Christian? *(According to Joel's prophecy, the baptism in the Holy Spirit is for all "born-again" devoted followers of Christ.)* Why was it "impossible for death to keep its hold" on Jesus? What does the outpouring of the Holy Spirit prove about Jesus? What's significant about the fact that Jesus is "both Lord and Christ"? *(Jesus being Lord means He is Ruler and Leader over everything. As Christ, He is the Anointed One and Savior.)*

PRAY: Pray that the power of the Holy Spirit flows through you to effectively communicate Jesus' message.

ACT: Make a deliberate effort to talk to at least one person about Jesus today. Spend time worshipping God and asking for His power to fill you.

Fire Starter

Acts 2:37-47

THINK: Many churches today aim to pattern themselves after the Church described in the New Testament, hoping to experience the same supernatural power, selfless devotion, and extraordinary growth. If you're looking to emulate the priorities of the first-century Church, this passage describes them in specific and practical terms.

RESPOND: Although water baptism itself does not save a person, what is the significance of this act? What is the ongoing significance of Peter's challenge to "Save yourselves from this corrupt generation"? *(One can't have a thriving relationship with God if they don't turn from and refuse to participate in corrupt activities. Relationships which promote sin should be broken and ungodly practices repented of and given up.)* What were the primary disciplines and activities of those in the early Church, which serve as a pattern for Christians and churches today? What's the significance of each of these disciplines? What were some of the selfless characteristics and practices of those in the first-century Church, and what can we learn from their example (verses 44–47)? What were the powerful results of the early believers' devotion to Christ and to each other? (verses 43,47)?

PRAY: Ask God to keep the Holy Spirit's presence fresh in your life. Ask Him to help you and the people in your church to develop the disciplines and characteristics of those in the first-century Church. Ask Him to help you personally develop a selfless and generous attitude toward others in the church.

ACT: If you are participating in any activities or relationships that could negatively affect or corrupt you spiritually, pull away from these things at once. If this involves relationships that must still be part of your life in some way, determine to be the positive influence on others. Also, make sure that you're developing each of the four disciplines mentioned in verses 42–47 by participating in ministry contexts that allow you to practice these things consistently.

Fire Starter

Acts 3:1-26

THINK: While many people dream of wealth, power, and the ability to go wherever and do whatever they want, few will experience this illusive fantasy. Those who do usually find little satisfaction and no real fulfillment. Regardless of whether you attain any degree of worldly wealth, power, or freedom, your life can be characterized by the ultimate power and provision that comes from a personal relationship with Jesus.

RESPOND: Whether they are rich or poor, what should all Christians possess above any material wealth (verse 6)? Who was responsible for the miraculous power displayed by Peter and John (verses 12,13,16)? What does it mean to pray for something "in the name of Jesus"? Who is the prophet Moses spoke about long ago (verse 22) and what would He do? *(Jesus was like Moses in many ways: [1] Moses was empowered by the Spirit; so was Jesus. [2] God used Moses to usher in the old covenant based on laws; Jesus introduced the new covenant based on spiritual salvation because of Jesus' sacrifice. [3] Moses led Israel out of Egypt; Jesus freed people from spiritual slavery. [4] A lamb was often sacrificed in the Old Testament as payment for sins; Jesus became the Lamb who paid for everyone's sins. [5] Moses pointed people to God through God's Law; Jesus pointed to himself and the Holy Spirit as a way of having a relationship with God.)* What happens to those who do not listen to Jesus (verse 23)? What is the condition for receiving God's blessing? *(Having true saving faith and receiving the baptism in the Holy Spirit are dependent on a person turning away from willfully sinful choices and habits.)*

PRAY: Ask Jesus to keep your life spiritually pure and prepared so He can work through you in powerful and miraculous ways. When He does, pray that you are faithful to give all credit and honor to Jesus.

ACT: Think of someone who has a need—physically, financially, relationally, etc.—that you do not have the ability to meet through your own efforts or resources. Contact the person and ask if you can pray for him or her.

Fire Starter

Acts 4:1-31

THINK: Are you willing to pay the price? If you want to have an impact for God, you've probably dreamed of powerful results from your ministry. It's not necessarily a pride issue. You simply want to influence as many people as possible for Jesus. But great pains precede great gains, and rejection usually comes before results. If you're willing to take risks for God and suffer for the cause of Christ, the returns on your investment can be extraordinary.

RESPOND: What "risks" and consequences can come from speaking boldly about Jesus? What positive results can come when people are persecuted for proclaiming Christ (verse 4)? What enabled Peter to respond so boldly to the religious leaders? *(Being filled with the Spirit isn't a one-time thing. As in Peter's case, there will be specific situations in which we need fresh inspiration, wisdom, and boldness with which to share God's message.)* How does this challenge and inspire you personally? What does Peter and John's response tell you about their commitment to Christ and His message? What did the believers expect would happen to confirm the message of Jesus as they boldly delivered it? Should we expect the same things today? Why or why not? How did God respond to their prayer? What does this indicate about the ongoing work, purpose, and effect of the Holy Spirit in believers' lives? *(After a person begins their faith journey, they can be baptized in the Holy Spirit. Though the initial baptism in the Holy Spirit is powerful, fresh fillings are part of God's purpose in the lives of believers. We should pray for and want those fillings so that we can experience unusual empowerment and boldness to serve and speak for Jesus.)*

PRAY: Ask for boldness from the Holy Spirit so you can speak about Jesus and respond effectively to those who confront you about your faith.

ACT: If you've been challenged or confronted regarding your faith in Christ, ask God for the opportunity to address the situation again, trusting Him for wisdom and boldness to meet the challenge. If appropriate, you may choose to write a note or e-mail in response to the situation. Be gracious, not combative, speaking from the perspective of what Jesus and your faith mean to you personally.

Fire Starter

Acts 4:32 through 5:11

THINK: When experiencing tough times, we tend to feel we don't deserve what we're getting—and this may be true. On the other hand, when experiencing success or prosperity, we tend to feel we've worked hard and deserve everything we have. But if you've been blessed with opportunities and resources, it has little to do with your own ingenuity and everything to do with the fact that God intends for you to be a channel of His blessing to others.

RESPOND: What characterized the apostles' preaching and why? *(Spirit-filled preaching is marked by "great power" and by messages firmly based on God's Word.)* Do you feel that ministry today is marked by this same power? Why or why not? How did people in the early Church meet one another's needs? How could we see this same result through the ministry of churches today? In what way was Ananias being deceptive and why was that considered lying to the Holy Spirit? *(Lying to the Holy Spirit is equivalent to lying to God.)* Why do you think that God's punishment was so severe in this situation? *(The deaths of Ananais and Sapphira reveal God's attitude toward selfish pride, hypocrisy, and deceitfulness amongst those who consider themselves followers of Christ.)* In what way does this account serve as a warning to believers regarding their motives and actions? How did the other believers respond to what happened to Ananias and Sapphira? *(It's interesting to note that rather than freak out and storm the exit door, the rest of the people responded in humility and fear—that intense reverence God deserves because of who He is . . . the fear that reminds us that we're ultimately accountable to God.)*

PRAY: Ask Jesus to give you a generous attitude toward others in the Church and to use you to meet people's needs when it is within your capability to do so. Pray that you remain humble, sincere, and honest in all the ways.

ACT: Think of someone in your church or circle of friends who has a need that you could meet. It may be financial or material, but it could also require help with a task, studies, or personal care if someone is ill or incapacitated in some way.

Acts 5:12-42

THINK: How do most people today view Christians and the Church? Often, it may not be in a favorable light. Of course, even if Christians do everything right in their conduct toward others, Jesus said that the world at large would still reject them. Ironically, Christians lose a lot of their influence because they worry too much about relating to the world and what people think. In the process, churches trade God's power for people's perceptions.

RESPOND: Do you think that Christians today are "highly regarded by the people" (verse 13) as they were in the early days of the New Testament Church? Why or why not? Can believers ever have this kind of favor with people in today's culture, and if so, how? Why don't we seem to experience the number of healings as they did in the early Church? *(The early believers were so consumed with God that His miraculous power was present wherever they went.)* How can following people keep you from obeying God? What are some examples of how people's desires, ideals and authority conflict with God's desires, commands, and authority? To whom does God give the Holy Spirit, and what does the Spirit help them do? *(People who live in the fullness of the Holy Spirit also submit their will to Jesus. After all, if Jesus doesn't influence every area of our lives, what's the point? He influences us through His Word and the Holy Spirit. So God gives His Spirit to the person who obeys Him and is submitted to Jesus' lordship—His authority, standards, and desires.)* In what way do people today oppose believers and end up fighting against God?

PRAY: Ask God to give you the wisdom, determination, and power to always obey Him, regardless of what people want from you or how they pressure you.

ACT: Make a deliberate choice and effort to live in a way that will earn respect and be well-regarded by others. By living this way, God will give you favor with the right people and help you bring honor to Him. If in any way you're following people rather than obeying God, make an immediate change and do what God wants you to do, regardless of what others think or do.

Acts 6:1-15

THINK: Who is more important in your church, the lead pastor or the groundskeeper, the worship leader or the maintenance man, the person on the platform or in the pew? It's true that some positions are more prominent than others. Some may have more responsibilities or more influence. God may even hold some to a higher standard of accountability because of their position. Depending on your God-given gifts, your efforts might be better spent on some things rather than others. Yet, God intends for all who serve Him to be guided by His Spirit and be full of His power to accomplish His purpose.

RESPOND: How do you think we can tell if people are "full of the Holy Spirit and wisdom"? *(This has to do with the condition of having the Spirit's presence and power in one's life in obvious ways—evident by thoughtful, wise, and godly conversation, self-controlled and selfless behavior, and engaging in activities that matter to God, and cultivating relationships that bear fruit [Galatians 5:22,23].)* Can these things be said of you? Why is it important for wise, Spirit-directed people to be serving in every capacity of church ministry? In what ways and for what reason did ministry leaders lay their hands on people? *(The laying on of hands is one way in which God commissions people to use their gifts to serve Him. In the New Testament it was associated with miracles and healing, blessing people, baptism in the Holy Spirit, commissioning people for service in a specific area, and recognizing spiritual gifts by church leaders.)* What do you think it means that Stephen's "face was like the face of an angel"? In what ways should God's life show through us like this?

PRAY: Ask God to help you live full of the Holy Spirit and wisdom and to give adequate attention to prayer so you can serve God and communicate His message to others.

ACT: Spend some extra time in prayer and in God's Word today. Perhaps during a study period or break at work you can review some of your Bible study over the past few days. Also, find a couple of practical ways in which you can serve people today and help meet their needs.

Acts 7:1-53

THINK: Notice that in face of extreme pressure and injustice, Stephen didn't get defensive or even address the false charges. Instead, he simply stated the truth—the message on which he had staked his reputation and life. Yet, even when you do this, realize that most people will remain stubbornly defiant toward God, refusing to accept the truth.

RESPOND: In what ways did Stephen's speech summarize the message being spread by Jesus' followers? *(Stephen not only recounted Old Testament history, but connected what God had done in the Israelites' lives and peoples' response to Old Testament prophets. Stephen defended the message Jesus preached and set the example for all who defend biblical truth.)* Reviewing this passage, what prophecies did God reveal to His people about what would happen to them (verses 5-7,34,37,43)? What promises did God make and fulfill to His people throughout history (verses 6,7,37)? In what ways did God provide for His people (verses 8,10,14,17,35-38,45)? How did the people rebel against Him (verses 9,39-43,51-53)? What can happen to people who persistently rebel against and reject God? *(Those who continually reject God are given over to the influence of evil, allowing them by their own free will, to risk their eternal salvation by making choices to break God's laws and reject truth. God loves everyone and forgives those who open their hearts and yield their wills to Him.)* In what ways do people "resist the Holy Spirit"? How can you guard against this tendency in your own life?

PRAY: Ask God for insight from His Word to understand how His plan has unfolded and progressed through history, culminating in the work and message of Christ. Pray that you'll follow the pattern His Word has set for ultimate living and that you'll never rebel against His plan for your life.

ACT: Take your Bible with you and review Stephen's speech from this passage. It provides a concise and relevant summary of the history of God's people and His plan as it unfolded. This is key to understanding how the Old Testament laid a foundation for the New Testament.

Fire Starter

Acts 7:54 through 8:8

THINK: Tough times tend to bring out the best in some people. Combine this with the fact that many people in the world are looking for a cause and purpose to stake their lives on. When Christians stand true in the face of persecution, they reveal the reality of their faith and prove that the relationship they have with God is worth dying for.

RESPOND: What distinction does Stephen have among all followers of Jesus? *(Stephen was the first apostle to be killed for defending biblical truth and opposing those who distort it.)* Who was Saul (8:1), and why is he significant to the New Testament? In what ways were Jesus' first followers persecuted following Stephen's death? What effect did this have on those in the early Church? *(God used Saul's persecution of believers as a catalyst for a great missionary work in the Church.)* How did this actually promote the message of Jesus and turn out for the good of the Church (verse 4)? *(This difficult time was the beginning of the fulfillment of Jesus' Great Commission—His command to spread His message throughout the world.)* What did Philip's ministry to the Samaritans reveal about the connection between receiving God's message, accepting Christ, and the ongoing work of the Holy Spirit? *(Philip preached Jesus and God confirmed his Word with miracles. Many Samaritans believed in Jesus and were water baptized.)* Why did people pay attention to Philip's message? What do you think would inspire people today to pay attention to the message of Jesus?

PRAY: Ask God to help you grow in boldness and devotion to Him so that you would be willing to give your life for Him if necessary.

ACT: Think of any resistance, opposition or rejection you've faced for your faith in Christ. Consider how these situations present opportunities to honor Jesus. For example, if a teacher has challenged your spiritual views, let this inspire you to do some Bible study and research that could be used for a paper or project on a Christian theme. Show exceptional kindness to those who have given you trouble. This can be the best witness of the life-changing power of Christ.

Fire Starter

Acts 8:9-40

THINK: Money, power, prestige, and influence may seem to open a lot of doors and provide a lot of things for some people. But none of these worldly benefits can get you any farther with God or gain you anything spiritually. Only sincere surrender to God and acceptance of Christ's leadership in your life will give you access to His power and special blessing. And nothing else in this world can give you greater influence on others than the Holy Spirit working in and through you.

RESPOND: How could someone like Simon the sorcerer have such influence on people? Where do you think his apparent power came from? What happened when the Samaritans encountered real power from God? What did it mean, "the Holy Spirit had not yet come upon any of them [Samaritan believers]"? *(They hadn't experienced the power of, nor demonstrated the expressions that typically accompanied the baptism in Holy Spirit as Christ's followers did on the day of Pentecost.)* What does this indicate about the relation between salvation and the baptism in the Holy Spirit? *(These two distinct experiences weren't abnormal for Christ's followers. It's clear that baptism in the Holy Spirit didn't save them, neither was it required for salvation; rather, it was a subsequent, welcome and empowering experience. Just as water baptism is an outward gesture of what God has done inwardly through salvation, baptism in the Spirit prompts outward confirmation of the Spirit's presence in a Christian's life.)* How was Philip's response to God's direction (verse 29) key in the Ethiopian's conversion to Christ? Why is it so important to respond when you sense God directing you to reach out to someone?

PRAY: Ask God to help you be responsive to His guidance so that you'll always be prepared to talk about Jesus.

ACT: Is God leading you to reach out to someone who is open and ready to respond to Him? You may need to develop a friendship first, or perhaps God wants you to show kindness to the person. Then again, he or she may be ready to talk about God. Do whatever you sense God leading you to. If you haven't yet been baptized in the Holy Spirit, ask God to give you this powerful gift.

178

Acts 9:1-31

THINK: No one is beyond God's reach. We may misjudge individuals and make assumptions about their openness to God or even about God's ability to reach them. But God can take people who are radically opposed to Him and turn them into radically committed followers of Jesus. And He may use you to help someone make that transformation. Be open to the possibilities in people's lives—and in God's plan—to turn them around for His glory.

RESPOND: What can you tell about Saul's intensity and commitment, even before he encountered Jesus? How did people first refer to the Christian faith (verse 2), and why did this description fit? In what ways did Saul's response immediately following his encounter with Jesus indicate a true change of heart? *(After Saul's—Paul's—conversion, he obeyed Jesus' instructions, committed to becoming a servant and witness of Jesus, a missionary to non-Jewish people.)* How would you have responded to God's instructions if you had been in Ananias' position, knowing Saul's reputation (verses 13,14)? Why does serving God's purposes often involve suffering and hardship? *(This is one of the mysterious paradoxes in Christian service, that suffering is often the path to effectiveness and depth in one's character and ministry to others.)* Why do you think Barnabas was willing to trust and accept Saul? In what way was Barnabas' encouragement vital to Saul's ministry?

PRAY: Pray that you'll be accepting of those whom God calls to minister to you and to serve alongside you. Ask God to help you be more like Barnabas, encouraging and supporting those who are new in faith—and even those in leadership—who struggle to find acceptance among some Christians.

ACT: Be a Barnabas—a defender and encourager—for someone whom others might not readily trust, accept or give a chance. If this involves Christian friends, gently and humbly remind them of God's acceptance and the fact that people need support and encouragement in order to serve Him with ultimate effectiveness.

THINK: Has God ever used you to perform a miracle? Perhaps He has and you didn't even realize it. Of course, it's doubtful that you would forget praying for someone who was supernaturally healed—or raised from the dead! But if you typically take advantage of the opportunities God gives you to help people, meet practical needs and contribute to ministry, then there's a good chance you've been a part of something supernatural. While extraordinary occurrences may stand out, it's often the common kindnesses shown at just the right time that make the biggest differences in people's lives. Perhaps your helpful hand, generous gift, or simple act of compassion will be an answer to prayer for someone in a desperate situation, providing the miracle they've been waiting for.

RESPOND: How does the way God worked through Peter compare to the way He worked through Dorcas (verses 34,36)? *(While God healed people through Peter, He used Dorcas to show acts of kindness to those in need.)* Is one way more important than the other? Are miracles more significant than doing good and helping the poor? Why or why not? How can help and good works honor Jesus just as much or more than supernatural signs? How could your simple act of kindness or generosity turn out to be someone else's miracle? In what ways can you do good to others? How can you ensure that God is honored through your actions? In what ways can you help the poor? What types of things can you do even if you have little or no resources yourself?

PRAY: Ask God to show you what good you can do for people as a means of honoring Him. Pray that through these opportunities you'll be able to influence others to trust and follow Jesus.

ACT: Look for as many ways as possible throughout the day to do good to others. Many of these opportunities will involve simple acts of kindness or assistance. Some may involve tangible or material gifts of some sort. Allow God to bless people and show compassion through you.

Fire Starter

Acts 10:1-23

THINK: How comfortable are you reaching beyond your social circle and associating with other believers who may not seem to fit your personality, style or social profile? If you seldom branch out to build new relationships—with both Christians and non-Christians—your growth and influence will be limited. God intends for His people to grow in community with each other. He uses others to sharpen, challenge, and inspire us spiritually, mentally, socially, and in many other ways. Don't diminish God's work in and through you by refusing to relate to people outside of your comfort zone.

RESPOND: How did Cornelius demonstrate his devotion to God? In what ways are prayers and gifts to the poor an offering to God? *(Prayer both feeds and reveals closeness with God; giving to the poor feeds and reveals compassion for people.)* What part did prayer play in the lives of Jesus' early followers and church leaders, and why? *(New Testament Christians understood that life in God's kingdom could not be experienced or conveyed by squeezing God into a few minutes, if they had time. Early Christians patterned their prayer lives after Jews, who prayed two to three times a day.)* When, how, and in what situations does the Bible tell people to pray? What was God illustrating for Peter through the vision? How did Peter's attitude begin to change after his vision? In what ways do Christians sometimes struggle to accept "outsiders" or relate to people who are different from them? In what way has God changed your attitude and helped you open up to others so you could be more effective in reaching them for Jesus?

PRAY: Ask God to help you overcome and eliminate any prejudice that could keep you from reaching out to people with His love and message. Pray that you'll not hesitate to accept those whom God wants you to influence for Him.

ACT: At some point today (or during the next couple days), plan to give a full hour to God, uninterrupted. Spend this time worshipping, praying, reading His Word, etc. Among other things, pray that God would make you more sensitive to His voice and more open to reaching out to all kinds of people with His love and message.

Fire Starter

Acts 10:24-48

THINK: Have you ever been surprised by how God spiritually saved, transformed, and worked through someone who you felt was almost beyond hope or God's reach? Perhaps you were one of those astonishing transformations. The fact is that all of us who follow Christ should be eternally grateful that God doesn't see us as people might tend to see us. We must be careful to never diminish or stand in the way of anyone's part in God's plan.

RESPOND: What does it mean that "God does not show favoritism"? How should that affect your attitudes and actions—in ministry and otherwise? What's the real condition for God's acceptance of people (verse 35)? How can you be sure to "fear him and do what is right"? *(It's important to remember who God is and what He's done through Jesus. We show "the fear of the Lord" when we humbly care for people who may never say thank you; God does it all the time. We also show we "fear the Lord" when we trust and obey Him, even when it's inconvenient; Jesus knows what that's like.)* Though God's plan of salvation and the message of Jesus originally went out through the Jews, who is Jesus' message for and for whom is He the Lord (verse 36)? What did Peter emphasize about Jesus in His testimony to Cornelius? Why do you think Peter's companions were astonished by the Holy Spirit's work within the Gentiles? What was the outward evidence that they also had been filled with the Holy Spirit? *(They spoke in unlearned languages as inspired by the Holy Spirit.)* How did their experience compare with that of Jesus' first followers on the day of Pentecost (cf. Acts 2:1-4)?

PRAY: Ask God to keep you from showing favoritism or prejudice toward others for any reason—particularly when it comes to reaching out or receiving ministry from those with whom you find it more difficult to relate.

ACT: Ask God to reveal any way in which you've shown favoritism or prejudice toward anyone. Consider how this may have affected your acceptance or outreach toward certain people. Make a deliberate effort to befriend or show kindness to these individuals in the hope of showing Jesus' love.

182

Acts 11:1-18

THINK: How does it feel to be misunderstood? How well do you take it when you're denied an opportunity you deserved simply because people don't know you? None of these experiences are pleasant, none are fair, and none have a place among Jesus' followers. We misjudge people at times, and it can certainly be difficult to accept those we don't understand at first. But when God exposes our misguided notions and demonstrates His acceptance in people's lives, we must be quick to change our attitudes, to accept one another, and to get in line with God's plan for us to work together.

RESPOND: Why do you think that the Jewish believers were closed-minded toward people of other backgrounds and nationalities? What was the sign that God had accepted the Gentile believers and that they had accepted the message of Jesus? How do we know that God's gifts of salvation, baptism in the Holy Spirit, and eternal life are for all who accept Jesus and entrust their lives to Him? *(The baptism in the Holy Spirit was not exclusive to Jewish believers. God showed that He wanted to and would pour out His Spirit on everyone who received God's forgiveness and entrusted their lives to Christ.)* How do we know that baptism in the Holy Spirit is a gift people can receive only after accepting Jesus the Forgiver of their sins and Leader of their lives (verse 17)?

PRAY: Pray for individuals at your school, workplace—or wherever—who you may have misjudged, particularly regarding their openness to God, and perhaps even in regard to God's ability to reach them. Ask God to adjust your attitude toward these individuals and to give you the opportunity to influence them for Jesus.

ACT: Perhaps there is someone in your church or youth group that you've misjudged. Maybe you've been unduly skeptical of their commitment to God or have not given them the benefit of the doubt. You may need to apologize and ask forgiveness for wrong attitudes you held toward them. Then encourage that person in their commitment to God and place of service in the church.

Fire Starter

Acts 11:19-30

THINK: Think of a time when someone encouraged you, and it made all the difference in that situation. One of the most effective ways to influence people in a positive way is to be an encourager. People like to be around those who lift their mood, inspire them to new heights, and simply offer hope. But most people have few, if any, significant encouragers in their lives. Of all people, Christians—confident in their identity with Christ—should be the greatest encouragers. By offering words of kindness, gratitude, and inspiration to people you encounter every day, you can influence them to receive the ultimate encouragement that comes through a personal relationship with Jesus.

RESPOND: What happened when the followers of Christ who were scattered by persecution began to spread the message of Jesus to people of other nationalities (verse 21)? What was the result of the Lord's blessing on the messengers? What did Barnabas do for the new believers? Why was his challenge important? *(New believers are susceptible to old temptations. Barnabas sets the example of encouraging those still near the beginning of their spiritual journey. We, too, should constantly help new believers to grow in faith, love, and closeness with Jesus.)* Judging from his defense of Saul (Acts 9:26,27) and his work among the new believers in Antioch, what kind of a man was Barnabas (verse 24)? Why is encouragement so vital, particularly to newly committed Christians?

PRAY: Ask God to use you every day to encourage people you meet, and particularly to those you know who are new in their Christian faith. Pray that the Holy Spirit will help and empower you to conduct yourself in a way that is worthy of identifying with Jesus.

ACT: Encourage as many people as possible today—Christians and non-Christians, those you know well and people you don't know at all. Don't underestimate the influence of simple words of kindness, thanks and inspiration. Befriend those whom others neglect. Thank everyone from teachers to cafeteria workers for jobs well done. Don't forget to be a help and inspiration to members of your family.

Acts 12:1-25

THINK: Have you ever prayed and been surprised when God answered? It's one thing to be amazed by how God answers our prayers, but to be surprised by the very fact that He does answer seems a bit odd. After all, why pray if you don't expect that God hears and answers prayer. He certainly isn't reluctant to respond to His people. But since you don't always know what's best in many situations, you may not recognize or realize when God answers. Then there are times when His answer is "no" or "not now." Still, God wants you to depend on Him and to pray at all times and in all circumstances. When you do—at some point— you are bound to see an answer in the form of a miracle.

RESPOND: Who was the first of Jesus' closest disciples to be put to death for following Him? How would you explain why James was allowed to die while Peter was rescued to continue ministry? How did the church respond to Peter's predicament—and to most situations where they encountered opposition? *(In times of crisis and opposition, the New Testament Church continued to meet and pray.)* Why do you think they responded this way? What does Peter's liberation from prison indicate about the power of prayer? Why is prayer so crucial to the life and ministry of a church? Why is it such a serious offense to accept praise that belongs to God alone? How do people sometimes accept undue praise or rob God of praise?

PRAY: Give God thanks for the connection you have to Him and the access you have to His power through prayer. Commit to making prayer your first course of action whenever you face opposition and difficult times.

ACT: Give extra time to prayer during your free time today, or take time from something else and give it to God in prayer. Pray for your church, it's leaders, and it's ministries. Pray particularly for any difficulties or big issues your church is facing. Pray that the members of your congregation grow in their desire to pray and that God inspires people to participate in and initiate prayer ministries.

Fire Starter

Acts 13:1-12

THINK: What do you picture when you think of a missionary? In reality, all followers of Christ are called to take part in Christian missions. Whether you ever set foot on a foreign field, you can contribute to the cause through prayer and giving. But you too are called to be a missionary right where you are, accepting responsibility for reaching spiritually lost people with the message of forgiveness and new life through faith in Christ.

RESPOND: In what atmosphere, or under what conditions, did the prophets and teachers hear the Holy Spirit? Why are believers particularly sensitive to God during such times? What is fasting as it relates to prayer and worship? What type of work were Paul and Barnabas commissioned by the Church to do? *(They preached the gospel, introduced men and women to Jesus, established local churches, and developed leaders.)* What does genuine, New Testament missionary service involve? What's the primary purpose of modern missionaries? What's the relationship between churches and missionaries? Who must be the real guide in any minister's life and service (verse 4)? *(Through prayer and fasting a local church discerns and aligns itself with the Holy Spirit's leading and plans so they can confirm God's call on certain individuals to missionary work. Through the laying on of hands—to bless and commission people for service—the local church affirms its commitment and support of the missionaries sent. The believers in a local church are responsible to pray for and financially support missionaries.)* Where did Paul get the power to firmly and effectively oppose the sorcerer? What do Paul's Holy Spirit-inspired words indicate about the nature of sorcery and other such practices (verse 10)?

PRAY: Ask God to help you grow closer to Him and more sensitive to the guidance of the Holy Spirit. Pray for missionaries you know or whom your church supports. Ask God to encourage them and make them ultimately effective in spreading the message of forgiveness and new life in Jesus Christ.

ACT: Get a list of missionaries your church or youth ministry supports. Commit to praying at least one day a week for these faithful servants. Also, if you're physically able to do so, fast one meal this week, and give that time to worship and prayer.

Acts 13:13-52

THINK: Before Jesus returned to heaven, He told His followers that they would be His "witnesses" (Luke 24:48; Acts 1:8), starting in their own community, then spreading His message throughout the world. Christians in contemporary churches talk about witnessing. A lot of them understand that it's their responsibility to "witness," yet few seem to really know what "witnessing" involves.

RESPOND: According to Paul's message, how did God bless and provide for Israel? Why did God consider David "a man after my own heart" (verse 22)? How did the people's rejection of Jesus fulfill prophecies about Him (verse 27)? What is a Christian "witness"? *(A witness is something you are as much or more as something you do. Christian witnesses confirm the saving work of Jesus by their words, actions, lifestyle, and in some cases, their death.)* What do true witnesses do, how do they do it, and what will they experience as a result? *(Christian witnesses communicate the message of Jesus to all people in all cultures, allow the Holy Spirit to work through them to convince people of their need for Jesus, and separate themselves from ungodly practices. They may suffer at times because of their witness. In fact, martyr comes from the Greek word for witness.)* What does Jesus offer everyone who entrusts their life to Him (verse 38)? What does faith in Jesus do that following the law cannot (verse 39)? Why did Paul and Barnabas turn their ministry attention to the Gentiles (i.e., people of other nationalities who aren't Jewish or Israelite)?

PRAY: Give God thanks for His plan of spiritual salvation, fulfilled through His Son, Jesus. Thank Jesus that He died to pay the price for your sins, providing forgiveness and eternal life through the power of His resurrection. Pray that you continue to be full of the power and joy of the Holy Spirit so you can be an effective witness for Jesus.

ACT: Review the above definition of a Christian witness. Write down how you have fulfilled any part of this definition. Then write down specific ways you can be a witness, first in your family, then in your school and community.

Acts 14:1-28

THINK: Who doesn't want to feel appreciated? Everyone likes to get credit for what they've done. Many will even take credit for things they don't deserve if others will give it to them. But few people are willing to give up glory or pass up praise. Paul and Barnabas were hailed as "gods," but they refused to accept praise and to draw attention away from the true God they served. They suffered greatly as a result. But God spared their lives and continued to use them powerfully.

RESPOND: Why did those who refused to believe the message of Jesus (verse 2) feel the need to cause division and discourage others from accepting Him? What was the purpose of the "miraculous signs and wonders"? *(God intended these miracles to confirm the truth and power of His Word.)* Is this purpose still valid today? In what way do people sometimes accept praise that belongs to God alone? How did Paul and Barnabas direct people's attention back to God? What price did Paul pay for honoring Jesus and doing what's right? Why did God allow Him to suffer this way? Why will God's people often suffer for the cause of Christ? *(Living in a world hostile to Jesus and His message, believers then and now must engage in spiritual warfare against sin and Satan. Those faithful to Jesus, His Word and mission, can expect opposition in this world, always mindful that their hope is not in this world's accommodations or approval, but in eternal life with Jesus.)*

PRAY: Ask God for boldness to do what's right, even when it costs you dearly. Pray that you'll never accept praise for using your God-given gifts and opportunities, but that you'll always direct attention and honor back to God.

ACT: When you face situations in which it would be easy to compromise your principles and faith, rely on God for strength and do what's right. Don't hesitate to tell why you're doing the right thing—because of your faith in Christ. Also, resist the tendency to take credit for your accomplishments. When God allows you to effectively use your talents, gifts, and opportunities, give humble and sincere praise to God, acknowledging Him as your source and inspiration.

Acts 15:1-21

THINK: Life can be tough enough. Why make things more difficult than they need to be—especially when it comes to spiritual matters and knowing God? Even God doesn't make it difficult to receive His gifts of forgiveness and eternal life. Of course, actually living for God—following His plans, serving His purposes and influencing others for Him—is not easy amid the pressures of a world opposed to Christ. But the decision to enter a personal relationship with God isn't complicated, nor is it a matter of our own efforts. It's an unearned, undeserved gift of love for those who willingly admit and turn from their own God-defying ways and surrender the leadership of their lives to Christ.

RESPOND: Where does God look to determine whether someone's faith in Jesus is genuine? How did Peter know that God had accepted the Gentiles' faith (verses 8,9)? Why is it wrong to add extra conditions to receiving spiritual salvation (verses 10,11)? What's the real condition for spiritual salvation? What does God give us that allows us to be saved and what must we demonstrate toward Him? *(Faith in Jesus Christ is the only condition for receiving God's free gift of spiritual salvation. Faith is not only a matter of belief, but it is also an active response from one's heart.)* How does a person demonstrate that they've truly accepted God's saving grace? *(God's grace—unearned favor and spiritual enablement is given to those who repent and turn from God-defying ways, and believe in and trust their life to Jesus.)* What's the significance of the proposed restrictions for the Gentile believers (verse 20)? How would these things apply to Christians today—particularly the issues of associating with "idols" and abstaining from sexual immorality?

PRAY: Give God thanks for His grace and for not making it difficult to receive salvation. Express your gratitude by committing to live in a way that honors God and to abstain from anything that could compromise your devotion to Him.

ACT: Make a conscious effort to demonstrate God's grace (i.e., unearned favor, love, kindness, help) to people, including anyone you know who may be struggling in their faith.

Acts 15:22-35

THINK: We all need boundaries and guidelines. Problems arise when we try to determine all of these according to our own preferences. Left to ourselves, none of us—even as Christians— would adopt the same values, and most of us would give little consideration to how our freedoms and restrictions affect others. That's why God gives us commands in His Word. He also gives us the Holy Spirit to guide us in making appropriate decisions that honor Him and benefit others. One of the marks of Christian maturity is when we become sensitive enough to the Spirit to willingly refrain from activities that could not only compromise and corrupt our own morals but could also offend or mislead others spiritually.

RESPOND: How did the Church leaders arrive at their decision regarding how the Gentiles should follow up their commitment to Christ? *(Jesus promised that the Holy Spirit would guide His followers into all truth, and in this instance we see that the Holy Spirit directed those at the Jerusalem council in these decisions.)* Why must you depend on the Holy Spirit's guidance in making decisions? What's the significance of the specific standards and restrictions that the Church leaders presented to the Gentile believers? *(These particular guidelines enable non-Jewish and Jewish believers to live in harmony without offense and moral compromise.)* How do these moral restrictions apply in practical ways to believers today—particularly the issues of "idols" and abstaining from sexual immorality? Why must you look past your own preferences and what you feel is okay and consider how your actions may influence others? What are some examples of how consideration for others could affect your own lifestyle choices?

PRAY: Pray that you'll refrain from activities that could compromise your own faith and moral values, and that you will also demonstrate the maturity to refrain from things that may offend or mislead others in their faith and morality.

ACT: Give God opportunity to voice His guidance, and be sure to listen for the Holy Spirit's direction in making your decision. Also, allow God to expose ways in which you may be compromising your moral standards or setting a questionable example for others. Demonstrate maturity by making a change and doing what's best.

Acts 15:36 through 16:15

THINK: Have you disagreed with anyone lately? Disagreements aren't the main problem. How you handle them are. When you find yourself in a dispute you have a choice. Allow the situation to deteriorate, tearing down those involved, or reach a compromise that allows for growth. This doesn't mean you have to reach the same opinion. People can go different ways, do different things and still benefit both ways if they keep the right attitude, aim to honor God and pursue His purposes more intensely.

RESPOND: What does the sharp disagreement between Paul and Barnabas indicate about relationships even among mature Christians leaders? Why do such tensions sometimes arise? Can God still have His way through contentious issues among believers? How so? When people agree to disagree, how should they handle things from that point on, and how should this affect their relationship? *(Often because of personalities, different perspectives and leadership styles, as well as past experiences, even Christian leaders who love Jesus and each other will disagree. There's no sin in these things if all parties have been respectful and considerate of God's laws and one another. When disagreements can't be resolved, it's best to disagree agreeably and trust God to work in the lives of all those affected.)* What was the result of Paul and Barnabas' proper handling of this situation (15:40 and 16:5)? When Paul had Timothy circumcised, what did this demonstrate about the need to accommodate others' standards in order to effectively minister to them? In what ways can this involve both loosening and tightening your own personal preferences, standards, and restrictions?

PRAY: Ask God to help you handle disputes with other Christians in ways that honor Him, so that everyone involved can continue serving God's purposes.

ACT: If you've had a significant disagreement with someone—particularly another Christian—connect with that person and make every effort to either settle the difference or agree to disagree in a gracious and constructive manner. Also, make a mature decision to adjust your personal freedoms and preferences, depending on what will give people a more accurate impression of Jesus.

Acts 16:16-40

THINK: Who can tell when you're in a bad mood—your closest friends, or everyone around you? Can they recognize what you're going through based on emotions? Are you down and depressed when things are rough or you've been mistreated? Do you show joy and excitement only when things are going great? Paul and Silas didn't let circumstances determine their mood or rob their joy.

RESPOND: Where did the slave girl get her supposed ability to predict the future? *(This young woman was doubly bound, spiritually—because of the demonically influenced spirit speaking through her—and economically, because her owners benefited financially from her future telling.)* In what way do the girl's actions and words as she followed Paul indicate how God's power is far superior to any other power? *(Satan is not equal with God. He is a created being and totally subordinate to God. Unlike God, Satan is not omnipresent—everywhere at once, omnipotent—all-powerful, or omniscient—all-knowing. So even though the demonically influenced spirit was making true statements through the girl, Jesus was not being glorified, and in His name and authority, the spirit was decisively ejected from the girl.)* What are some examples of how people today show far more concern for their own wealth and success than for the good of others? Why did the authorities punish Paul and Silas? Why and how could Paul and Silas praise God after all they had been through? What does this demonstrate about true Christian joy? How can you learn from their example? According to this passage, what must a person do to be saved?

PRAY: Give God thanks for His matchless power, authority and love. Ask Him to give you uncommon joy in all situations—so much that others will notice and be influenced to accept and trust Christ for themselves.

ACT: Practice maintaining and expressing an attitude of joy and gratitude in difficult and unfair situations. Whenever someone mistreats you for no good reason, or you encounter opposition for doing right, or you simply hit a hard time, make a deliberate effort to keep a good attitude.

Fire Starter

Acts 17:1-15

THINK: Some people aren't content just to ruin things for themselves. They have to ruin things for everyone else as well. If they can't have it or don't want it, no one else is going to get it either. If they're going down, they're taking others down with them. Many people who reject Christ are like this, whether they realize it or not. If only more people who follow Christ were like this as well—not taking others down, but determining instead to bring them up. Make it your aim to help people find a relationship with Jesus and to take as many as you can to heaven with you.

RESPOND: What does Paul's practice of reasoning with others from God's Word (verses 2,3) indicate about the importance of knowing the Word? In what ways do people in the world stir up opposition against God, His standards and His purposes in an attempt to keep people from following Him? What does the Bereans' example reveal about the value of Bible study and how we should approach it? *(Rather than swallowing all Church teaching whole, we must carefully study God's Word for ourselves to determine whether that teaching measures up to biblical truth.)* How did the Bereans' attitude toward God's Word demonstrate good character? In what way do the Bereans serve as a model for all Christians and churches? How does their example challenge you personally? What are the personal benefits of Bible study? How does knowing and studying God's Word benefit an entire church? How does knowing and loving God's Word help you to understand and communicate the message of Jesus?

PRAY: Give God thanks for His powerful and precious Word. Ask Him to give you a fresh love for and commitment to knowing and understanding it. Ask Him to give you insight from the Holy Spirit whenever you read and study it.

ACT: If you're reading this, it's likely that you're already committed to spending daily time in God's Word. Continue to dig deeper into God's Word and gain a better understanding of how it applies to your daily life.

Fire Starter

Acts 17:16-34

THINK: How do you think God feels when He sees the ravages of sin on His creation, and when people reject Him to pursue to worthless things? Now consider how those who love God should feel when they observe these things. Deeply devoted followers of Jesus sense His grief over the moral corruption and spiritual destruction all around them. But they don't lose hope. Instead, they take action, reaching out to spiritually lost people, finding common ground and communicating Christ's message without compromise. They find ways to relate people's search to God's solution.

RESPOND: Why was Paul distressed over what He saw in Athens? *(Paul's spirit was saddened and troubled over people who were spiritually lost. Those truly committed to Christ are grieved by moral corruption and want to take action.)* What can a person's attitude toward sin and its effects indicate about his or her spiritual condition and relationship with God? How can you keep a balance between being grieved by the effects of sin and still demonstrating hope of what Christ can do in people's lives? What are some of "the latest ideas" (verse 21) people are listening to today? How is Paul's response to the Athenians an example to us? How did He get their attention, find common ground and appeal to their openness (verses 22,23,28)? How did He relate the people's search to God's solution? How can we engage our culture in conversation about God without being negatively influenced by the corruption in the culture?

PRAY: Pray for insight from the Holy Spirit about how to engage others in conversation about God. Pray that the minds of spiritually lost people will be aware of the deception all around them and open to the truth of Jesus.

ACT: Throughout the day, pay attention to how people follow and prioritize other things above God, rejecting His authority in their lives. At the same time, notice those who seem to be searching for answers or hope and may be open to the truth. How could you convey Jesus' love and message to them without compromising godly principles? Look for common ground, and try to get into a couple of conversations today based on this exercise.

Fire Starter

Acts 18:1-23

THINK: Every individual follower of Jesus is a minister—one who serves on behalf of Jesus. Whether you're a student, an office worker, a part-time pastor, or a life-long missionary you share the opportunity and responsibility to spread Jesus' message, and influence others for Him wherever you are. Do whatever it takes to make the most of the ministry Jesus has given you.

RESPOND: What does Paul's tent-making indicate about some ministers' need to work another job to support themselves? Are ministers in this situation less involved in ministry than those who receive full time support from their ministries or churches? Why was Paul confident in continuing to talk about Jesus despite the opposition he encountered? How does it encourage you to know that God is with you in a special way when you take a stand for Him? Why is it crucial to recognize and rely on God's presence when ministering for Him? Why did Paul return to places where he had previously ministered? *(Paul never forgot about the people he'd led into a relationship with Jesus. He followed up on new believers and helped them grow.)* What example does this set for all followers of Jesus who work to influence others for Him? Why is ongoing contact so vital for people who are new in Christian faith?

PRAY: Give God thanks for His constant power and presence in your life. Pray for anyone you've led to Christ in the past. Pray that they remain faithful to God or that they return to Him if they've abandoned their faith. Pray for any ministers you know who must work outside of their ministry.

ACT: Follow up with someone whom you've led to Jesus. Ask how they are doing and if there's anything you can pray with them about. Try to answer their questions, but don't feel the need to have all the answers. If you've talked to someone in-depth about God or your faith in Jesus but they've not yet accepted Him, try to renew that conversation in order to help them grow closer to receiving a personal relationship with Jesus.

Fire Starter

Acts 18:24 through 19:7

THINK: The baptism in the Holy Spirit is a gift God wants us to have. A person can be "born again" or "saved" spiritually—which means that the Holy Spirit lives within them—but still not be baptized in the Spirit. The primary purpose of the baptism is to immerse a Christian's life in the boldness and power of God's Spirit so that he or she can accomplish Jesus' purposes with His authority.

RESPOND: While it's fairly obvious that Apollos knew God's Word, believed in Jesus, and had accepted Him as Savior and Lord, what had he not yet experienced that would help him grow deeper and be even more effective in ministry? What happened when the Holy Spirit came on them and why is that significant? *(They spoke in tongues and prophesied. This took place about twenty-five years after the first outpouring of the Spirit at Pentecost, but the pattern, as written in the above parenthetical remarks, is consistent with the pattern seen throughout Acts.)* What does this situation indicate about the outward evidence of baptism in the Holy Spirit and the ongoing validity of speaking in tongues? *(Acts never presents the outpouring of the Spirit as being so subtle that it takes places without any outward evidence. Instead, it reveals it to be an identifiable experience that could be verified: the initial evidence of speaking in tongues—a Holy Spirit-inspired way of speaking, praying or praising God in a language the Christian has never learned—and prophesying. Perhaps God chose something as unusual as speaking in tongues because the tongue is the most unruly part of the body [see James 3:5].)*

PRAY: Give God thanks for His gift of the Holy Spirit. Thank Jesus for sending the Spirit to baptize His followers.

ACT: If you've been baptized in the Holy Spirit with the evidence of speaking in tongues, pray in your heavenly language, allowing the Spirit to strengthen and inspire you to serve God more passionately and effectively. If you haven't received this gift since accepting Christ, spend time worshipping God and waiting for His power to fill you.

Acts 19:8–41

THINK: There's a battle waging. Though you can't see it with natural eyes, you can see it's effects in people's lives. It's a spiritual battle for our souls. Most people don't even realize that they're caught up in this battle and that their lives are at stake. But you cannot wage war in your own strength or ingenuity. You must be personally connected to the Commander-in-Chief of God's forces: His Son, Jesus.

RESPOND: What was the significance of Paul's aprons and handkerchiefs bringing healing to the sick? Is this unusual occurrence meant to be imitated? Why or why not? *(Paul's life was so God-saturated that some of the many extraordinary miracles that marked his ministry happened through indirect contact with his handkerchiefs and aprons. These objects weren't magic or holy in themselves, but they represented a point of contact and faith involving someone who had a powerful relationship with God (Matthew 9:20). Note that Paul didn't use these items to gain a following, money, or to impress people with spiritual brawn. Any minister who attempts to gain recognition or financial support by advertising items like this in exchange for healing isn't modeling Paul's motive and Spirit.)* What was the main problem of those who tried to drive out demons by referring to Paul's ministry? What did this indicate about their own relationship with and reliance on Jesus? Like the rioting crowd in the theater, how do people today get caught up in rebellion against Christ without really knowing what they're doing or why (Acts 19:32)?

PRAY: Ask God to help you never rely on anyone else's experience with Jesus, but to help you deepen and strengthen your own relationship with Him so that you'll have His sensitivity to the Holy Spirit and His authority over evil.

ACT: If you're relying on anyone else's relationship with Jesus or reputation in ministry to define your own spiritual experience, confess this to Jesus and determine to develop a deep personal relationship with Him through time in prayer, His Word, and devoted service.

Fire Starter

Acts 20:1-26

THINK: Most of us have probably joked about dozing off during a long-winded sermon. But outside of a little embarrassment, it's doubtful that any of us have suffered from our slumber as Eutychus did. His experience gives whole new meaning to the concept of "falling asleep" in church. But Paul loved the people and held nothing back from them. No doubt it was difficult to take at times, but it was for their good. And nothing was going to interrupt God's instructions and encouragement to His people.

RESPOND: Why was encouragement so important to Christians in Paul's time? Why is it still important among Jesus' followers? If you had been there, how would you have felt for the rest of the night after seeing Eutychus raised to life? What did Paul mean when he said, "I served the Lord with great humility and with tears"? *(Paul's tears weren't a sign of either weakness or over-emotionalism. Paul was deeply grieved over peoples' sins, the consequences of sin, and the distortion of the gospel.)* How is this an example to all followers of Christ? If you were in Paul's place, how would you have felt about going to Jerusalem after the Holy Spirit's warnings? (verses 22,23.) Why do you think the Holy Spirit was leading him into this situation and why did the Spirit warn him about what was ahead? What did Paul mean when he said, "I consider my life worth nothing"? *(Paul's priority was finishing the work God gave him to do, regardless of what happened to him.)*

PRAY: Ask God for strength to face challenges that will test you spiritually and help you grow closer to and more dependent on God. Ask Him to spend your life as He chooses and to honor himself through you, regardless of the cost.

ACT: Encourage as many people as you can today with your words and actions. Show particular compassion to those who don't know God and are obviously hurting or living in rebellion against Him. If concern over your own comfort or reputation has kept you from doing or saying something God has been directing you to do, ask God to forgive you. Then put yourself aside and follow God's direction.

Fire Starter

Acts 20:27-38

THINK: Church ministry is serious business. That doesn't mean we should approach it with a sour or stuffy attitude or that we shouldn't use humor or creative communication. But we must fulfill our roles of service in the Church with great passion, intensity, and devotion because Jesus gave His life to save people and to make them part of His Church. The Church is His primary channel for reaching a lost world with His message of hope and new life. Understand that some will try to infiltrate churches to deceive their people and destroy their work. For these reasons, you must be seriously devoted to knowing God and living by His Word.

RESPOND: In what ways must you keep watch over yourself spiritually (verse 28)? How can you help keep watch over others? What does it mean to be a shepherd of the Church (verse 28)? Who are the "savage wolves" that come into the Church, what motivates them, and what do they do? *(Some leaders, motivated by selfish ambition, pride, money, power, or popularity, will try to build their own kingdom. They may distort the gospel, emphasizing one particular scriptural principle over every other biblical mandate, or mix biblical teaching with worldly or humanistic philosophies that don't promote salvation through faith in Jesus.)* In what ways is it "more blessed to give than to receive"?

PRAY: Ask the Holy Spirit to help you guard yourself spiritually as you are faithful to God's Word and to His plans for you. Ask Him for discernment to recognize deceptive ideas and individuals. Pray for your church leaders, that they will remain true to God's Word and will have wisdom in guarding God's people.

ACT: If you're involved in a church ministry, take time today to invest in that ministry by practicing your gifts, planning future events, making contacts, etc. If you're not actively involved in ministry, find a place of service right away. Talk to a pastor or ministry leader for direction.

Acts 21:1-16

THINK: A lot of people will give you a lot of advice about a lot of things. Sometimes this is helpful. Often it's confusing. But regardless of what you hear and from whom, there's always one source of sure guidance and direction: God's Word. No counsel that is truly from God will ever contradict what He's already revealed in His Word. Even when God uses other people to speak into your life, it will only be to confirm what He shows you through personal time with Him in the Word.

RESPOND: Was the Holy Spirit trying to direct Paul away from Jerusalem? *("Through the Spirit" means "on account of what the Spirit said." The Spirit had told Paul he would suffer, [Acts 20:22,23]. The Spirit wasn't forbidding Paul, but was warning him of what awaited.)* Why was Paul willing to continue on to Jerusalem, despite the risk? What is the first place you should look for God's guidance? How will God sometimes use prophecy in relation to His Word? *(The New Testament doesn't record the legitimate gift of prophecy being used to give personal guidance to people in situations that could be decided by clear biblical principles. Sometimes God will use a legitimate prophetic message to confirm direction He's given a person, or comfort and encourage them.)* How should the views and advice of the majority of your well-meaning Christian friends affect your decisions in regard to following God's plans? How can you best determine God's will (i.e., His desires, plans and intentions based on His character and purposes) for your life in any given situation?

PRAY: Pray that you never turn from God's plans, regardless of who or how many try to dissuade you. Ask God to always draw you to His Word as your source of guidance and to help you understand how it applies in every situation.

ACT: If you've backed away from anything you know God wants you to do because you've feared the difficulty you'll likely encounter, ask God for strength. Then face the challenge and begin boldly pursuing God's plan. If you're facing a significant decision, take extra time today to search God's Word for insight regarding the choice you need to make.

Acts 21:17-36

THINK: Have you ever tried to do something to help someone or made a sincere effort to relate to them and had them not only reject your efforts, but turn on you personally? Perhaps they've lied about you, or believed a lie. Maybe they've misjudged your motives, or even turned abusive. Such unjust treatment can leave you confused, if not angry. But that would defeat your purpose in reaching out. This is part of the reason that God gives example after example in His Word, showing how Christ's followers are bound to endure opposition and treachery. It simply comes with the territory of communicating God's love and truth to a spiritually rebellious world.

RESPOND: What does it mean that the Jewish Christians were "zealous for the law"? Was this appropriate? Why or why not? *(Though James and Paul knew that religious ceremonies could not produce salvation in anyone, they recognized that some parts of the Law and Jewish custom were simply expressions of the believer's faith in Jesus. Jewish believers had a personal relationship with Christ. Their zeal for the law wasn't based on legalism—reliance on rule-keeping and good works primarily to gain salvation and God's favor—but dedication to Jesus and loyalty to God's ways.)* Do you think Paul expected the reaction he got in the temple? Why or why not? Why couldn't the commander get the truth about Paul and the situation from the angry mob? What does this show you about the way you may be treated for trying to relate to people and tell the truth?

PRAY: Ask God to help you know whom and what to trust—and not to trust. Ask Him to prepare you for the disappointment, rejection and pain you will unjustly suffer at times for compassionately conveying the truth.

ACT: Write down a few traditions you have followed in your family or church. Look up verses in the Bible that support or at least refer to that tradition. Be committed to always knowing what you believe about the traditions you uphold.

THINK: Have you ever had to defend yourself against false accusations? As a Christian, you'll be misjudged and unfairly confronted at times. When you are, resist the tendency to get overly defensive. In most cases, the best thing to do is keep quiet and let your gracious actions speak for themselves. But sometimes you can't back away and you must speak up in your own defense. That's when it pays to be close to God and to know His Word so you can stand confident, responding with His wisdom and character.

RESPOND: In what ways did Paul—because of his background— relate to the crowd? What distinct privileges and responsibilities had Jesus given to Paul (verses 14,15)? What's the significance of baptism in water as it relates to spiritual salvation through Jesus? What does baptism demonstrate and symbolize? At what point should a person be baptized in water? How does water baptism specifically relate to Jesus' life and work? *(Water baptism was a ceremony used since the beginning of the Church to indicate that a person was committing himself or herself fully to Jesus. Water baptism symbolizes someone identifying with Jesus in His death, burial, and resurrection, as well as the beginning of new life in Christ.)* Does baptism save people spiritually or remove sins? Why or why not? *(Baptism does not save a person. It is a public testimony of God's forgiveness and transforming work in a person's life.)* Why did Paul leave Jerusalem in the first place, and how did his predicament in this passage confirm the Lord's warning? To whom did the Lord send Paul with His message (verse 21)?

PRAY: Express your gratitude to Jesus for allowing you to identify with Him and to spread His message.

ACT: If you've not yet been baptized in water since receiving Christ and entrusting your life to Him, regardless of how long ago you entered a personal relationship with Jesus, follow this biblical directive and identify with Jesus in this way. Talk to your pastor or a church leader about arranging to be baptized. If you've already been baptized, encourage Christian friends who have not been baptized to do so as a public testimony of their faith in Jesus.

Fire Starter

Acts 22:22 through 23:11

THINK: Do you sometimes find yourself at odds with friends or peers, when they seem to be okay with doing something that you simply don't feel right about? Do you ever wish that the little voice inside you would keep quiet and loosen the restrictions that don't seem to tie others down? The times when you feel like that are the times you must listen even more intently to that inner voice—your conscience—which is really a God-given awareness of right and wrong. While having a strong conscience may at times feel like you're on a short leash, it can also keep you closer to God, His standard, and His purpose for your life. Don't regret having a strong conscience, which allows the Holy Spirit to keep you in line with God.

RESPOND: Why was the crowd so offended by what Paul had just said? What is your conscience and what does it do for you? *(It is a God-given awareness confirming to our mind and personality the rightness or wrongness of our actions.)* Why was Paul able to have a clear conscience? Is your conscience a fool-proof guide that's always right? Why or why not? How can your conscience become weak and insensitive? How can you keep your conscience clear and clean? In what way was Paul gracious toward his accusers, even in the face of false accusation (verse 5)? In what way was Paul wise and shrewd in the way he responded to the council, even getting some of the leaders to defend him (verses 6–9)? How did God comfort and assure Paul in his trouble?

PRAY: Ask God to keep your conscience strong and in line with His heart and principles. Pray that you'll respond appropriately to your conscience, keeping it clear and honoring God in all you do and don't do.

ACT: Pay strict attention to how the Holy Spirit is speaking to your conscience throughout the day. Do what you know is right in all situations. Don't compromise your conscience by doing anything that is questionable. If you've allowed your conscience to become weak, insensitive, or misguided in any area of your life, ask God to forgive you and to restore your conscience to full sensitivity and strength.

203

Fire Starter

Acts 23:12-35

THINK: Isn't it ironic that Paul's accusers—those who were so irate because they thought Paul was undermining their laws and so smug in their claim to uphold the Law—were actually planning to violate God's Law by lying about their motives and plotting to murder Paul without legal appeal (verses 12-22)? But human plots and opposition could not hinder God's plan for Paul to testify about Jesus to more leaders. God can use whatever means necessary—including soldiers, horsemen, and armed defenders (verses 23,24)—to get His people exactly where He wants them.

RESPOND: What do you suppose were some of the thoughts running through Paul's mind as he waited in the barracks through the night and into the next morning? Since the Jews' main complaint and accusation against Paul was that He had disregarded their law and incited others to do so (which was not true), what was ironic and hypocritical about the men's plot against Paul? Why do you think that so much effort and manpower was put into protecting Paul (verses 23,24)? How can you see God's plan and hand of protection at work in all of this? In what ways has God guarded and protected you in order to get you where you needed to be?

PRAY: Give God thanks for His care, guidance, and protection. Praise God for His ability to get you exactly where He intends for you to be, despite the efforts of both spiritual and human enemies to prevent you from fulfilling His plans.

ACT: Perhaps you've sensed in the past that God had a particular plan or course of action for you, but you don't see any way to fulfill that plan or to reach the goal from where you are now. Allow God to renew your hope and vision and to begin revealing to you day by day how you are to proceed on a path toward that goal. Don't get overwhelmed by the destination or by the fact that you don't understand everything. Take one day at a time, and do what you feel God is directing you to do at the moment. Trust Him to help you fulfill your destiny in His time and way.

Fire Starter

Acts 24:1-27

THINK: The world today is full of religion, and perhaps more than ever, people are searching for something spiritual. But many people want "spirituality" on their own terms. They want a religion that fits their lifestyle and a faith that is convenient for their personal belief system. Most people don't realize that their deepest desires can only be satisfied by self-surrender to Christ.

RESPOND: In what way was the lawyer, Tertullus, trying to win Governor Felix's favor? Had Paul been a troublemaker? Why or why not? Who really instigated the riots that seemed to follow Paul (21:27; 22:22; 24:19)? What was the one "accusation" to which Paul admitted? What was the significance of referring to salvation through Jesus as "the Way"? *(Spiritual salvation provided by Jesus was called "the Way." The Greek word—bodos—implies a path or road. New Testament Christians saw salvation not just as an experience, but also a path to walk by faith. We, too, must determine to walk this road for the rest of our lives so that we can enter the final salvation of an eternal relationship and home with God.)* Why did Paul have favor with the governor (verse 22)? What does this likely indicate about Felix's past encounters with or impressions of people who belonged to "the Way"? How does this challenge you regarding your conduct toward people who don't follow Jesus? In what ways is it evident that people today—like Felix (verse 25)—want to listen to and follow only religious views and practices that are convenient?

PRAY: Ask God to give you wisdom and grace in responding to opposition and accusation. Ask God to give you favor with unbelievers as you strive to honor God, and keep a clear conscience toward Him and others.

ACT: If in any way you've set an unfavorable example to non-Christians by behaving or responding to them in a harsh, arrogant or less than gracious way, go and apologize to the individuals involved. This includes times when you may have tried to defend your faith and ended up arguing about spiritual issues, but it also includes times when you simply talked or acted inappropriately.

Acts 25:1-12

THINK: Have you ever known someone who was out to get you for no good reason? Perhaps they were jealous. Maybe they thought you wronged them in some way. Then again, maybe they were trying to impress others by trying to make themselves look tough, cool or in control, and you were the most accessible victim. For Paul, personal opposition was a way of life. But he knew what his accusers were up to, and with God's help he was able to refute them time and again. You, on the other hand, may have no idea what someone has against you. God, however, knows what you're facing, and He will help you just as He helped Paul. The situation may not go away, but it won't stop God from getting you where you need to be and giving you the influence He intends for you to have.

RESPOND: Why were the religious leaders still bent on killing Paul after more than two years? What was it about Paul that worried them so much? Why was Paul confident that he had done nothing to violate the law? Why are people often willing to compromise what they know is right just so they can please or impress other people? Why was Paul unafraid to die? Why do you think God took Paul through such a long and difficult ordeal in order to send Him to Rome when he could have gotten him there through an easier way?

PRAY: Ask God to help you patiently trust Him when He takes you the long, hard way to your destination.

ACT: Are there people in your life—at school, work, or even at home or church—who seem like they're on a mission to bring you down in some way? Pray for the situation and the individuals involved. Then approach them humbly and graciously to see if there is an issue and if there is anything you can do to help resolve it. Continue to pray for them whenever you think of or see them.

Acts 25:13 through 26:1

THINK: If you asked people who Jesus is, what do you think most would say? Whether or not they know the Bible or believe that Jesus' life has anything to do with theirs, most will still likely claim that His greatest influence came from His sacrifice—His death. If they believe He rose from the dead, some would accurately conclude that His greatest influence and triumph came through that act. Either way, Jesus' greatest impression on humanity—those who accept Him and those who don't—came through the most difficult and uncommon aspects of His life. The same is true with His followers. Their greatest influence most often comes through difficult and unusual circumstances. As with Jesus, the journey to your destiny will not be an easy road, but it will likely be an adventurous one.

RESPOND: Why was the governor confused about Jesus and whether He was dead or alive? In what ways are people today confused about Jesus because of the mixed signals they get from both religious and nonreligious people? What are some of the misconceptions people have about Jesus? What was unusual about the way Paul got to meet with and testify to so many influential leaders? Why does God often take His people through difficult times and unusual routes in order to give them the greatest opportunities?

PRAY: Ask God to help you conduct yourself in ways that won't send mixed signals, but instead convey to others an accurate impression of Jesus. Ask God to give you influence with those in authority, even through difficult situations.

ACT: Show special kindness, consideration, and helpfulness to any leaders in your life—parents, teachers, administrators, supervisors, pastors, etc. Go out of your way to serve them in practical ways, realizing that this is one of the best ways to gain favor and influence with people in authority.

Acts 26:2-18

THINK: If you've followed Jesus for a while, chances are you've heard powerful testimonies of how God used admittedly unlikely mouthpieces to dramatically influence others to accept Christ—sometimes changing entire schools or communities. Hearing stories like that, it's easy to envy those involved and to wonder what it would be like to be used by God in an extraordinary way. But these kinds of results typically came at a price—a price that included the boldness to step out at some point and start a tough conversation. Those who make a habit of speaking boldly and compassionately about God will eventually be part of something supernatural.

RESPOND: What was the "hope in what God promised our fathers" (verse 6) for which Paul was on trial? As radical as Paul had been in persecuting Jesus' followers, what does his dramatic life-transformation prove? What did it take to turn Paul's life around? What evidence have you seen of God's life-transforming power? In what way are spiritually lost people under Satan's power, and how does Jesus' message turn people "from the power of Satan to God" (verse 18)? What does it mean that Jesus' followers are "sanctified by faith in me [Jesus]" (verse 18)?

PRAY: Pray for people you know who seem far from God or are opposed to Jesus. Ask God to transform their lives and to use you in the process. Pray that whenever Jesus' message is presented through the ministries of your church—or through you personally—it has the intended effects in people's lives, bringing hope, inspiration, healing, and life.

ACT: Look for people who have made it fairly obvious that they don't follow Jesus. Though you can't typically judge by appearances, you may be familiar with their views toward God or Christianity. Initiate conversation with a couple of these individuals about what they believe and why. Exercises like these require a bold step, but they stretch your faith and help you become accustomed to talking about spiritual issues, faith and Jesus in a variety of situations. Doing this a time or two can take you to a whole new level of spiritual boldness.

Fire Starter

Acts 26:19-32

THINK: There's a reason most people don't fulfill their full potential and make the impact they could on the world. It's because they are too image-conscious. They're afraid to look ridiculous or foolish. It's not that you should actually be ridiculous or foolish or "out of your mind" (verse 24), but most people who have done great and worthwhile things were considered to be that way at some point by other people. But the criticism and rejection didn't stop them from saying, doing, or being the kind of people God could use to bring positive change to the world.

RESPOND: How do people demonstrate that they've truly repented (i.e., turned from their own way to follow Jesus)? *(While good deeds don't spiritually save a person, they prove the sincerity of one's faith and commitment to living life by God's principles of service and compassion.)* Why had people not been able to kill Paul, and why had God kept him alive (verse 22)? What does this indicate about why God protects and preserves the lives of His followers? How can you be more effective in testifying about Jesus and conveying His message? What had Moses and the prophets predicted about Christ (verse 23)? Why did Festus think Paul was insane (verse 24)? What was Paul's desire for all who heard him (verse 29)? Why do you think Paul appealed to Caesar even though he probably could have been set free?

PRAY: Ask Jesus to help you to more effectively hear from Him and communicate His message. Ask Him to help you recognize and take advantage of the opportunities He gives you every day to impact lives for Him.

ACT: Throughout the day, look for ways that God may be opening doors or setting up opportunities for you to do or say things that would honor Him. These don't have to be big or unusual events, but simple occurrences that provide an opportunity to serve someone, to meet a need, to offer encouragement, to invite someone to a ministry event, to talk about spiritual issues, or to get into a conversation about Jesus.

Acts 27:1-26

THINK: What do you do when you turn out to be right and someone else turns out to be wrong and you're tempted to say, "I told you so!"? Knowing that you don't like to hear those words any more than anyone else does, can you resist the urge to prove yourself and instead be considerate of others? You see, even when Paul said, "you should have taken my advice" (verse 21), he wasn't trying to prove a point or make himself look better. Rather, he was looking out for those around him, trying to encourage them and offer hope in a seemingly hopeless situation.

RESPOND: Why do you think that Julius showed kindness and favor to Paul (verse 3)? Why do you think Paul warned the ship's crew of impending disaster (verses 9,10)? Where did he get his insight? How could Paul be so courageous while everyone else, including the experienced sailors, feared for their lives? *(Though physically and legally a prisoner, Paul was spiritually a free man because of his relationship with Jesus. That relationship and experience with Christ gave Paul a keen awareness of God's presence and, therefore, freedom from fear.)* How would you have felt throughout this entire adventure?

PRAY: Ask God to give you wisdom, insight and discernment regarding His plans and purposes so that you can effectively help and influence others for Him. Pray that God gives you such an uncommon courage through severe circumstance that it will be an inspiration and example to everyone around you.

ACT: If you're facing a difficult or troubling situation—particularly one that involves other people, such as your family or your Bible club—trust God to help you display uncommon courage and peace through this situation. If others ask you about your calm attitude, let them know that you're trusting God, and encourage them to do the same. You might even ask them to pray with you about the situation. Also, pay attention to all of the suggestions and advice you get today. Consider how each of these might or might not fit with God's principles, plans, and purposes. In each situation, make the choice, and take the action that seems most pleasing to God.

Acts 27:27-44

THINK: How do you respond in a crisis? How would you respond in a truly desperate, life-threatening, all-hope-seems-lost emergency that's completely out of your control? Would you be calm, collected, and comforting to those around you? Or would you have a major meltdown? In times like that, a person's faith, character and priorities are put to the test. That's when it becomes apparent what—or who—they are really relying on for life. Would God's peace, power, and confidence shine through you in your darkest, stormiest moment?

RESPOND: After God had already promised Paul that He would spare the lives of all those sailing with him, how could Paul now say that "unless these men stay with the ship, you cannot be saved" (verse 31)? *(Throughout the Bible, we can see that his promises to people are usually conditional on their obedience to his will.)* Why do you think that the centurion and soldiers believed Paul and were willing to stake their lives on his advice (verses 31,32)? Why do you think Paul's words were encouraging to the men (verses 33-36)? Do you think you would have been as calm and confident as Paul was throughout this entire ordeal? Why or why not? Why was he so certain of a positive outcome?

PRAY: Ask God to give you a greater understanding of His Word and a greater sensitivity to His voice as you spend time in prayer. Then pray that you always take Him at His Word and that you follow His direction with confidence and without hesitation. Pray that God uses you to encourage people who have lost hope.

ACT: Look for people today who seem to need hope or encouragement. Allow God to use you to inspire these individuals through simple acts or words of kindness. Spend as much time as you can with these people, perhaps eating lunch with them, walking to class with them, or giving them a ride. If you know of anyone whom you won't see today but you know they're struggling with hope, contact them by phone, e-mail, text message, etc.

Acts 28:1-16

THINK: Are you ready for God to use you without even a moment's notice? Would you be prepared for Him to work powerfully through you in even the most unsuitable circumstances? Are you close enough to Jesus that His power flows through you almost automatically? Are you so in tune with His desires that you can sense what, when, and where He wants you to do something that will unquestionably bring honor to Him? That's how Paul lived. How about you?

RESPOND: Why did the islanders go from thinking Paul was a murderer to thinking he was a god (verses 3-7)? What does this reveal about their beliefs? Why didn't Paul suffer any ill effects from the snake bite? *(Note that Paul didn't go looking for a snake to handle. He was neither testing God nor showing off his spiritual power or faith. Under the dire circumstances, God protected him.)* What do the events at Publius' estate indicate about Paul's readiness to do God's work (verses 7-9)? In what way does this challenge you personally? Do you think you're prepared to minister in any situation? Why or why not? What would it take for you to become prepared? How does being with other Christians encourage you? Are people typically encouraged by spending time with you? Why or why not? How can you be more encouraging?

PRAY: Ask God to help you become better prepared to serve His purposes in all situations at all times. Pray that you grow closer to Him and more sensitive to His direction in the process. Ask God to make you an encouragement to the people you are around every day—those who follow Jesus and those who don't.

ACT: Ask God to open your eyes spiritually so you can recognize all of the opportunities He gives you throughout the day to offer encouragement, help, healing, and to talk outright about Jesus. Boldly act on each of these opportunities, trusting God to use you to influence as many people as possible for Him. Conduct yourself in such a way (including your attitude) that everyone who comes in contact with you has a positive, uplifting experience.

Acts 28:17-31

THINK: The vast majority of people will always reject the truth about Jesus. His message will offend them. It won't make sense to spiritually closed minds and hard hearts. God's Word makes it clear that apart from Him we're spiritually blind and under the influence of evil, so people reject the Word's testimony about Jesus. And yet, the Church and it's mission prevails. Jesus' message will continue to spread. So never lose heart. You're called to be part of this victorious mission, which evil forces will never defeat as the supernatural acts of the Holy Spirit continue to flourish through Jesus' followers for all time.

RESPOND: How was Paul's preaching different from some ministers' today when they find that their message offends people (verse 31)? While you must be able to convey Jesus' message to people in understandable and relevant terms, in what ways must you still deliver the message "boldly and without hindrance" (verse 31) and without compromise? In what ways is the open-ended conclusion of the Book of Acts appropriate as it relates to Jesus' followers and the Church to this day? *(Jesus' mission for His Church—His true followers worldwide—isn't complete, and won't be until His return. Until then, God intends the working of the Holy Spirit and preaching of the gospel to continue.)* In what ways do the events in Acts serve as a pattern for God's people today?

PRAY: Pray for peers at school, co-workers at your job, people in your community, and even your family members whose spiritual eyes, ears, and hearts are currently closed to Christ. Pray that they would encounter His love through you in a way that makes them more receptive to a bold and uncompromised message of Jesus.

ACT: If you're not already part of a Bible or prayer group at your school, investigate the opportunities and join an existing group. If there are none, talk to your youth leader for advice on starting one. If you're already part of a club, start a dialogue about innovative ways to grow and reach your campus through acts of service and outreach.

Romans 1:1-17

THINK: "My faith is a personal issue." You've probably heard someone make a statement like that. Often, this is a person's excuse for keeping quiet about what he or she believes, or it's an attempt to silence others who would be more vocal about their faith. Certainly, a relationship with Jesus is deeply personal, but it's not meant to be a private issue. Christians are not supposed to keep the message of Jesus to themselves. So don't keep your faith to yourself, and don't be ashamed of the only message that has the power to save people for eternity.

RESPOND: What is the relationship between obedience and true, saving faith? *(True, saving faith is identified by a willful choice to join one's life to God, and follow His Son, Jesus, in love, devotion, gratitude, and obedience.)* What can you tell about Paul's relationship with the Roman believers from the opening of this letter? How does this challenge you regarding your relationship with those whom you lead, serve and work alongside in the church? Why was Paul "not ashamed of the gospel"? In what way are verses 16 and 17 key to the entire book of Romans? How would you define or describe spiritual "salvation"? What is "righteousness" and what does it mean to be righteous? *(Biblical righteousness is being in right relationship with God through faith in Jesus and obedience to God's Word.)* How are faith and righteousness related? (One who is righteous—in right standing with God—lives by faith, growing from one level of maturity to another.)

PRAY: Ask God to help you demonstrate your faith by obeying His Word. Pray that you'll never be ashamed of Jesus' message but that you'll trust it's power to transform lives as you boldly share it. Thank Jesus for your spiritual salvation.

ACT: Sometime today, actually demonstrate your faith by obeying something specific from God's Word or the prompting of the Holy Spirit (He will only prompt you to do things in line with God's Word and will). Ask someone to hold you accountable or just encourage you to be obedient. Also, look for ways to instigate spiritual conversations.

Romans 1:18-32

THINK: Have you noticed that a lot of people who are considered intelligent by human standards are skeptical of—or outright opposed to—spiritual issues, particularly Christian faith and the standards of God's Word. This proves that worldly wisdom is essentially the opposite of true, godly wisdom. But those who are humble and open-minded enough to consider how God has revealed himself and to take Him at His Word will discover the truth.

RESPOND: What is "the wrath of God" and what provokes it? *(The wrath of God is not a cosmic temper tantrum or an out-of-nowhere angry outburst. Rather, it's a demonstration of God's justice and justified anger over anything defiant to his standards and character. God's wrath is provoked by the evil behavior of people, nations, and by the unfaithfulness of God's people.)* How is God's wrath evident at present, and how will it be unleashed in the future? How can people escape God's wrath? In what ways do people who defy God demonstrate foolishness? What does it mean that people exchange God's truth for a lie, and how does this relate to honoring other things above God? What does this passage indicate about homosexual behavior? *(Even though the word "homosexual" or "homosexuality" isn't used in this passage, it must be considered that this was written in another language, and it describes homosexual activity in plain and literal terms.)* What other behaviors result from failing to honor and follow God (verses 29–31)? How can God transform people's lives, helping them overcome sinful tendencies?

PRAY: Give God thanks for who He is and for specific things He does in your life. Pray that people you know who are caught up in God-defying behaviors and lifestyles will recognize God's truth and trust Him to transform their lives.

ACT: Look through several news and information sources, making mental note of how people approve of ungodly behaviors. Pray for the people and situations you come across in this exercise.

Romans 2:1-29

THINK: God isn't saying that we shouldn't use judgment. In fact, chapter 1 concludes by emphasizing the evils of excusing or approving bad behaviors. God's "tolerance" (verse 4) isn't like the world's, which basically allows people to do as they choose regardless of what the Bible says. Still, God is patient, giving people time to see the error of their ways so they can turn to Him for forgiveness before He judges them. The primary judgments Christians make must be toward themselves personally. Certainly we should stand for what's right and influence others to do the same. But we must ensure that our own lives are free from hypocrisy, setting an example of what it means to follow God.

RESPOND: Why were those to whom Paul originally addressed his remarks wrong in judging others? Jesus' followers are supposed to inspire others—by actions as well as words—to trust God, follow Him and do right. However, under what conditions is it not right for people in the church to challenge others about ungodly behavior? (verse 3) What must Christians do before attempting to influence others to do what's right? In what ways do some who claim to follow God actually dishonor God among others who don't follow Him? *(The benefits of God's Law became a liability when Paul's fellow Jews failed to live by them. For many, there was a disconnect between what they professed and what they practiced. This hypocrisy gave non-Jews reason to curse, doubt, and disregard God. In the same way, today, compromise in churches and by inconsiderate Christians makes a mockery of the gospel, giving many an excuse to slander Jesus' name and reputation.)*

PRAY: Ask God to help you never overlook ungodliness in your own life and to expose ways in which you're being judgmental and hypocritical. Ask Him to forgive such attitudes and actions and to make you a worthy example to others.

ACT: Stop judging others for the types of things you're still struggling with in your own life. If you're doing anything that could possibly dishonor God, ask Him to forgive you, then stop that behavior immediately.

Romans 3:1-31

THINK: The fact that most people choose not to trust God doesn't diminish the fact that He's proven to be completely trustworthy (verse 3). Through the personal sacrifice of His Son, Jesus Christ, God has made a way for us to enter a right relationship with himself and to fulfill His ultimate purpose for our individual lives. Jesus' sacrifice completely satisfied God's justice and completely provides for your forgiveness and eternal life—if you completely trust Him.

RESPOND: How does our unrighteousness bring out God's righteousness more clearly (verse 5)? In what way are "all under sin"? *(Everyone in the world is born in spiritual slavery to a sinful nature—an innate tendency to go their own God-defying ways. Consequently, all are guilty in relation to God and deserving of death and permanent separation from Him. Of course, God's loving response to this truth is by the grace, forgiveness, and spiritual salvation offered through His Son Jesus.)* What does it mean to have "no fear or God" (verse 18), and how does that contribute to people's persistently sinful condition? *(Fearing God is having a deep awe and reverence for Him, which keeps us aware of our accountability to Him.)* In what way does God's Law make us aware of sin (i.e., our own God-defying nature, verse 20)? What is the "righteousness from God," and how can a person receive it? *(People could never earn God's mercy on their own merit, so God has provided a way to be restored to Him and made righteous through faith in Jesus Christ.)* Why can't anyone boast about how they are saved spiritually (verses 27,28)? Does the fact that we receive spiritual salvation through faith make following God's Law unnecessary and obsolete? Why or why not?

PRAY: Give God thanks for His standard of living that makes you aware of your sin and your need for His forgiveness. Thank Jesus for providing that forgiveness and a fresh start with God by dying in your place.

ACT: Practice how you would explain to someone in practical terms what Jesus has done and how they can receive His gifts of forgiveness and eternal life.

Romans 4:1-25

THINK: What was it about Abraham's faith that was so outstanding? It had little to do with Abraham and everything to do with God. Abraham was fully persuaded that God had the ability to fulfill His promise, despite the circumstances. You see, it's one thing to believe in God's ability—the fact that He can do anything—but it's another thing to trust that He actually will do anything He promises. Do you take God at His Word to the point of proving your faith by actions?

RESPOND: Why was Abraham credited with being righteous—in right relationship with God? *(Abraham was loyal and devoted to God and believed His promises, and responded with obedience to God's instructions.)* How does faith allow a person to enter and maintain a right relationship with God? Why can't we work for or earn a right relationship with God? What are the traits of true saving faith? How would you describe God's grace, and how it relates to spiritual salvation? *(If salvation were earned by obedience strictly, no one could make the cut. Since salvation is through faith by God's grace, everyone can be saved spiritually.)* What does verse 17 indicate about God's character and power, and how does this relate to Abraham's personal experience in trusting God (verses 18–21)? How does Jesus' life provide "for our justification," and how does this apply to believers' lives on an ongoing basis? *(Justification is our "not guilty" verdict in relation to God, and is a life-long spiritual condition of staying close with Jesus.)*

PRAY: Give God thanks for His grace—His unmerited favor, unearned benefits and undeserved love—that made spiritual salvation available to you. Ask Jesus to strengthen your faith and to help you trust not only in His ability, but also in His promises so that you always take God at His Word and rely on Him in all circumstances.

ACT: Consider the decisions you are currently facing or will soon face. In each of these situations, exercise your faith and make the choice that best reflects your trust in Jesus.

Romans 5:1-11

THINK: Why do people reject Jesus because of other things in life or because of what other people think? Why do His own followers often tend to be timid about their relationship with Him? After all, Jesus did for us what no one else ever would or could. Jesus died for the entire human race that, for the most part, totally disregards and defies Him and will never even care to know Him. Yet He gave everything for the opportunity to have a relationship with such people. It shouldn't matter what anyone else does or thinks. No one will ever love you like Jesus does.

RESPOND: What kinds of "sufferings" is Paul referring to in verse 3, and how can suffering be a blessing and reason to rejoice for Christ's followers? *(In the middle of suffering God assures us of His presence, helps us depend on and grow closer to Him. Through challenges, we develop strength and maturity.)* How has suffering in your life produced character in you? How does character produce hope (verse 4)? What kind of hope does verse 5 talk about, and why does it not disappoint those who trust Jesus? *(Biblical hope isn't just wishful thinking about what might happen. It a confidence from God, sure because it's based on God's Word.)* According to verse 8, what is significant about how and when Jesus died for us? What does it mean that "we were God's enemies," and why is that significant regarding God's actions toward us? What does it mean to be reconciled to God, and how did Jesus provide for this?

PRAY: Thank Jesus for making a way for you to become right with God by giving His life for us while we still opposed Him. Ask God to help you grow in character and to strengthen your hope in Him as you go through tough times. Give thanks for the presence of the Holy Spirit that enables you to continuously experience God's love.

ACT: Consider any tough times you're currently experiencing, as well as things you've suffered in the past. How can these be faith-builders and character-builders in your life? Apply what you've learned in the past about trusting God to your present situations.

Fire Starter

Romans 5:12-21

THINK: Consider all of the death and destruction that human sin and rebellion against God has caused in the world. How much more can God's gracious gift of salvation provide life and restoration to those who trust Him? Eventually, His judgment will rid the world of sin and restore everything to perfect harmony (Revelation 20:11 through 21:4). Are you relying on the Holy Spirit to help you convey Jesus' message of hope and new life to those who are still enslaved by sin?

RESPOND: How did sin gain entrance into the human race, and how has it affected individual lives and the world ever since? *(When Adam gave in to temptation, rebellion against God gained entrance into the human race. The result is that sin earned "star status" as a normal element of being human; everyone born has inherited Adam's sinful tendency.)* Why and in what way are all people responsible for their own sin? What is the ultimate consequence of sin? (verse 14) What is God's gift, what does it do, and how is it "not like the trespass" (verse 15)? *(Jesus provided spiritual salvation and restoration to undo the effects of the "trespass"—humankind's rebellion against God. If sin could cause so much destruction, how much more can God's salvation provide restoration?)* How would you define or describe God's grace?

PRAY: Pray that you'll never make excuses for your own wrongdoing, but that God will help you to always recognize and confess your sin to Him, trusting His grace to keep you in right relationship with God. Give Him thanks for His great gifts of forgiveness, spiritual salvation, and eternal life with Jesus.

ACT: Re-read verses 15 and 16. Make a short list of death-inducing sins in your life (all sin plants seeds of spiritual, emotional, relational, or physical death). Next to your list, take a red pen or marker and write the words: the gift—salvation through Jesus—followed this trespass and brought justification for me. As a recipient of God's grace, also consider yourself an agent of His grace toward others. Treat them in ways that honor Jesus and may initiate spiritual conversations.

Fire Starter

Romans 6:1-14

THINK: Part of what it means to be "dead to sin" (verse 11) is being in a condition where the devil's temptations and your own tendency to defy God does not entice, provoke, or get the best of you. You must rely on the Holy Spirit, continually surrendering your will to God's and refusing to engage in attitudes or actions that will allow temptation to gain a hold.

RESPOND: What is "sin"—its characteristics, causes, and effects? *(Sin is any act of disobedience or disregard for God's instructions or standards. The essence of sin is selfishness.)* How is it an abuse of God's grace to deliberately go our own ways, disobeying and defying God? What's the significance and symbolism of baptism in regard to Jesus' death, burial, and resurrection? *(Water baptism for Christ's followers is symbolic of identification with Jesus' death, burial, and resurrection. It also represents a spiritual cleansing—rejecting sin and embracing obedience to and grace from God.)* Since Jesus was sinless, what does it mean that "death no longer has mastery over him" and "he died to sin once for all"? *(Jesus, though sinless, suffered from and was humiliated by the power and punishment of sin for our sake.)* In what way must a follower of Jesus continually die to sin, and how does one do this? *(Making a deliberate choice to neither feed nor exercise your sinful tendencies—which requires you to be honest with yourself and others about what exactly your sinful tendencies are.)* How can Jesus' followers resist and overcome sin's tendency to regain control of their lives (verses 12,13)?

PRAY: Thank Jesus for dying in your place to provide freedom from sin and its ultimate consequences. Ask Him to help you die daily to the sinful tendencies of your human nature and to continually serve His purposes in all you think, say, and do.

ACT: Don't be surprised if you struggle with certain sins over and over if you're doing things that feed those tendencies and temptations. Instead, choose attitudes and activities that will feed and strengthen your spirit, enhance your relationship with Jesus, and promote your service for Him.

Fire Starter

Romans 6:15 through 7:6

THINK: A lot of people think that they aren't getting what they deserve in life. For Jesus' followers, this is certainly true—and that's a good thing. What all people really deserve for going their own way and defying God is death (6:23) and eternal separation from God. But God offers the gift of forgiveness and eternal life to all who accept and entrust their lives to Him.

RESPOND: Does the fact that Jesus' followers are "under grace" mean that they don't need to be concerned about sin or that they can sin without punishment? Why or why not? *(The choices to serve God and not to sin were never a one-time deal. These choices should be made daily.)* What can happen if a Christian stops resisting sin's influence or persistently chooses to defy God? (verse 16) Where can Christians today find the standards and patterns God has given to guide their lives? What does it mean to "become slaves to righteousness" (verse 18) and "slaves to God" (verse 22)? How does this lead to "holiness" (verse 19,22), which means moral purity? In what way is death earned? In what way is eternal life a gift, and how does a person receive it? What does it mean that Jesus' followers have "died to the law through the body of Christ"? *(We no longer live by Old Testament rules, rituals, and sacrifices. Jesus is the fulfillment of that Law. Because of Jesus' life, death, and resurrection, He has become our access to God.)*

PRAY: Ask God to keep you aware of the sinful tendencies of your human nature and to help you follow the pattern of His Word to overcome sin and fulfill His purposes. Give God thanks for not giving you the punishment you deserve for sin, but giving you instead the priceless gift of eternal life through faith in Jesus.

ACT: Ask God to expose any area in your life in which you may be taking His grace for granted and toying with sin. Then rely on His help to deal with that issue and to replace it with something that will benefit you spiritually.

Romans 7:7-25

THINK: Some feel that in this passage Paul is simply being candid about his ongoing struggle with sin. However, In light of what he said about dying to sin (chapter 6) and about the power Christ gives us over our sinful nature (chapter 8), it's unlikely that Paul consistently gave in to sin (verse 19). It's more likely that he's speaking of his experience before encountering Christ (Acts 9), when he depended on strict adherence to God's Law to be "righteous" and to find favor with God. Ultimately, he found that pleasing God is impossible apart from Christ (verse 25).

RESPOND: What purposes does God's Law serve—both in relation to sin and in relation to following Jesus (verses 7,13)? Why is it useless to attempt to live right and please God by our own efforts? *(Without depending on God's grace, mercy, and strength, our own efforts are weak and inconsistent.)* What does God's Law expose in our lives, and how does it point us to Jesus? What condition does Paul describe by saying, "I am unspiritual, sold as a slave to sin"? *(Paul is clarifying the inability of the Law to rescue a person who hasn't been renewed by a personal relationship with Jesus.)* In what way is a Christian's struggle with his or her sinful human nature different from someone who struggles to do right apart from a relationship with Jesus? Why is it impossible to find favor with God, overcome sin, and live by God's standard apart from a personal relationship with Jesus? *(Without a relationship with Jesus, a person's sinful nature remains dominant.)*

PRAY: Thank Jesus for the ongoing victory that is yours over sin as you continually rely on His power and obey His Word.

ACT: Are you trying to overcome a sin or temptation, or trying to do something for God, in your own strength—without completely relying on Him? Spend time listening to God and searching His Word for direction regarding this issue. Then take the action you feel He desires. Simply trust Jesus and aim to honor Him in what you do or don't do.

Romans 8:1-17

THINK: Most crime, destruction, depression, and other ills in society could probably be traced to a persistent sense of guilt and regret in individuals' lives. If only more people understood that they could truly be forgiven, freed from guilt, and given a fresh start. That's the power of Jesus' love to change individuals, communities, societies, and the world.

RESPOND: What does it mean to be "in Christ"? What is "the law of the Spirit of life" and how does it free believers from the law of sin and death? *(This phrase refers to the life-regulating and motivating power of the Holy Spirit working in a Christ-follower's life.)* Can a person follow their sinful nature and the Holy Spirit at the same time? Why or why not? *(Those who don't rely on the Holy Spirit's power to resist sinful tendencies and ungodly desires become spiritually weakened. Eventually, without repenting of sin, they will rebel against God.)* Who has the Holy Spirit living in them and how does that affect their lives? *(From the moment people enter into a surrendered relationship with Jesus, they have the Holy Spirit living in them.)* What's it like to be "led by the Spirit of God"? *(The Holy Spirit's leading—often inner promptings or motivations—come by reading God's Word, praying and listening to God so regularly that it becomes natural [1 Corinthians 12:7–10].)* If you follow the Spirit, what is your relationship with God the Father? What does it mean to be "heirs of God and co-heirs with Christ" (verse 17)?

PRAY: Thank Jesus for freedom from guilt, for the presence of the Holy Spirit, for power over sin, and for strength to do right. Thank the Father for accepting you as His child and for giving you an eternal inheritance with Jesus.

ACT: If you're struggling with guilt from past experiences or present temptations, consider the great lengths to which Jesus went to provide forgiveness and victory over those things. Don't neglect His gift. Move on in the Father's love and the Holy Spirit's power. Focus on attitudes and actions that feed and strengthen your spirit.

Fire Starter

Romans 8:18-39

THINK: While there are legitimate victims in any society, Jesus' followers never have to view life as a victim. Regardless of what happens to them, they are overcomers. Nothing can rob them of their joy and ultimate reward. Christians are victors who are free to focus on what they can do for others.

RESPOND: What "sufferings" do we experience as humans and as followers of Jesus? What perspective should Christians have regarding these troubles and why? How does the Spirit help our weaknesses? *(The Holy Spirit empowers us to be victors instead of victims in our circumstances.)* What does it mean that "the Spirit himself intercedes for us with groans that cannot be expressed"? *(The Holy Spirit communicates with God through our inner cries and longings of our hearts when we don't have adequate words to express our needs.)* What does it mean that God "foreknew" us and "predestined [those He foreknew] to be conformed to the likeness of His Son"? *("Foreknew" means God chose to demonstrate His love to people before we knew Him through Jesus. "Election" refers to God's choice to claim for himself a people, based on their choice to accept forgiveness from Him and enter into a relationship with Jesus. "Predestination"—to decide beforehand—is what God has determined will happen to His people as a result of their choice to follow and serve Him.)* How do you feel about the fact that God is for you (verse 31) and Jesus "is also interceding for us" (verse 34)?

PRAY: Thank Jesus for the fact that no trouble or suffering in this life can compare to what He has in store for you in eternity. Thank Him that these things help you rely more on Him and that He's given you ultimate victory through it all.

ACT: Consider any trouble, hardship or suffering that you currently face. Knowing that you have God's love and strength to help you through it all, ask Him to show you how to turn these situations for good. A good attitude through tough times can inspire others and may lead to opportunities to talk about your faith.

Fire Starter

Romans 9:1-29

THINK: God can certainly do whatever He desires and chooses; His authority and power are infinite. Though He's always looking out for our best interests, if we choose to resist or reject His plans, we will become calloused and hardened to His guidance, purposes, and persistent love. But if we choose to trust Him, He will take care of us, guide us, and use us for His honor. In addition, we'll become even more sensitive to His presence and responsive to His purposes.

RESPOND: What caused Paul "great sorrow and unceasing anguish"? Are there people in your life about whom you feel this way? What are you doing to influence them for Christ? What do verses 15 and 16 indicate about God's mercy and about your responsibility? *(God's mercy cannot be earned or controlled by people. He has purposed to have mercy on all people, but it's up to people how they will respond to it.)* To whom does God show mercy? *(God shows mercy to people who repent—admit and turn from God-defying ways, accept His forgiveness, and enter into a relationship with Jesus.)* What really causes some people to become hardened toward God? What does it mean that God is sovereign, and how does His character affect His choices and actions? How can a person who is headed for God's wrath become an object of His mercy?

PRAY: Ask God to give you a heart of desperate compassion for spiritually lost people and to help you recognize and capitalize on the opportunities He gives you to reach them with His message of hope and new life. Pray that you'll never resist His love or take it for granted, but that you'll pass it on to others.

ACT: As you go through the day, try to view the people around you through God's eyes of compassion. Notice those who appear to be particularly hardened by the situations of life and try to say or do something to help, encourage and demonstrate God's love to them. Even a simple smile can make a difference.

Romans 9:30 through 10:21

THINK: Receiving spiritual salvation and eternal life is not complicated. It's as simple as asking God to forgive you and surrendering leadership of your life to Jesus. But simple as it is, people can't make this decision unless they receive and believe Jesus' message. That's where your part comes into the process. Whether you're spreading the word yourself or helping to send someone else to deliver it, you can ensure that people everywhere receive the life-saving message of Jesus.

RESPOND: In what ineffective way did many Israelites try to pursue a right relationship with God (verse 32)? In all of their efforts to live by the Law, what part of God's Law did many Israelites miss that kept them from being right with God (verse 4)? What's the significance of confessing "Jesus is Lord"? *(Jesus is referred to as Savior sixteen times in the New Testament and Lord over four hundred and fifty times! No one can truly accept Jesus as Savior without receiving Him as Lord.)* What are the implications of the statement, "Everyone who calls on the name of the Lord will be saved" (verse 13)? *(When someone recognizes their need for God, humbly confesses their sin, and calls on God for mercy, they can receive His forgiveness, and therefore, spiritual salvation.)*

PRAY: Give God thanks for the simplicity of surrendering to Him and receiving His gift of spiritual salvation. Pray that you'll always submit to His authority as Lord of your life. Ask Him to help you do what you can to communicate His message to others, including helping to send others to places you will never be able to go with the message.

ACT: Buy a soft drink for someone who doesn't claim to be a Christian. After small talk, ask what they think of spiritual issues. Listen well, then share how you're growing spiritually, and how your life is different because of salvation through Jesus. Also, set aside extra money this week to give to missions efforts through your church. Give up one monetary birthday gift or allowance to give to missions.

Fire Starter

Romans 11:1-24

THINK: Many people would like for God to prove himself to them. But history has persistently proven that people will fail to acknowledge God, regardless of what He shows them. Israel is a prime example. Despite God's revelations throughout history and through His Word, people of all nationalities and walks of life still choose to remain rebels against God. Yet, His gracious offer of spiritual salvation stands. All who accept and live by it receive the relationship with God that He's always intended for His people—those who have chosen to take their place in God's kingdom.

RESPOND: Did God completely reject the people of Israel who rejected Him? Why or why not? What does it mean to be "chosen by grace"? *(Salvation through Jesus and gifts from God cannot be earned by doing good things. They are a matter of God's grace—His undeserved favor because of Jesus' sacrifice.)* Why are people "broken off" or excluded from a relationship with God? *(The nation of Israel chose to reject God's grace in Jesus.)* What attitude should you have about your relationship with Jesus? Considering how often God's Word says, "Do not fear" or "Do not be afraid," why would He say in verse 20, "Do not be arrogant, but be afraid"? Why must we consider both God's kindness (verse 22) and His sternness? What does it mean to "continue in his [God's] kindness," and how do you do this? What can happen if you do not do this?

PRAY: Give God thanks for your spiritual salvation and for making a place for you in His kingdom. Pray for the nation of Israel, for peace and salvation of Jewish people who have yet to recognize and receive Jesus as Savior. Ask God to encourage those Jewish people who do recognize and serve Jesus as Savior and Lord.

ACT: Go to an online news source or somewhere you could access information on current events pertaining to Israel. Pray for the situation described in these news stories.

Romans 11:25-36

THINK: Have you ever felt that you had at least a little bit about God figured out—and then He surprised you? Or perhaps you tried to give God some advice, only to be relieved that He didn't take it after all. While God wants you to know Him deeply, He doesn't expect you to understand many things about Him or the way He works. Simply know this: God will always do what's best, He will always keep His Word, and He will ultimately accomplish His purposes. It's just a matter of whether you choose to trust Him and follow Him, even when you don't understand.

RESPOND: What is Paul referring to when he talks about "the full number of the Gentiles" coming into God's kingdom? *(This phrase pertains to the completion of God's purpose in inviting people from all nations into a personal relationship with himself. At that time, Jesus will return to judge people in the world.)* During what particular time period will an exceptional number of Jews turn to God and finally accept Jesus as their Messiah (i.e., Savior, Christ)? In what way are all people "bound . . . over to disobedience" (verse 32), and in what way has God shown mercy to all? What do verses 33-36 tell you personally about God? What are some of God's awesome and outstanding traits as highlighted here? What does this passage indicate about God's wisdom and His judgments in relation to us? What does it mean that "from him [God] and through him and to him are all things (verse 36)"? What is Paul's response to God in light of God's awesome attributes?

PRAY: With verses 33-36 as inspiration, praise God for His awesome attributes, including wisdom, justice, and mercy.

ACT: Take two brief prayer walks today. During one, walk through a crowded place—perhaps your school halls, a shopping mall, or a downtown area. Pray silently for the people you see that they would submit to God, receiving forgiveness and renewed purpose in life. For your second walk, go somewhere more secluded, where you can ponder the beauty and mystery of creation. As you walk, worship God for His awesome power and creativity.

Fire Starter

Romans 12:1-16

THINK: What does it mean to worship God? Is it just something you do during a church prayer or song service? In reality, worship is much more than songs or words of praise. True, godly worship involves a lifestyle that honors Jesus in attitudes and actions, as well as words. This includes using your God-given abilities and opportunities to serve and honor Jesus and to benefit others in a way that helps them become more receptive to Him.

RESPOND: What does it mean to "offer your bodies as living sacrifices"? *(Out of gratitude, we should show our devotion to God by loving Him, living by His standards, and serving His purposes. The sacrifice comes in separating ourselves from God-defying practices and patterns so we can pursue depth, maturity, and complete submission to Him.)* In what way is this an "act of worship"? *(True worship isn't simply a church or a music thing, but authentic Christian worship involves God-honoring speech, behavior, and lifestyle choices.)* In what ways do people tend to conform to "the pattern of this world"? Why and how must Jesus' followers resist this? What does it mean to "be transformed by the renewing of your mind," and how does this happen? What does it mean that we all have different "gifts"? What are the main purposes of these gifts? Why do you think it mentions sincere love directly following the gift descriptions (verses 9,10)?

PRAY: Ask God to continually renew your mind so that you can resist conforming to the world's pattern of thinking and living. Pray that all you do today—and every day—will be an act of worship, worthy of identifying with Jesus. Also, give God thanks for the unique abilities He's given you with which you can serve and honor Him.

ACT: Make a conscious effort to view everything you say and do today as an expression of worship—an offering of yourself to God—something that honors Him and conveys His character. Also, consider the study notes related to each specific gift mentioned in verses 6–8. See if your interests and inclinations identify with any of these gifts.

Romans 12:17 through 13:14

THINK: Are you interested or involved in government? God may not be asking you to serve on a political campaign or support one party over another. But He does want you to be involved in the sense of conducting yourself respectfully toward authorities and, more importantly, by being faithful to pray for those in leadership over you.

RESPOND: Why is it important—especially for Jesus' followers—not to repay evil for evil (12:17)? What does it mean that we should try to "live at peace with everyone"? How does God's vengeance differ from human revenge? *(God's vengeance is about His perfect justice in punishing those who willfully rebel against His ways.)* What influence can you have on those who oppose you by doing good to them (Proverbs 25:21,22)? What does it mean to "submit . . . to the governing authorities" (Romans 13:1), why is this important (verse 2), and what are the exceptions to this command? In what way does loving others as ourselves sum up and fulfill the entire Law (verse 10)? Though love is positive, what types of restrictions does it put on people's behaviors? In what ways might Christians sometimes use their rights and freedoms in a way that might mislead, confuse or harm others? What does it mean to "clothe yourselves with the Lord Jesus Christ"? *(To identify with Jesus is to adopt His values and principles, obey His commands, and become like Him in character, faith, and lifestyle.)*

PRAY: Ask Jesus to help you be a person of peace in your relationships and associations with others. Pray for individuals in all levels of government, that they'll lead with wisdom and that they'll come to know Christ if they don't already.

ACT: If you're currently experiencing conflict with anyone, be the peacemaker, and try to settle the issue by making an apology, conceding to the other person's preferences, showing kindness, etc. If you have time, send a letter or e-mail to your mayor, congressional representative, or senator, letting them know that you are praying for them.

Romans 14:1 through 15:4

THINK: Are there certain issues and activities that you feel okay about that other Christians seem to have a problem with? Or perhaps others seem free to do things you can't do in good conscious. We must be careful not to use this passage to justify morally questionable behavior. Our primary concern regarding issues of conscience and personal preference should be to do what best promotes God's work and builds others up.

RESPOND: What criteria should you use to evaluate your choices regarding issues of personal preference? *(Biblical principles should always be the first criteria you use to evaluate personal preferences. Second, ask yourself if God would consider your actions or behaviors to be the best for you spiritually or if they could affect how others view you as a Christian.)* How should concern for others affect your decisions (verse 7)? What does it mean "not to put any stumbling block or obstacle in your brother's way"? *(Paul's warning should help Christians remember they'll not only answer to God for their conduct, but we should be responsible to behave in a way that sets a godly example.)* What are some contemporary issues of conscience in which Christians must be careful not to mislead or misjudge others? How should love affect your decisions (verse 15)? Why are morally questionable activities that affect the mind and spirit completely different from the debatable issues discussed in this passage? How can we destroy God's work by approving certain behaviors that may be questionable to others (verse 22)? In what way did Jesus set the prime example of how we must consider others ahead of ourselves?

PRAY: Ask God to always help you consider how your discretionary choices affect His work in others. Also ask for guidance to do what promotes His purposes and puts the good of others ahead of your personal preferences.

ACT: Make sure that you're not looking down on those who are more restrictive in their behavior. On the other hand, refrain from judging those who seem to take more liberty than you do with certain activities. In all things, don't put your personal preferences ahead of others by approving of activities that may influence them to defy their own consciences.

Fire Starter

Romans 15:5-33

THINK: One of the most effective ways to expand your influence in ministry is to partner with other Christians, particularly those who minister to you. Start by helping to support them. In addition to encouragement, practical service, and financial support, the best means of support is to pray faithfully for those who have ministered to you and alongside of you. In this way, you share in the work God does through them, allowing you to influence many more people for Christ than you would have ever been able to reach on your own.

RESPOND: Why is unity of heart so vital among Christians (verses 5,6)? How can you demonstrate acceptance toward other Christians in the way God does toward you (verse 7)? How does trusting God give you joy and peace (verse 13)? Is it wrong to speak boldly about what God does through you? Why or why not? What must you keep in mind when testifying about great things God does through you? How should you evaluate and measure "success" in ministry? How does Paul's desire expressed in verse 20 inspire you personally? *(Paul's passion was to take Jesus' message to lands and cultures not yet exposed to the gospel.)* In what ways can you personally help to convey Christ's message in places and among people where He is not known? In what way can you be a blessing to those from whom you have benefited spiritually?

PRAY: Pray for spiritual leaders who have had a positive influence on you, that God would continue to guard, refresh, inspire, and use them effectively in His service.

ACT: Do something practical and tangible to help and encourage one of your ministry mentors or leaders. Also, demonstrate acceptance to someone in your church or youth group who has not seemed to fit in yet.

Fire Starter

Romans 16:1-27

THINK: Ordinarily, it's a good thing to develop skills in as many areas of life as possible. But there is at least one way that God wants His people to remain "unskilled" and that is in practicing evil. Becoming "experienced" in ungodly behavior simply gives Satan more opportunities to tempt and trouble us with sin and guilt in the future. But when we avoid evil and refuse to participate in ungodly behavior, we deny Satan the opportunity to tempt us with certain things because we have chosen to remain "innocent" in those areas.

RESPOND: What ministry role did Phoebe fill in the Church, and how is she an example to women and to all believers? *(Phoebe, assistant to the ministers with respect to church business, is believed to have carried this letter to Rome.)* What do verses 3-16 indicate about relationships in ministry and about giving proper recognition to those who faithfully serve the Church? What does it mean to be "innocent about what is evil"? *(The idea of separation from evil isn't a matter of being afraid of the world so much as fearing God in a healthy, reverent way.)* Why must Christians be extremely cautious about the activities in which they participate and the things to which they expose themselves? *(God wants us to grow in our spiritual salvation, our faith, in personal purity, and in service and devotion to Him, and influence of others.)*

PRAY: Ask God to help you remain "innocent about what is evil" by helping you recognize and avoid situations that would tempt you to participate in ungodly behavior. Pray also that you would recognize and avoid teaching that distorts the true message of Jesus and that you would always believe and obey His Word.

ACT: This week, consider if you're allowing yourself to participate in spiritually questionable activities or relationships that may be exposing you to temptations and behaviors that could distract you spiritually. Ask God to purify your mind and spirit from corrupting influences to which you've exposed yourself in the past.

1 Corinthians 1:1-31

THINK: No church is perfect. Most have issues of some sort, and the Corinthian church was no exception. Still, God was working through them, having gifted them with all they needed to serve His purposes (verse 7). Understand that God has placed you exactly where you need to be to learn, grow, and stretch your faith. In addition, He's given your group—through its people—all the abilities needed to pursue God's purposes at this time and place. Humbly do your part, while encouraging others and praying that all of you will work together to reach your part of the world for Christ.

RESPOND: How is your life enriched by your relationship with Jesus (verse 5)? What is a "spiritual gift"? *(Spiritual gifts are God-given abilities enabling people to serve the Church in a way that. honors God and helps people in some way.)* When Paul talked about having no divisions and "being perfectly united in mind and thought," did he mean that Christians should always agree and have the same opinions? Why or why not? Why were the Corinthians quarrelling? What problems arise when Christians get too attached to leaders and follow people more than Christ? Why is worldly wisdom like foolishness to God? *(Worldly wisdom celebrates self-interest and self-sufficiency, and elevates human knowledge above God's knowledge.)* What does Paul mean when he refers to "the foolishness of what was preached"? *(God's message doesn't make sense to people's self-exalting mind-set.)* What do verses 25-29 indicate about how God's values compare to the world's, and why is this an encouragement to many people? What does it mean that "Jesus . . . has become for us wisdom from God"?

PRAY: Ask God to help you keep your eyes on Him and never to put loyalties to leaders ahead of Christ.

ACT: If you're struggling with attitudes about your church or individuals in your group, ask God to help you understand and appreciate how all the people have been uniquely put together to build each other up and accomplish His purposes. Make sure that you're not depending on one of your leaders more than Jesus.

1 Corinthians 2:1-16

THINK: Often, the best known, highest regarded, most sought after ministers are those who demonstrate the sharpest communication skills and seem to posses the most unique insights. While this may be a result of God's gifting, it doesn't make someone's ministry more worthy, more powerful, or more effective in God's view. Regardless of peoples' gifts, God wants your attention to be on His message, His power and His purposes, not on how much you enjoy listening to the speaker.

RESPOND: Though Paul's speaking ability was apparently not impressive, why was his preaching powerful and influential (verses 1-4)? In what ways can the Holy Spirit's power work through godly preaching? *(Recall a time when you experienced or felt God's power through someone's godly preaching.)* How does God reveal what He has prepared for us (verse 10)? *(As you study God's Word, the Holy Spirit can deepen your understanding of truth and God's character and the way He leads people, including you.)* When speaking of Jesus' followers, what does it mean that "we have the mind of Christ"? *(Having the mind of Christ is comprehending His will—His desires and intentions based on His character and purposes, evaluating things from His perspective, and adopting His values. It implies humility, servanthood, and selflessness, putting priority on other's needs, just as Christ did in giving His life for all people.)* Why is this mind-set vital for Jesus' followers and how does it affect their lives?

PRAY: Pray that you would never depend on human abilities and personalities in doing or receiving ministry, but that you would rely on the Holy Spirit's power, guidance,, and insight to understand and apply God's Word.

ACT: As you go through the day, practice having "the mind of Christ" (verse 16) in all situations. Try to maintain attitudes you believe Jesus would have. Do for others what you feel Jesus would do, and say what you feel He wants you to say. Rely on the Holy Spirit to guide you in this way, and be prepared for God to use you to bring encouragement, help, and healing to people.

Fire Starter

1 Corinthians 3:1-23

THINK: People tend to follow rather than lead. In a spiritual sense that's not all bad, since true discipleship involves following Christ and those He places in leadership. However, we must never become so attached to people that we distinguish ourselves from other believers based on our favorite leaders. A mark of spiritual immaturity is disunity that arises from idolizing people (pastors, leaders, musicians, celebrities, etc.). This takes honor from God, the only source of real spiritual growth and power and it's dangerous because of the destruction it causes in churches and individual lives. Anyone who stirs up this kind of trouble will find themselves in deeper trouble with God.

RESPOND: What does it mean that Paul planted and Apollos watered (verse 6)? How does that relate to the various purposes God has for His followers? Why must we keep in mind that God brings spiritual growth (verses 6,7)? What "one purpose" must all God's people work together to fulfill? What does it mean that a person may "be saved, but only as one escaping through flames"? *(Though a Christian is saved because of their relationship with Jesus, there is still a future judgment of their faithfulness and opportunities given them on earth.)* Who or what is God's temple? *(God's Church is His temple. Though the Bible also refers to individual believers' bodies as God's temple [6:19], in this passage, "temple" refers to the Church body as a whole—the dwelling place of His Spirit.)* As a dwelling place for the Holy Spirit, how must those who are part of the Church conduct themselves? Why do you think Paul brings this whole passage back to the issue of not bragging about those we regard as spiritual leaders (verses 21,22)?

PRAY: Pray that you'll never idolize people, but that you'll always depend on God for your spiritual growth. Ask Him to keep you from discouragement when you don't see results from your ministry and to keep you humble when you do.

ACT: Plant some spiritual seeds today by showing kindness and help to people and by looking for opportunities to talk about your faith in Christ.

Fire Starter

1 Corinthians 4:1-21

THINK: It's popular advice these days to "be true to yourself." While this may be a well-intended notion, it's not completely appropriate. Your primary responsibility is to be true and faithful to God. To do so, you must know and rely on His Word, because even your own conscience can fool you when you feel okay about something that's contrary to the principles of God's Word. You must ask God to continually expose your motives and to guide your thoughts and behaviors so you remain faithful to Him, regardless of what happens or how you feel.

RESPOND: What does it mean to have a clear conscience, and why does that not guarantee that you're doing what's right? *(Our conscience is our internal God-given awareness that confirms the rightness or wrongness of our choices. However, just because we feel confident about our actions and motives, we shouldn't presume that we're always correct in our views and actions.)* From verse 8 on, Paul uses sarcasm to challenge and warn the Corinthians against what kinds of attitudes? *(Some in the Corinthian church took pride in their superior knowledge and spiritual gifts, and thought they were above Paul's instruction. There's no place for spiritual arrogance in God's people. On the contrary, Paul went on to show the Corinthian Christians that those who identify with Jesus may very well experience suffering and hardship before glory.)* Why and how did Paul want the Corinthians to follow his example (verse 16)? Why is it so important for Christians' actions to be consistent with their message (verse 17)? Why is it vital to remember that "the kingdom of God is not a matter of talk, but of power" (verse 20)?

PRAY: Ask God to help you be faithful with all He's entrusted to you—including the opportunity to communicate His message and demonstrate His love. Pray that you'll never become prideful about your spiritual opportunities, knowledge, or progress, but that your motives for serving Him will always be pure.

ACT: Find a way to express gratitude to the person who led you to Jesus or who became your main spiritual mentor.

Fire Starter

1 Corinthians 5:1-13

THINK: Sometimes, the church can do a person a favor by letting him or her go their own way—removed from church participation—so he or she can experience the bitter consequences of ungodly actions and reach the point where they have nowhere to turn but to God. While churches need to open their doors to people who don't know God, they must not tolerate God-defying behavior from people who claim to be Christians.

RESPOND: How should Christians feel about immoral behavior among those who claim to follow Christ, and why should they feel this way? What does Paul mean when he says, "Hand this man over to Satan, so that his sinful nature may be destroyed and his spirit saved on the day of the Lord"? *(When a church is forced to expel from its congregation someone who refuses to repent and perhaps influences others to sin as well, it's allowing them to go their own God-defying way. This severe discipline may turn them to God for help and forgiveness, ultimately saving them.)* In what ways are Christians to judge and respond differently to those inside the Church—who claim to be believers—than to those outside the Church? *(The judgment of Christ's followers shouldn't be aimed at those outside the Church, who are still caught up in sinful behavior. However, those who claim to follow Christ but willfully dishonor Him should be held accountable by other believers.)* Why and in what way must people within the Church hold each other accountable?

PRAY: Ask God to help you make right judgments about your own life and accountability to God, and to help you encourage others in the Church to remain true to Him. Then ask Him to give you a heart of compassion for those outside of the Church who naturally defy God.

ACT: Allow God to search your life, exposing any hidden sin. Confess your faults to God, accept His forgiveness, and trust Him to help you make a deliberate change before He enacts further judgment or discipline regarding this issue.

Fire Starter

1 Corinthians 6:1-20

THINK: Some people who claim to be Christians seem to think—or at least act—like it doesn't matter what they do with their bodies. Since salvation is essentially a spiritual matter, they feel that they can use, treat and flaunt their bodies as they desire—without spiritual consequence. But for those who have accepted Jesus' sacrifice to redeem—to buy back—their lives from sin, His ownership extends to their entire being. They are to reflect and honor Jesus with all they are and all they do—body, mind, soul, and spirit.

RESPOND: Why should Christians try to settle minor disputes among themselves rather than taking one another to court? What should happen when church members are involved in immoral or unlawful activity or have neglected their social responsibilities? What types of persistent behaviors keep people out of God's kingdom? *(Spiritual death is the inevitable consequence of habitual sin. No one can live for selfish or immoral pleasure and still be part of God's eternal kingdom [see Romans 6:23]. It's important to note that Paul isn't talking to the unchurched, but to the Christian community as a whole.)* How do you know that there's hope for people who are struggling with these behaviors (1 Corinthians 6:11)? Do Christians have the right to do whatever they please? Why or why not? How does sexually immoral behavior rob a person of God's purpose for them? What does the fact that "your body is a temple of the Holy Spirit" imply about how you should treat your body? How can you honor God with your body?

PRAY: Thank the Holy Spirit for taking up residence in your life. Ask Him to help you honor Jesus with your body.

ACT: Try to settle any minor disputes you have with other Christians. Talk directly with those involved. If that doesn't work, ask church leaders or pastors for advice and help in resolving the issue. If any behavior, habit, or lifestyle is keeping you from honoring God with your body, ask Him to forgive you. Then trust Him to help you make the necessary changes.

1 Corinthians 7:1-40

THINK: Is marriage in your future? Who knows? God does—and He's not anxious about it, so don't you be. For now, focus your attention on your relationship with Jesus and how you can best serve Him. If you do, the rest of your relationships will fall into proper place and perspective. And if dating is part of the picture, be wise and spend that time only with individuals who share your faith in Jesus and will understand that God's plan takes priority in your life.

RESPOND: What are God's intentions for marriage, and what's His view of divorce? *(Paul acknowledges God's plan for lifelong marriages, but he also recognizes that sometimes separation is necessary. Paul isn't referring here to divorce because of adultery or abandonment. He's speaking of separation. Today, conditions such as adultery, addiction, or abuse, in which the spiritual or physical life of the spouse or children may be in danger, may warrant such separation or even divorce.)* Is a Christian's spouse or children automatically right with God even though they personally don't believe? Why or why not? *(The unbelieving spouse and children are ultimately responsible for their response to the gospel message. However, because of the believing spouse/parent, they are under God's influence; through the Christian's faithfulness to Jesus, the impact on their family may lead to their salvation.)* Why does Paul say, "Keeping God's commands is what counts"? What are the benefits of remaining single if one is able to do so? What does verse 39 indicate about the type of person a Christian is to marry?

PRAY: Pray for the marriage relationships in your immediate family. Pray for your future spouse if you believe that marriage is in your future. Also pray for any older single adults you know, asking God to be especially near to them and that they would invest their lives even more in serving Jesus.

ACT: If you have Christian parents or grandparents, express gratitude to them for the heritage and example they have set for you in following Christ. If none are believers, thank another adult who has been a godly influence in your life.

Fire Starter

1 Corinthians 8:1-13

THINK: Many Christians are convinced that they can do whatever their conscience allows. But your conscience is not the final judge, and Jesus' followers are not to live simply for themselves. Real maturity means being willing to put aside your own rights and preferences out of concern for others. In most cases, the things you give up are no big deal, and there are likely much better things you could do to enhance your relationship with God.

RESPOND: What should be your primary consideration in making choices about issues of conscience? What is meant by a "weak" conscience? *(Those with weak consciences didn't fully understand that since the gods represented by idols weren't real, it wasn't a moral issue whether to eat meat offered to idols.)* How might this passage be taken out of context and misused to justify activities that are morally and spiritually inappropriate or destructive? *(In this passage, the issue is food. We must be careful not to twist the meaning to apply to matters affecting one's thought life or spiritual health. One couldn't use these verses to justify questionable media choices or immodest clothing, for example.)* How do those who willingly refrain from certain activities often demonstrate a stronger faith and conscience than those who take a lot of liberty? Why must we be careful about how our example influences others—both Christians and non-Christians? How can exercising your freedom become a "stumbling block" to others? Why is this a direct offense against Christ? Why should you not consider it inconvenient to give up some of your own rights so you don't offend or mislead others?

PRAY: Ask God to help you keep love and consideration for others ahead of your own rights and preferences. Pray that your actions will never become spiritual stumbling blocks to others who are sincerely trying to serve Christ.

ACT: If you're participating in something that is reasonably debatable and may influence others to defy their own consciences or get a wrong impression of Christian's values, replace that activity with something that will benefit you and others spiritually.

242

Fire Starter

1 Corinthians 9:1-27

THINK: Many Christians are more than willing to take great liberty in their behavior and to loosen their personal preferences, believing that this will help them relate to their culture. But few are willing to go the other direction when necessary, restricting their rights or limiting their freedoms out of consideration for others who are sincerely trying to keep their consciences clear toward God. Those who are willing to practice this for the good of others will ultimately discover that you can never surrender anything to God that He doesn't replace with something even better.

RESPOND: What do verses 3-14 indicate about supporting those who serve in ministry? What does verse 16 indicate about a genuine call to preach about Jesus? What does it mean that Paul made himself "a slave to everyone," and why did he do this? *(Paul is an example of self-denial in favor of consideration for others—particularly, for their spiritual convictions.)* What does it mean to "become all things to all men," and what's the aim of this practice? *(Paul wasn't so prideful or stuck in his ways that he couldn't adjust his personal preferences in order to influence someone's perspective of Jesus and hopefully come into a personal relationship with God.)* What kind of discipline does it take to "win the prize" of eternity with Christ and to help others receive that reward? Why must we approach life as a matter of surrendering to Christ and His purposes? How can you ensure that you don't forfeit the prize for serving Christ?

PRAY: Ask God to help you put the good of others ahead of yourself. Pray that you would be willing to either loosen or limit your own freedoms—without compromising biblical principles—depending on what helps others get the most accurate impression of Jesus. Ask God to help you develop the discipline to keep surrendering your will to His.

ACT: As you go through the day practice the principle of doing what's best for others in all you say and do. Without compromising biblical principles, make a deliberate effort to befriend and relate to people who don't know Jesus, demonstrating special consideration for them.

Fire Starter

1 Corinthians 10:1-13

THINK: Christians today have every reason to trust God to guide and provide for them. At the same time, they have no excuse for failing to trust God and behaving in ways that displease Him and bring destruction on themselves. The Bible is packed with examples—both of faithfulness and of rebellion—that serve to challenge, warn and inspire you to trust God, to grow in your relationship with Him, and to follow His plans for your life.

RESPOND: What fact is Paul illustrating about spiritual salvation by his remarks in this passage? *(Paul uses Israel's history as an example of how people could experience the benefits of a right relationship with God and later choose to stop living a devoted life, therefore being rejected by God because of their evil conduct.)* How does Moses' leadership of Israel relate to Christ's leadership over those who submit to Him? How do God's miraculous provisions for Israel in the desert illustrate how God provides for His people through Christ? *(The rock providing water for Israel and the manna were symbolic of the supernatural life God offers people through Jesus, who is both the water and bread of life.)* According to this passage, why must Jesus' followers be careful regarding their attitudes and actions? What encouragement can you take from verse 13 regarding temptation? *(We're all tempted; it's not a sin to be tempted. However, God gives believers adequate spiritual strength and opportunity to overcome every temptation.)* How does God provide help and "a way out" when you're tempted? What have Christians failed to do when they give in to temptation?

PRAY: Thank Jesus for His leadership and provision in your life. Also thank Him for the power He provides over temptation. Pray that you'll never take these things for granted.

ACT: Think about specific struggles and temptations you currently face. Make yourself accountable to a mature Christian; someone you can call or text when you feel tempted or frustrated concerning those struggles. Hopefully, you are or will be that kind of encourager to someone else who's struggling.

1 Corinthians 10:14 through 11:1

THINK: Where and how do you spend your social, recreational, entertainment, and leisure times? How do these times and places influence you and others? Are you a better person for the time spent on these activities? Do others benefit? And above all, is God honored by your attitudes and behaviors associated with these times and places? Be sure that you're not compromising your faith and that you're truly influencing people for Christ.

RESPOND: To what occasion do verses 14–16 refer by using the illustration of the cup and the loaf? In what way do Christians partake of and participate in Jesus' sacrifice? *(The "cup of thanksgiving" was drunk from at the Jewish Passover, the same celebration at which Jesus instituted the Lord's Supper, or Communion.)* How can our own spiritual freedoms and preferences sometimes cause us to disregard what's best for others (verses 23,24)? What's your spiritual responsibility if you're aware that your actions or choices may offend or mislead others who are sincerely trying to follow Jesus or are looking to you for an example (verses 27,28)? Why must a follower of Jesus consider other people's consciences and not just his or her own? What should be the goal of a Christian's life and choices—first in regard to God, then in regard to others? How should following Jesus' example affect your life, faith, character, actions, and overall relationship with God?

PRAY: Ask God for wisdom, guidance, and discipline not to associate with things that honor ungodly practices and could mislead others in their efforts to see and serve Christ. Pray that you'll honor God in all you do and don't do.

ACT: Jesus set the example for unselfish love and devotion to God, His concern for and commitment to God's glory, His focused willingness to do God's will, and His love for people. Rate yourself on how strong you are in each of these four areas—1 being strongest, 4 being weakest. Ask someone who loves you and whom you respect to tell you how they would rate you. Then ask God to help you take focused steps to follow Jesus' example in these areas.

Fire Starter

1 Corinthians 11:2-34

THINK: Whether you realize it or not, your life has a direct influence on others. This is especially true if they know you're a Christian. Your attitudes, your words, your actions, and even your appearance will send impressions—right or wrong—about what God is like and what He values. Be sure that the "image" you convey is worthy of reflecting God and associating with Christ.

RESPOND: In what ways are men and women equal under God and in relation to Christ? *(In relationship to Jesus, men and women are spiritually equal. Both are recipients of God's offer of spiritual salvation and have a part in building His Church and spreading His message.)* Why has God established an order of authority? What does it mean that man is the "head" of the woman? *(A husband must recognize a woman's worth to God, leading her in a way that encourages her to fulfill her God-given role in life.)* How does modesty enhance a person's beauty, dignity, and worth? How and why must Christians be distinctly different from others? What's the significance of the Lord's Supper? *(Established by Jesus himself, the Lord's Supper, or Communion, is an opportunity to remember, acknowledge, and show gratitude for Christ's sacrifice on the cross.)* What does it mean to eat and drink in "an unworthy manner"? *(A person who takes communion with an irreverent attitude with no intention to turn away from known sins shows blatant disregard for Jesus' sacrifice made to provide forgiveness.)* How can you ensure that you participate in communion in a worthy manner?

PRAY: Ask God to help you demonstrate modesty in your appearance so that you draw attention to Christ and not yourself. Pray that you'll be sensitive to the culture in which you live so you can relate Jesus to people in a proper and effective manner. Thank Jesus for His sacrifice for you. Ask Him to help you share His grace with others.

ACT: Be sure that your clothing and fashion choices are modest, not drawing inappropriate attention to yourself. Also, be careful not to exclude people from social and ministry settings. Deliberately include people who don't know Jesus.

1 Corinthians 12:1-31

THINK: What part of your physical body could you do without? You'd probably rather not dispense of any parts, because they all serve a purpose—and they're meant to work together. This is a good picture of how God fits Jesus' followers together in the Church. All members are to function in harmony, each serving a purpose that benefits the whole body. This doesn't mean that things will always operate smoothly. But the Church is resilient, and through the power of the Holy Spirit is able to compensate for loss, bring healing to hurting parts, and gain the strength to fulfill God's purposes.

RESPOND: What are "spiritual gifts"? *(Spiritual gifts are God-given abilities and desires for the purpose of honoring Jesus and building up people in the church—a community of believers.)* Why is it important for Christians to understand how the gifts operate? How do spiritual gifts relate to Jesus? *(Jesus is the leader of the Church, and therefore, all gifts and demonstrations of the Spirit should honor and give attention to Jesus.)* In what ways are God's people like parts of a body? How does the Holy Spirit unite all true followers of Jesus? Why and in what ways do Christians need each other? Why must we never be prideful in using spiritual gifts? Why must spiritual gifts never be the basis of honoring one person over another? Who determines how to dispense the ministry gifts (verses 27-31) and what purpose they serve? Does this passage list all ministry leadership gifts? Why or why not?

PRAY: Give God thanks for His gifts to the Church. Ask Him to help you develop your specific gifts and to use you as He chooses to honor Him and benefit others. Pray for a greater appreciation for all church members and their gifts.

ACT: After re-reading this passage and the above notes, write down what you believe your spiritual gifts might be. Make a list of possible ways God could use them in your future.

Fire Starter

1 Corinthians 13:1-13

THINK: People fill roles of service and strive for great achievements for a variety of reasons: pride, duty, adventure, compulsion, responsibility, and destiny. But when it comes to serving God and fulfilling His purposes among people, the primary motivation must be love—for Jesus and for others. Apart from this, no other motive really matters. Only when we serve in love do we reflect God's character and give others a compelling reason to follow Jesus.

RESPOND: Why must godly love be the main motivation for exercising all spiritual gifts and ministries? Why is it meaningless to have, use, and experience spiritual gifts apart from love? *(Religious activities without love are just a show without meaning.)* What are some of the specific traits of godly love? In what ways do these traits demonstrate love for God and others? In what way is love both a practical action and an ongoing lifestyle? *(Love is an activity and behavior beyond feeling. Note how all the traits listed in this passage characterize God the Father, Son, and Holy Spirit.)* How does growing in love make a person more like Jesus? Why are spiritual gifts still needed now but not "when perfection comes"? What are the implications of love being greater than faith and hope? What does this reveal about whom God honors as part of His kingdom?

PRAY: Ask God to help you develop a more Christlike love and all of the traits that go along with it. Pray that you'll never attempt to use your spiritual gifts or serve God's purposes without demonstrating His love.

ACT: Look back over the list of traits that characterize true godly love (verses 4-7). Consider if you are lacking any of these in regard to specific situations in your life right now. If so, make the necessary changes, which may involve contacting some people and settling some issues. Also, make a deliberate effort to apply and practice these traits in all of your interaction with people throughout the day.

1 Corinthians 14:1-25

THINK: Many Christians base their church attendance and participation on what they get out of the worship and ministry time. But spiritual maturity requires a shift in focus from, "What do I get from this?" to a more selfless perspective that says, "How can I serve and help ensure that others benefit and receive what they need from God?"

RESPOND: Why should we desire the spiritual gifts described in chapters 12–14? *(Christ followers should ask God regularly for them, so that they will be more empowered to serve, encourage, comfort, and strengthen others.)* In what way were the Corinthians overemphasizing and misusing the gift of tongues? *(They were giving tongues "star status" but overlooking the other gifts. Plus, they were speaking in tongues publicly without waiting for God to enable someone else to interpret in plain language what the message was saying.)* How would you describe the gift of prophecy, its function and its purpose in the church? *(Prophecy is a gift enabling a Christian to communicate a Holy Spirit-led message from God to encourage the Church. The emphasis is on strengthening the spiritual life of the Church more than telling the future.)* Why is it important that the gifts and ministries we exercise in church build and benefit others as well as us? What is one of the surest signs that the Holy Spirit is at work in a church or gathering of Christians? *(The Holy Spirit brings conviction of sin, righteousness, and judgment, meaning He exposes an individual's sin to their conscience, convincing them of their need to enter into a right relationship with God through Jesus' forgiveness.)*

PRAY: Ask God to have His way in your church services and to use your leaders and others as He chooses to deliver messages of conviction and encouragement to all.

ACT: If you've received this gift through the baptism in the Holy Spirit, exercise it effectively in your personal prayer and worship time with God. If you have not received the baptism in the Spirit, ask God for this powerful gift.

1 Corinthians 14:26-40

THINK: Anything that draws attention away from God and puts it on us is out of place in a worship service. God is infinitely creative, and we can never fully comprehend how He chooses to operate among His people. But we must submit to God and let Him work in His way, without self-serving disruptions on our part.

RESPOND: What's the primary purpose of all spiritual gifts and ministries when used in public worship? *(The gifts are to strengthen and promote the maturity and character of the Church and individuals.)* What are the guidelines for using the gifts of tongues and prophecy in a church service (verses 27–31)? *(All public speaking in tongues should be done one person at a time, and evaluated by the congregation for its authenticity.)* Why must we "weigh carefully" or evaluate prophetic messages? *(People must always use discernment and consider whether a prophetic message is consistent with God's Word and relevant to their situation.)* Why did Paul say "women should remain silent in the churches"? Since this mainly concerned disruption in worship, does this passage contain any direct implications that women cannot hold certain ministry positions in a church? Why or why not? *(New Testament women would ask their husbands questions about philosophical matters or engage in disruptive discussions right in the middle of a meeting. Paul isn't forbidding women to speak as much as discouraging disorderly interruptions.)* Does the fact that "everything should be done in a fitting and orderly way" limit freedom and spontaneity during a church service? Why or why not?

PRAY: Pray for God's guidance and direction in your church services. Ask Him to give your leaders discernment in directing the ministry and wisdom in lending guidance as people exercise spiritual gifts for the congregation's benefit.

ACT: Next time you're in a church service, make a conscious effort to take the primary focus away from what you can get out of the service, and instead, look for ways that you can help and encourage others to receive from God during the time you're together.

Fire Starter

1 Corinthians 15:1-34

THINK: It's one thing to believe in Christ with your mind, but it's another thing to believe with your heart that He's alive and at work in and through you. Only an active faith—demonstrated by unreserved trust and obedience to God—will keep you courageous when pressure and opposition mount. When others try to influence you to compromise your values and to abandon your devotion to God, will you depend on the power of the living Christ to help you stand strong? And will you trust the promise of His Word that this earthly life is only a preface to eternity with Christ?

RESPOND: How would you summarize the "gospel" that Paul and other faithful ministers preached (verses 3,4)? How can you "hold firmly" to the message of Christ, and why is that crucial to your spiritual salvation? How would you describe a true believer in Christ? How would you describe God's grace, and how does it change people like Paul—or anyone who turns to Christ for forgiveness? *(Grace is God's undeserved favor and help for believers to experience His mercy and power to fulfill His purpose for their lives.)* Why is Jesus' literal physical resurrection crucial to the gospel message and the Christian faith? *(People who deny the resurrection are denying the entire Christian faith.)* How did Paul's own ministry and experience demonstrate a firm conviction that Jesus had risen from the dead (verses 30-32)? Judging from verses 33 and 34, where were people getting distorted views about Jesus and the resurrection? In what ways does bad company corrupt good character, and what can you do to prevent this in your life?

PRAY: Thank Jesus for His grace and for the hope of resurrection and eternity with Him. Also, ask Him to help you make wise decisions about the company you keep.

ACT: Examine your relationships to see if you're keeping company with people who are having a negative influence on you. If so, either break off those relationships, or demonstrate the boldness and discipline to be a positive influence on others.

Fire Starter

1 Corinthians 15:35-58

THINK: Countless people over the centuries have dreamed of immortality. Many have invested their entire lives trying to leave a legacy they hoped would span the eons of time. The truth is, we will all live forever. But only those who have entrusted their lives to God and experienced His forgiveness have the hope of eternal life with Christ. His followers can look beyond the pain, suffering, and hardship of earthly life because these things will all pass away with their physical bodies. Those who do not know God do not have this assurance because when they pass from this life, their troubles will linger forever. But when Jesus' followers are taken from this life, they are transformed by the same power that raised Jesus from the dead so that they can enjoy eternity and immortality with Jesus.

RESPOND: In what ways will Christians' heavenly resurrected bodies be different from their earthly physical bodies (verses 42–44)? In what ways were Jesus and Adam different in their being and in their activity (verses 45–49)? What's the "mystery" Paul describes from verse 51 on? *(When Jesus returns for His true followers, the bodies of believers who are alive at that time will be transformed and made permanent, indestructible, and immortal.)* When will all of this be fulfilled? How does the final resurrection and spiritual transformation of the body assure a Christian's ultimate victory through Christ (verses 53–57)? In what way does this hope enable you to "stand firm" (verse 58) and to give yourself fully to the Lord's work?

PRAY: Thank Jesus for the ultimate victory that is yours over sin and death because of His death and resurrection. Ask God for the strength to stand firm in your faith and the diligence to fulfill the work that He's given you.

ACT: Choose a verse related to resurrection to memorize. Write it on a slip of paper to look at throughout the rest of this week. This can inspire hope and assurance of the ultimate victory that is yours because of your personal relationship with Jesus.

Fire Starter

1 Corinthians 16:1-24

THINK: You've probably heard the phrase "tough love," which typically refers to strict discipline placed upon a person by someone who cares deeply for them and hopes to teach them a valuable lesson. In most instances, people don't view toughness and tenderness in the same context. In fact, these traits are typically placed on opposite ends of the character spectrum. But for followers of Jesus, strength and sensitivity, courage and compassion are meant to go together. If you want to be more like Jesus, you will submit to God, develop greater discipline, and gain spiritual strength by growing in godly love.

RESPOND: What is the "collection for God's people" to which Paul is referring in verse 1? *(This was a collection of funds for the poor Christians in Jerusalem.)* Why was this offering necessary and appropriate? What does verse 9 tell you about taking advantage of ministry opportunities, despite apparent opposition? What do verses 10-12,15, and 16 indicate about accepting one faithful minister as well as another? Why do you think that Paul issued the specific challenges and encouragements in verses 13 and 14? How do things like courage and strength go together with love? To whom does Paul give a strong warning at the conclusion of this letter? Why and in what way is it vital to demonstrate authentic love and devotion for Christ? What was the constant desire of the first Christians, and how should this serve as an example to Christ's followers today? *(The early Church prayed regularly that Jesus might return soon. Christ's true followers long for his appearing and express this desire in words, attitudes, and actions.)*

PRAY: Pray for your church leaders, that God would encourage and guide them in their ministry and that He would bless them in their personal life. Also pray for people in your church who are in need materially or financially.

ACT: Set aside some extra money this week that you would have spent on yourself, and put it toward a missions project through your church or youth ministry. Trust God's direction and empowerment, and follow up on a ministry opportunity to honor Jesus.

253

THINK: Have you ever gone through a difficult time and felt you were alone—that no one really understood what you were going through? Chances are you've heard this more than once: "I know how you feel." While people mean well, those words only go so far—until they come from someone who has actually experienced what you're going through. That's one reason why God allows you to go through difficulties. Beside the fact that they teach you to rely on Him, experiencing tough times enables you to effectively encourage, help, and pray for others who may face the same troubles God has brought you through.

RESPOND: How have you experienced God's compassion? What's the ultimate means by which God provides comfort? *(The Greek word for "comfort"—paraklesis—is to stand beside, encouraging and helping in a time of trouble. God fulfills this role ultimately by sending his Holy Spirit to comfort his children.)* Why does God sometimes allow trouble in our lives? What must you keep in mind when going through difficulty beyond your ability to endure? *(God has not abandoned you. He sometimes allows us to experience challenges so "that we might not rely on ourselves but on God," verse 9.)* How can your prayers help others? What does "Amen" mean? *("So be it." A modern-day version might be, "True.")* What are some ways God works in people's lives through the Holy Spirit? *(The Holy Spirit draws people into a relationship with Jesus. He renews them spiritually, helps them gain a solid spiritual foundation, grow in their faith, empowers Jesus' followers to communicate Christ's message and accomplish His purposes.)* How had Paul shown "tough love" to the Corinthians, and why is this essential for spiritual leaders?

PRAY: Give God thanks for comfort through life's difficulties and for teaching you to depend on Him. Thank Him for the Holy Spirit, who encourages, enriches and empowers your present life, and guarantees an eternal inheritance with Christ. Pray for at least three other people.

ACT: Show God's compassion in a practical way to someone who's going through a difficult or dangerous time.

2 Corinthians 2:5 through 3:6

THINK: As a Christian, have you ever wondered how people can passionately resist and even be repulsed by the very things that bring you the greatest joy and fulfillment? What you know as true freedom and salvation, another person may mistake for fanaticism or slavery because they don't know God or understand His purpose for their lives. Let your sense of renewed life, ultimate purpose, and assured victory inspire you to reach out to those who may still unknowingly see God as their enemy. They may already be watching to see if what you have is really worth crossing the line of resistance and giving their lives for.

RESPOND: How would you describe the New Testament pattern of discipline for those who commit serious offenses affecting the life and reputation of the Church? *(Someone who has committed a deeply consequential sin should be held accountable and corrected in a way that produces true spiritual change. Yet, they mustn't be punished so severely that they lose hope for restoration back into the Church community. Forgiveness and acceptance should be offered to a truly repentant offender.)* What typically determines how a person reacts to Christ's message? What does it mean that God makes Jesus' followers "competent as ministers of a new covenant"? *(The Greek word for "competent" is* hikanosen, *meaning "qualified and adequately empowered." God has qualified Jesus' followers to spread His message of forgiveness and new life, and empowered them to do so, with the help and leading of the Holy Spirit.)* How do God's Law and Spirit work together to bring someone into a personal relationship with Jesus?

PRAY: Ask Jesus to keep you alert to Satan's schemes, deceptions, and attacks. Thank Jesus for the victory He gives you over these things as you rely on Him.

ACT: If you know anyone who has left a church because of a past failure, contact them and encourage them to let God and His people back into their life. Also, make a conscious effort to converse, behave, serve, and treat others in ways that reflect a positive image of Jesus and make His message appealing (without compromising godly principles).

Fire Starter

2 Corinthians 3:7 through 4:18

THINK: Have you ever tried to talk to someone about your relationship with Christ and been frustrated that they didn't seem to understand or accept certain things? What you may have failed to understand is that until people experience God's Spirit working in their hearts, it's as if they have a veil over their minds that keeps them from seeing their need for God. Only God's Spirit can remove the veil as people respond to the Spirit's promptings and open their hearts to Him. That means you need to let God's Spirit work and show through you, and then trust the Spirit to work in those He wants you to influence for Christ.

RESPOND: How is the "veil" removed when someone turns to Christ? What freedom does God's Spirit bring? Does this mean that Jesus' followers can do as they please? Why or why not? *(True freedom in Christ is not the license to do as you please; rather, it's the power to do what you should. Spiritual freedom should never be an excuse to do questionable things in the name of grace.)* How has the "god of this age" (Satan) "blinded the minds of unbelievers"? How should this affect your attitude and actions toward those who don't know Jesus? How is God's power evident through human weakness? How do your present difficulties and troubles compare to the honor that will ultimately be yours if you know Christ? Why is it important to focus attention on what is unseen rather than what is seen, and how can you do this? *(While some things we observe and experience are frustrating and painful, we don't have to lose heart because we know that they are temporary.)*

PRAY: Thank Jesus for opening your spiritual eyes so you can glimpse His glory and comprehend His plans for you. Ask Jesus to give you active compassion for those who don't know Him and are still blinded and deceived by Satan.

ACT: Respond with compassion, patience, and graciousness to people, situations, news, etc., that reflect how people are blinded by Satan. Take a prayer walk around your campus, workplace, or neighborhood and ask God to remove the veil from those around you so they can clearly see His truth and receive His Word.

2 Corinthians 5:1 through 6:2

THINK: There are Christians who claim that believers can sometimes be so heavenly-minded that they are no earthly good. But the truth is that Jesus' followers who make the most positive and significant impact in this life are those who have their minds and affections focused firmly on the next life—eternity with Christ.

RESPOND: As a follower of Jesus, what hope do you have if you die or if Jesus returns before that? How should this affect your life now? For a follower of Christ, what happens as soon as he or she dies? *(When a Christian dies, they come into the heavenly presence of God.)* What will happen when we stand before the judgment seat of Christ (verse 10), and how should this affect your life now? For Jesus' followers, what old things have gone and what new has come? How must we respond to Jesus and live from then on? *(Reconciliation with God becomes effective through personal repentance—admitting and turning from God-defying sins. Then Christians are empowered to help others be reconciled to God.)* What does it mean to be "Christ's ambassadors"? In what way did God make Christ—who is sinless—"to be sin for us"? *(Jesus didn't become a sinner; however, He took all our sins on himself and carried God's judgment against humankind when He died on the cross.)* How does Jesus' sacrifice allow you to "become the righteousness of God" (verse 21) and how should this impact your daily life?

PRAY: Give God thanks for the hope you have beyond earthly life. Pray for a strong sense of accountability to God. Thank Jesus for re-creating your life to fit His plan and for allowing you to represent Him to others.

ACT: Think of some "old things" in your life that you would like to change or that you know God has been wanting you to change. This includes attitudes, habits, etc. With God's help, make a deliberate effort to do something new and better in those areas today and from now on.

THINK: In what ways have you suffered and sacrificed for your faith in Christ? People throughout history and even to this day all around the world have endured unimaginable hardship and persecution for following Christ and spreading His message. Who will benefit from your unquenchable devotion to Christ and your willingness to endure whatever it takes to serve His purposes and reach others for Him?

RESPOND: How did Paul's suffering and hardship (verses 3–10) lend credibility to his ministry? Is being materially disadvantaged by worldly standards any indication of a person's spiritual condition? Why or why not? *(God wants those who have a gift, work ethic, and tenacity for making money to bless those in need. However, material wealth isn't necessarily an indication of spiritual wealth.)* In what way do Christians who seem to have nothing actually possess everything (verse 10)? What is God telling His children by the command to "come out from them and be separate"? Does this mean that Christ's followers should not associate with unbelievers? Why or why not? What is the condition for claiming God's promises? *(Those who live a life of holiness—moral purity, spiritual integrity, rejection of evil, and devotion to God—can claim God's promises.)* What does it mean to "purify ourselves from everything that contaminates body and spirit"? Why and how must we do this? How should this affect your lifestyle choices?

PRAY: Ask God to help you endure difficulty with Christlike character so you never compromise your influence for Him. Pray for wisdom regarding your relationships, that they will always honor Christ. Ask God for discernment and discipline in avoiding anything that could contaminate your spirit and compromise your relationship with Him.

ACT: Think of aspects in your life and material resources in which God has blessed you with more than you need. Determine some practical ways that you can in turn bless others in these areas. Do so with a humble and gracious attitude. Get rid of anything in your life that you are "idolizing" or prioritizing above God or beyond where it should be.

2 Corinthians 7:2-16

THINK: Love is tough. It has to be for all it must endure. In order for your love for Christ to grow stronger and deeper, it will need to be challenged, tested and refined. That requires discipline— exercising it and receiving it when needed. So don't resent it when those God has placed in your life have to show you some tough love to teach you valuable lessons and spare you from lasting consequences of bad behavior and poor choices. And if God directs you to get tough toward a friend, be true to God and your friend by confronting them with compassion.

RESPOND: In what ways were Paul's words to the Corinthians both challenging and encouraging? How can you tell that he genuinely loved them? What does this indicate about leaders who authentically care for their people and how such leaders will respond to people? Did Paul's troubles and fears indicate any problem or lack of faith in his spiritual condition? Why or why not? *(Just as wealth in itself doesn't indicate God's blessings on a person, neither do hard times in and of themselves mean that a person isn't in a right relationship with God.)* Why is godly sorrow a good thing? Why does genuine, godly sorrow not leave any regrets? What are some other positive results of godly sorrow (verse 11)? *("Godly sorrow" is genuine repentance which leads to a restored relationship with God, often resulting in renewed closeness with him, whereas "worldly sorrow"—being only sorry for the consequences of sin—is shallow and leads to death and judgment.)*

PRAY: Ask God to keep you humble and receptive to challenges and discipline from Him and from godly leaders. Thank Jesus for the times He has allowed you to sense sorrow for things that needed to change in your life. Thank Him for the opportunity to serve Him without regrets.

ACT: Thank someone who loves you enough to have given you a tough challenge or word of correction in the past.

Fire Starter

2 Corinthians 8:1 through 9:15

THINK: Hyper-speed computers, personal digital assistants, Internet shopping, GPS systems, iPhones, and drive-up windows for everything. Our culture is obsessed with convenience. While there's nothing wrong with taking advantage of technological advancements, we must remember that no great gain comes without personal sacrifice. Some of the people described in this passage gave more than enough when things were tough.

RESPOND: How are the Macedonians an example to all Christians? What giving principles do these chapters highlight? *(Everything we have—including ourselves—belongs to God and must be invested for Him and in His name.)* What attitudes should you have about giving to God and to those in need? How does giving demonstrate sincere love and faith? What does it mean to "excel" in giving? *(God never asks us to give more than we're able with His help, knowing that when we willingly give beyond what might be expected, we demonstrate great faith and dependence on Him.)* How did Jesus provide the ultimate example of giving? Why is it important to keep commitments and to finish what you start (verses 10–12)? What's the difference between giving generously and giving grudgingly (verse 5)? How will a person's giving habits come back on him or her? What's "a cheerful giver"? *(The Greek word for "cheerful" is* hilaros, *and actually indicates that we get to experience an overwhelming sense of joy and fulfillment which accompanies sincere and generous giving.)* Who should get the credit for your giving (verses 11–13)? What is God's "indescribable gift," and how should it affect your generosity?

PRAY: Ask God to give you a heart of gratitude toward Him that demonstrates sincere generosity toward others.

ACT: Think of someone who lives with an inconvenience (physical ailment, bad home situation, etc.) that you could do something to relieve. Helping the person may not be convenient, but it can give you a fresh perspective on giving. Also, put something extra toward your missions giving goal this week, and be sure you plan to fulfill your overall goal.

2 Corinthians 10:1-18

THINK: Are there temptations, habits, insecurities, or attitudes that frequently get the best of you? The devil isn't stupid; he will use what has worked against you in the past. By the same token, he will not waste time with ineffective weapons. The key is getting to the point where things that once troubled you become simple reminders to turn to God and do what pleases Him. Eventually, Satan will put down those old weapons, because the last thing he wants to do is remind you to rely on and honor God.

RESPOND: What's the main source of opposition and conflict for Christians? *(Satan and his demons are powerful and actual existing influences in the world. They, not people, are our real enemy.)* What types of weapons must Christ's followers use to wage spiritual warfare, and why are they effective (verse 4)? What does it mean to "take captive every thought to make it obedient to Christ" (verse 5)? How does this strategy work in practical terms? *(When a morally impure or destructive thought comes into your mind, "seize" it mentally. Turn sinful thoughts over to God and replace them with helpful Scripture and prayer, especially if there's an issue that triggered the harmful thoughts in the first place.)* How can you keep your mind on things that honor God? *(Practice dwelling on Scriptures and godly thoughts and plans. Refuse to allow your eyes and ears to take in corrupt, sensual, or degrading games, TV, movies, books, magazines, Internet sites, or downloads. It's not worth the harmful effects.)*

PRAY: Ask God to help you effectively use the weapons He provides for victory in spiritual warfare. Pray that you'll always measure your attitudes and actions by God's standards, not your own.

ACT: Think of people with whom you have conflicts. Realize that they are not your real enemy. Also, think of one or two things Satan typically uses against you. The next time you face these thoughts or situations, let them remind you to immediately turn to God for help and to do something to honor Him.

Fire Starter

2 Corinthians 11:1-15

THINK: In most circumstances, sarcasm is uncalled for. However, that is the tone Paul uses as he talks about people's tendency to follow dynamic but deceptive leaders while disregarding his ministry because he served at his own expense. Too often, the devil is able to fool people by masking his lies and evil intentions in ways that seem innocent and good. But the end result will be disastrous unless someone loves people enough to tell the truth and to confront their issues head-on.

RESPOND: What is it about the way false teachers often handle biblical truth that makes their message and approach so deceptive and appealing? *(False teachers may mingle biblical truth with human or anti-biblical philosophies that sound "positive" but don't line up with God's standards.)* Why was it easy for some people to disregard, take advantage of or look down on Paul (verses 7–9)? In what way were "deceitful workmen" masquerading as genuine messengers of Christ? *(Deceitful leaders are influenced by Satan—knowingly or unknowingly. They may do great things "for God" and preach attractive messages that indirectly encourage self-worship. They may even be good, moral people. But if they deny Jesus' life-giving sacrifice or his deity and rightful lordship, they are leading people astray.)* What is it about Satan and his schemes that make him so deceptive, and why are so many persuaded by his lies? In what ways does Satan masquerade "as an angel of light" (verse 14)? What evidence do you see of this in society?

PRAY: Pray for discernment so that you'll never be deceived by leaders who may have charisma but are not completely loyal to the truth of God's Word. Pray that you'll always demonstrate a good attitude toward authentic godly leaders. Also, pray for God's wisdom and insight in recognizing Satan's deceptive schemes, especially when they are masked in attractive packages, innocent-looking activities, and seemingly good causes.

ACT: Convey your appreciation to a godly leader in your life, thanking him or her for their faithfulness to God and their positive influence on you and others. Pray for all who are deceived by Satan and his schemes, asking God to open their spiritual eyes.

Fire Starter

2 Corinthians 11:16-33

THINK: In order for people to understand, you typically need to speak their language. In this passage, Paul continues to talk from an admittedly unspiritual and somewhat worldly perspective. He was trying to expose the petty, foolish, and ungodly attitudes and behaviors of a few in the Corinthian church—particularly those who were being misled by selfish messengers. Paul's message had credibility because he backed it up with devotion to God, love for the people, and personal sacrifice that exceeded anything his opponents could claim.

RESPOND: How was Paul's behavior toward the Corinthians different from those who were opposing and slandering him? In what ways had Paul demonstrated his devotion to Christ and to the Corinthian church? What specific sufferings had Paul endured, and what do they reveal about his character and determination? *(Paul rejoices in suffering that exposes his weaknesses because through his weaknesses, Jesus' power and competence are demonstrated. It's the same with us today!)* What do they reveal about how he depended on and identified with Jesus? What things caused Paul particular grief? In what ways does his attitude toward God, sin, and the Corinthian church serve as an example to all who truly desire to follow and please Christ? How would you have felt if you had endured what Paul did, yet still faced rejection from people whom you loved and served? How do Paul's sacrifices and hardships challenge and inspire you? How do they provide encouragement and hope? In what ways did Paul empathize with other believers (verse 29), and how does this serve as an example to you?

PRAY: Ask God for strength, determination, and devotion to endure whatever hardships are necessary to influence others for Him. Pray that you'll learn to depend more fully on God through these things and that you will gain a greater sense of His compassionate heart for people.

ACT: Consider some of the difficulties you currently face, particularly if they stem from devotion to Christ. Ask God to reveal what He wants you to learn in each situation and how you can use your circumstances to honor Him and help others.

2 Corinthians 12:1-21

THINK: Many people are preoccupied with what they perceive to be their inadequacies, flaws, and weaknesses. However, these often present the greatest opportunities for God to work through you in ways that honor Him alone. What may appear to be your greatest imperfections are the very aspects of your life from which God intends to shine the most, revealing His glory and making your life a thing of beauty for His honor.

RESPOND: Why do you think the Bible never specifically identifies Paul's "thorn"? What does God's response to Paul indicate about the way God sometimes answers prayer? What was God teaching Paul by allowing the "thorn" to persist? *(God's grace—which involves His strength, presence, and love—gives us power to depend on Him for help.)* How is God's "power made perfect in weakness"? In what way has God shown His strength through one of your weaknesses? Why is harsh and hurtful speech such a serious offense among Christians? Even when the church must be firm in confronting its people, what attitude should be evident in those who offer the discipline and correction? Why should true Christians and their leaders grieve over those in the church who refuse to turn from sin? *(Ministers should grieve and share God's sorrow over those who refuse to admit and turn from sin.)*

PRAY: Think of something you've persistently prayed for God to change or take away. Instead of asking God once again to spare you from this difficulty or hardship, ask Him to make you more dependent on Him and to reveal His power in a greater way through your weakness. Ask God to help your speech be uplifting and character building.

ACT: Is there anything that has been a "thorn" and challenge for you to endure? Ask Christ to honor himself through this weakness. Then let God use you in a way that defies your fear and insecurity and reveals to others Christ's grace, message and power. Also, if you've hurt someone with your words, confess any wrongdoing to God and ask for His forgiveness. Then apologize and seek forgiveness from the person you offended.

2 Corinthians 13:1-14

THINK: How teachable are you? Do you respond humbly to correction? Can you take a tough challenge or firm rebuke and come out better for it? If you want to develop godly character and "aim for perfection" (verse 11) in your relationship with Christ, you're going to have to accept discipline, learn hard lessons, and keep yourself accountable—to God first, but also to other trusted friends and leaders who will challenge and inspire you to new heights of faithfulness and greater depths of devotion to God.

RESPOND: In what way would Paul show tough love the next time he visited the Corinthian church? Why is such firm leadership important for a church? *(God's honor and the good of the church community must come before tolerating someone who, by their sin, is harming themselves and the body of Christ.)* Why and in what way must those who claim to be Christians examine themselves regarding their faith? How can tough challenges from leaders like Paul actually build the Church up rather than tear it down (verse 10)? What does it mean for people in the Church to "be of one mind" (verse 11)? What is significant about the way Paul refers to God at the close of this letter? *(Paul's closing affirms the NT belief in the Holy Trinity. As long as God is with believers in these ways—through Jesus' grace, God's love, and the Holy Spirit's companionship, their spiritual salvation is assured.)*

PRAY: Ask God to search your heart and expose anything that isn't pleasing to Him and that could adversely affect your relationship with Him. Ask Him to help you do your part and fill the role He intends for you in your local church.

ACT: Examine the current status of your faith and relationship with Jesus. Are you growing, or falling back? Is your character becoming more Christlike? If you don't have someone to whom you've made yourself accountable, find a trusted Christian friend or leader who will meet with and check up on you regularly.

Fire Starter

Galatians 1:1-24

THINK: Not everything or everyone that claims to be "Christian" is Christlike. Not everything that seems to come from the Bible is the truth. Few people who wear a cross are willing to accept the humiliation that accompanies its message. And most people who identify themselves as spiritual are not actually led by God's Spirit. There are a lot of people spreading a lot of messages that sound good, but in reality they distort the real "good news"—the gospel message of Jesus Christ as we have it in the Bible. That message is the measure of truth. Anything that is not consistent with God's Word is a "different gospel."

RESPOND: How does Jesus' sacrifice "rescue us from the present evil age" (verse 4)? Why were some of the Galatians "turning to a different gospel" (verse 6)? Why is Paul's warning so strong against the false teachers, and in what way is this a warning to us? *(Those who distort the original gospel of Christ, thereby distorting peoples' perception of God, lead people to spiritual death and eternal separation from God. The deception of false teachers is literally a matter of eternal life and death.)* How and with what attitude should you respond to false teachers and their teaching? What are some key elements of the message of Christ and spiritual salvation that we must never compromise? In what way is each of Jesus' followers "set apart" to serve His purposes and to spread His message?

PRAY: Ask for discernment regarding how ideas, messages, and behaviors measure up to the truth of Jesus. Pray for a proper balance of firmness and gentleness in dealing with situations and people that distort the truth of God's Word.

ACT: Who are the most significant influences in your life—whether they follow Christ or not? Do their words and lifestyles set a worthy example and support the truth of Christ? Do something to encourage those who have a positive, godly influence on you. Do something to positively influence those who might cause you to compromise your commitment to Christ.

THINK: Can you recall a time when you knew what was right, but gave in to pressure and did otherwise? Or have you ever tried to do the "right" thing, but with wrong motives? God wants you to do the right things for the right reasons. Knowing God isn't a matter of following rules and routines; it's about a personal relationship with the One who gave everything for you. If you could gain that relationship by your own efforts, Jesus wouldn't have had to pay the price to make a way to God.

RESPOND: What legitimate and necessary role does God's law serve regarding salvation and a relationship with God? *(While keeping God's standards is good and often protects us, obeying God's Law alone simply makes us good, moral people; it can't save us. Only Jesus' sacrifice and forgiveness provides salvation.)* What should your motivation be for following God's standards? What was the key issue in Paul's letter to the Galatians (verse 16)? *(Paul emphasizes that sinners are made right with God, not by observing the Law, but by a living, active faith in Jesus.)* What does it mean to be "crucified with Christ" (verse 20), and how does that enable Christ to live in and through a person? *(In a sense, all Jesus' followers can identify with Jesus' crucifixion in that their old God-defying ways were "put to death" with Jesus as He took their sin on himself on the cross.)* How would you define God's grace and how it relates to His mercy and justice? *(Grace is God's unearned favor. Justice means getting what we deserve. Mercy implies that we are spared the judgment we deserve.)*

PRAY: Pray that you won't be swayed by people's opinions and behaviors, particularly in how you treat others. Give God thanks for His saving grace, and for enabling you to entrust your life to Him.

ACT: Are you compromising your Christian influence or setting a bad example for others by how you treat them or what you expect of them? Take notice if your attitudes and actions stem from worrying about what others think of you.

Fire Starter

Galatians 3:1-14

THINK: Nearly every religion in the world is based on some set of routines, rituals, or regulations that attempt to direct people toward a deeper spiritual experience or personal fulfillment. But the Christian faith is different. It is based on the fact that God took the initiative toward us, making the way back to Him. Christianity is not about routines, rituals, and regulations. Instead, it's about a personal relationship with the God who created us.

RESPOND: How does a person receive God's Spirit as part of their spiritual salvation? *(We receive forgiveness, a relationship with God, and the indwelling presence of His Spirit through faith in Christ—period.)* What are some of the benefits provided by God's Spirit that are available to Jesus' followers? *(The Holy Spirit provides leadership for our lives, comfort for our hearts, insight, empowerment to serve God, and special gifts and expressions through the baptism of the Holy Spirit for the purpose of strengthening the Church, encouraging individual believers, and helping them mature in their faith.)* What does it mean that "the righteous will live by faith" (verse 11), and where does that righteousness come from? *(True inward righteousness comes from having a right relationship with God through faith in Jesus, and involves character attitudes and actions based on His rightness, not our own.)*

PRAY: Give God thanks for rescuing you from the curse of your offenses against Him and for all the benefits of His Spirit in your life. Ask God to help you live in a way that demonstrates complete dependence on Him.

ACT: Is there any way in which you are depending on your own strength and efforts to please God as opposed to relying on Him to help you serve His purposes? While God wants you to give your best, make sure that you are trusting Him and allowing Him to stretch your faith. This will likely mean stepping out and doing something you ordinarily would not dare to do on your own.

Galatians 3:15-25

THINK: One of the first things a person must do in order to get help in dealing with a personal problem or addiction is to recognize and admit the problem and the need for help. Thankfully, God has exposed our shortcoming and our need for His help as the only hope of breaking our sin addiction. Once we accept what Christ did for us and entrust our lives to Him, we can be forgiven of our sin, freed from it's penalty, and fulfilled through a personal relationship with God.

RESPOND: What is the covenant promise that God established with people through His Son, Jesus? What does faith have to do with receiving this promise? What is God's "Law" and what is its primary purpose? Does God's Law in any way contradict His promises? (See verse 21.) How does God's Law relate to His promise of spiritual salvation through faith in Christ? How does the law point us to Christ and reveal the need to put our faith in Him? *(The word for "Law" is translated "teaching" or "direction." The Law refers to the Ten Commandments, the Pentateuch—the first five Old Testament books—or any Old Testament commandment. The Law was a temporary guide for God's people, protecting and pointing them to righteousness until Jesus provided ultimate spiritual salvation.)*

PRAY: Express gratitude to God for His promise of spiritual salvation through faith in Christ. Thank Him for His righteous laws and standards that exposed your sin and revealed your need for spiritual rescue and a personal relationship with Christ.

ACT: Think of an area of your life in which you've been challenged by your time in God's Word recently. In what way is it pointing you to Jesus? Is it challenging questionable behavior? Is it inspiring you to depend more fully on God? Is it stretching you in regard to a particular character trait? Respond by taking action or making changes so that Jesus is honored and you become a little more like Him today.

Galatians 3:26 through 4:20

THINK: Have you ever caught yourself feeling envious of people who inherit a life of privilege simply because of who their mother or father is? From an earthly standpoint, you may never lead a life of luxury. Yet if you are a child of God through faith in Jesus Christ, you have the ultimate privilege of relating to God and experiencing spiritual freedom. In addition, your inheritance is out of this world—beyond anything you could imagine—and it will last forever.

RESPOND: What rights and privileges do you have as a child of God? In what way are all people who are in right relationship with God equal in regard to His promise? (See 3:28.) Why and in what way was Jesus able to rescue people from slavery and make them full-fledged "sons" of God? (See 4:4-7.) What kinds of things are people enslaved to before coming to Christ (verse 8)? Why do people who have been freed by Christ often return to the same things that once enslaved them—particularly things they thought could bring them spiritual help or enlightenment? According to verse 18, spiritual zeal and enthusiasm are only good under what conditions? What did Paul's concern for the Galatians indicate about the spiritual condition and needs of many in the church? (Paul was anguished over those Galatians who abandoned their faith in Christ to follow false teachers.)

PRAY: Give God thanks for making you His child through faith in Jesus. Thank Him for the fact that He shows no favoritism in extending the promise of eternal life with Him. Pray that you too will not discriminate in your attitudes and actions toward people—particularly those who share your faith in Christ. Give thanks for the care and benefits that God's Spirit brings to your life. Pray that you will not depend on anything or anyone else but Christ and the Holy Spirit to keep you in right relationship with God.

ACT: Make sure that the things you are most passionate, enthusiastic, and energetic about are worthy purposes and are in line with God's truth and consistent with His character.

Fire Starter

Galatians 4:21 through 5:15

THINK: Do you always do what you're told? Probably not. We all have rebellious tendencies, but by no means does that excuse such attitudes and behaviors. Yet God himself knows that it's much easier and more desirable to do things because you want to, not because you have to. God wants you to follow Him not out a sense of obligation, but out of love and gratitude for who He is.

RESPOND: In what way did some of the Galatians risk being "alienated from Christ" and falling "away from grace"? Does this mean that following God's commands and living by the moral principles of God's Law is unnecessary for Christians? Why or why not? What should be your motivation for living by God's standards? What is the connection between faith, love, and obedience when it comes to serving God and following Christ? Why are love and obedience crucial to your faith? What two patterns does false teaching in the Church usually follow? *(False teaching either challenges the truths of Jesus, or changes or adds something to biblical standards that God never intended.)* What are the standards by which we should evaluate spiritual teaching? *(We can't evaluate teaching based on feelings, experience, what others' say, or even miracles. The New Testament is the standard for truth.)* What serious caution does Paul give regarding the way you use your spiritual freedom? *(While Christians are free from rule-based religion, they are still accountable to follow biblical standards.)* How should this affect your attitude toward questionable behaviors?

PRAY: Ask God to help you demonstrate your faith and to live by His principles, standards, and commands out of love and gratitude to Him. Pray that you will never abuse your spiritual freedom by indulging in questionable behavior that does not benefit you or others spiritually.

ACT: Find a way to demonstrate Jesus love to someone in a way that reflects your love for and faith in Christ.

Fire Starter

Galatians 5:16-26

THINK: What grows on an apple tree? How about a pear tree? Or a grapevine? The answer is obvious. You know a plant or tree by its fruit. The same is true of people, but can people figure out who you are by your "fruit"? In other words, can they tell that you follow Christ by observing your life? If not, are you displaying another kind of fruit, or any at all? Jesus wants growth in your life to reflect His character, and He wants His love and life to flow through you by the power of His Spirit within you.

RESPOND: What is "the sinful nature"? Why and in what ways is it so opposed to your spiritual life (verses 17,18)? How would you describe the inner conflict between your sinful human nature and your spirit that has been renewed by Christ? What does it mean to "live by the Spirit," and how does that keep you from gratifying the desires of your sinful human nature? What are some of the behaviors of the sinful nature? (verse 19.) What do people forfeit when they behave in these ways? (verse 21.) What is "the fruit of the Spirit," and what character traits should be evident in people who are growing spiritually? What does it mean that "there is no law" against such things (verse 23)?

PRAY: Ask God to help you make choices that will exercise your faith and strengthen your spirit so that you can consistently overcome the ungodly tendencies of your sinful nature. Pray that you will take advantage of every opportunity to develop Christlike character traits.

ACT: Is there any attitude, behavior or aspect of life in which you consistently give in to your sinful nature and allow it to prevail in the conflict with your spirit? Rely on God to help you "live by the Spirit," making deliberate choices to behave differently in that aspect of life. Also, look back through the list of spiritual qualities that comprise the "fruit of the Spirit." Select two of these traits that you often struggle with. Throughout the day, look for opportunities to grow in these areas.

Fire Starter

Galatians 6:1-18

THINK: At one time or another you've probably strained yourself trying to lift something that was too heavy. But perhaps you were able to move that same object with ease once you had a little help. A load always seems lighter when someone helps you lift it. That's one of the reasons God links us together with other Christians. It allows us to share His love and it helps us get through the difficulties of life with a little more hope and encouragement.

RESPOND: How should you respond to a fellow believer who gets "caught in a sin"? (verse 1) What type of failure is Paul referring to and how does this instruction relate to spiritual leaders? What does it mean to "carry each other's burdens," and how can we do this? *(Bearing others' burdens includes praying like you'd want someone to pray for you in the same situation, and meeting practical needs as God enables you.)* What problems can stem from comparing ourselves to others (verses 4,5)? In what way might a person mock God (verse 7), and what stern warning does this passage give in this regard? What is the end result of indulging one's sinful nature and the end result of living to please God's Spirit (verse 8)? What encouragement can you take from verse 9, and who should benefit from your good deeds (verse 10)? According to verse 15, what really matters?

PRAY: Ask God to help you respond with grace and compassion to Christians with legitimate struggles and to leaders who invest their lives ministering to you. Pray for strength to stand for Christ in a world that continues to defy Him.

ACT: Find a way to help another Christian with a problem, struggle, or tough issue. Perhaps he or she simply needs encouragement. But also look for an opportunity to help the person in a more tangible way. Also, do something to help, encourage or meet a need for one of your pastors or leaders.

Fire Starter

Ephesians 1:1-14

THINK: Though God already knows all that will take place and has a specific plan for your life, He doesn't cause or force you to make the choices you do. God's ultimate purposes will be accomplished, but you must choose for yourself whether or not to be part of God's overall plan and eternal purpose for His people. And while He will always be faithful to you, it's up to you to rely on Him so you can remain faithful and fulfill His plan for your life.

RESPOND: What does it mean to be "in Christ Jesus"? *(Being "in Christ" means a believer is united with Jesus through personal relationship and lives under his influence.)* What does it mean to be "adopted as his sons through Jesus Christ" (verse 5)? *(Being chosen and adopted through Jesus as God's own is among the highest honors of a Christian's salvation. Being His child is the basis for faith and trust in God.)* In what way is God's will a "mystery"? *(This speaks, not of the difficulty in discovering God's will, but of God's unique purpose for people.)* Do verses 5 and 11 mean that God determined who would follow Him and that people really have no choice in the matter? *(Though God knows everything that will happen, He neither causes nor forces us to make the choices we do. We have free will and choose for ourselves whether or not to be part of God's eternal purpose for people who follow Him.)* What roles and functions of the Holy Spirit are mentioned throughout Ephesians?

PRAY: Give God thanks for having a plan already established for your life. Thank Him for adopting you into His family and laying up an inheritance for you in heaven. Pray for strength and devotion to accept and follow His plans.

ACT: Has God given you a specific opportunity to honor Him—something He's planned that could help you grow spiritually or influence others for Christ? Perhaps you've hesitated to act because of doubts or fears. Choose today to venture boldly toward God's destiny for you.

Fire Starter

Ephesians 1:15 through 2:10

THINK: Sometimes it may seem that in order to get the best opportunities in life you need to know certain people and have the right connections. But God isn't dependent on other people's reputations and influence to get you where you need to be. As you rely on the Holy Spirit, you will be able to endure anything that comes your way and accomplish anything that God intends for you, influencing others for Christ along the way.

RESPOND: In what way do Paul's prayers for the Ephesians reflect God's desire for all followers of Christ? Why do we need God's power, and what does it provide and accomplish for us? *(To grow in spiritual strength and ability, overcome Satan and sin, and communicate Jesus' message well, Jesus' followers must have God's power infused in them by His Spirit.)* What do verses 20–22 indicate about Jesus' authority? What do the first few verses of chapter 2 indicate about "those who are disobedient" to God and who follow "the ways of this world"? Why should this give Jesus' followers a deep sense of compassion for those who do not follow Him? *(People who don't know Jesus and live apart from Him are under the influence of Satan, their minds blinded to God's truth and enslaved by sinful cravings. Without God's grace, those who haven't been transformed through a personal relationship with Jesus can't fully understand God's truth. Christians need to see people caught up in immoral behavior and pride, not with self-righteous judgment, but from this biblical perspective, with compassion and Jesus' passion for souls.)*

PRAY: Pray for the people you will encounter today who don't know Jesus. Ask God for the opportunity to share His grace and to help you influence them in a positive way for His honor.

ACT: Show compassion in a practical way to someone who doesn't know Jesus. This may be through a simple act of kindness, a word of encouragement, a helpful gesture, etc. Perhaps you could invite the person to join you and some friends for an activity that will show them the type of good time those who follow Jesus can have.

Fire Starter

Ephesians 2:11-22

THINK: Young people in particular will do almost anything to be accepted, to become part of a family, to discover purpose and to find peace. Jesus has provided a way to experience all of these things through a personal relationship with God. No one can satisfy your search for significance like Jesus can. By accepting His gifts and staying true to Him, you become part of something infinitely greater than yourself—something ultimately and eternally fulfilling.

RESPOND: What enabled you to enter a relationship with God and to become part of His eternal kingdom? What benefits and hope does this provide for you at the present time? What "barrier" or "wall of hostility" did He destroy and whom has He brought together? (God, through Jesus, has united all people of all nations and backgrounds, by taking the focus off His Law as the basis for relationship with Him. The basis is now His grace through faith in Jesus.) How and why did He do this? In what way do followers of Jesus have access to God the Father (verse 18)? What are some of the benefits of our access to God? Why and in what way is the Holy Spirit vital for our access to God?

PRAY: Thank Jesus for sacrificing His life so you could enter a personal relationship with God. Thank Him for the continual access He provides to the Father. Thank Him for the other Christians He has placed in your life. Ask Him to help you fill your role in His Church.

ACT: Do something to build a new or better relationship with another Christian at school or church. Get together with a group of Christian friends and plan a new ministry venture or event for your youth group, Bible club, or community.

Fire Starter

Ephesians 3:1-21

THINK: Do you have a good imagination? Do you ever find yourself dreaming of "what could be"—if you dared to venture into the unknown? Think of your biggest dreams and deepest desires. Now consider this: none of those thoughts can compare with what God is able to do in and through you. This doesn't mean that His plans will resemble your expectations or that the course of your life will follow the route you imagined. What God chooses to do with you may or may not appear to be a big deal to other people in this life. But from God's perspective, your life can have an extraordinary impact on eternity.

RESPOND: What is "the mystery" Paul refers to several times in verses 3-9, and how has it been revealed to us? *(The mystery is God's purpose to "bring all things . . . under . . . Christ" [1:10]. The fact that Gentiles—non-Jews—would be equal in sharing the promises and purposes of God was also a "mystery" before God revealed it through his plan of salvation through faith in Jesus.)* How would you define or describe God's "grace"? In what way did the apostle Paul receive and experience God's grace, and in what way have you experienced it personally? What does it mean to be strengthened "with power through His Spirit in your inner being"? What does this enable you to do? What are the implications of God's people "being rooted and established in love"? In what way does this give God's people power? In what way does Jesus' love surpass anything we could comprehend or imagine? How should the fact that God "is able to do immeasurably more than all we ask or imagine" affect your faith and prayer life?

PRAY: Give God thanks for His grace—His undeserved favor and unearned benefits—in your life. Thank Him for the strength and guidance of the Holy Spirit and for the opportunity to come to Him with freedom and confidence.

ACT: Think of something you've been asking God to help you with. Have you done your part to bring this request to reality? Take a bold and deliberate step today and let God involve you in the answer to your prayer.

Ephesians 4:1-16

THINK: Are you a leader or a follower? In God's kingdom, both of these roles are vital in each of our lives. As faithful followers of Christ, we must serve under the leadership and authority He establishes. Even so, godly leaders are to set the prime example of servanthood, following the example of Jesus himself. Their primary role is to equip God's people for service in their churches and communities. All of us are to get involved. God doesn't need spectators who stand by as leaders do the work of ministry. Instead, we are to learn from the instruction and example of godly leaders so we can become more effective in serving God's purposes and leading others to Christ.

RESPOND: What are some of the character traits of a person who is living "worthy of the calling" (verse 1)? According to verses 7 and 8, what is one of the ways Christ has demonstrated His grace to us? Why does He distribute various leadership gifts? What is the primary task and purpose of spiritual leaders (verse 12)? What does it mean to be a spiritual "infant," and why is it important that Christians not remain that way? *(Spiritually immature people—spiritual infants—are unstable in their spiritual commitment and easily led astray by false teaching. God wants Christians to become spiritually mature, able to respond appropriately to His Word, take an active role in serving and building His Church, and communicate His message effectively.)* According to verses 15 and 16, what are some of the key aspects of continuing to "grow up" in Christ?

PRAY: Express gratitude to God for the Christian leaders who invest in your life and for those who have had significant influence on your spiritual journey. Pray that God will give these leaders special wisdom and encouragement to serve others in an effective, God-honoring way.

ACT: Send a note of appreciation to one or more of your pastors or leaders. Get involved in a new ministry venture.

Fire Starter

Ephesians 4:17 through 5:2

THINK: Do you tend to think before you speak? Or are you more likely to say what's on your mind? The fact is that your words mean things. They reflect not only what's on your mind; they reveal what's in your heart. God doesn't take your words lightly, and neither should you. As His representative, you must be careful in your conversations, making sure that they honor God, reflect Christ's character, and build up those who hear.

RESPOND: According to verses 17 and 18, what are some characteristics of those who do not know or follow Christ? When people lose sensitivity to God, why are they so susceptible to sensuality and "every kind of impurity" (verse 19)? *(Life without God leads to frustration, inner discontent, and fruitless plans. Eventually people who close their minds and lives to God and His truth, lose sensitivity to Him, giving themselves over to a God-defying lifestyle.)* What does it mean to "put off your old self" (verse 22) and "put on the new self" (verse 24)? What are some ways that Christians must become "new in the attitude of your minds"? In what way can anger "give the devil a foothold" in your life (verse 27)? What would you classify as "unwholesome talk" (verse 29)? What kinds of words build people up? What does it mean to "grieve the Holy Spirit"? *(Christians grieve the Holy Spirit when they resist and ignore his presence or leading, engage in conversations or behavior involving or encouraging sin.)* Why and in what ways must we be careful not to grieve the Spirit? What behaviors can help us avoid this (verse 32)? In what ways can we be "imitators of God" (5:1)?

PRAY: Pray that you develop greater sensitivity to God, so you can grow in purity as He intends. Ask for God's help in controlling your anger and developing attitudes that honor Him and reflect His character.

ACT: Pay attention to your words and conversations throughout the day. Make sure they are appropriate for a follower of Jesus. If you have hurt anyone lately with angry words, apologize and settle things with that person.

Fire Starter

Ephesians 5:3-20

THINK: Have you ever kept something secret until someone convinced you to give them a hint? It doesn't take much, does it? A little bit can prove to be quite revealing. When God says, "there must not be even a hint of sexual immorality, or any kind of impurity," He's not saying that you can entertain just a little impurity, as long as you don't get into the really obvious stuff. He's telling you not to let the least little bit into your life. That includes conversations, actions, relationships, and what you allow into your mind through things like entertainment. The Bible makes it clear that while these things may seem perfectly acceptable to most people in society—and even to some in the Church—they are completely inappropriate for those who uphold God's standards and reflect His character.

RESPOND: What does it mean that among God's people "there must not be even a hint of sexual immorality, or any kind of impurity"? What kinds of thoughts and behaviors must you be extremely cautious about (verse 4)? *(While we can't completely avoid all associations and influences, we can choose what's best over what's merely good or "okay" and certainly over what's bad in our relationships, activities, and entertainment choices.)* What warning does verse 7 give regarding the people with whom we associate? What implications does verse 12 have for a Christian's conversation and behavior? Why is it so important to be careful how you live and to "make the most of every opportunity" (verse 16)? Why is it so important to "understand what the Lord's will is" (verse 17), and how can you do this? In the context of verse 18, what does it mean to "be filled with the Spirit," and why is this so vital?

PRAY: Pray that God will keep your conscience strong so you can recognize and avoid conversations, activities, and behaviors that could convey any degree of sexual immorality or impurity. Pray that you will recognize and take advantage of every opportunity to reflect Jesus' character and illuminate the way to God.

ACT: Express gratitude to at least two people for something specific they've contributed to your life.

Fire Starter

Ephesians 5:21 through 6:9

THINK: Submission isn't easy. Most people like to feel in charge—especially of their own lives. But when the Bible says that we are to submit to one another, God isn't giving anyone a license to control others. In every situation—whether you're in charge or not—you never lose the power to choose how you'll respond to God and to others. This is particularly true in regard to your attitudes. That's one of the reasons submission is so important. It's the opposite of selfishness, which is spiritually devastating. But submission is also God's way of allowing you to help others in your life to fulfill their God-given roles of both leadership and service.

RESPOND: What does it mean to "submit to one another"? *(To submit is to yield one's rights for another's sake.)* In what way does humble submission to others show reverence for Christ? In what way is the husband the head of the wife, and how is he to exercise his leadership? *(The family is the basic foundational unit in any society. God has given the role of family leader to husbands. His leadership must be exercised in love, gentleness, and consideration to his wife and children.)* In what way are husbands to be servant-leaders? What are the implications of husbands loving their wives as Christ loved the Church? In what way is the union between a husband and wife like the relationship of Christ with His church (verse 32)? What is significant about God's command for children to "honor your father and mother" (verses 2,3)? What cautious instruction does God give to fathers in this passage (verse 4)? How should those who fill the role of a servant carry out their duties? What are they to keep in mind so as to serve with the best attitude (verses 7,8)?

PRAY: Ask God to help you serve and submit to others in the appropriate ways that demonstrate Christlike character. Pray that you will fulfill your daily duties in all aspects of life as if you are doing things directly for Jesus.

ACT: Practice serving others in any way you can today. Pay particular attention to helping those in leadership or authority.

Fire Starter

Ephesians 6:10-24

THINK: Many teens are into gaming, and among the most popular games are those with combat or war themes. Most people who get into these computer simulations would have no desire to engage in real-life warfare. But the games allow them to do "battle" with no "real" consequences. But whether we recognize the fact or not, we all are in a very real battle against a powerful enemy. In this war, it's not points that are at stake, but people's eternal souls. By choosing to follow Christ, you are already destined for victory, but you must still engage in battle. You must choose to "put on the full armor of God" (verse 13).

RESPOND: Why is it absolutely imperative to rely on the Lord's strength and "mighty power"? What are some of "the devil's schemes" that you must be aware of and prepared to stand against? *(Satan attempts to influence and throw us off track through "schemes" like discouragement, temptation, unforgiveness, fear, accusation, habitual sins, self-centeredness—whether extreme self-love or extreme self-hate, rebellion, and spiritual laziness.)* Why must you "put on the full armor of God"? *(We can't fight Satan with logic, human skill, or willpower. We will be defeated if we don't combat the true enemy of our souls with God's power and "weapons.")* What kind of prayer must we engage in to do effective spiritual battle? *(Satan is a spiritual being, and Christians must combat him spiritually. Prayer, beyond being a spiritual weapon, often has a major role in an actual conflict. Scripture-based and Spirit-led prayer is part of the battle.)* Why is it so imperative to "be alert and always keep on praying for all the saints" (verse 18)?

PRAY: Ask God to help you rely on His strength and mighty power as you engage in spiritual warfare. Ask God to help you effectively employ faith and His Word to gain victory over your spiritual enemy.

ACT: Whenever you encounter challenges or difficulties today, take time to pray for God's help and guidance. Also, try to recall something from God's Word that applies to each situation, and let it inspire your faith and action.

Fire Starter

Philippians 1:1-30

THINK: What makes you happy? The thing about happiness is that it usually depends on something else. But joy is different. Joy doesn't rely on circumstances or things—or even emotions. True joy is something you can have no matter what, simply because of your relationship with Christ. Nothing can undo what He's already done for you, and nothing can take away what He has in store for you. This is not to say that your circumstances will be ideal or that your sense of joy won't be tested.

RESPOND: From the opening of the letter to the Philippian church, what can you tell about its main theme? How would you describe true joy, and why can Jesus' followers always have it? *(Joy is based on God's extreme—translate: crazy, ridiculous, over-the-top—love for us, and the comfort that comes from His nearness. Joy is one of the "fruits" of the Holy Spirit—character traits He develops in Christians.)* How does it make you feel that God is still working in your life and will finish that work as you rely on Him? How and why does persecution often make people bolder in faith (verse 14)? Why was Paul able to rejoice even though people were stirring up trouble for him (verse 18)? What did Paul mean when he said, "to live is Christ, and to die is gain"? *(Jesus was Paul's source of joy and purpose in life. Continuing life here on earth meant more joy, purpose, and Jesus. However, the "gain" in dying would be literally being with Jesus. The same is true for Christians today, which is why they shouldn't bring death on, but they don't have to fear death. Death is merely the end of a Christian's mission on earth, and the beginning of an even better, eternal life with Christ.)*

PRAY: Ask God to help you adjust your perspective so that circumstances don't dictate your attitudes. Thank Him for the joy that is always available to you through your relationship with Jesus.

ACT: If there is anything you've started for God but not completed, particularly because of difficulty or opposition, pick up where you left off, and trust God to help you finish it.

Philippians 2:1-18

THINK: The term "Christian" literally implies being like Christ. As His follower, that should be your aim—to consistently become more like Jesus in thought, behavior, and character. Perhaps more than any passage in the Bible, this one tells what that means in the most practical terms. Having the mind of Christ (verse 5) means living with humility and putting others ahead of yourself (verses 3,4). That's how Jesus gave us hope (verse 6). If you follow Jesus' example, He can use you to bring hope to others who need to see what Jesus is like so they too can follow Him.

RESPOND: Why is humility vital for Jesus' followers? *(One of the monstrous enemies of Christian unity is individual pride and promoting of self-interest. Humility is key to unity, not to mention personal holiness and closeness with God. It is the simple awareness of one's own weakness and inadequacy, coupled with crediting God with salvation, provision, and accomplishments in life.)* In what way does humility make us more like Jesus? What does it mean to "work out your salvation with fear and trembling"? What does this process involve? *(Salvation is intended to involve ongoing growth, lived out through a continual process of surrender to Jesus. This doesn't imply earning or working for salvation through human effort; rather, Christians rely on God's grace and the Spirit's power to live for and serve God.)* According to verses 14–16, why should God's people avoid complaining and arguing?

PRAY: Ask Jesus to help you demonstrate humility and to put others' interests ahead of your own. Thank Him for prioritizing your need for spiritual salvation and laying His life down for you. Ask God to help you avoid complaining and to keep a positive outlook on life as an example to everyone of the hope God has given you.

ACT: All day, practice putting others before yourself. Let them go ahead of you. Give them the best choices. Allow them to have their way. Meet their needs. If anyone asks why you do this, point out how Jesus did the same for us.

Philippians 2:19 through 3:11

THINK: What are the most important things in your life—the people, the passions, the priorities, the possessions? What motivates and excites you most? These are the things that could potentially control you if you're not careful. But the crucial question is where all of this stands in regard to your relationship with Jesus. Many things in your life may be worthwhile and important, but none should compare to Christ. Your devotion to Him should be in a class by itself—far above anything else. Is your passion to know Jesus the ultimate priority in your life? And is that priority evident in the way you spend your time, efforts and resources? If not, what changes are in order?

RESPOND: In what way was Timothy a great example to all followers of Jesus? *(Timothy was a passionate and obedient student of God's Word. He had a good reputation, was dependable and genuinely concerned for others.)* What does it mean that Paul and other true believers "put no confidence in the flesh" (3:3)? What was Paul's greatest desire in life? (verses 8–11.) How did everything else in Paul's life compare to his relationship with Jesus? What does it mean to "know Christ and the power of his resurrection and the fellowship of sharing in his sufferings"? *(Paul desired to experience the same spiritually renewing, life-changing, miraculous, sin-annihilating power that God used to raise Jesus from the dead. And so should we. To share in His sufferings means self-denial and suffering for Jesus' sake and His cause.)*

PRAY: Pray that your priorities and affections will always remain in proper perspective so that nothing in your life compares to your devotion to Christ. Ask God to help you live in a way that is worthy of demonstrating His power.

ACT: Pick up where you left off yesterday. Continue to set a good example of putting others ahead of yourself and looking out for their good. If there is anything in your life that has taken priority over your devotion and service to Christ (consider your use of time and resources), make a definite change to put things in their proper place.

Fire Starter

Philippians 3:12 through 4:3

THINK: Chances are, there are some things in your life you'd like to forget, and a few other things you should forget. While there are things you can learn, appreciate, and celebrate from your past, there is nothing you can do to change any of it. For that reason, your primary focus must be on what is still ahead. Too many people have trouble getting past the past—the good and the bad—which prevents them from pursuing the priorities and purposes God intends for their future. Don't let the past hold you back. Press forward with God so you can experience all He has in store for you.

RESPOND: In the process of pressing on in his faith and in God's purposes, what did Paul choose to forget and why? In what way must you follow his example? What will it take to "press on" toward God's ultimate purpose for your life? What does it mean to "live up to what we have already attained" (verse 16), and what does that have to do with maturing as Christians? *(Mature believers continue to grow in their relationship with God, continually living up to what they have "already attained"—areas they've learned and become mature in. Maturity means putting into practice the biblical knowledge you have, applying what God has shown you. As you grow, you should break the up-and-down cycle of spiritual victory followed by defeat that stifles the growth of many immature Christians. Circumstances will change and some will challenge you morally, but you can make steady spiritual progress by growing closer to God and applying His Word.)*

PRAY: Ask God to help you put the past in the past, so that you aren't distracted by your failures or successes. Pray for diligence in fulfilling God's purposes for your life. Ask Him to help you handle conflict with other Christians with wisdom and grace.

ACT: If there is an issue from your past that still troubles you, take appropriate action to settle that issue once and for all. If you have an unresolved conflict with another Christian, make an effort to settle things and to maintain a loving and productive relationship—even if you still disagree.

Fire Starter

Philippians 4:4-23

THINK: There's an ailment that's reaching pandemic proportions in America: chronic discontentment. People are changing careers, spouses, locations, hobbies, and everything in between, yet nothing seems to satisfy. But there is a remedy. When Paul says, "I can do everything through him," he isn't just talking about the things we can accomplish. Rather, he is saying that we can experience joy, peace, and contentment through any situation by relying on Christ. Contentment doesn't come from focusing on your own needs and wants. If Jesus is not the central focus of your life, then everything else will be out of focus and you'll never be content. Contentment is not something you have to chase or earn. It's something God gives to those who are in right relationship with Him.

RESPOND: What does it mean to "rejoice in the Lord" (verse 4), and why is Paul so emphatic about it? It what way is Christian joy a powerful example to others? Why do you not have to worry or be anxious about anything? What's the best remedy for worry, and why (verse 6)? In what ways can prayer benefit us even when we don't understand what's going on or don't see the answers we expect? *(God's peace is the opposite of anxiety. We experience His peace when we pray from hearts fully devoted to Jesus and His Word.)* Why is your thought life crucial to having God's peace? *(We risk losing God's peace, closeness, and joy when we're mentally occupied with ungodly thoughts. Our thoughts and attitudes influence our behavior, our conversations, and our faith.)* What kind of attitudes, issues, and traits should occupy your thoughts? How can your thoughts influence your entire life? What does it mean, "I can do everything through him who gives me strength"?

PRAY: Give God your worries and anxieties, and thank Him for peace even when you don't recognize the answers to your prayers.

ACT: Make a deliberate choice not to worry about something that has been bothering you lately. If you are doing what you sense God wants you to do, leave the issue in His hands, and accept His peace.

Fire Starter

Colossians 1:1-23

THINK: Imagine you went to the mall and did a survey asking, "Who is Jesus, and what is He all about?" What kinds of responses do you think you'd get? Many people might define Jesus as a wise teacher who started a religion and had a lot of good things to say. Some may consider Him to be a prophet. A few might see Him as a fictional character or even have a negative opinion of Him. Of course, some would actually describe Him as the Son of God who died for our sins so we could be forgiven by God and live with Him forever. But how would you answer the question, "Who is Jesus?" This passage can help you comprehend and clarify who He truly is.

RESPOND: To be "holy" (verse 2) implies being morally pure, spiritually whole, devoted to God, and set apart for His purposes. Why is it imperative for people in the Church to be "holy and faithful"? What is God's will (verse 9), how can you know it, and how do you follow it? *(God's will for your life is based on His character and purposes. The more you know and apply God's Word and steadily develop a deep personal relationship with Him, the more confidence you will have in hearing His voice and knowing what He's purposed for you to do and be in life. Always remember that being something in and for God is more important than doing something for him.)* From what has God rescued us and how (verse 13)? What are some things you can tell about the nature and character of Christ from verses 15-23? What does it mean that He reconciled all things to himself? What responsibility do you have in remaining in a right relationship with God?

PRAY: Pray for the insight to know God's will and faithfulness to follow it. Give God thanks for the hope of being with Him in heaven.

ACT: Spend a few extra minutes in prayer today. Pray for people you know (perhaps your youth group, Bible club, church, or family) using the principles of Paul's prayer in verses 9-12.

Colossians 1:24 through 2:5

THINK: Bank tellers and others who frequently handle money are typically taught to recognize counterfeit currency. They do not learn this by being exposed to a variety of phony bills. They learn the skill by handling real ones. By becoming extremely familiar with the real thing, they can easily recognize a fake. The same principle applies to recognizing spiritual truth. The better you know Jesus, the less likely you are to be fooled by false teaching.

RESPOND: In what way do Christ's followers continue to share in His sufferings? *(Paul considers Jesus as still suffering, not for our sins, but with His people as they serve His purposes, often through persecution and difficulty. Christians in numerous countries still suffer persecution for sharing Jesus' message and standing for biblical principles.)* How can your suffering for the cause of Christ affect and benefit others—those who know Christ and those who don't? What is significant about "Christ in you," and what ultimate hope does that provide? In what way do spiritual challenges and true teaching help "perfect" Jesus' followers? What kinds of "treasures of wisdom and knowledge" (2:3) are "hidden" in Christ"? How can truly knowing Jesus keep you from being deceived?

PRAY: Ask God for the strength to share in His sufferings and to reach others with His message of love and life. Give Jesus thanks for living and working through you by the Holy Spirit.

ACT: Go through the day with an intense awareness of Jesus living through you by His Holy Spirit. Let this guide your thoughts, attitudes, and behaviors. Let it inspire faith and boldness to say and do things that will honor Christ, even if this brings opposition. Go online and look up information on the persecuted church. Then pray for Christians around the world who are suffering for their faith.

Colossians 2:6-23

THINK: Educated people are often convinced that knowledge brings freedom and enlightenment. But this is the case only if it's based on truth. Otherwise, human knowledge ultimately proves to be "hollow and deceptive" (verse 8). In reality, people who subscribe to worldly values and humanistic philosophies are held captive by their knowledge. That's because true freedom and enlightenment come only by knowing God through a personal relationship with Jesus Christ.

RESPOND: What does it mean to be "rooted and built up in [Christ]" (verse 7)? *(Jesus' followers "being rooted" in the revelation—clear, confident, deep understanding—of God's love are like plants with deep roots in the ground. "Being established" in His love is like a building with a strong foundation. Both comparisons imply depth instead of superficiality.)* In what way has Christ "disarmed the powers and authorities"? From what types of regulations and judgments are Jesus' followers freed (verse 16)? What does it mean, "you died with Christ to the basic principles of this world"? What kinds of worldly principles and regulations don't apply to Christians, and what principles and regulations still apply to them? Why did the human regulations "lack value"? *(Rule keeping and ritual following, while they can help us to be disciplined and may even deepen our commitment to moral purity, don't totally control sinful desires themselves.)* In what way do routines and regulations that apply to outward, physical issues differ from true godly principles regarding what enters your mind and spirit?

PRAY: Pray for people you know who still follow the world's ways rather than God's. Give God thanks for the freedom you have through Christ. Pray for discernment and discipline to live by God's moral and spiritual principles.

ACT: Are there any activities or behaviors you've tried to justify in the name of Christian "freedom," but you really compromised biblical principles and filled your mind and spirit with questionable images? If so, make the necessary changes, using your spiritual freedom in ways that honor God, build your spirit, and set a godly example for others.

Fire Starter

Colossians 3:1 through 4:1

THINK: What's the focus of your life? What are you known for? What are your highest priorities? What gets your time and attention? If you follow Jesus, then He should not just be a major part of your; He must be your life. That means allowing His Spirit to live through you and develop His character in you, resulting in the holiness this passage talks about. Many people view holiness in terms of what they can't or shouldn't do.

RESPOND: What does it mean to "set your minds on things above"? How should this affect your life in practical ways? What does it mean for Christ to be "your life"? How do you put to death the things belonging to your earthly nature (verses 5,8,9)? In what way is greed a form of idolatry? *(Giving anything priority over God and allowing it to become the focus of your desires, values, and dependence is a form of idolatry.)* How does a follower of Christ put on a "new self" (verse 10), and how is it continually "renewed in knowledge in the image of its Creator"? *(Jesus' followers must resist the tendency to adopt the world's ungodly thinking and behavior because the current world system is under Satan's rule, and therefore evil, hostile to God and His people, and built on human wisdom and values. See Romans 12:2 and 13:14.)* Why are the traits and actions in Colossians 3:12-14 vital among Christians? How does love bind these virtues "together in perfect unity" (verse 14)? What must you do for the Word of Christ to "dwell in you richly," and why is this important? What is meant by "whatever you do, whether in word or deed, do it all in the name of the Lord Jesus"?

PRAY: Pray that your thoughts and affections will focus on what matters for eternity. Ask God for a greater hunger for and understanding of His Word.

ACT: What issues in verses 5, 8, and 9 do you struggle with? Trust God to help you exercise discipline in overcoming these. Consider which of the godly character traits in verses 12-14 need to improve most in your life. Make a deliberate effort today to practice these traits.

Fire Starter

Colossians 4:2-18

THINK: Have you ever prayed for God's direction, then waited—and waited—seemingly with no response? When seeking God's guidance, we might wish to hear an audible voice or receive a supernatural vision of things to come. But God is not likely to provide answers that are so obvious that they don't require faith. Just as you can't steer a car unless it's moving, God doesn't intend to steer lives that are idling in neutral. Many times when God opens or unlocks doors, you'll still need to move ahead, turn the knob, and walk through. This requires active trust and persistent prayer. But those who are ready to respond to God discover a world of wide-open opportunities.

RESPOND: How is devotion to prayer related to "being watchful and thankful" (verse 2)? *(Christians must be "watchful" and alert to the fact that Satan, the enemy of our souls, loves to distract people from focused prayer.)* What does it mean to "be wise in the way you act toward outsiders" (verse 5), and why is this important? How can you ensure that you "make the most of every opportunity" (verse 5)? What does it mean to "let your conversation be always full of grace, seasoned with salt, so that you may know how to answer everyone"? *(When a Christian's speech is encouraging and gracious, people who don't follow Jesus are more likely to identify the Christian's kind conversation with Christ.)* Why is this important in influencing others for Christ? What do you think it means to wrestle in prayer? Why and when is intense prayer vital for you personally and for others?

PRAY: Ask God to strengthen your passion for prayer. Pray that you remain spiritually alert and that you always maintain a grateful attitude. Ask God to help you recognize when He is opening and closing doors in your life.

ACT: Has God opened for you a door of direction, opportunity, or ministry through which you have not yet ventured? Step through that open door today and trust God to help and guide you.

1 Thessalonians 1:1 through 2:16

THINK: Is your life making a mark for God on the world? Are you inspiring hope in others, or are you letting others dictate your destiny? Regardless of what you see or don't see, one thing is certain: God is doing His part. He's saved you, restored your purpose, given you opportunities, and empowered you for spiritual success. Are you doing your part? Are you letting His joy show? Are you living worthy of identifying with Jesus? Are you relying on the Holy Spirit to help you communicate Christ's message, not just in words but in power? This doesn't mean that things will be easy or automatic. Remember, God's power is most evident in the face of opposition and is best demonstrated by people who aren't inhibited by what others may think or do.

RESPOND: In what ways are faith, love, and hope crucial to your work for Christ (verse 3)? What is significant about the fact that "God has chosen you"? *(God took the initiative through Jesus' death on the cross to pursue a personal relationship with people.)* What are your responsibilities in living up to that calling? Why is it so important for Christ's message to be conveyed not only in words, but with power? What are the effects and results of the gospel when delivered in power? How can showing joy through suffering inspire and influence others for Christ? Where does such joy come from (verse 6)? Why is it important for those who serve and minister for Christ to be "holy, righteous, and blameless"? How can we ensure that we "live lives worthy of God"? *(Christians must always examine themselves to ensure their lives represent Jesus' character. We can only do this by relying on God's grace and his Spirit's power.)*

PRAY: Ask God to help you live in such a way that you can convey His message not just in words, but in undeniable power. Ask Him to help you maintain obvious joy, even through the most difficult times.

ACT: Is there any issue or aspect of life in which you're showing more concern for people's approval than for God's? Change your perspective and do what honors God, regardless of the fallout with people.

1 Thessalonians 2:17 through 3:13

THINK: Some believers obsess over their spiritual enemy, seeing the devil behind every obstacle in their lives and giving Satan more "credit" than he deserves. Then again, many people disregard the devil or even doubt his existence, which can be even more devastating spiritually. You need to be sober about Satan and his schemes, while recognizing that as God's child, you have power over the enemy and need not fear him.

RESPOND: What does Paul mean when he says, "but Satan stopped us"? *(Satan is permitted by God to orchestrate circumstances to oppose and hinder Jesus' followers from doing what they believe God has called them to do. The good news is that Satan's power is subject to God's authority.)* What insight does this provide into Satan's strategies, power, and ultimate subordination to God and God's people (verses 8,11)? Why and in what way must Jesus' followers prepare to face "trials"? *(Christians must be mature and wise to the fact that tough times are part of life—even a believer's life. The question is not if, but when trials will come and how the Christian will deal with them.)* Though they should not fear or obsess about the devil and his activity, why is it still crucial for Christians to take Satan seriously and be alert to his schemes? *(Although Satan is a spiritual being, he can affect things in the physical reality. Christians mustn't be naïve to this. If Satan tempted Jesus, he is certainly capable and willing to tempt others—especially Jesus' followers. Again, the good news is that Jesus is not Satan's "opposite"; Satan does not have equal power with Jesus. No, Jesus is all sufficient and all-powerful, as He is an equal part of the Trinity, having the same overruling power and authority of His Father. Therefore, through Jesus, Christians have the power to overcome Satan and his evil influences.)*

PRAY: Pray for wisdom and insight to recognize Satan's strategies and for strength and discipline to overcome temptation during difficult times.

ACT: Write out the areas where Satan seems to continually try to deceive you. Doing so will help you recognize his strategy the next time he tries to deceive you.

Fire Starter

1 Thessalonians 4:1-18

THINK: Do you like to do the dishes? Possibly not. But that's what dishwashers are for, right? While most people would prefer not to wash dishes, no one likes to eat off of dirty plates or drink from dirty cups. Neither do we put our most precious possessions in filthy containers. The same is true of God. When you accept His forgiveness and entrust your life to Him, He cleanses you spiritually and reserves you for His purposes. But He also continues to refine, purify, prepare, and perfect you for the day you will join Him for eternity.

RESPOND: Why is self-control (verse 4) so vital to the process of sanctification? What is "sexual immorality," and what precautions can you take to avoid it? *(Sexual immorality isn't merely an issue of not having premarital sex. It includes avoiding temptation or taking pleasure in sexually suggestive games, images, or entertainment. It's not just avoidance. Our author has never heard a youth pastor or abstinence speaker say, "Sex is bad!" as some anti-abstinence advocates claim. But because sex is not only good, but a gift from God, remaining pure in thought and behavior before marriage is a matter of hopeful anticipation of the joy and sexual fulfillment that comes in marriage when one has remained pure in mind, body, and heart.)* In what way does sexually immoral behavior not only offend God, but also harm, rob, and violate others (verse 6)? *(Having sex with someone other than your spouse is, in a very real sense, stealing what isn't yours. You're stealing from their treasures—purity, innocence, physical and emotional wholeness, and a good conscience toward God. These things, taken not only through intercourse, but other sexual involvement, can't be returned.)* What does it mean to be spiritually "pure," and why does God expect this of His people (verse 7)?

PRAY: Ask God to help you develop and exercise greater self-control. Commit to avoiding all sexual immorality, in thought and behavior. Pray for a passion for purity in every aspect of life. Thank Jesus for the hope of His return.

ACT: Examine your life for any trace of sexual immorality. Make the changes necessary to rid your life of spiritual impurity.

Fire Starter

1 Thessalonians 5:1-28

THINK: Though Christ's return for His followers will be at an unknown time, it should not be unexpected. God's Word offers ample warning of this glorious event, which provides ultimate hope and joy to those who receive Christ but ultimate devastation and judgment for those who reject Him.

RESPOND: What is "the day of the Lord" and what are its end-time implications? *(This isn't talking about a 24-hour period; rather, it refers to a time when God's enemies are overthrown—Isaiah 2:12–21, Jeremiah 46:10, Zechariah 14:1–3, followed by Jesus' earthly reign—Revelation 20:4–7.)* What does it mean that "the Lord will come like a thief in the night"? *(This metaphor simply means Jesus' return will be unexpected—especially for those unprepared, who don't have a personal relationship with Jesus.)* Why is it important to remain alert and self-controlled in the last days before Christ returns? How can faith and love guard your heart like a "breastplate"? How does "the hope of salvation" (verse 8) guard your mind like a helmet? In what way can you show respect for your spiritual leaders (verse 12,13)? Why is it important for Christians to "be joyful always" (verse 16)? What does it mean to "pray continually"? *(Praying continually has more to do with an open heart and mind than an open mouth. God wants us to go through our day in two-way communication with Him, open to His promptings and ready to follow His lead, as well as asking and talking to Him about things.)* Why and how can you "give thanks in all circumstances"? What does it mean that we must "not put out the Spirit's fire"? *(This refers to devaluing or rejecting the Holy Spirit's supernatural expressions and demonstrations among His people. It also means refusing to facilitate God's Spirit operating through people by spiritual gifts.)*

PRAY: Give God thanks that you can look forward to "the day of the Lord" as a time of hope and salvation. Pray for those you know who don't follow Jesus and are headed for destruction and judgment on that "day."

ACT: Is there any aspect of life in which you've become spiritually lazy and lacking in alertness? Make the changes necessary to better prepare for Christ's return.

2 Thessalonians 1:1-12

THINK: We all know that life can be unfair. For Jesus' followers, it can seem even more so in a world that persistently defies God and opposes His people. But God's Word assures us that in the end, justice will be served, and everything will work out right for those who know God. While that should give comfort as we endure difficulty and opposition, it should also stir in us compassion for those who don't know God and are headed their own way toward judgment and destruction.

RESPOND: What does it take for your faith in God to keep growing and your love for others to continually increase (verse 3)? How can this happen through "persecutions and trials" (verse 4)? In what way did the Thessalonians' faithfulness to God through intense persecution demonstrate God's justice? *(God judged the Thessalonians as worthy to represent Jesus and His kingdom for which they suffered. Of course, God didn't abandon them, but provided strength and resources to help them endure their trials, which developed great moral character and spiritual resolve, proving God was on their side.)* When will God demonstrate both sides of His justice—salvation for His people and judgment on His enemies (verse 7)? *(When Jesus returns, God will repay rebellious and evil people as He begins to unleash end-times judgments.)* What will ultimately become of those who do not know God (verse 9)? In what way will Jesus' followers be glorified in Him (verse 12)?

PRAY: Ask God to help your faith in Him to grow and your love for Him and others to increase. Pray that you recognize and capitalize on opportunities He provides for you to grow spiritually, particularly through difficult times. Give God thanks for His justice that ultimately will reward faithfulness and punish wickedness.

ACT: Find a practical way to demonstrate faith in God today. Take a bold step and do or say something to honor Christ— something you might not have attempted without this challenge. Also, find a practical way to demonstrate God's love to someone who already follows Jesus and to someone who doesn't.

Fire Starter

2 Thessalonians 2:1-17

THINK: In many ways, the world is in desperate shape, and it's only going to get worse. While that's no cause for alarm among those who will be rescued from God's impending judgment, it is a cause for urgency and compassion. We must not stand idly by while the world brings disaster on itself. It's not our place to pass judgment; God will do that in His time. For now, we must remain faithful to Christ, letting our lives serve as a gracious warning of things to come. For some, this will feed their misguided notion that Christians are a scourge on society. Let God use you to influence as many as possible to accept the truth. That may bring persecution for you now, but it can spare others from destruction forever.

RESPOND: What will signal the arrival of "the day of the Lord"? *(Two significant things will precede the Lord's return: [1] Both the Church and the world will experience a "rebellion" in which many people abandon their faith, rejecting and defying God and His standards, and [2] the "man of lawlessness"—the Antichrist—will be revealed.)* Who or what is currently "holding him"—the Antichrist—"back" and why? *(God's restraining influence through the Holy Spirit and the Church holds back the Antichrist. When that restraint is lifted, the time frame called "the day of the Lord" will begin.)* What does it mean that "God chose you" (verse 13), and what does your choice have to do with this? *(This implies that God has determined what will happen to those who willingly follow Him and those who don't.)* How can you continue to "stand firm" (verse 15) and what "eternal encouragement and good hope" has God given to help you?

PRAY: Give God thanks for hope and comfort regarding Jesus' return. Pray for people you know who aren't following Jesus.

ACT: Go through the day with a strong awareness of how many people are spiritually deceived. Be prepared for God to use you to convey—and to demonstrate—God's truth.

2 Thessalonians 3:1-18

THINK: Do you like hard work? Or do you prefer to take it easy? While there's nothing wrong with rest and relaxation, there is no place for outright laziness among God's people. In fact, Christians should have a reputation as the hardest and most competent workers and employees. To people outside the church, there is hardly a better example of character and commitment than hard work. On the other hand, people with too much idle time on their hands are bound to cause trouble for themselves and for others. When it comes to getting things done and taking advantage of the opportunities God provides, work hard, focus on God's priorities and let your actions speak for themselves.

RESPOND: Why is prayer so vital for the spread of Jesus' message? *(Faithful intercession is a catalyst to accomplishing God's purposes, frustrating Satan's schemes, and revealing the Holy Spirit's power.)* In what way does prayer protect people from evil influences (verse 3)? What comfort do you personally derive from God's faithfulness? Why is laziness disgraceful for God's people, and why is hard work important (verses 8-10)? Who are "busybodies," and for whom do they cause trouble (verse 11)? What instruction does this passage give these individuals, and how does this apply to all Christians? Why and how should we treat and warn those in the Church who consistently refuse to obey the instructions of God's Word (verses 14,15)? How does the Lord "give you peace at all times and in every way" (verse 16)?

PRAY: Pray for ministries you know and work with, that they will be effective in spreading the message of Jesus and influencing others for Him. Give God thanks for His continual faithfulness to you. Pray that you continue to be faithful to Him and diligent in the work He provides for you.

ACT: Make every effort today to be diligent in your work— that includes your studies for school, chores at home, job responsibilities, and ministry involvement. While you also need time to relax and refresh, don't catch yourself being lazy. Take extra time to pray for specific people and ministries you know about.

1 Timothy 1:1-20

THINK: Christians often pray that God would give them a deeper understanding of His Word. But knowledge isn't God's primary aim. You can know the Word without letting it into your heart and allowing it to change your life. The fact is that most Christians know more of the Word than they put into practice. So why should God show us more when we have yet to enact much of what He's already shown us? God's Word reveals His character, and putting it into action leads to deeper love and purity. This keeps your conscience clear, which allows you to exercise greater faith and accomplish God's purposes. As you spend time in the Word, make it your goal to practice its principles and live what you learn.

RESPOND: Why had Paul told Timothy to stay in Ephesus, and why was this task so important (verses 3,4)? How does genuine spiritual change based on God's Word lead to love and purity? How do love and purity lead to a clear conscience and sincere faith? Why is it important for those who teach God's Word to model the truth in their own lives? Why is it good and necessary that God's Law confronts and exposes everything that defies and contradicts the standards, commands, principles, and guidelines in God's Word? Why did Jesus come into the world (verse 15)? What can happen if we don't hold on to our faith and a good conscience (verse 19)?

PRAY: Pray that you always take God's Word to heart by applying it to your life. Give God thanks for His Law that exposed your sin and for His grace and mercy that rescued you from your sin.

ACT: Think of something (or ask God to remind you of something) that you know from His Word but have not fully put into practice. Ask God to show you a specific way today that you can live what you have learned.

Fire Starter

1 Timothy 2:1-15

THINK: Have you noticed how many things today are aimed at giving people opportunity to draw attention to themselves? It would seem that it's all about "you." But today's passage gives instructions regarding true worship, which is all about God. In fact, anything that draws attention to self is completely out of place in authentic Christian worship. This is true not only in church services, but in all of life. God's people must exercise humility, discretion, and purity in how they present themselves.

RESPOND: Why are our prayers so vital to everyone in our lives, including family, friends, leaders, etc.? According to verse 4, what is God's desire, and how can our prayers help fulfill it? *(God's Word reveals that His perfect will is that no one be spiritually lost or condemned. Yet, His permissive will—what He allows—is peoples' free will; God permits them to choose whether to accept or reject His forgiveness and salvation through Jesus.)* If God wants all people to be saved and come to know Him, why is it that most still don't? What does it mean that Jesus Christ is the only mediator between God and people, and why is He the only one who could ever fill this role? What does it mean "to dress modestly, and with decency," and why is this important for both women and men? *(Beyond a literal choice of what to wear, the source modesty is first one's heart. The fashion choices people make as a result of what's in their heart are the outward demonstration of their inner purity. Modesty involves dressing in a way that reflects a person's respect of God and themselves, and doesn't draw inappropriate attention to one's body.)*

PRAY: Pray by name for your individual family members, best friends and spiritual leaders. Thank Jesus for being the ultimate Mediator—for making the way for you to have a personal relationship with God.

ACT: Whether you're a guy or a girl, practice modesty and discretion today in the way you act, dress and talk, as a way of reflecting spiritual purity in every aspect of your life.

1 Timothy 3:1-16

THINK: What do you think a pastor's life is like? Preach or teach a time or two a week? Visit people? Give out advice? Attend meetings here or there? Most of us have little idea of how hard and long most pastors work, or what is expected of them—by people and by God. Pastor's today fill the roles of teacher, counselor, manager, business executive, custodian, and more. They work mostly with volunteers and are constantly under scrutiny from those they serve. At times, it can be a thankless job, but make no mistake, ministry is a special calling and can be a most fulfilling way of life. Expectations are high, but God equips and empowers those who accept His call to serve the Church.

RESPOND: Why must a pastor have a good reputation both inside and outside the church? Who are "deacons" in the church? *(A primary role of a deacon—servant in Greek—is to assist pastors with business and material affairs of the church in order to free pastors up give more time and energy to prayer and ministry.)* How do qualifications for deacons (ministry assistants, board members) compare to the qualifications for pastors? How do you think they are to be "tested" (verse 10)? What is expected of ministry leaders' spouses (verse 11)? Why should spouses of ministry leaders be trustworthy and cautious in their conversations? What does it mean that the church is "the pillar and foundation of the truth" (verse 15), and what does this imply regarding the faith and conduct of its leaders and members? *(God's people—followers of Jesus—are responsible to uphold the truth of His Word by obeying it [Matthew 13:23], hiding it in their hearts [Psalm 119:11], communicating it effectively and lovingly [Philippians 2:16] and through the Holy Spirit's guidance and enablement, demonstrating His power.)*

PRAY: Pray for your pastors and church board member and their families.

ACT: Write, e-mail, text, etc., one or more of your pastors, expressing appreciation for all they do. Ask God how He wants you to serve in ministry—whether occasionally in now-and-then volunteer roles, or lifelong service in some way.

Fire Starter

1 Timothy 4:1-16

THINK: Are you practicing a "compartmentalized Christianity"? In other words, are you separating your spiritual life from other aspects of life so that your faith has little influence on things like your relationships, school life, entertainment choices, spending habits, etc.? While such a lifestyle comes easily and seems acceptable for many who attend church today, it is not acceptable to God. He expects your faith and relationship with Him to pervade your entire life, positively influencing all you are and all you do.

RESPOND: What does it mean that in the end times "some will abandon the faith and follow deceiving spirits and things taught by demons" (verse 1)? *(Many believers—even gifted ministers—will abandon faith in Christ because they don't love the truth enough to defend and obey it in the face of opposition [2 Thessalonians 2:10]. The increasing popularity of God-denying and God-defying trends and beliefs will undermine true biblical teaching in the lives of those not completely dependent on and loyal to God and His Word.)* What can you do to guard against this in your own life? What do you think it means that "such teachings come through hypocritical liars, whose consciences have been seared as with a hot iron" (verse 2)? What does it mean that God "is the Savior of all men, and especially of those who believe"? *(God offers salvation to any and everyone, though only those who entrust Jesus with their lives will be saved.)* Why is it important for youth in the Church to set an example of godliness and purity? What influence can this have on a church congregation?

PRAY: Pray for spiritual discernment so you won't fall for deceptive ideas in the days ahead. Ask God to help you become more disciplined in spiritual matters and to help you set a worthy example for young and old alike.

ACT: Determine a specific way in which you will practice greater discipline and "training" in spiritual matters, just as you may already do in a physical way for an activity in which you participate.

1 Timothy 5:1-25

THINK: You've likely heard of the "generation gap." Essentially this refers to a disconnect in style, preference, communication, understanding, etc. between younger and older people within certain groups or segments of society. In some ways, this is obvious and understandable. But younger people can learn a lot from people who have more life experience, and older folks can gain insight about innovation and where things are going by spending time with youth. There are fascinating stories to be told both ways. Among young and old in a church family, there should be mutual care, respect, and contribution to ministry. Bridging the generation gap provides a road to enrich us all.

RESPOND: What is significant about the instructions in verses 1 and 2 about treating others in the Church as beloved family members? What guidelines does this passage give regarding the correction and discipline of pastors and ministry leaders who fall into sin? (See verse 20 note.) Why is it so important to follow biblical instruction "without partiality" (verse 21) or favoritism? Why must the Church use caution and godly judgment in appointing, commissioning, or electing Church leaders? *(Because godly leaders are essential to the Church community, when it's been confirmed that a pastor or church worker has defied God's standard, leaders, while compassionate and grace-giving, must not cover up the sins of other leaders that hurt the entire community and dishonor the name of Jesus. Any public rebuke should aim to be a warning to others in the Church to maintain a healthy fear of defying God.)* In what way will both sins and good deeds eventually become obvious (verses 24,25)?

PRAY: Pray for the men and women in your church whose spouses have died. Ask God to meet their needs in a special way. Pray for all of your pastors and church leaders, asking God to bless them and their families.

ACT: Do something practical to help or encourage an elderly family member or church member. Even a brief visit might make someone's day. Throughout the day, be careful to avoid gossip and foolish conversations.

𝔉𝔦𝔯𝔢 𝔖𝔱𝔞𝔯𝔱𝔢𝔯

1 Timothy 6:1-21

THINK: Our economy used to be based on manufacturers who created products to meet specific needs. But in recent years, marketing strategies have shifted drastically to create "needs" that require their products. So advertisers aim to convince you that you "gotta have it" because their product will make you more popular, successful, and satisfied. But it's still stuff, and it won't last. The only thing we really can't live without is a relationship with God, and the only thing of eternal value is what you invest in God's purposes.

RESPOND: What are some indications of whether a teaching is biblical or unbiblical? *(Messages that line up with Jesus' New Testament teachings will call for and promote godly character, moral purity, faith in and obedience to God, and separation from evil.)* Why is some false teaching appealing to certain people? In what way do "people who want to get rich fall into temptation and a trap" (verse 9)? Why and in what way is "the love of money . . . a root of all kinds of evil" (verse 10)? Rather than financial and material gain, what things are Christians to prioritize and pursue (verse 11)? How do you "fight the good fight of the faith"? *(Paul considered the Christian life a struggle requiring perseverance and absolute loyalty to Jesus. The goal of this struggle is not political, legal, or material, but to spread God's message of forgiveness and a personal relationship with Jesus, recognizing that opposition isn't so much from other people as it originates from spiritual forces of evil.)* What's one of the reasons God provides everything we need (verse 17)? What do you think it means to "be rich in good deeds"? Why is it vital for God's people to "be generous and willing to share" (verse 18), and how does this "lay up treasures" for eternity?

PRAY: Ask God to help you be content with your needs being met. Pray that you won't get caught up in a selfish pursuit of wealth and materialism.

ACT: Take some money you were going to use for a luxury item or something you don't really need, and give it to a missions project through your church or youth group.

Fire Starter

2 Timothy 1:1-18

THINK: When it comes to following Jesus, life can be an adventure. But because God doesn't often show us what's in store, it's easy to get anxious or even a bit fearful about what lies ahead. That's where faith comes in; though one thing is certain: where God guides, He provides. Whatever God gives you to do or calls you to endure, as you rely on Jesus, He will provide more than adequate power and capability to see you through.

RESPOND: In light of Paul's circumstances at the time, what's so significant about his plea for Timothy to remain faithful to God (verse 8)? *(This was the second time Paul was a prisoner in Rome. This time, he's likely in a dungeon, whereas the first time, he was under house arrest. Most of his friends have abandoned him and he now anticipates execution.)* What did Paul mean when he told Timothy to "fan into flame the gift of God"? *(Paul compares Timothy's gift to a fire that he must fan into flame. It most likely refers to empowerment from the Holy Spirit to fulfill his ministry. Our gifts from the Holy Spirit must be fueled by God's grace through our prayers, faith, and obedience to God, continually exercised like a muscle, to keep them strong and active for our good and the benefit of the church.)* What does this imply about God's gifts to people through the Holy Spirit? According to verse 9, why has God saved us and called us to a holy life? What is "the pattern of sound teaching"? *(The basis of Paul's instruction here is the foundational revelation and teaching of Jesus and the apostles.)* Why and how must we guard this message, and who helps us do it (verse 14)?

PRAY: Express thanks to God for those who have influenced you most spiritually, asking Him to bless them in a special way. Pray that you will be an inspiration to others through tough times. Ask God to help you fully develop and boldly use the gifts He's given you.

ACT: Exercise the power and discipline God has provided for you and take a step toward using your gifts to honor God and to benefit others.

Fire Starter

2 Timothy 2:1-26

THINK: Are there issues and temptations that constantly get the best of you? Many Christians live with a self-induced sense of frustration and failure because they give in to the same sins over and over. They feel that in order to prove their spiritual strength and maturity, they must eventually reach the point of being exposed to a troublesome temptation without caving in. But God never told us to put ourselves to the exposure test. In fact, if we foolishly keep putting ourselves in compromising situations, we are setting ourselves up for a fall every time. We never gain spiritual strength by toying with temptation. The Bible says to exercise the wisdom and discipline to stay away from or "flee the evil desires" (verse 22). That's how you develop strength to win spiritual victories, by leaving evil behind and vigorously pursuing what's right.

RESPOND: In what way does verse 2 describe the discipleship process? *(Discipleship involves training Christians in the practical disciplines of following Jesus so that they can, like Timothy, in turn, disciple others.)* Why and how must you prepare to endure hardship (verses 3-6)? *(All Christians, especially ministers, encounter opposition, testing, or adversity in some form.)* In what way does this compare with how a soldier (verse 4), an athlete (verse 5), and a farmer (verse 6) must pursue their goals and tasks? *(They must be willing and committed to spiritually fight opposition, discipline themselves as they prioritize their spiritual "race," and work hard planting spiritual seeds and tending their "fields" before reaping benefits of their fruitful spiritual harvest.)* What must you do and what must you avoid "to present yourself to God as one approved, a workman who does not need to be ashamed" (see verses 15,16)? According to verse 22, what must you "flee" from and what must you "pursue" in order to serve God out of a pure heart?

PRAY: Thank Jesus for the strength He provides to overcome temptation as you flee evil and pursue righteousness.

ACT: If you are constantly giving in to the same temptations, make the changes necessary to get away from these things and quit exposing yourself to them.

Fire Starter

2 Timothy 3:1-17

THINK: Many "experts" today claim that a lack of love for oneself is the root of destructive behavior and personality disorders. However, God's Word reveals that the problem lies in self-centeredness that disregards God and others. That tendency will increase in the days ahead—in and out of the Church. Many who claim to follow Christ will lack the authentic spiritual power that characterizes Christ's true followers—those who trust God fully and live by His Word without compromise.

RESPOND: What are "the last days" (verse 1), and what kinds of "terrible times" are included? What does it mean, "people will be lovers of themselves"? In what way is self-centeredness the cause of many other sins and destructive behaviors? How does love for pleasure hinder love for God (verse 4)? What does it mean that people will have "a form of godliness" but deny its power"? *(Christians shouldn't be afraid of or hide from the evil influences of world. While they should build positive relationships with people who don't follow Jesus, they shouldn't invest time, emotion, and energy into relationships with hypocritical people who pretend to follow Jesus but are in actuality distorting His message, misleading others, and causing divisions in the Church.)* How can we identify false teachers in the Church? *(False teachers neglect certain aspects of God's Word, take Bible truths out of context, or distort Jesus' claims and teachings for their own purposes.)* What does it mean that "all Scripture is God-breathed" (verse 16)? *(The Bible, both Old and New Testaments, is the only authoritative Scriptures of the Christian faith. They are reliable and backed by solid evidence. The inspired Word of God—the Bible—is the expression of His wisdom and character; able to give wisdom and spiritual life through faith in Jesus. Jesus himself taught that Scripture is God's inspired Word, affirming that everything He said was from his Father and all true.)*

PRAY: Ask God to help you recognize and resist the ungodly behaviors and tendencies that will be increasingly prevalent in the last days. Pray that you will demonstrate genuine love and godliness, backed with power.

ACT: Make an effort to avoid any self-centered behavior.

Fire 🔥 Starter

2 Timothy 4:1-22

THINK: Are you ready? Ready to run your race? Ready to serve? Ready to speak up? Ready to face opposition? Ready to defend the truth? Ready to be patient with people? Ready to resist false teaching? Ready to finish what you've started for God? Ready for the Lord's return? With Jesus by your side, you can always be ready.

RESPOND: In regard to ministering for Christ, what does it mean to "be prepared in season and out of season" (verse 2), and why is this important? *(There's no designated "spiritual moment in time" versus not spiritual moments. Jesus' followers—especially ministers—must be ready at any given moment to provide an appropriate word, whether for encouragement, inspiration, correction, or a humble but direct response to challenge, all with the goal of making Jesus known and glorified.)* What is "the truth" that people will turn from, and what will they rely on instead (verse 4)? What are the implications of Paul's words, "I have fought the good fight, I have finished the race, I have kept the faith"? How should all true Christians follow that example? Why is it important for Christians to live with intense longing and anticipation for Jesus' return? *(Living in expectation for Jesus' return kept New Testament believers prepared for His return and faithful in serving Him as they wait. A distinctive mark of Christians is that they don't feel at home in this world; they recognize and look forward to their heavenly home.)* How did a strong awareness of the Lord's presence help Paul through tough times? In what way should Paul's life serve as an example and encouragement to all followers of Christ, regardless of their circumstances?

PRAY: Pray for readiness at all times and in all situations to serve God's purposes and influence others for Christ. Ask God for strength to stand up to the persecution you will face for remaining faithful to Him in the days ahead. Pray for endurance to "finish the race" marked out for you. Thank Jesus for His constant help and presence.

ACT: Be ready for God to use you in an unexpected way to accomplish something or to influence someone for Him.

Fire Starter

Titus 1:1 through 2:15

THINK: Do the people around know that you follow Jesus? Have you told them? Have you shown them? Can people who don't know you tell that there is something different about you, just by the way you conduct yourself? Do you say "No" to anything that could compromise your devotion to God or His standards? Do you say "Yes" to opportunities to do good, to honor God, to encourage others and to influence them for Christ? Could people get an accurate impression of what Jesus is like by what they see in you?

RESPOND: In what way should knowledge of the truth lead to godliness? What do you think it means that "to the pure, all things are pure"? *(Paul is most likely referring to the ceremonial Jewish food laws. Some in his time were obsessed with what was considered "pure" versus "impure" food, at the expense of attention to moral character, inward purity, and outward demonstration of godliness.)* What does true spiritual purity involve? How do some people who claim to know God actually deny Him by their actions? *(It's imperative to follow up knowledge of God with God-honoring behavior and attitudes.)* What behaviors and character traits should be evident in those who follow Christ? What is significant about the instructions given to each age and gender group (2:1–10)? Why and in what way is it important for older people in the Church to train and influence younger people (verses 4,5)? What special purposes and responsibilities do women have regarding their families and homes? Having received God's grace, what should you be able to learn and do in response to temptations and ungodliness (verse 12)? What does it mean to say "No" to these things? What is the "blessed hope" that Christ's followers are waiting for? What insight does verse 14 provide about why Jesus gave His life for us? How should this affect your daily life?

PRAY: Pray for your pastors and their families. Pray that your faith will be confirmed by your actions.

ACT: Pay particular attention to your attitudes and behaviors today. Exercise self-control by saying "No" to ungodly or questionable behavior and "Yes" to all that is Christlike.

Fire Starter

Titus 3:1-15

THINK: While God doesn't want us to dwell on the past—the good or bad—He does want us to remember where we would be without Him. This inspires humility and compassion toward those who don't know Jesus. After all, we don't receive a relationship with Christ because of good works or right things we do. Rather, it's only by God's mercy that we are "born again" and renewed spiritually, as we simply surrender to Jesus and entrust our lives to Him.

RESPOND: What should be your attitude and conduct toward leaders and those in authority? *(Unless asked to disobey God's Laws and standards, Christians should obey civil and governmental authorities, follow the law, be good citizens, and respectful neighbors so that the influence of Jesus' message isn't compromised.)* What does it mean that we are spiritually saved "through the washing of rebirth and renewal by the Holy Spirit"? *(This refers to the spiritual birth in the life of someone who accepts God's forgiveness, submits their life to Jesus, and begins following His purposes for their life.)* In what way has God poured out His Spirit on us generously? *(This points to the outpouring of God's Spirit at Pentecost and ever since [Acts 2:33, 11:15]. Thankfully, God is still generously pouring out His Spirit.)* Why are controversies and quarrels typically "unprofitable and useless" (Titus 3:9)? What does Paul have in mind when he says, "Our people must learn to devote themselves to doing what is good" (verse 14), and why is this important?

PRAY: Pray for leaders and authorities outside of your church, including teachers and school administrators, coaches and directors, job supervisors and government officials. Pray that God will give them wisdom and guidance.

ACT: Send a note or e-mail to one or more of the leaders you prayed for, expressing appreciation for their work and letting them know that you're praying for them. If you've recently had a tense quarrel with someone, contact the person to apologize and try humbly to settle the issue—without quarreling further.

Fire Starter

Philemon 1:1-25

THINK: It's one thing to believe that people are created equal, but it's another thing to actually treat them as such. It's one thing to know what's right, but it's another thing to actually do the right thing—without having to be pressed or persuaded. Still, from time to time, we all need to be reminded, challenged and encouraged to respond to others in a way that reflects our faith and devotion to God. The fact is that we are all subject to God and equally accountable to Him for the unique responsibilities and opportunities He gives us. Yet through faith and dependence on His Son Jesus, we all have the opportunity to experience ultimate freedom and eternal life, regardless of our earthly situations or status.

RESPOND: Why does Paul call himself "a prisoner of Christ Jesus"? *(Philemon was written during Paul's two-year imprisonment in Rome.)* What does it mean to "be active in sharing your faith"? According to verse 6, how does sharing your faith benefit you personally? In what way will this help you "have a full understanding of every good thing we have in Christ"? *(There is a sense of purpose and fulfillment when you help someone enter a personal relationship with Jesus. It is the greatest good we can do for another person in life.)* Why is it almost always more productive to appeal to people on the basis of love rather than to tell, order or demand that they do something that they ought to do (verses 8,9)? In what way does a relationship with Christ "equalize" people and put them on common ground (verse 16)? How should Philemon's faith cause him to respond to Paul's request and to Onesimus personally? In what way was Paul following Jesus' example by offering to cover any debt for Onesimus? *(Jesus willingly paid our debt for sins against God, freeing us from sin's slavery.)*

PRAY: Ask God to help you become more active in sharing your faith and to recognize every opportunity to do so. Pray that you become known as a person who "refreshes" others.

ACT: Take any and every opportunity to do good and to do the right thing—without being asked.

Fire Starter

Hebrews 1:1-14

THINK: Remember when you were a kid—during the first few years of school—you might have looked forward to "show and tell," when you could bring a favorite thing from home and tell the class all about it. It was likely a proud moment for you, and hopefully informative for others. These times helped everyone get to know each other just a little better. Actually, people never outgrow the tendency to learn best about others by what they see and hear from them directly. That's part of why God chose to reveal himself to us through His Word and ultimately through His Son, who is the living Word (John 1:1)—God in human form. He came to clearly show and tell us the way to God. And because He did, we not only know about God, we can know Him personally.

RESPOND: What does the opening of Hebrews reveal about the nature, character, power, and authority of Jesus Christ? What did Jesus do after He had paid the price and provided the means for us to be cleansed from sin? *(Jesus took His rightful place of honor in heaven.)* In what ways is Jesus superior to the angels? What does it mean that Jesus is God's "firstborn" (verse 6; Colossians 1:15)? *(Jesus wasn't a created being like angels or humans. Rather, this phrase refers to the Old Testament meaning, "first in position," "heir," or "supreme.")* How can we grow in love for righteousness and hatred of wickedness? *(When Jesus' followers grow in compassion for those whose lives have been destroyed and twisted by sin, and when they experience a deeper and greater union with God, who also "loved righteousness and hated wickedness" [Psalm 94:16, Proverbs 8:13, Romans 12:9], their love for what's right and disdain for what's wrong will increase.)* What does Hebrews 1:10-12 clearly indicate about Jesus?

PRAY: Take time to worship Jesus for who He is—the all-powerful Son of God, the Creator of the universe, the eternal King with authority over all. Ask Jesus to give you His love for what's right and His hatred for evil.

ACT: Make a conscious effort to do the right thing in all situations.

Hebrews 2:1-18

THINK: As chapters 1 and 2 point out, Jesus came to earth as God in human form. He did so to relate, rescue, and restore to us the opportunity to know God. And because God devised a way to relate directly to us, we now can relate personally to Him. Because He took our punishment for sin, we can live with His power over sin. Because He is holy, we can be made holy—like Him. This is often an uncomfortable, even painful process. Living a God-honoring life in a God-defying world often brings suffering. But that's one way we develop Christlike character.

RESPOND: Why must we "pay more careful attention . . . to what we have heard" (verse 1) regarding the message of Jesus? What can happen if we become careless in our relationship with God? In what ways did God confirm His message of salvation to us? *(Jesus first delivered His message of spiritual salvation. It was confirmed by those who'd actually heard and knew Jesus, then validated by God with "signs, wonders and various miracles" and the "gifts of the Holy Spirit" [Acts 1:1-4, 1 John 1:1, 1 Corinthians 2:4-11].)* What does it mean that Christ tasted death for everyone (Hebrews 2:9)? To whom is God's forgiveness available? What does it mean that Jesus was made "perfect through suffering" (verse 10)? Does this mean that Jesus wasn't morally or spiritually perfect already? Why or why not? *(The already perfect Son of God became the perfect Savior "through suffering." Jesus' obedience in life and his ultimate sacrifice on the cross qualified Him to be the perfect representative for all people.)* Why and how is Jesus able to help "those who are being tempted" (verse 18)?

PRAY: Thank Jesus for becoming human in order to rescue us from sin and destroy the devil's work. Thank Jesus for the powerful works that accompany salvation—including the gifts of the Spirit—and help in overcoming temptation.

ACT: If in any way you've become spiritually careless or neglected your relationship with Jesus—by lack of time with Him, service for Him, or obedience to His Word—pick up the slack and revive your devotion to Christ in attitude and action.

Fire ♨ Starter

Hebrews 3:1-19

THINK: Perhaps you've heard the term "backsliding" used in a spiritual context. The theological term is "apostasy" (Greek: *apostasia*). Hebrews 3:12 uses the verb form (*aphistēmi*), which literally means "standing away" from God, implying spiritual rebellion or abandoning one's belief and experience with Christ. While this is a danger for all who turn away from the faith, ultimate apostasy resulting in the hopeless condition described in this chapter doesn't occur without constant, deliberate resistance against the Holy Spirit. Just as we aren't saved by our own efforts (Ephesians 2:8,9), neither are we fully condemned to separation from God by our actions alone. People are saved by accepting God's grace and putting faith in Christ; and people are condemned by rejecting (or not accepting) God's grace and refusing to put faith in Christ.

RESPOND: As followers of Christ, why is it crucial that "we hold on to our courage and the hope of which we boast" (Hebrews 3:6)? In what way is it apparent that the writer of Hebrews regards Scripture (God's written Word) as the words of God rather than mere human words (verse 7)? In what way are verses 7-11 a warning for Christ's followers? What does it mean to "harden your hearts"(verse 8), and why is this a serious offense against God? *(The longer we ignore God's voice, the more likely our hearts will grow unresponsive, to the point of total insensitivity and cynicism.)* What are the implications and consequences of turning "away from the living God" (verse 12)? Why is it important for Christians to "encourage one another daily"?

PRAY: Ask God to keep you hopeful and courageous in your devotion to Christ. Pray that you always take seriously the challenges and warnings of God's Word.

ACT: Make a specific point to encourage one or more fellow Christians today. Send a note, call, e-mail, or text message to these friends to see how they're doing, commend them for something, or let them know you're praying for them.

Fire Starter

Hebrews 4:1-13

THINK: God's Word stands forever (Matthew 24:35). Yet it's not stagnant or inactive; it's dynamic and powerful, like a sword (Hebrews 4:12). It pierces our inner being, discerning whether our thoughts and motives are worthy or unworthy—spiritual or unspiritual. Like a surgeon's scalpel, it cuts corruption from our lives and brings spiritual healing as we submit to the Word in faith.

RESPOND: In what way must the message of Christ be combined with faith to be effective and of value to a person? *(Knowing Jesus' message and God's promises aren't the same as responding to them in true, life-surrendering faith.)* What must a person do—and continue to do—to enter God's rest? *(When we trust our lives to Jesus' leadership and care, He takes our sin, guilt, and concerns, giving us the "rest" of his forgiveness, salvation, and the Holy Spirit.)* What does it mean, "there remains, then, a Sabbath-rest for the people of God" (verse 9)? *(God's promised rest is both earthly in the peace of God and eternal in heaven after death.)* Why and how must we "make every effort to enter that rest" (verse 11)? Why and in what way is God's Word "living and active" and "sharper than any double-edged sword" (verse 12)? What does it mean when it talks about the Word "dividing soul and spirit" (verse 12)? *(God's Word penetrates our inner beings so precisely so as to discern worthy or unworthy, spiritual or unspiritual thought and motives. This New Testament reference to the human spirit is the spiritual dimension of our being—our life in relation to God. "Soul" refers to our inner life in relation to our emotions, thoughts, desires, and choices.)*

PRAY: Give God thanks for the rest that awaits you as you remain faithful to Him. Thank Him for His Word that exposes your needs, brings life, and makes you aware of God's promises to you and your accountability to Him. Pray that you always respond to God's Word with faith.

ACT: Take your Bible with you wherever you go today. It is your guidebook for life, your weapon for spiritual warfare, and your inspiration to influence others for Him. Whenever you have spare time, take it out and read some key passages of your choosing.

Hebrews 4:14 through 5:10

THINK: Do you ever wonder how Jesus can relate to your failures, since He never failed God's plan? And if He never sinned, how can He truly understand the frustration and guilt of giving in to temptation as we often do? While this passage doesn't mean that Jesus experienced every exact temptation we have, it does imply that He endured every kind of human temptation, so He can personally empathize with all we go through. He endured more than all of us put together. And since He never gave in to sin, He endured temptation more intensely than we ever will, pressing through to victory every time. Because of this, He knows exactly how to help us overcome.

RESPOND: Why and in what way is Jesus able "to sympathize with our weaknesses"(verse 15)? What's significant about Jesus having "been tempted in every way, just as we are—yet . . . without sin"? *(See THINK above.)* In what way can this provide comfort and help? Why can you approach God with confidence? What does it likely mean when it refers to Jesus offering "prayers and petitions with loud cries and tears," and in what way was He "heard" by His Father? *(This probably refers to Jesus' agony in the Garden of Gethsemane when Jesus' intensity in prayer caused Him to sweat blood [Luke 22:39-44]. God "heard" Jesus not by removing all the pain involved in Jesus' death, but in the sense that He gave Jesus grace to endure His appointed suffering. In the same way, God will give His children grace to endure difficulties.)* What does it mean that Jesus was "made perfect" (Hebrews 2:10)? *(As a result of Jesus' perfect obedience, He became qualified to be our perfect sacrifice, Savior, and leader of our lives.)*

PRAY: Thank Jesus for making the way for you to have a relationship with God. Give God thanks that you can approach Him with confidence whenever you need help. Pray that you'll endure suffering if that's what it takes to fulfill God's plans for you.

ACT: Wisely avoid situations that could unnecessarily expose you to temptation.

Hebrews 5:11 through 6:20

THINK: Some people think that once a person is truly "saved" spiritually, he or she can never lose that salvation. Or, if a person who formerly appeared to follow Jesus is obviously defying Him now, then that person was never really saved before. But it seems clear from this passage that a person who once accepted forgiveness and truly entered a relationship with Jesus can later turn from that faith and abandon Jesus to the point of losing their salvation and condemning themselves for eternity. (See the "THINK" introduction to the Hebrews 3:1–19 daily reading.)

RESPOND: What does Hebrews 5:12–14 tell you about the need to grow and mature in your faith? What ability and insight do you gain from spiritual maturity, and why is this vital? What does it mean that it's impossible for those who have experienced God's gift of new life (6:4,5), "if they fall away, to be brought back to repentance" (verse 6)? *(The author of Hebrews presents "falling away"—forfeiting one's spiritual salvation—as a real possibility.)* What does this indicate about the possibility of accepting God's truth and entering a personal relationship with Christ, but later abandoning the faith and rejecting Christ? In what way is the illustration in verses 7 and 8 a warning to those who claim to know God? What confidence can you have regarding your love, faith, and work for Christ (verses 9–15)? Why are faith and patience vital in order to "inherit what has been promised" (verse 12)? The fact that "it is impossible for God to lie" provides what encouragement regarding His Word? What does it mean that God-inspired hope is "an anchor for the soul"? *(Like an anchor holding a ship in place, as long as we stay anchored to Jesus Christ, our faith and hope in Him assures our safety and security.)*

PRAY: Pray for the faith and patience to continually endure, grow and thrive in your relationship with Jesus. Thank Jesus that your relationship with Him is secure as you continue to entrust your life to Him.

ACT: Conduct yourself in ways that demonstrate spiritual growth and maturity.

318

Fire Starter

Hebrews 7:1-28

THINK: Most religions represent human ideas and efforts aimed at understanding and connecting with "god" or some higher good, purpose, or enlightenment. But if there is a true God— one that can be known, is worth knowing and wants to know us—wouldn't He know how to connect with us? Wouldn't He be capable of showing us that way? And wouldn't we be better off following His way? In reality, the One true God has made His way to us—not based on our imperfect efforts, but on His perfect plan—not requiring religious rituals and routines, but a personal relationship with our Creator. God gave a glimpse of His plan throughout history, but He actually made the way through His Son, Jesus.

RESPOND: Who was Melchizedek and what was his relation to Abraham, forefather of the Israelites? In what ways is Melchizedek symbolic of Christ? *(They both filled the dual roles of king and priest.)* In what way did Jesus "become the guarantee of a better covenant" (verse 22)? Why and how is Jesus "able to save completely those who come to God through Him" (verse 25)? What does it mean that Jesus "always lives to intercede," and how does this benefit us? *(Jesus continually mediates for His followers according to His Father's purposes. Through intercession, people experience Gods love, presence, and help.)* Why is Jesus' role crucial to a relationship with God? *(Without the grace and help that happens through Jesus' intercession, people would fall away from God. Jesus is our only heavenly go-between with people and God.)*

PRAY: Thank Jesus for providing the ultimate means for you to relate to God. Thank Him for being both your Priest and King. Thank Him for constantly interceding with His Father on your behalf.

ACT: Jesus made a way for people to receive a personal relationship with God if they entrust their lives to Him. Just as Jesus bridged the relational gap between us and God, make an effort to build bridges of relationship with individuals you hope to influence for Jesus. Aim to eventually help lead them into a personal relationship with Him.

Fire Starter

Hebrews 8:1-13

THINK: Have you ever done something over and over—something that worked, but with a lot of effort. You may have even wondered, "There has to be a better way." Then perhaps someone showed you that better way, and suddenly, things got a little easier. Or perhaps you used a product for a long time and it seemed to work just fine—until the "New and Improved" version came out. Then it became apparent that something was lacking all along. When Jesus came into the world, the way He made for us to God was more than an improvement; it was the perfect and permanent method God had planned for all along. Everything that came before was aimed at showing us what was missing in our lives and giving us a full appreciation for what Jesus has accomplished for us.

RESPOND: In what way does Jesus serve as our high priest? *(After Jesus took our sin's punishment on himself, He entered heaven, where He serves in God the Father's presence on behalf of those who have entrusted their lives to Him.)* Why is His heavenly priesthood ultimately more effective than any earthly priesthood (verses 1-6)? Why was it so important that exact specifications be followed in building the Old Testament tabernacle (the portable worship center used by the Israelites from the time of Moses until the building of the temple under King Solomon; verse 5)? In what specific ways is Jesus' New Testament ministry superior to that of the Old Testament priests? *(A covenant is a formal "life agreement" between two people committed to one another—like marriage. The "old covenant" was God's prescription for Israel to maintain a right relationship with Him and receive forgiveness for sins until He sent Jesus to ultimately give His life to pay the penalty for peoples' sins—"the new covenant.")*

PRAY: Thank God for making a new "life agreement" with you, based on Jesus' sacrifice.

ACT: As a devoted follower of Jesus think of activities you're involved in and your primary character traits. Ask God to show you what might change about those things if you weren't devoted to Him.

Fire Starter

Hebrews 9:1-10

THINK: Have you ever seen a picture or a media image of someone before you actually met him or her? Did they look any different than you expected in person? Regardless of the differences, an image or preview can never replace the real thing. Throughout history, God gave people a preview into His plan, preparing them for the perfect time when He would fulfill all of it through His Son, Jesus. Sadly, some still rely on the old images for their concept and connection to God. Others reject the real thing because He isn't what they expected. But those who open themselves to Christ discover what real life is meant to be.

RESPOND: What do you think is the author's purpose in describing the features, functions, and regulations of worship surrounding the Old Testament tabernacle (the portable worship center used by the Israelites from the time of Moses until the building of the temple under King Solomon)? What was "the ark of the covenant," and what was its significance in regard to worshipping God under the old covenant? *(The ark contained the Ten Commandments, a container of manna, and Aaron's rod that budded. It was the most sacred furnishing in the tabernacle, as it represented God's presence among the people.)* What did the "inner room" (verse 7) of the sanctuary symbolize and what restrictions applied to it? *(The inner room, or "Most Holy Place," symbolized God's presence. Under the old covenant, access was restricted to once a year by the high priest.)* Who could enter the Most Holy Place, when, and for what reason? For whom did the high priest offer the blood sacrifice, and why (verse 7)? Why did such sacrifices need to be made over and over (verse 9)?

PRAY: Thank Jesus that you don't have to make ritual sacrifices or follow religious routines in order to have forgiveness and access to God.

ACT: Throughout the day, enjoy your access to God and your freedom of worship by using your "between-time" (i.e., getting ready for school or work, driving, breaks, etc.) to express praise to God.

Fire Starter

Hebrews 9:11-28

THINK: Sin is defiance against God, and the entire human race is guilty of this offense. It's so serious that it requires the most extreme penalty: death and separation from God. Forgiveness is possible only at the cost of a life. But imperfect lives and sacrifices could never pay the ultimate price to permanently remove sin and guilt. Only God himself could provide a sacrifice that satisfies His perfect justice and pays the penalty for sin once and for all. God's provision came through the willing sacrifice of His Son, Jesus Christ. He is the only one capable and worthy of destroying the sin barrier, bridging the gap between God and people, and reuniting the Creator with His greatest and most beloved creation.

RESPOND: Why was His sacrifice good enough to be made "once for all" (verses 12-14)? What was accomplished and made available to us through "the blood of Christ"? *([1] Forgiveness, [2] Ransom from Satan's control and the power of evil, [3] Justification—made right with God, [4] Cleansing of conscience from guilt, [5] Sanctification—purifying, refining, and setting apart for God's service, [6] Direct and continual access to God, and [7] Guarantee of promises of the new covenant.)* What does it mean, "Christ is the Mediator of a new covenant? If you have accepted the sacrifice Jesus made for you the first time He came to earth, what hope do you have for the future?

PRAY: Thank Jesus for the Blood He shed for you when He died on the cross in your place and for your sins, for the forgiveness and cleansing available through His perfect sacrifice, and for the spiritual freedom He provides.

ACT: No one needs another person to go between them and God. Only Jesus could provide us access to the Father. Yet Jesus uses His followers to influence others and lead them to Him, so they too can receive forgiveness and find ultimate purpose. Aim to influence as many as possible today by demonstrating Christlike character, helping others in a practical way, or engaging in conversations about spiritual issues. Try to inspire others—Christians and non-Christians—to consider Christ, to grow closer to Him, or to depend on Him for help or healing.

Fire 🔥 Starter

Hebrews 10:1-18

THINK: Perfection—many strive for it; a few even expect it. But as the cliché goes, nobody's perfect. From a human standpoint, that's true, and most people can accept that. But God is the Author of perfection. His character is perfect. His plans are perfect. And He's able to bring us into those plans if only we surrender our own imperfect way of life and follow Him. We can't do this by our own imperfect efforts, and we certainly won't appear perfect in the process. Yet God has a perfect plan for each of us, and He will work to perfect those of us who entrust ourselves to Him until the day we leave this imperfect world to be with Him forever. Then we'll experience true perfection. Why settle for anything less?

RESPOND: In what way was God's Old Testament Law, with its sacrificial system, "a shadow of the good things" to come? In what way were the repetitive sacrifices of the Old Testament a constant reminder (verse 3)? What could these sacrifices never do (verses 4,11)? How did Jesus solve this problem? In what way did Jesus accomplish His Fathers will (verses 5-10)? What did Jesus do after He had made the perfect sacrifice for sins (verse 12), and what does that position signify? Why is no further sacrifice needed for a person's sins once he or she receives the forgiveness provided by Jesus Christ?

PRAY: Thank Jesus for doing what no religious systems, sacrifices, rituals, or regulations could do—bring people into a right relationship with God, including complete forgiveness and open-access to Him. Give God thanks for writing His perfect Law into your heart and mind. Praise Jesus for claiming His rightful place of authority at His Father's right hand.

ACT: Accept God's forgiveness once and for all for any past issues that have caused persistent guilt or condemnation. Also, demonstrate godly character by extending forgiveness to anyone who has hurt or offended you in the past. If appropriate, do this in person. But either way, give the situation to God and accept His freedom from the past.

THINK: Many people get nervous at the thought of meeting someone of prestige or influence. Some have the impression that nobody of great importance would care to associate with them. But think about this: The Almighty Creator of the universe wants to know you and spend time with you. He's given you an open invitation to a personal relationship with Him, and He's even made a way for you to be with Him forever. But only those who humbly accept God's invitation, delivered through His Son, Jesus, will receive an "all-access" pass to God, with eternal rewards.

RESPOND: What does it mean to "have confidence to enter the Most Holy Place," and why can we have it (verses 19,20)? What does it mean to "spur one another on toward love and good deeds," and how can we do this? Why is it important that Christians not neglect opportunities to gather for worship? *(As Jesus' return approaches, we will increasingly face opposition and spiritual deception. Meeting together regularly with other believers will provide the necessary encouragement to help each other hold firmly to faith in Christ. Jesus expects, as part of His intention for His Church, that we grow in community as well as individually.)* What will eventually happen to people who have known God's truth and experienced His forgiveness if they abandon God and deliberately keep defying Him (verses 26,27,30,31,39)? Why do some who seem intensely devoted to Christ at first, later turn from faith and lose confidence in Him (verses 32–34)? What will happen if you persevere in faith and devotion to Christ (verses 35,36)? What does "my righteous one will live by faith" mean?

PRAY: Thank Jesus for His personal sacrifice, which cleanses you from sin and allows you to serve God with a clear conscience. Pray for anyone you know who has turned from faith in God, that they would again submit their lives to Him.

ACT: Encourage fellow Christians today, inspiring them to do what's right and good. Take advantage of opportunities you have this week to gather with others for worship and service.

Fire Starter

Hebrews 11:1-16

THINK: You've probably heard the phrase, "seeing is believing." Perhaps you've even said, "I'll believe it when I see it!" Either way, God doesn't want His people to take that posture when it comes to faith in Him. It's one thing to have cautious reservations when dealing with people, but God expects you to trust Him completely, regardless of what you see or don't see. He's not asking for blind, baseless trust, since His Word has proven totally reliable.

RESPOND: At the opening of chapter 11, how is faith defined, and what does this mean to you? What is authentic Christian faith based on? What will true faith inspire you to do? In what kinds of circumstances is faith best demonstrated? How does faith enable you to understand God's creative work? *(We spiritually and intellectually grasp the knowledge God gives through our physical senses, natural reasoning, and through revelation by God.)* Why was Abel's sacrifice better than Cain's? *(Abel, in an act of true worship, gave his very best to God in the way God prescribed.)* How was faith involved in Abel's actions? Why do you think it's impossible to please God without faith (verse 6)? What must a person who comes to God for help or salvation believe? *(A person must believe in the existence of a personal, infinite, caring and holy God, and that He will respond to and reward those who look to Him in faith, recognizing that God himself—His presence and personal involvement and influence in our lives—is the ultimate reward.)* In what ways did Abraham demonstrate faith in God (verses 8-11)? How are faith and obedience related?

PRAY: Ask God to help you grow stronger in faith and to trust Him through all circumstances, regardless of how things appear. Pray that you live with an eternal perspective that looks forward to your home with Christ.

ACT: Demonstrate faith in God by obeying what you know He's told you, by trusting Him to help you with every task and challenge, and by boldly aiming to influence others for Him.

Hebrews 11:17-40

THINK: When reading about the great feats of faith in the Bible, it's easy to feel inadequate about your own faith. After all, it's difficult to imagine ourselves in some of the situations described in Scripture. Looking back on these events, we often forget that most of the people involved had no idea what was about to happen. They were ordinary people who trusted God for extraordinary things. If you're willing to trust God like that, you too can experience His power and guidance in extraordinary ways.

RESPOND: What extreme test of faith did Abraham experience, and how did he respond (verse 17)? In what way did this incident demonstrate extraordinary faith in God's promise (verses 18,19)? Why do you think God allows faithful people to suffer? *(Through the same faith, some of God's people were rescued from suffering; some were not. As it was then, so it is today: authentic faith will lead people to do great things for God, but at times, lead them into great difficulties. Faith in God doesn't make anyone immune to suffering. And, because everyone has free will, faith won't always protect us from people exercising theirs for evil purposes. However, faith assures us that we'll have God's help and strength to endure times of trouble.)* What do you think it means that their "weakness was turned to strength" (verse 34)? What can you learn from these examples, and what must you be prepared to endure for your own faith? *(Refusing to conform to the world's low standards or take part in its momentary pleasure caused God's followers to face ridicule and trouble. The New Testament teaches Jesus' followers to expect difficulty and opposition [2 Timothy 3:12] and identify with Jesus' suffering [Matthew 10:38].)*

PRAY: Pray that God will help you be willing to sacrifice anything for Him. Thank Him for the fact that nothing you put aside in following Him can keep you from fulfilling His purposes and being who He wants you to be.

ACT: Attempt something bold and out of the ordinary for God today—something that could set the stage for God to do greater things through you in the days ahead.

Hebrews 12:1-13

THINK: Some people think that faith means believing that God will rescue them from nearly every problem and pain with little consequence. They feel that being spared from suffering and blessed with success are unmistakable evidence of faith. While faith can definitely be a factor in these situations, the reality is that true, God-inspired faith is tested and proven through difficult circumstances. It takes greater faith to endure a trial with unfailing trust in God than it does to escape a trial without really relying on Him. God doesn't want you to look for trouble or bring difficulty on yourself.

RESPOND: In what way can the faith of those who have gone before us inspire us to greater faith and devotion to Christ? How is the Christian life like a race that requires perseverance? *(The Greek word for perseverance is hupomone—"with persistent patience and endurance.")* What must you do to run the race effectively? What does it mean to "throw off everything that hinders and the sin that so easily entangles," and why is this crucial in fulfilling God's plans for you? *(Just as a track runner wears the lightest weight clothing to minimize the potential of slowing themselves down, Jesus' followers must "throw off everything that hinders and the sin that so easily entangles," literally translated, "our most troublesome, sidetracking sins.")* What kind of things must you put aside, and what disciplines does this require? *(We must become accountable for and make choices to oppose the sins that repeatedly get the best of us and keep us from growing in our relationship with Jesus. We also should put aside things that are not necessarily sinful but aren't helpful in our spiritual growth, activities and choices that are dead weight, keeping us from devoting greater time and focus to our relationship and purpose in God.)*

PRAY: Give God thanks for all of the inspiring examples of faith in His Word. Pray for the spiritual strength, stamina, and discipline to finish the course God has set before you.

ACT: With God's help, exercise the discipline to put aside sin or bad habits, so you can "run with perseverance the race marked out" for you.

Fire Starter

Hebrews 12:14-29

THINK: Many Christians have a mistaken notion of what it means to live a "holy" life. Certainly, by definition, holiness implies the highest standard of moral purity, spiritual wholeness, separation from evil, and complete devotion to God and His purposes. But holiness is not simply a matter of negative restrictions and things we avoid. It's more a matter of positive actions and things we pursue. By focusing on all of the positive things God gives us the opportunity to do, we will have little time or desire to get caught up and distracted with the negative behaviors He wants us to avoid.

RESPOND: What do you think it means to "make every effort to live in peace with all men and to be holy" (verse 14)? What does it mean to be "holy"? *(Re-read THINK above.)* In what ways does receiving the good new of Jesus stand in contrast to the receiving of God's Old Testament Law? Though the message of Christ brings a complete joy and freedom that the Law could not, in what way are the consequences of rejecting Christ even more severe than the consequences of rejecting the Law (verse 25)? *(The Old Testament covenant included many unattainable standards, fearful warnings, and severe punishments. New Testament believers don't have such a threatening covenant.)* What does it mean that God "will shake not only the earth but also the heavens" (verse 26), and why will He do this? *(God will someday destroy the current world system and material universe, replacing it with a "new heaven and earth" [Revelation 20:11; 21:1; 2 Peter 3:10-13].)* In light of this, how should we worship God (Hebrews 12:28)?

PRAY: Pray for a greater pursuit of holiness in your life. Pray that you will never become bitter or defiant toward God's discipline. Ask God to help you never compromise His long range plans for short-term satisfaction.

ACT: If to any degree you've become bitter, resentful, or resistant toward God or someone else because of the Lord's work in your life or theirs, let God help you change your attitude, settle the issue and take appropriate positive action.

Fire Starter

Hebrews 13:1-25

THINK: Have you ever been in a church service and not felt like worshipping? Perhaps you didn't feel "spiritual," or maybe you felt hypocritical or unworthy. But your feelings don't change God's worthiness. If you're truly living in a way that honors God, then you can praise God regardless of how you feel, because you're simply expressing the truth about your life. That's part of what it means to "offer to God a sacrifice of praise" (13:15). The place where praise truly becomes a sacrifice is outside of the church, where your life should bring positive attention to Christ. An authentic lifestyle of worship means honoring God in words, attitudes, and actions, no matter where you are, what you're doing, or how you feel.

RESPOND: What does it mean to "keep on loving each other as brothers," and why is this important for Christians? Why is it important to empathize with those who are going through difficult times (verse 3)? Why must you keep your life "free from the love of money" (verse 5), and how can you do this? *(Notice how the New Testament connects greed and immorality [1 Corinthians 5:11, 6:9–10, Ephesians 5:3, Colossians 3:5]. Often the constant desire for material things causes a person to be more vulnerable to sexual sin.)* How should Christians view their leaders, and why is it important to obey them (Hebrews 13:17)? *(Obedience, respect, and faithfulness to Christian leaders should be based on a higher loyalty to God. In the context of Church relationships, a Christian's loyalty must be to God first, the local church community next, as long as it remains faithful to God and His Word, and finally, to godly leaders in the Church community, as long as they remain faithful to God, His Word, and His mission for the Church.)* What does it mean that Jesus is the "great Shepherd"?

PRAY: Pray for those you know who are going through difficult times. Ask God to give you empathy and understanding so you can pray more effectively.

ACT: Encourage someone you know who is going through a tough time. Be careful not to come across in a way that makes them feel as if their faith is failing.

James 1:127

THINK: Do you ever forget a face? Probably so—but not your own! It's an absurd notion that you would forget what you look like after walking away from a mirror. Yet, that's what it's like to read or hear God's Word but then fail to take action. Looking into the Word provides a reflection that reveals the way you really are and helps you see what needs to change. In order for God's Word to become part of your life you must live what you learn.

RESPOND: What are "trials of many kinds" (verse 2), and why can you face them with joy? *(God can use trials—difficulties or pressures in life—to strengthen our faith and develop godly character and perseverance in us. Though frustrating and painful, we can still take joy in trials because of the positive results from what God does in us through them.)* In what way do trials help you grow and mature? What does it mean to be "double-minded" (verse 8), and why does that keep people from receiving from God? What are the differences between trials and temptations? *(Trials result from outside sources beyond one's control, to be endured with faith and trust in God. Temptations come from Satan and one's own inner moral struggles.)* How should your approach and response to "trials" differ from your response to temptations? Left to ourselves, without relying on the Holy Spirit, where will our own desires eventually lead us? *(The natural progression between unresisted temptation and spiritual wreckage is that ungodly desire can lead to moral deception, which leads to morally wrong choices, which leads to spiritual death.)* How is failing to put the Word into practice like walking away from a mirror and forgetting what you look like (verse 24)?

PRAY: Ask God to help you face difficulties with joy and faith so they become opportunities for growth. Ask Him to help you avoid, resist, and overcome temptation. Pray that you will be a doer of God's Word, not just a hearer.

ACT: Think of something specific God has shown you from His Word regarding what He wants you to do, to develop, or to change. Take immediate action and put His Word into practice.

Fire Starter

James 2:1 through 3:12

THINK: Lots of people claim to believe in Jesus, and they think that's enough. After all, the Bible says that to be saved, you simply need to believe (Mark 16:16; John 3:16, 36; 6:40, 47; Acts 16:31; Romans 1:16; 10:9-10). Yet, this is more than intellectual belief that Jesus is God's Son who died for our sins. Even demons believe that (James 2:19). Biblical belief implies faith—an active trust that surrenders control of one's life to Christ and His purposes. That means action. Good works can't save you, but if you're truly saved, you'll do good things. Faith without works is dead faith (2:17).

RESPOND: Why and in what ways must Christians refrain from showing favoritism? In what way does discrimination stem from "evil thoughts" (2:4)? In what way is faith "dead" (verse 17) or "useless" (verse 20) without action? *(True faith is more than an intellection conclusion or verbal confession; it is expressed by obedience to God and active compassion for others.)* In what way was Abraham a great example of faith in action? What was God's response to Abraham's active faith (verse 23)? What kinds of actions stem from a right relationship with God? How can a tongue control and effect one's entire being (3:2-7)? In what way is the tongue like a "fire" (verse 6)? What can words reveal about what's inside of us? *(The words and even the way we talk reveal what's in our hearts, not just what mood we're in at the moment [Matthew 12:24]. Mature believers control their tongues by relying on the Holy Spirit and taking "captive every thought to make it obedient to Christ" [2 Corinthians 10:5 and James 1:19].)*

PRAY: Ask God to help you avoid discrimination so that you demonstrate His love to all people equally. Pray that your faith will always be backed by action and that your words and conversations will always honor Christ.

ACT: Find a way in which your faith has not been sufficiently demonstrated by action, and make an effort to change that starting today. Also, keep control of your tongue, and make sure your words and conversations are pleasing to God.

THINK: Can you recall a time when Satan tried to get the best of you, but you resisted him—like it says in James 4:7—except that he didn't "flee from you"? In fact, he pressured you relentlessly until you finally gave in. What went wrong? Why didn't that strategy work for you? Like many Christians, you may have tried to gain spiritual victory by focusing on the last part of that verse and trying by sheer determination to resist Satan's schemes on your own.

RESPOND: How does "bitter envy and selfish ambition" reveal a lack of godly wisdom (3:14,15)? Why and how does envy and selfish ambition lead to "disorder and every evil practice" (verse 16)? What causes fights and quarrels among Christians? What's one reason that people don't get answers to prayer (4:3)? What does it mean "that friendship with the world is hatred toward God"? *(In this context, the Scripture isn't referring to God's love for people in the world [John 3:16]. "Friendship with the world" here refers to embracing the world's ungodly attitudes, values, and practices. God is jealous for our undivided love and loyalty.)* What's the key to resisting the devil and causing him to "flee from you" (James 4:7)? What is involved in submitting to God? What's a key to developing a deeper relationship with God? *(As we depend on God through time in His Word and prayer, and following the leading of the Holy Spirit, God commits himself to us through His presence, blessing, and love, making himself known to us in special and personal ways.)*

PRAY: Ask God for wisdom and the discipline to use it. Pray that you'll not get caught up with selfish ambitions. Pray that you will avoid quarrels with other Christians and that you will demonstrate humility toward God and others. Ask God to help you always submit to Him so that you can resist the devil.

ACT: Take steps to remove any selfish ambition from your life and settle any quarrels with other Christians. If you've spoken in a slanderous way about anyone, apologize to those who have been affected.

Fire Starter

James 4:13 through 5:20

THINK: Most Christians view sin as the bad things in our lives we need to confess and give up for God, and the bad things we must continually avoid. But sin isn't just the bad stuff we knowingly do; it is also a matter of the good stuff we knowingly neglect. Even the devil understands this, and one of his most potent strategies is to turn this principle against us, making us feel guilty for not doing enough. But guilt should never be your motivation for doing good.

RESPOND: Why is it so important to spend time with God when making plans and setting goals for your life (See 4:14,15)? What does verse 17 say about someone who deliberately neglects the good he or she ought to do? In 5:1-6, what is James saying about the potential effects of wealth? What attitude should Christ's followers have while waiting for His return? What do verses 13 and 14 tell us to do in every circumstance—whether happy or in need of help? What is God's invitation and instruction to us when we are in need of healing (5:15)? What is the key to effective prayer? *(Prayer must be offered in God-dependent faith. People may not be healed instantly, but Jesus' followers should persist in prayer and reliance on the Holy Spirit's healing power, knowing that God's presence and peace are available for those who trust in him. Regardless of the outcome, God's people can trust God to be present.)* In what ways are the prayers of godly people "powerful and effective"? What can Elijah's example teach us about prayer and how God responds to it?

PRAY: Ask God to help you see and understand His will for specific aspects of your life. Ask God to help you recognize and do the good you ought to do.

ACT: Take an opportunity to publicly and sincerely give credit to God for something He helped you achieve. Do whatever good you have opportunity to do today.

Fire Starter

1 Peter 1:1-21

THINK: What comes to mind when you think of holiness? Many people think that holiness puts large limitations on life, viewing it in terms of all things we shouldn't do. But in verses 13-16, God calls us to prepare for action and be holy in all we do.

RESPOND: What is "the sanctifying work of the Spirit" (verse 2)? What does it mean to be sanctified? *(Sanctification is to be made holy—morally pure, spiritually whole, separated from evil and devoted to God's purposes. Sanctification is not absolute perfection; rather, it's relating rightly to God and doing right according to His standards—demonstrated by moral purity, godly obedience and God-honoring, Christlike character.)* In what way is sanctification immediate, and in what way is it ongoing? *(Upon entering a relationship with Jesus, sanctification is a decisive act of grace in which a believer is set free from Satan's control, making a clear break with sin and a God-opposing lifestyle. At the same time, it's also a lifelong process by which a Christian continues to reject sinful choices and habits, develop a greater love for God and people, and fulfill God's purpose in their life.)* What does it typically take to prove genuine faith (verse 7)? In what ways has the Holy Spirit worked to deliver the message of Jesus (verses 10-12)? What does it mean to be holy, and why are we to be holy (verse 16)? What does it mean to be "redeemed" (verses 18,19)? How is "the precious blood of Christ" involved?

PRAY: Surrender to the Holy Spirit's spiritually purifying, refining, and developing work in your life. Ask Him to help your faith grow through tough times and to help you pursue holiness.

ACT: Go through the day with two specific thoughts or aims. (1) Look for the positive actions God would like you to take to develop your spirit and character. Watch your attitude through challenging circumstances. Do what you can to help others, and take steps to convey your faith in both words and action. (2) Maintain a strong awareness that regardless of what you encounter, you are "shielded by God's power." That awareness should inspire faith and boldness.

Fire Starter

1 Peter 1:22 through 2:25

THINK: When you were a child, you may have been afraid of "aliens," and you were probably told not to talk to "strangers." For kids, both terms can carry negative, even fearful connotations. But when the Bible tells us to live as "aliens and strangers in the world" (2:11) it implies a positive, beneficial difference. God isn't asking us to be odd or isolated, but He wants us to understand that to a large degree we will be outsiders whose way of life is foreign to most people. Our lives can provide hope and inspiration to all who are searching for something beyond what this life can offer.

RESPOND: How enduring is God's Word, and why is this significant regarding its message of spiritual salvation? What does it mean that Jesus' followers are "a holy priesthood" (verse 5), and how should this affect our lives in practical ways? *(In the Old Testament only Aaron's descendents qualified for priesthood. Now, through Jesus, all His followers are "priests" to God [Revelation 1:5-6; 5:10; 20:6]. This means believers have [1] direct access to God through Jesus, [2] are obligated to live holy lives, [3] must offer "spiritual sacrifices" including living obediently to God, [4] refusing to conform to the world, [5] must intercede—pray for others' needs and concerns, [6] defend God's Word, and [7] spread Jesus' message.)* In what way can Christians follow Jesus' example through suffering, and what can this produce in their lives (1 Peter 2:21-23)? What's the primary purpose of Jesus' death, and how should this affect our daily lives?

PRAY: Give God thanks for His eternal Word, and pray that you'll gauge your behavior by its instructions, commands, principles, and guidelines. Pray that your life stands out with a positive difference that draws attention to God.

ACT: Make a deliberate, humble effort to stand out in a positive way today. Be considerate, cooperative, and helpful in ways that most people overlook. Make sure that your conversations and behaviors reflect godly character and devotion to Christ. Don't be a passive follower, but instead set an example that others can follow.

Fire Starter

1 Peter 3:1-22

THINK: From the moment we awake each day, our senses are bombarded with images and impressions of what society perceives as beautiful, successful, and satisfied. Almost inevitably, these are the opposite of God's standards of beauty and success. In fact, the world's false impressions set unrealistic and unattainable standards that often lead to dissatisfaction and hopelessness. But Christ's followers have something inside of them that reflects true satisfaction—something that stands in such positive contrast to worldly images that people are bound to ask about it.

RESPOND: Where should true beauty come from, and how should it show? *(The word "gentle" describes a humble and unassuming character of a person who shows concern for others. "Quiet" refers to attitude and behavior not obnoxious or disruptive; rather, respectful and peaceful. This is less about a girl's personality—shy versus not shy—and more about her character and disposition—how evident the "fruit of the Spirit" is [Galatians 5:22–23]. These traits will be tested in a world saturated by materialism, self-will, manipulative fashion, obsession with sex, and contempt for godly values in the family.)* How should a husband treat his wife and why? What is God's promise to Christians who suffer for doing good (1 Peter 3:14)? As a follower of Christ, why and how are you to "always be prepared to give an answer to everyone who asks you to give the reason for the hope that you have"? Why did Jesus give His life, and what did that ultimately accomplish? How is water baptism related to spiritual salvation through faith in Christ? *(While water baptism doesn't provide spiritual salvation, it symbolizes Jesus' death, burial, and resurrection.)*

PRAY: Pray for anyone you know who is struggling in their marriage or family. Pray that you focus more on inner beauty than outer beauty—both in yourself and others. Ask God to help you set a humble and submissive example in all you do. Pray that you'll always be prepared to share your faith and hope in Jesus with a gracious attitude.

ACT: As you get ready for the day, give greater attention to inner beauty than outer beauty. Make a deliberate effort to get along with everyone today.

Fire Starter

1 Peter 4:1-19

THINK: Since becoming a Christian, have you ever gone through a really difficult time or faced incredible opposition and wondered: *Why me? What went wrong?* But of all the things that might be unexpected in life, painful rejection, opposition and suffering should come as no surprise for Christ's followers. Jesus himself warned that they would have trouble in the world (John 16:33) and that they would be hated and persecuted (Matthew 5:11; 10:22).

RESPOND: In what way are you to arm yourself with the same attitude as Christ (1 Peter 4:1)? What does it mean that "he who has suffered in his body is done with sin" (verse 1), and how does that apply as we endure spiritual trials and difficulties (verses 1-4; 3:18)? *(People who patiently endure opposition for Jesus' cause find it easier to resist sin and follow God's plans— often because they tend to depend on God more.)* What is a "gift" as used in verse 10? How should each of us view our God-given gifts, and how are we to use them (verses 10,11)? *(God has given each person specific interests, abilities, and talents that He expects them to use to serve Him and others.)* Why and in what way must "judgment begin with the family of God"? *(The practice of self-examination and turning from sin must begin with God's people before they attempt to judge those outside the church community. This is critical for seeing any degree of spiritual revival among believers and any significant influence for Jesus in their communities.)* How should this affect your attitude toward those who don't follow Christ?

PRAY: Ask Jesus to help you follow His example when experiencing difficulty and suffering. Ask Him to help you graciously face and respond to misunderstanding and rejection. Thank Jesus for the privilege of suffering for His sake.

ACT: Examine yourself to see if you have any of the issues, character flaws, or sinful shortcomings that you might tend to see in others. It's likely you'll discover some, so be prepared to take corrective action in your own life. If you're holding any sort of grudge against anyone, give it up.

Fire Starter

1 Peter 5:1-14

THINK: Are you a self-motivated, driven, and ambitious person? While those traits can be beneficial and productive, they must also be held in check by Jesus' followers because of the potential dangers they present. In a drive to achieve success, many people get caught up in a destructive quest for wealth and power. The world system often seems to reward such a pursuit.

RESPOND: Who are "the elders" (verse 1), and what are their primary responsibilities? *(Elders—overseers, pastors, or church leaders—were, and still are, to lead and care for the church community, teaching them from God's Word and discipling them—training them in practical disciplines of following Jesus and learning from God's Word.)* What attitude and motivation should ministry leaders have in serving the Church? What two dangerous desires must leaders—both in and out of the Church—be cautious to avoid (verses 2,3)? What attitude and character trait can help a person overcome these dangerous tendencies (verse 5)? What does it mean to clothe yourself with humility, and why must all of Christ's followers be characterized by this trait? *(Humility must be the distinguishing characteristics of Jesus' followers. It's the absence of selfish pride and a know-it-all attitude. Humility includes a humble consciousness of one's weaknesses—though not putting one's self down—and the character to give God and others credit for their part in one's achievements.)* Why must you "be self-controlled and alert" (verse 8), particularly regarding the devil's activity? What hope and awareness can strengthen your resolve and inspire you to keep standing firm in your faith, even through suffering and opposition?

PRAY: Pray for your pastors and church leaders, that they would depend on God to help them serve effectively. Ask God to help you avoid the temptation to pursue money and power, and to always look for ways to honor Him and to help others with a humble attitude.

ACT: Find a way to help, serve, or encourage one of your pastors or church leaders today.

Fire Starter

2 Peter 1:1-21

THINK: Most people spend their lives trying to accumulate more—more stuff, more knowledge, more power, more friends, more security, and on and on. But God has already given you access to all the resources, promises, and power to be all He created you to be. You may not always recognize what you have, and you might still need to discover and develop what's available to you. And He will continue to provide everything at the right time and place as you trust Him for all of it.

RESPOND: By what means has God "given us everything we need for life and godliness" (verse 3)? How do God's provisions help us develop Christlike character? *(God's love and His Word, salvation through Jesus and His intercession—praying earnestly for people, the inner presence of the Holy Spirit, and the companionship of other Christians provide everything we need for godly character development.)* According to verse 4, what causes corruption in the world, and how do we escape it (verse 4)? What character traits must Christ's followers develop along with faith (verses 5-7)? What happens "if you possess these qualities in increasing measure" (verse 8)? What happens if you lack them (verse 9)? What does this passage imply about spiritual growth? *(All these qualities are to be developed together and continually, not necessarily in the order Peter writes them here. A person can't serve God or people productively if they aren't growing in faith and character.)*

PRAY: Give God thanks for providing everything you need for life and godliness, and for the light and authority of His Word. Ask God to help you grow in these character traits.

ACT: Look back over the list of character qualities in verses 5-7. Write these on a piece of paper or note card that you can carry with you this week. Circle the two you've matured the most in the past year. Underline the two you most need to grow in and ask God to help you do just that. Refer to your card frequently and make every effort to practice and develop these traits.

Fire Starter

2 Peter 2:1-22

THINK: What do you love to do? What excites and motivates you? Consider this: whatever excites you the most is likely to control you the most. As this passage points out, a person "is a slave to whatever has mastered him" (2:19). Is your relationship with God the controlling influence in your life? Is devotion to Him your ultimate priority? People who haven't given God control of their lives are enslaved by their own desires. But if God's highest purposes are your greatest passion, you're free to be all He created you to be.

RESPOND: Why does the Bible warn us about false teachers in the Church? What kind of "stories" do the false teachers make up? *(Some false teachers will use emotional manipulation and dramatic stories to gain money and loyalty from those who don't know what they believe from the Bible.)* In what way are God's past judgments an example to us (verse 6)? What encouragement can we take from what happened to Noah's family and to Lot (verses 5,7,9)? What can we learn from Lot's distress and faithfulness while he was in Sodom? *(Truly godly people love righteousness, hate evil, and grieve over sin in the world.)* Why will false teachers experience certain judgment? What do you think it means, "a man is a slave to whatever has mastered him" (verse 19)? Why are people who have known Jesus but then turned their backs on Him worse off than if they had never known the truth in the first place?

PRAY: Pray for discernment and wisdom to recognize and avoid deception that could compromise your devotion to God and His Word. Give God thanks for providing protection and rescue from the world's corrupt influence. Pray that you would never be mastered by ungodly behavior or desires, but that God would always have control of your life.

ACT: Take special notice today of things in your life—your schedule, your activities, your priorities—that seem to control or "master" you. Do these things honor God? Are they His priorities for your life? If not make the changes necessary to give Him complete control of your life.

Fire Starter

2 Peter 3:1-18

THINK: Many people today think the noblest cause to be involved in is to "save the earth." While efforts to protect the environment and make better use of natural resources are usually well intended and beneficial, there are higher priorities. To be thoughtlessly wasteful or abusive to our planet is wrong. Still, we should be good stewards of God's creation with the sober understanding that no matter how much effort we put into preserving the planet, according to God's Word, it's destined for destruction. Many people are at least vaguely aware that God's Word prophesies an end to the world as we know it, but they don't give it any thought because they don't recognize the signs of the "last days."

RESPOND: Peter wrote both of his letters (1 & 2 Peter) to stimulate what kind of thinking? What warning did Peter give regarding the last days before Christ returns (2 Peter 3:3)? What will the "scoffers" say and do (verse 4)? What doubts will they raise, and why is this attitude so dangerous? What's the main reason why Christ has not yet fulfilled His promise to return (verse 9)? How should this inspire and motivate Jesus' followers? What will ultimately happen to the earth as we know it? In light of this fact, how should we live as we wait for Jesus' return (verse 11)? In light of what will happen to the present heavens and earth, what can God's people look forward to (verse 13)? *(See Revelation 21.)*

PRAY: Ask God to help you keep your thoughts pure and wholesome. Pray that you will not be swayed by doubts regarding Jesus' return. Ask Him to help you use that time to influence as many people as possible to come to know Jesus.

ACT: Make every effort today to put time and resources into things that will last beyond this world—things with eternal significance. Instead of spending money on perishable or material things, set it aside for a missions offering. Take time to help others or to prepare for a ministry you're involved in. Above all, look for ways to influence others for Christ through conversations or service.

Fire Starter

1 John 1:1 through 2:14

THINK: Jesus has gotten a lot of attention in recent years from some unlikely sources—movies, television documentaries, magazine articles, etc. And yet people still wonder—who is Jesus? Is He for real? And what does He have to do with me? Thankfully, Jesus has given us a completely reliable record of His character, His claims and His purpose regarding our lives. In order for people to see Jesus as more than a fabled philosopher, religious leader, or moral teacher who lived a long time ago, they need to see evidence of how He changes lives, restores hope, and provides the peace and purpose they desire. They must see Jesus' life and love through His followers.

RESPOND: What is "fellowship," and how do we experience it with God and each other? *(Fellowship in Greek is koinonia, translated "having in common" and involves sharing and participation with other Christians.)* What does it mean to "walk in darkness"? How does walking "in the light" free us from sin? What does it mean to "confess our sins" (verse 9), and what is God's promise if we sincerely do so? What assurance do we have if we sin? What does it mean that Jesus is "the atoning sacrifice for our sins"? *(God's holy nature and justice required a penalty be paid for humanity's sins against Him. Out of love for us, God provided Jesus as the ultimate atoning—sin-covering, forgiveness-providing—sacrifice.)* What does it mean to "know" Jesus? What kind of person claims to know God but doesn't do what God commands? Why do some people feel they don't need to obey His commands?

PRAY: Thank Jesus for becoming human and ultimately giving His life so we could be forgiven and have eternal life with Him. Ask God to help you sincerely show His love to others.

ACT: If you're currently struggling or holding on to unconfessed sin, accept God's forgiveness and help in overcoming it. If you are aware of any way in which you have not obeyed God, do so without further delay. Since Jesus wants to demonstrate His love through you, make a conscious effort to be like Jesus "with skin on" to everyone around you today.

1 John 2:15 through 3:10

THINK: Though God created the world, the world rejects God. Though God invites all people to be part of His family, some exercise their free will by refusing His invitation. Defying God has been the norm, ever since the first humans gave in to Satan's temptation, disobeyed God and brought the curse of sin into the world. As a result, humankind forfeited authority over creation that God originally delegated to them (Genesis 1:26-30). Satan then seized control (John 14:30; 16:11) and began to dominate the world with his evil purposes (1 John 5:19).

RESPOND: Why are we not to love "the world" or anything in it (2:15-17)? *(The term "world" used in the New Testament frequently refers to the world system existing independently of God and opposed to Him.)* How should this affect your life? What temptations and tendencies come from "the world" (verse 16)? What will eventually happen to the world (verse 17)? What does it mean to be "children of God"? What are the benefits of that relationship? How does the hope of being with God promote purity? *(The hope of spending eternity with Jesus will motivate His followers to avoid anything that offends Him and, with the Holy Spirit's help and God's grace, will keep themselves spiritually pure.)* What does it mean to live "in him [Jesus]"? What does this passage reveal about "the devil"? Why is it impossible for someone in a right relationship to persistently sin? (God's children cannot make habitual sin their way of life because God's life can't exist in those who make a practice of sinning [1:5-7, 2:3-11,15-17, 24-29.) What distinctions exist between "children of God" and "children of the devil"?

PRAY: Pray that your desires and affections won't get tangled up in worldly things. Ask God for wisdom to recognize anything that opposes Jesus and His Word. Give God thanks for making you His child through a relationship with Jesus.

ACT: Are you in any way compromising with worldly behaviors or struggling with the same sin repeatedly? With God's help, take deliberate and perhaps difficult steps to deal with the issues before they take a greater toll on you spiritually.

343

Fire Starter

1 John 3:11-24

THINK: Jesus gave His life for you. Would you be willing to do the same for Him? Perhaps that thought raises anxiety in your heart and mind. Yet there is something God asks of you that may at times be tougher than dying for Him; that is, living for Him. In reality, God has already asked you to lay down your life for His sake (verse 16). But He's not simply referring to a physical sacrifice of your life. Rather, God expects you to willingly put aside your own rights, interests, and concerns for the benefit of others, particularly to demonstrate Jesus' love and bring them closer to Him.

RESPOND: How will people whose actions are evil typically respond to and treat those whose actions are righteous (verses 12,13)? Why should the world's hatred toward Christians not surprise you? In what way is someone "who hates his brother" a murderer? *(All sin—evidence of our corrupt human nature—will, apart from God's grace, bring spiritual death and separation from God.)* Why must Christians take all sin seriously? *(All sin—even the less "serious" ones—if not repented of, can lead to a weak spiritual life, which can lead to a rejection of the Holy Spirit's influence, and ultimately to spiritual death and separation from God.)* How do we know what true love is (verse 16)? How are we to respond to Jesus' example of love (verse 16)? In practical terms, what does it mean "to lay down our lives for our brothers" (verse 16)? How, when and why are we to demonstrate true Christlike love in tangible ways (verse 17)? According to verse 18, how do we prove and demonstrate true love? What is one of the vital keys to an effective prayer life (verse 22)?

PRAY: Ask God to give you compassion for those who oppose, reject, or mistreat you because of your devotion to Christ. Pray that you will take advantage of every opportunity to demonstrate Jesus' love.

ACT: If God has given you the ability or opportunity to meet any of these needs, do so as a way of demonstrating Jesus' sacrificial love.

344

1 John 4:1-21

THINK: God is Love. That's one way He describes himself in His Word (verse 8). Even people who don't really know God or His Word often claim to know that "God is love." Some use His love to excuse their ungodly lifestyles. Others feel that if they show enough love to others they'll gain God's favor or automatically be in good standing with Him. God's love provides security only for those who respond to it with obedience to His Word. And God's love will bring reward only if our attitudes and actions are motivated by true love for Him.

RESPOND: What does it mean that we should "not believe every spirit"? What does it mean to "test the spirits"? *(We must test every spirit—someone inspired or influenced by a spirit, or the spirit behind a person's motives and message—as tolerance for spiritual error and unbiblical teaching increases. Use biblical standards to evaluate all professing Christian authors, speakers, prophets, or individuals who claim their message and work come from God.)* How did God demonstrate love for us (verses 9,10)? How can we develop and demonstrate His love for others? How can you know that you're in a right relationship with God and that He lives within you (verse 13)? What will provide confidence on judgment day? Why and in what way does perfect love drive out fear? *(If we're in a right relationship with God, we don't need to fear His judgment. His love for us, and our love for Him and others confirm our spiritual salvation.)* Why can't a person love God if he or she does not love others (verse 20,21)?

PRAY: Pray for discernment regarding ideas, behaviors, and people that could undermine your devotion to God's truth and purposes. Thank Jesus for His love that removes the fear of judgment.

ACT: Continue to look for practical, tangible ways to demonstrate God's love to people. Also, if you are harboring feelings of bitterness, resentment, or hate toward anyone, ask God to help you overcome these feelings with forgiveness and compassion. If appropriate, apologize and ask forgiveness from the other person or persons involved.

Fire Starter

1 John 5:1-21

THINK: Most religions involve people attempting to appease "god" or to attain some kind of enlightenment through rules, rituals, and routines. But Christianity is about knowing God through a personal relationship with His Son, Jesus Christ. Another major difference between true Christianity and nearly all other religions is that with religion, people are never sure of where they stand with "god" or where they are in some cycle of life. But Christ offers real hope and assurance of spiritual salvation.

RESPOND: How will genuine faith in Jesus express itself? How and why are faith and love connected? *(When we're reborn by faith—having accepted God's forgiveness and become His child—the Holy Spirit pours God's love into us.)* How can we know that our love for others is true Christian love? *(When our love for people is unselfish, we know it's the real deal.)* How will true children of God view His commands (verse 3)? What enables God's people to overcome the corrupt influences of the world and avoid the judgment in store for it? What should you do if you know a fellow Christian who is not deliberately defying God but is struggling with sin because of spiritual weakness (verse 16)? How can your prayers help a person in this situation?

PRAY: Pray that your love for God and others will always be sincere, purely motivated, and backed by obedience. Ask God to strengthen your faith to overcome worldly influences as you depend on the Holy Spirit. Thank Jesus for the hope of eternal life with Him and the opportunity to develop that relationship now.

ACT: Pray for and personally encourage anyone you know who is struggling in their relationship with Jesus but still desires to serve Him. As you go through the day, stay aware of Jesus' presence, and take every opportunity to interact with Him through prayer—not only speaking, but also listening to Him.

2 John 1:1-13

THINK: Though the ability to love comes from God, people certainly can exercise love for others without knowing God or being devoted to His Word. People who do this are essentially placing love, acceptance, friendship, and good works above the truth and commands of God. On the other hand, it is also possible for people in the church to promote biblical truth and defend the Bible's teachings, yet not show active love and compassion for others. But this is not showing a true love for God himself.

RESPOND: According to verse 2, how can we know "the truth"? How does being committed to the truth of God's Word enable us to love others more deeply? Why and in what way must devotion to God's truth and love for others go together? *(See THINK above.)* What are the conditions for continuing to live in God's grace, mercy, and peace (verse 3)? *(Love people [verses 5,6], and guard the truth [verses 7-11].)* Why is obedience to God inseparable from true love for God? How can we verify if a teaching about God or about Jesus Christ is true? *(Teaching about God which doesn't hold to the truth and standards of Jesus presented in the New Testament is incomplete and deceptive and must be rejected.)* How should those in the church respond to anyone who claims to follow Christ but whose teaching distorts, contradicts, or opposes authentic New Testament teaching (verse 10)? *(God tells His people not to encourage or financially support such teachers. Doing so not only joins you with them in their deceptive "ministry" but could compromise your ability to discern truth.)*

PRAY: Ask God to give you greater passion for His truth and greater compassion for others. Ask the Holy Spirit to challenge you if you are in any way failing to obey God's Word.

ACT: Be sure that your love for God is confirmed by love for others. Make every effort to behave in a kind way toward the people you come in contact. If you've behaved inappropriately toward anyone, make an apology and find a way to make up for your shortcoming with sincere kindness.

Fire Starter

3 John 1:1-14

THINK: When Jesus left the earth and told His followers to take His message throughout the world (Matthew 28:16; Mark 16:15), He was not simply offering a good suggestion; He was issuing a direct command. And it wasn't for a select few ministers or missionaries. God sent the Holy Spirit to guide and empower us for the mission, and He also links us with other Christians.

RESPOND: What does God want every aspect of our lives to reflect (verse 2)? *(God wants His followers' lives to reflect and demonstrate His care and provision.)* Why might we experience difficult circumstances or health issues? What can we learn through such times? *(The Bible teaches that God may allow us to experience times of need. Sometimes our need serves the purpose of challenging us to trust God, developing and strengthening our faith and spiritual endurance. Times of need also help us relate and effectively minister to others in need. Of course, times of need also occur because of natural disasters, war, famine, drought, or poor economic or social conditions.)* Does good spiritual health—a thriving prayer life and growing faith in one's life—ensure good physical health and material blessing? Why or why not? Why do Christian missionaries rely on churches for support, rather than taking support from those among whom they serve? *(For a missionary to depend on material support from those they're trying to reach with the gospel could hinder the message and bring the accusation of preaching for financial gain.)* Why does John remind us, "do not imitate what is evil but what is good"?

PRAY: Pray that Christ will be honored in every aspect of your life—whether through blessing or adversity. Give God thanks for providing for your needs and for teaching you to depend on Him at all times. Ask the Lord to help you take advantage of opportunities to spread His message by contributing to worthy ministries through prayer and material support. Pray for specific missionaries and evangelists that you know or that your church supports.

ACT: Make a commitment to give to missions and give offerings to help those ministering throughout the world.

THINK: Many Christians like to flaunt their spiritual freedom by disregarding anything that remotely resembles a religious rule or constraint. They feel that since spiritual salvation is a result of God's grace—His unearned, undeserved favor and love—they are not obligated to follow such "legalistic" standards. The problem is that they end up disregarding many of the moral standards of God's Law. Some people go so far as to think that it doesn't really matter what they do, as long as they believe the right things.

RESPOND: What does it mean "to contend for the faith"? *(The word "contend" in Greek is* epagonizomai, *literally means to "struggle," "suffer," "be under great pressure" or "fight." This describes the battle faithful believers must fight in defense of Jesus' gospel. This speaks more of being passionate and spiritually determined than of being obnoxious, self-righteous, and Pharisee-like toward the world. Christians are to be confidently reliant on the Holy Spirit to help them defend and stand firm for the truth of God's Word without becoming hateful, bigoted, or arrogant.)* How can you build yourself up in faith, and why is this vital? *(Diligently study God's Word, never making excuses for not applying the Bible's teaching to your life. Pray in the Spirit—communicate and interact with God, relying on the power of the Holy Spirit, depending on Him to inspire, guide, energize, sustain, and help you pray according to God's purposes.)*

PRAY: Thank Jesus for His ever-increasing mercy, peace, and love in your life. Ask Him to help you boldly, firmly, and graciously defend His truth. Pray that your beliefs will always be founded on God's truth and that your behavior will be consistent with those beliefs. Pray for discernment when people compliment you with selfish or deceptive motives.

ACT: Do a school project or paper on an issue related to your faith or godly standards. Do something practical to encourage someone you know who is struggling with doubts about the Christian faith.

Revelation 1:1-20

THINK: Are you ready to be blessed? That's God's promise to those who read and "take to heart" (verse 3) what's written in His Revelation. Some venture into the book out of strange curiosity, but God wants you to approach it with purpose. Some people avoid it because they feel it's too difficult or even frightening. But Revelation is a celebration of Christ's ultimate victory and conclusive triumph over evil. For those who love God, Revelation provides assurance that all things will be made right in the end. As you read Revelation, you'll notice the use of symbolic language and images to describe real events. Though it foretells the future, it speaks to the present. Looking through the lens of late first-century/early second-century Christianity, Revelation gives a glimpse of things that are unfolding even now as well as things to come.

RESPOND: What does the word that's translated "revelation" mean? *(The Greek word* apocalupsis, *"to take from what is being covered," implying unveiling or revealing.)* What's the primary purpose of Revelation? *(The primary purpose is to describe the ultimate triumph of God's kingdom and purposes when Jesus returns to destroy evil and establish His kingdom on earth.)* How does verse 7 describe Jesus' second coming—when He literally returns to earth? What will His coming mean for those who know Him, and for those who don't (verse 7)? What do the seven gold lampstands represent (verse 20)? What is the double-edged sword, and what does it do? *(This is God's Word, which cuts away sin from churches, bringing God's grace and forgiveness, or cuts a church off from God's kingdom in judgment.)* In what way does verse 19 give a general overview of Revelation and it's relevance then, now, and for the future?

PRAY: Thank Jesus for revealing himself and His plans for people, both now and for the future. Ask God to help you respond appropriately to His Word. Praise Jesus for His eternal and unchanging character, power, and authority.

ACT: Meditate on and consider memorizing Revelation 1:3 to bring back to your mind as you study this fascinating and unique book.

Revelation 2:1-17

THINK: Consider the spiritual condition of the churches addressed in this passage. Then ask yourself the following: Am I staying pure in spiritual beliefs but also passionate in spiritual practice? Am I doing things for Christ but not taking time to be with Him? Is serving Jesus a matter of convenience, or is it truly costing me something? Am I focused more on what I get from God than on surrendering to Him? Is my outward testimony being threatened by inward compromise?

RESPOND: For what did Jesus commend the church in Ephesus (verses 2,3)? What did the Lord have against this church (verse 4)? In what way had people forsaken their "first love"? What does it mean to "repent and do the things you did at first" (verse 5)? How can individual Christians and churches avoid losing their first love? Who are overcomers and what is their reward? *(Overcomers are Jesus' followers who continually rely on God's grace, remain passionately devoted to Jesus, live in consistent victory over sin, Satan, and the corrupt world system.)* How was the church doing, materially and spiritually? In what way was it "rich"? What warning and encouragement did Jesus offer this church (verse 10)? What is "the second death" that overcomers won't experience? *(This refers to spiritual death and permanent separation from God.)*

PRAY: Pray that you'll never abandon your love for Jesus, but that it would grow day by day. Ask God to help you resist influences that could lead to spiritual compromise. Ask Him to help you respond to His Word with obedience and action.

ACT: As you go through the day, consider whether any of your actions or behaviors could give anyone a wrong impression of Christ or what it means to follow Him. Make a deliberate effort to avoid and resist attitudes and actions that could compromise your character or mislead others spiritually. Do things that build people up and give them an accurate impression of Jesus.

THINK: Consider the spiritual condition of the churches addressed in this passage. Then ask yourself: Has spiritual "success" or recognition caused me to rationalize questionable behavior or overlook sin in my life? Am I coasting spiritually and relying on my image, reputation, or past experiences; or am I authentically alive and growing spiritually?

RESPOND: How can we tell that the church in Thyatira was growing spiritually (2:19)? What serious problem did they still have? What does Jesus' warning to this church reveal about His attitude toward "believers" who influence others to compromise godly standards and principles? *(Christians must reject the influence of those who put their words above biblical revelation and standards. No matter how nice or reasonable a spokesperson or author comes across, and regardless of how many Scriptures are included or positive references to Jesus, teaching which ultimately promotes ungodly behavior, self-promotion, and considering oneself equal to God is to be exposed and rejected.)* What is Jesus' promise to those who remain faithful to Him (3:5)? What is "the Book of Life" (verse 5)? How does a person's name get into this book?

PRAY: Pray that your spiritual growth would never allow you to become proud or complacent regarding spiritual problems in your life. Thank Jesus that your name is in His book of life.

ACT: Is there is any aspect of your spiritual life in which you've become less passionate or devoted to God's purposes? It could be your personal time in the Word and prayer. Perhaps your intensity in worship or your drive to tell others about Christ has diminished. With God's help, take deliberate and practical steps to reignite your passion in whatever area may be lacking.

THINK: Consider the spiritual condition of the churches addressed in this passage. Then ask yourself: Am I focused on myself—my needs, my desires, my goals—or am I focused on Christ, His purposes and how I can help others to know Him? Am I following Christ through open doors of opportunity that will allow me to grow in faith and influence others for Him? Have I taken God's blessings for granted and allowed them to erode my passion for Jesus personally?

RESPOND: What do Jesus' words in verse 7 indicate about His character, power, and authority? How had the Philadelphian church proven its faithfulness, and what would Jesus do for them as a result? What does it mean that Jesus will "keep you from" (verse 10) that trial if you keep His "command to endure patiently"? What does it mean that Jesus is "the Amen, the faithful and true witness"? *("Amen" in Hebrew means "surely" or "truly." It affirms important sayings throughout the Bible, drawing attention to God's authority, and closing blessings and prayers. The God of truth guarantees His Word to us through Jesus.)* When describing the church in Laodicea, what does Jesus mean "that you are neither cold nor hot" but are "lukewarm"? *(Jesus is referring to their spiritual condition.)* How do Christians get this way, and how does Jesus feel about this condition (verse 16)? What attitudes do spiritually lukewarm people have, and why can it be difficult to change (verses 17,18)? In what way were the people "wretched, pitiful, poor, blind and naked"? How did Jesus address the Laodicean's main sources of pride (verse 18)? In what way does Jesus sometimes exercise "tough love" with us (verse 19)?

PRAY: Thank Jesus for helping you through tough times, but also for rescuing you from the judgment that's coming on the world. Thank Him for providing correction and discipline when you start to become spiritually lukewarm.

ACT: Consider a specific way in which God has blessed you, then think of a practical way to pass that blessing on to others.

Fire ✸ Starter

Revelation 4:1-11

THINK: Are you good at explaining things to others in ways they understand? Regardless of your way with words, there are things that simply defy description. There is just no vocabulary to verbalize how extraordinary they are. More than anything, this applies to God. The Bible describes many aspects of His character, His attributes, His activity, and His purposes. At times it describes people's reactions to God's glorious presence, which typically rendered humans speechless, immobile, and virtually lifeless (Revelation 1:17). But mere words don't do justice in describing God himself. Even in this passage, John doesn't attempt to describe God directly, for His glory is too great for words and beyond describing in any shape or form.

RESPOND: At this point in the Revelation, what type of transition seems to take place in how things were revealed to John? *(This indicates that time passed between the revealing of various parts of the book to John.)* What do many scholars and interpreters think has happened prior to the events described in this passage and beyond? Why do they believe this? Why do you think John doesn't describe God directly? What do the four living creatures around the throne likely represent and what is the significance of their appearance? *(These fantastic creatures likely represent the entire living creation. All of God's living creatures will bring Him glory and honor and will eventually be liberated from the curse sin brought.)* What do these creatures "never stop saying" (verse 8)? What's the significance of repeating this continuously? *(God is completely separate from and above all creation in His character and purposes. The repetition of "Holy, holy, holy" emphasizes His absolute holiness from eternity past and future. Holiness is the most apparent aspect of God's nature and character.)* Why do the elders lay down their crowns as they worship God? What is the essence of their worship to God (verse 11)?

PRAY: Worship God the Father for His indescribable glory and perfect holiness.

ACT: Take extra time throughout the day to worship God. Notice the people and things around you and praise God for specific aspects of His creation, His work, His purposes, His power, and His protection.

Revelation 5:1-14

THINK: How often do you stop to consider where you would be without Jesus? In every conceivable way, we would be lost apart from Christ. No one else could do what Jesus has done and what He continues to do to bring fulfilment to God's plan for all things. He is truly the only One "worthy"—completely capable, infinitely valuable, and entirely right in every way. He's the only One worthy to judge all people and all things and to rule forever.

RESPOND: Why did John weep profusely over the scroll? *(John probably knows that if a worthy person isn't found to open the Book, God's purpose of judgment and blessing for the world will remain unfulfilled.)* Who is "the Lion of the tribe of Judah" and "Root of David," and what's the significance of those titles? *(Jesus is pictured as a lion—the king of beasts, indicating He will rule earth, fulfilling God's promise in Genesis 49:9,10 to raise up a ruler from the Israelite tribe of Judah and King David's lineage.)* Why is He worthy to open the scroll's seals (Revelation 5:9,10)? What's the significance of "the prayers of the saints" (verse 8), and why are they described as "golden bowls full of incense"? *(The bowls of incense indicate that the Book must be opened and its judgments taken place before these prayers can be answered fully.)* To whom are the worshipful acknowledgments of "worthy" now directed, and what is the source of His worthiness? *(Jesus is referred to as "the Lamb" twenty-eight times in Revelation, reminding hearers and readers that He is the worthy Lamb whose sacrifice on the cross "takes away the sins of the world" [John 1:29].)* Who offers this worship (Revelation 5:13)?

PRAY: Worship Jesus for His worthiness in sacrificing His life for the sins of the world, and for fulfilling all of God's purposes— past, present, and future. Worship Him for His right judgments regarding all people.

ACT: Continue to practice godly worship in all aspects of life. This time, focus on who Jesus is and what He's done. Approach Him with reverence, but also interact with Him as your closest friend. Find ways to honor Christ in all activities and conversations.

THINK: Perhaps you've heard a reference to the four horsemen of the Apocalypse or maybe even seen a graphic depiction of that imposing scene. But this is not just a mythical concept or fictional theme for a Hollywood horror movie. These images convey a future reality and mark the arrival of catastrophic events, the likes of which the world has never known, as God unleashes His divine judgment on the corrupt and evil world system and the ungodly people who are part of it.

RESPOND: What must happen before God's justice is fully revealed (verse 11)? How do we know that some will turn to God during the Tribulation period, and what will happen to them? How will people's response to Christ before the Tribulation affect their response to the judgments during the Tribulation? *(Some people will be given the chance to surrender to Jesus and be spiritually saved during the Tribulation. For the most part, this refers to people living during that period who never adequately heard or understood the message of Jesus. Those who heard the gospel before this time period but resisted God, continuing in sin, will not likely be given further opportunity for salvation during this time. Some think that those who knew the truth but rejected Jesus will naturally turn to Him during the Tribulation, but the Bible seems to indicate otherwise since this is a period of God's judgment, not His mercy [9:21; 16:9].)* How will people react to God's judgments (6:15,16)? What does "the wrath of the Lamb" indicate about Christ's character and view toward sin?

PRAY: Pray for greater sensitivity and compassion toward those around you who don't know Jesus. Pray that they would see Him in you and that you could influence them for Jesus so they can escape God's end-time wrath.

ACT: Encourage someone you know who has endured opposition for their faith. Build a friendship with someone who seems resistant to God but may be open to Jesus' message if they see His life and love in you. Look for an opportunity to engage in conversation about the end-times, perhaps related to cultural trends or current events.

Revelation 7:1-17

THINK: The Great Tribulation is a time of God's unprecedented judgment on a world that has persistently rejected Christ; but it's also a time of satanic assault against those who receive Christ and remain true to His Word. During this period, followers of Christ will suffer terrible persecution. The conflict between righteousness and wickedness will be so intense that it can only be called a "great tribulation" (verse 14). This phrase in Greek literally reads "the tribulation, the great"—the repeated article "the" adding forceful emphasis. Matthew 24:21 says, "For then there will be great distress, unequaled from the beginning of the world until now—and never to be equaled again." But through this time, those who receive Christ and remain true to Him have assurance of eternal peace and joy like the world has never known.

RESPOND: Who are the 144,000 and what will they do? Who is part of the "great multitude" standing before Christ in heaven (Revelation 7:9,13,14)? *(Some Bible interpreters believe these are new believers from the family lines of Israel who will be commissioned and empowered by the Holy Spirit to preach the message of Jesus during the Tribulation.)* Regarding the end-time judgments on the earth, what is implied by the phrase "great tribulation"? *(This will be a time of God's unprecedented judgment on those who have rejected Jesus. It will also be a time of satanically influenced assault on those who become faithful to Jesus and His Word during this time.)* During this time, how will God respond to those who rejected Him, and how will Satan respond to those who follow Christ? For those who remain faithful to Christ, what assurances are given in this passage (verses 15-17)? What does it mean, "God will wipe away every tear from their eyes"?

PRAY: Pray for the strength to endure persecution for Christ. Thank Him for His seal of protection on your life.

ACT: Encourage as many people as possible today—Christians and non-Christians alike—who are going through difficult times. Volunteer to pray for those to whom God directs you, even doing so in person.

Fire ✦ Starter

Revelation 8:1-13

THINK: The scene around God's throne in heaven is one of awesomely intense worship and wonder—flashes of light, rumblings of thunder, heavenly creatures and countless angels encircling the throne and crying out in praise (verses 4,5). Suddenly, the music, singing, and shouts of praise stop. The silence is as intense as the worship had been, bringing an overwhelming sense of the seriousness of what is about to take place as the Lord intervenes in human history and unleashes His judgment on the earth.

RESPOND: In regard to judgment, what do the trumpets symbolize? *(Trumpets were a sign of kingly authority, served to announce important events, give signals during war, and sound an alarm. The seven trumpets announce a series of end-time plagues more severe than the previous breaking of seals, but not as dreadful as when the bowls of God's judgment are poured out.)* How do "the prayers of all the saints" relate to God's purposes—including His enactment of justice on earth? *(Some interpreters believe the seventh seal [silence] is a time of God giving priority to His peoples' prayers—prayers about to directly effect earth's events. John mentions the prayers of all the saints, possibly indicating the prayers of those enduring the Tribulation are joined by the intercession of those in heaven. This passage may also imply the prayers for God's purposes and justice of God's people of all time.)* In what sense does God store up people's prayers? *(Although God may not answer all prayers immediately, He keeps them for fulfillment at the right time.)* In light of this, how should you pray at the present time? What kinds of devastation do the first four trumpets reveal? Who or what is affected?

PRAY: Pray for God's justice to be enacted and fulfilled on earth. Ask God to help you and your church have more effective influence on people for Christ. Give God thanks for mercifully providing more time for people to turn to Him.

ACT: Spend free periods today in silent consideration and compassionate prayer for those around you who don't know Jesus and are headed for judgment.

THINK: Many people have the impression that serving God is too restrictive and that following their own way—or following Satan's way—provides much more freedom. But those who reject God and follow Satan's deception will ultimately find that he has no loyalty to those who serve his purposes. As you continue studying Revelation, keep in mind that regardless of one's interpretation of the symbolic language in Revelation—whether descriptions are taken figuratively or literally—whenever symbols are used, they represent something or someone very real.

RESPOND: What is the Abyss (verse 1), and how does it fit into the events described in Revelation? *(The Abyss is the place of imprisonment for demons [11:7; 17:8]. The beast—the Antichrist—comes out of the Abyss. Satan will later be imprisoned there for a thousand years.)* What does the severity of these judgments reveal about God's justice and the effects of evil on people's lives? *([1] God demands judgment on unbelief, rebellion, and rejection of Jesus' message. [2] The destructive power of evil. [3] Opposing God and His truth and pursuing evil purposes instead opens one's life to satanic influence, making them easy prey for demonic activity and control of their very nature, eventually to have their life and soul destroyed.)* Why is it significant that forces of evil are the ones inflicting the pain and suffering at this point? Why will the people not killed by these plagues still not turn to God? *(The defiance and hard-heartedness of people during this period of time demonstrates the depth of human sinfulness and corruption.)* What will be among the most prominent sins in the last days and the Tribulation period?

PRAY: Pray that God works powerfully through the Church to combat the devil's schemes in individual lives and communities. Pray that the Holy Spirit opens people's eyes to the destructive effects of evil so they'll turn to God for mercy.

ACT: As you go through the day, take particular note of the destructive, devastating, yet sometime subtle effects that evil, wickedness, and immorality have on people's lives. Let this stir greater compassion in you.

Revelation 10:1-11

THINK: God's Word is not all sweetness; many parts are hard to swallow. While it speaks of mercy for those who humbly submit to God and entrust their lives to Christ, it also pronounces bitter judgment on those who defy God and reject the message of Christ. Revelation contains much sorrow concerning the judgments to come. Yet, for God's people, the message is ultimately one of sweet hope, culminating in the revelation of their eternal reign with Christ (22:5).

RESPOND: What do the seven thunders signify? *(The seven thunders' sounds represent certain aspects of God's coming judgment.)* What can we learn from the fact that John is forbidden to reveal the message of the thunders? How should this influence our views and perspectives on the end-time events conveyed in Revelation? *(This shows that during the Tribulation there will be certain judgments not revealed in the seals, trumpets, and bowls, which means no one knows ahead of time everything that will take place. For this reason, we should be flexible in our views about the sequence of events in Revelation.)* What's the significance of John being asked to eat the little scroll? What's the significance of the scroll tasting sweet but then souring his stomach? *(John doesn't offer an explanation for such an unusual act. However, it likely relates to a similar action in Ezekiel 2:8,9 and 3:1–3. The scroll's sweet-to-taste but sour-to-the-stomach affect is like God's message to people, a mixture of goodness and harshness, blessing and curse, mercy and judgment.)* In what way does this relate to how people respond to God and the message of Christ? *(For Jesus' followers, His message is sweet and increasingly nutritious. For those who reject Him, the message represents judgment they must face.)*

PRAY: Give God thanks for His sweet mercy and the fulfillment that comes from following His Word. Pray that He uses you to influence others who are currently headed for the bitter judgment that comes from rejecting Christ.

ACT: Make a deliberate effort to do and to speak things that may not be easy or convenient but will honor Jesus. Be sure to respond in a gracious way to anyone with whom you interact.

THINK: Many people in the world talk about compassion, civility, and open-mindedness. They pride themselves on their "tolerance" of different ideas, views, faiths, and lifestyles. But in reality, people have little patience or tolerance for anyone or anything that challenges or contradicts their own self-indulgent lifestyles. The harsh reality is that many people would celebrate the death and demise of those whose godly lifestyle exposes the wicked ways of the world at large. After all, many people feel that the world would be a better place without radically devoted followers of Christ. In the end-times, they will get a glimpse of such a dark world—and it will be nothing to celebrate.

RESPOND: Where do the events of chapter 11 take place, and what does the measuring of the temple and altar symbolize? *(Chapter 11 continues the interlude begun in chapter 10, still before the final judgments to be revealed. This passage, occurring in Jerusalem, refers to God measuring Israel's unbelieving spiritual condition.)* When the seventh trumpet sounds, what happens in heaven? *(The angel announces that the world is now the kingdom of Jesus, under His reign forever.)* Contrary to some interpreters' views, why is it unlikely that this is the "last trumpet" (1 Corinthians 15:52; 1 Thessalonians 4:16), which signals the rapture of the Church? *(The seventh trumpet involves events leading up to Jesus' return, including judgments, including the bowl judgments of chapter 16 and the subsequent victory. This is different than the "last trumpet" of 1 Corinthians 15:52 and 1 Thessalonians 4:16, when Jesus' followers are suddenly taken from the earth to heaven. That trumpet is the last prior to God's tribulation judgments. Here, the judgments are well underway prior to this seventh trumpet.)* What do the twenty-four elders prophesy will happen when Christ returns to earth?

PRAY: Pray for the spiritual salvation of those who don't know Christ. Pray that you will be a more effective witness for Jesus in the days ahead.

ACT: Do something today that will stretch or enhance your witness for Christ. Make a deliberate effort to talk about Jesus or God's work in your life.

Revelation 12:1-17

THINK: Guilt can be disheartening and devastating. While recognizing legitimate guilt is necessary for justice—even receiving God's life-liberating forgiveness—persistent guilt leads to overwhelming hopelessness. That's why guilt is part of Satan's strategy. As "the accuser," he constantly points to people's failures and unworthiness. He will even accuse you of not doing enough for God if the resulting guilt causes a rift in your relationship with Jesus. But those who surrender their lives to Jesus can enjoy forgiveness and freedom from guilt.

RESPOND: What conflicts involving Satan are depicted in this chapter? *(Satan's conflict is with Jesus and the redemption He provided, faithful believers in Israel and worldwide, and with heaven itself.)* How does the "war in heaven" relate to the Tribulation period? *(Satan and his dark angles will make one final effort to defeat God's angels. Michael, the chief angel, will lead a defeating attack on Satan, marking the beginning of the end his rule in the "heavenly realms" [Ephesians 6:12].)* In what way is Satan an "accuser," and how does this play into his strategy against people? *(The Hebrew meaning of Satan is "accuser." Satan accuses people before God, claiming their unworthiness and selfish motives for serving God [Job 1:6–11, Zechariah 3:1]. Satan and his demons use accusations to riddle Christians with guilt over past failures and forgiven sins.)* How do God's people ultimately overcome Satan's schemes and accusations? *(Christians overcome Satan by continually acknowledging to themselves and others that it's Jesus' sacrifice—the blood He shed on the cross—not their own efforts, which has provided forgiveness and spiritual salvation.)*

PRAY: Give thanks to God the Father for sending Jesus to die for your sin and open the way to a relationship with Him. Pray for persecuted Christians.

ACT: Continue your efforts from the previous day to strategically create and take advantage of opportunities to communicate your faith in Jesus. Ask friends questions to spark spiritual conversations. For example, "What is your purpose in life?"

Revelation 13:1-10

THINK: Taking a step back from the devastating images of end-time judgment, this section provides a symbolic description of persons and events that are part of the Great Tribulation, including a graphic depiction of the end-time antichrist, embodied in a satanic-empowered world ruler who will oppose God and all He has accomplished through Christ. This individual, and the God-defying world system he represents, will deceive people and engineer Satan's final assault against Jesus, His work, and His followers before Christ ultimately returns to earth to defeat the forces of evil and reign forever.

RESPOND: Who or what is represented by the beast coming out of the sea? *(Chapter 13 is still part of the interlude between the trumpets and bowls, symbolically describing events and persons of the Tribulation. Here begins the description of the clash between God and His people and the beast—history's final great world government, specifically, the Antichrist and his government.)* What kind of power will the Antichrist possess? *(The beast, while it represents the end-time world kingdom or government, also represents the ruler over it, someone who will gain political, economic, and religious power.)* How will the issue of "a fatal wound" enhance the Antichrist's deceptive influence (verse 3)? Who will be deceived by the beast's pretentious "miracles"? Who will people really worship because of the beast (verse 4)? How long will the beast exercise authority, and what will he do to God's people during this time (verses 6,7)? What choice will people have to make during the Tribulation, and how will that choice affect their lives? Who will worship the Antichrist, and why?

PRAY: Spend time in worship. Pray for people you know— Christians and non-Christians—that their minds and hearts will be open to God so they won't be deceived in the end times.

ACT: Make an effort to do good and to show kindness to someone who has a reputation for opposing God and Christians and who knows that you believe in Jesus. Pray that your actions will influence them to consider the truth of Jesus.

Revelation 13:11 through 14:20

THINK: You've probably seen or heard the number used somewhere other than the Bible—perhaps in literature, movies, or other media—referring to something sinister or ultimately evil. Christians often call it "the mark of the beast" (666). Much speculation has surrounded this description of the end-time antichrist. The important thing is being able to discern the deception of anyone who would undermine what Jesus has done to bring hope and true life to people. Those who faithfully follow Christ now won't have to endure the Antichrist's rule. Nonetheless, God's people always need His wisdom to avoid deception and recognize evil in all its forms.

RESPOND: How will the false prophet compel people to worship the Antichrist (13:15)? What "mark" will the false prophet force people to receive, what will it allow and what will it represent? What will happen to those who refuse the mark? Why do you think the Bible isn't more specific about the "mark" and how it will be applied? How are people blessed by giving their lives for Jesus during this time (14:13)? Who is seated on the cloud (verse 14), and why is there a sharp sickle in His hand? (Here Jesus is ready to execute judgment on a world ripe with evil [see John 5:22]. Revelation 14:14–16 is a prediction or preview of events of 16:12–16 and 19:11–21 occurring at the end of the Tribulation period.)

PRAY: Pray that no one you know will be fooled by eloquent words or deceptive displays of power. Pray for wisdom about things to avoid in the last days.

ACT: Pray for a strong sense of Jesus' leadership so you can "follow the Lamb wherever he goes" (verse 4). Let Him lead you to people who need encouragement or who may be open to Him. Let God's presence inspire greater purity in thought, speech, and actions.

Fire ❀ Starter

Revelation 15:1-8

THINK: Do you tend to finish most things you start? And when you complete a significant project, do you ever celebrate by giving yourself a special reward? Regardless of your personal tendencies, you can rest assured that God always finishes what He starts. At times there may seem to be a lot of incompleteness in the world, as well as loose ends in your own life. But thankfully, God's justice ensures that all will be made right in the end. You can be "confident of this, that he who began a good work in you will carry it on to completion until the day of Christ Jesus" (Philippians 1:6). That's cause for celebration.

RESPOND: What is significant about the "seven last plagues" mentioned at the beginning of this chapter? *(These judgments are more severe than those described to this point and come in rapid succession—the final warning that a holy God cannot leave sin unpunished.)* and what is "the tabernacle of the Testimony" (Revelation 15:5), and what is the connection between this and the final judgments? *(John saw in heaven what looked like the Old Testament tabernacle with its inner sanctuary, housing the ark of the covenant, containing the Ten Commandments [Deuteronomy 10:1-5; Exodus 40:17-21]. This signifies that the judgments are the result of God's opposition to sin and people who reject His Law.)* What are the "golden bowls filled with the wrath of God" (verse 7), and what does it mean that "no one could enter the temple until the seven plagues of the seven angels were completed" (verse 8)? *(This will be God's final judgments on unrepentant people prior to Jesus' return to destroy the Antichrist and his forces, then establish His reign on earth. No one can intervene to stop the judgment.)*

PRAY: Give God thanks for providing people with ample opportunity to turn to Him. Thank Him for His perfect justice that will prevail in the end, and for His ultimate victory over evil.

ACT: Think of something you've started but not finished—a chore at home, a project at school, a commitment at church, a promise, or a conversation about Jesus. Make every effort to complete or follow through on these efforts in a way that honors God.

Revelation 16:1-21

THINK: Considering some of the horrendous events described in Revelation, many people have difficulty understanding God's love in light of His judgments. But just a glimmer of God's perfect character and infinite goodness exposes the terrible reality of sin and how repulsive it is to God. It corrupts His creation and destroys people's lives. God's love and justice demand that sin's penalty be paid. His Son, Jesus, paid that penalty with His own perfect life. For now, God extends the opportunity to personally accept that sacrifice, receive forgiveness and escape the judgments to come.

RESPOND: What is God's "wrath"? *(God's wrath is His justified anger, judgment, and punishment for sin.)* How would you respond to someone who had difficulty understanding how a loving God could send these judgments on the world? *(Being completely holy—pure and separated from evil—God must oppose and punish the sin and evil which opposes His perfect nature. God's perfect justice requires the most extreme penalty, earned by sinful humanity, but paid by God's Son Jesus. Christ's sacrifice is our evidence that God's justice doesn't contradict his love and mercy.)* Who will be influenced by demonic spirits, working with and through Satan, the Antichrist, and the false prophet (verse 14)? What will happen among world leaders during this time? (Manipulated and influenced by these demonic spirits, world rulers will enter into an alliance with the Antichrist, plunging the entire world into a great holocaust.) What "natural disasters" take place near the conclusion of this time and what devastation will they cause (verses 11–21)?

PRAY: Give God thanks for His ultimate love and justice, and for exposing the horrendous nature of sin by displaying His perfect justice against it.

ACT: Do all you can today—even going out of your way—to show love and kindness to people you know who have caused opposition or grief to Christians. If they react harshly or indifferently, respond graciously. If they outright ask you what you're doing, don't hesitate to let them know that you're trying to do what God desires and to be more like Jesus.

Revelation 17:1-18

THINK: Many who reject Christianity believe that religion is among the most deceptive, destructive things on earth. Following Jesus isn't about "religion"—it's about a relationship with the Creator. Since religion is based on human initiative, it's highly susceptible to corruption and compromise. In the end times, the union between humanistic religion and world government will be complete but short-lived, eventually destroying all who are involved.

RESPOND: What does "Babylon the Great" symbolize (16:19; 17:5), and what does it imply about the wicked activities that will be prevalent in the end times? *(Babylon represents the God-defying, God-denying world system dominated and influenced by Satan throughout history. Babylon symbolizes humanity's pride and rebellion against God.)* How will the Antichrist and the end-time world government use world religion, and what will they eventually do with it? *(The false religious system will throw aside foundational teachings of Jesus and enter into partnership with corrupt political, economic, and social systems under the leadership of the Antichrist, who will unite religion with political systems in order to manipulate and take spiritual control over the world. But there will come a point when the Antichrist and his supporters will come to resent this "great prostitute"—the world's religious system. He will use her for his own purposes but then diminish and finally block out its influence in the world.)* How will they serve God's purposes by doing this (verse 17)?

PRAY: Pray against the spirit of false religion that pervades the world with its corrupt system. Pray that you'll never compromise your relationship with Jesus.

ACT: Make a deliberate effort—as always—to conduct yourself in a way that demonstrates authentic Christian character and commitment. Refuse to compromise God's principles for people who think they can follow Jesus yet disregard the standards of God's Word or tolerate behaviors that don't reflect His purity.

Revelation 18:1-24

THINK: Considering the apparent wealth and prosperity of many people in the world, it's easy to dream of getting in on the action—particularly if you feel that you're missing out. But even those who enjoy worldly "success" seldom seem to be satisfied. That's because worldly wealth often comes at the expense of one's own integrity. This passage clearly displays the Lord's hatred for businesses and governments founded on greed, dishonest gain, and oppressive power. Eventually He will repay those who live in selfish luxury and pleasure. Since they refused to be humbled by His mercy, they will be humbled by His judgment.

RESPOND: Why and in what way must God's people separate themselves from this corrupt system (verse 4)? What will determine the degree of suffering and punishment that will come upon the corrupt world system and those who gained wealth and power from it (verse 7)? *(The rich and corrupt enterprises that rejected God and earned wealth at the expense of others will be stripped of their power in one awful day.)* When "Babylon" is judged and destroyed, how will the reaction of God's people in heaven differ from the reaction of people on earth (verse 20)? How will these reactions stand in contrast to what many of God's people experienced on earth? When will it happen and why must the world's system be completely destroyed forever? *(The God-defying, God-denying world system will be annihilated at "the battle on the great day of God Almighty" [16:14], when Jesus returns to earth. With the corruption of this present world destroyed, Jesus millennial kingdom—His thousand-year reign of peace on earth—will come.)*

PRAY: Pray that you won't envy worldly wealth and prosperity that come from selfish desires and ungodly methods. Give God thanks that His economy ensures complete justice and eternal reward in the end.

ACT: If in any way you're overly concerned with money, material things, status or success, adjust your priorities accordingly. Back your decisions with practical actions, such as putting extra money toward godly endeavors like missions, rather than material things.

Revelation 19:1-10

THINK: Think about how exciting it is to get a special invitation. When you were younger, this may have been an even bigger deal. Then again, you may recall a time when you felt severely let down or excluded because you weren't invited to something. Perhaps you've even wondered what it would be like to be invited to a particular event or celebration. As a follower of Jesus, you can do more than wonder; you can anticipate the day when you'll take part in the greatest and most spectacular celebration ever—when Jesus is united with the love of His life: His church.

RESPOND: In what way does chapter 19 represent both an ending and a beginning? *(Chapter 19 is a picture of the end of the Tribulation and of Jesus' awesome second coming!)* What are some specific reasons why those in heaven praise God so intensely in this passage (verses 1-7)? What does it mean that "the wedding of the Lamb has come, and his bride has made herself ready"? *(The chronology of chapter 19 leads many interpreters to place the Church—Jesus' faithful followers prior to the Tribulation—in heaven before Jesus' return to earth. Here the Bride is completely dressed in "the righteous acts of the saints" [verse 8] and ready in heaven for the "wedding of the Lamb." For these acts of faith by God's people to be complete, they must be in heaven, free from spiritual and moral impurity.)* What does "fine linen" represent (verse 8)? What is "the wedding supper of the Lamb" (verse 9), when does it take place and who is invited? *(This incredible banquet—think of it as the ultimate church fellowship dinner or potluck—celebrates Jesus' union with His faithful followers—His "bride.")*

PRAY: Spend extra time praising God for His goodness, right judgments, and ultimate reward for His people. Pray for a greater devotion to godly purity and purpose in your life.

ACT: Make sure that every way in which you use your voice or communicate today is pleasing to Jesus and demonstrates His character and purpose.

Revelation 19:11-21

THINK: The first time Jesus came—by birth—few people witnessed the event. During His time on earth, few recognized Him as the world's Savior. Yet, when He sets foot on earth again, all will witness His return (Revelation 1:7); no one will mistake His identity. He won't arrive as a helpless infant or suffering servant, but as a warrior and conquering King. Those who rejected the reason for His first coming—to forgive and save them—will not escape the "fury of the wrath" (19:15) of His second coming.

RESPOND: Verse 11 begins the final revelation of what climactic event? *(This is Jesus' second coming to earth as conquering King of kings and Lord of Lords, Warrior-Messiah, and victorious Savior to establish perfect truth and justice, to judge the nations and wage war against evil. This scene makes Hollywood blockbusters look like amateur videos!)* What are the implications of the title "KING OF KINGS AND LORD OF LORDS" (verse 16)? In what way will Christ's future return to earth differ greatly from His coming by birth? *(Re-read THINK above.)* What will happen to the Antichrist and his false prophet (verse 20)? In the last days, why must those who want to remain faithful to God be cautious and rely on the Holy Spirit (verse 20)? *(The false prophet, having performed miracles, could very well deceive people with these acts. People mustn't base their evaluation of truth and reality on the appearance or success of these miracles.)*

PRAY: Worship Jesus as the Faithful and True King of kings and Lord of lords, and for being greater than you can comprehend. Thank Him for the opportunity to be part of His victorious army when He returns to earth to defeat the Antichrist and his allies.

ACT: Go through the day with an awareness that you serve and are empowered by the victorious King of kings and Lord of lords. Allow this thinking to inspire a humble faith and boldness to honor Jesus in all you say and do. Create a poem, song, drawing, or other artistic work conveying the hope and splendor of Jesus' return to earth at the end of the Tribulation period.

Revelation 20:1-15

THINK: While we need to live in a way that gives people an accurate impression of Jesus and what it means to follow Him, it's a reality that most people who reject Christ under less-than-ideal circumstances would still reject Him under the most ideal circumstances. Astoundingly, many who are born and live during the Millennium will reject Christ's authority and choose instead to believe Satan's lies, even after experiencing the perfection of Christ's reign.

RESPOND: What will happen to Satan at the conclusion of Armageddon (verse 2)? Who is resurrected at this time, and what privilege will they have? Why will Satan be released at the end of the thousand years, and what will he do (verses 7,8)? *(It appears that God will allow Satan to test those who have lived under ideal conditions during Jesus' millennial reign, not already saved prior to the start of the Millennium. In this, the last rebellion against God in history, many born during the Millennium will evidently choose to reject Jesus' authority and instead believe Satan's lies. Because human nature will remain the same, some may think they've missed out on something or don't have complete freedom under Jesus' rule. People with weak commitments or insincere motives will always deny or defy God when tempted.)* What will happen to Satan after his final assault is abruptly defeated (verse 10)? Who is involved in the "Great White Throne Judgment," and how will they be judged? *(Jesus Christ is the judge who will give the final verdict on the spiritually lost. Their lives will be completely exposed before God.)* What happens to those whose names are not found in the Book of Life (verse 15)? How should these realities motivate and inspire Jesus' followers?

PRAY: Thank Jesus for the victory He's already won over Satan and for the promise to ultimately destroy evil. Pray for the spiritual salvation of those you know who don't know Jesus.

ACT: Look for an opportunity to share your faith or talk about Jesus with someone who doesn't know Him.

THINK: Have you ever bought something and been pleased with it—until the "new and improved" version came out? Perhaps then you weren't satisfied until you got your hands on the new model. Or have you ever had something go wrong with a product while it was still under warranty? Although the manufacturer typically reserves the right to repair or replace the item, depending on the condition and problem, wouldn't you prefer a brand new one? Someday, God will make everything new. He won't simply refurbish, update, or renovate the old. Instead, there will be a complete destruction of what was—earth, stars, galaxies, the entire cosmos—erasing all traces of sin and imperfection. Then God will replace it all with a new and transformed world where Christ will live forever.

RESPOND: What does John see at the beginning of this passage, and what drastic changes have taken place? Why will everything be made new? In what way will God's relationship with His people be different in the new earth (verse 3)? What does it mean that God "will wipe every tear from their eyes"? What kinds of people will have no part in this place, but instead end up in "the fiery lake of burning sulfur" (verse 8)? Why is there no temple in the city (verse 22)? What purpose will the New Jerusalem serve (verses 24–26)? *(It's likely that the New Jerusalem will be the capital city of the new earth.)* What assurance do God's people have about what will never happen in the New Jerusalem or anywhere in the new heaven and earth (verse 27)?

PRAY: Give God thanks for the fact that someday, all things in earth and heaven will be made new, perfect and incorruptible, with no traces of sin, suffering, or evil.

ACT: As you go through the day, notice the signs and effects of sin, corruption, and imperfection—not just in people but in your surroundings and environment. If you have the opportunity, take a walk through your city and observe these same things. As you do, consider the drastic and unimaginable difference between what you see now and what will exist in the new heaven and earth.

Fire Starter

Revelation 22:1-21

THINK: God concludes His personal revelation to us—His written Word—with a warning, a promise, and an invitation. Be true to His Word, or suffer the consequences (verses 18,19). Take heart in following Jesus, because He's returning soon with His reward (verses 12,20). If you lack a life-transforming relationship with God, there's still time to receive His gift (verse 17). And if you've already accepted His invitation to eternal life, it's your responsibility and privilege to share it with others.

RESPOND: Why is it essential to accept, retain, and live by "the words of the prophecy in this book"? What does it mean, "Let him who does wrong continue to do wrong . . . let him who does right continue to do right"? *(The angel is essentially warning the there's going to come a time when it will be too late to be saved.)* What causes some to "continue to do wrong" and what enables others to "continue to do right"? *(Those who become spiritually hardened will continue to do wrong. Those who choose to serve God receive His spiritual power to continue to do what's right.)* How does all of this relate to people's response to the prophecies and promises of Revelation, as well as the whole Bible? Why and in what way are dishonesty and deceit condemned as this book comes to a close? *(These last two chapters of the Bible focus on the issue of lying and all that involves. Lying is the last on a list of sins condemned in the Bible, possibly because it was a lie that introduced sin to humanity [Genesis 3:1-5 and John 8:44].)* What invitation does Jesus extend in verse 17? In what way are Jesus' followers responsible and empowered to share the invitation with others?

PRAY: Pray that you'll remain true to God's Word. Thank Jesus for extending His invitation to eternal life, and ask for His help in sharing it with others.

ACT: Set a strategy to share Christ's invitation to eternal life with as many people as possible. Pray for five friends who don't know Jesus, and extend an invitation to them to receive Christ.

373